THAILAND
The Versatile Guide

THAILAND
The Versatile Guide

Julia Wilkinson

Duncan Petersen

This first edition published 1996 by
Duncan Petersen Publishing Ltd
31, Ceylon Road
London, W14 OYP

Sales representation in the U.K. and Ireland by

World Leisure Marketing
Downing Road
West Meadows Industrial Estate
Derby DE21 6HA

Distributed by
Grantham Book Services

Conceived, edited, designed and produced by
Duncan Petersen Publishing Ltd from a concept by Emma Stanford

Typeset by Duncan Petersen Publishing Ltd
film output by Reprocolour International, Milan

Originated by Reprocolour International, Milan

Printed by GraphyCems, Novarra

A CIP catalogue record for this book is available from the British Library

ISBN 1 872576 53 2

Editorial director Andrew Duncan
Assistant editor Leonie Glass
Art director Mel Petersen
Design assistants Beverley Stewart, Chris Foley
Maps by Chris Foley and Beverley Stewart
Illustrations by Beverley Stewart
Ko Samui and Ko Pha-Ngan written by Jeroen Snijders

Photographic credits
All photography by Jeroen Snijders

In 1978, fresh out of Cambridge, **Julia Wilkinson** left England for the Far East, planning to visit Thailand before going to Australia. The visit changed everything: deciding she wanted to discover more of Asia, she based herself in Hong Kong and became a freelance travel writer and photographer, travelling throughout the region and writing for a variety of international publications including *The Independent*, *Discovery* and *National Geographic Traveler*. A PATA award winner, she has also written and contributed to guides on Hong Kong, Tibet and Portugal. Thailand remains her special interest: since that first visit, she has frequently returned, travelling by bus and boat, tuk-tuk, truck or elephant to reach the remotest corners. She and her guide book author husband now divide their time between Hong Kong's outlying island of Cheung Chau and a cottage in England's Wiltshire countryside where Julia indulges her other travelling passion, flying hot air balloons. She has yet to make it to Australia.

Steve Rosse, who contributed our sections on Phuket and Bangkok, has lived in Thailand since 1988. He is a columnist for *The Nation*, *Thailand Tatler*, *Phuket Magazine*, *The Phuket Gazette* and *South East Asian Fishing World*. He lives on Phuket with his wife, Mem, and their son, Andaman C. Rosse.

Master contents list

This contents list is for when you need to use the guide in the conventional way: to find out about where you are going, or where you happen to be. The index, pages 254-6, may be just as helpful.

HOWEVER...
There is much more to this guide than the region by region approach suggested by the contents list on this page. Turn to pages 8-9 and also see pages 10-11.

Contents

Thailand Overall
- master map

Thailand Overall, pages 34-133, is a traveller's network for taking in the whole country, or large parts of it.

Each 'leg' of the network has a number (ie, Thailand Overall: 1). Each route 'leg' features a whole region, and describes many places both on and off the marked route. Think of the overall routes not only as physical trails, but as imaginative ways of connecting all the main centres of Thailand and of describing and making travel sense of the country as a whole.

They are designed to be used in these different ways:

1 *Ignore the marked route entirely:* simply use the alphabetically arranged gazetteer of Sights & Places of Interest, and the map at the start of each route, as a guide to what to see and do in the region, not forgetting the hotel and restaurant recommendations.

2 Follow the marked route by public transport (see the transport box), boat, or by car. You can do sections of the route, or all of it; you can follow it in any direction. Link the routes to travel the length and breadth of Thailand.

Bangkok has a section of its own, pages 134–55

8

Contents

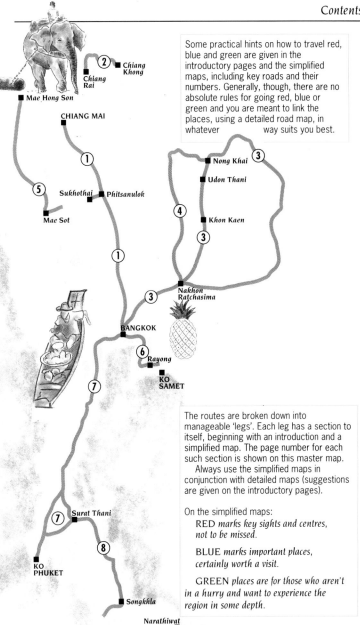

Some practical hints on how to travel red, blue and green are given in the introductory pages and the simplified maps, including key roads and their numbers. Generally, though, there are no absolute rules for going red, blue or green and you are meant to link the places, using a detailed road map, in whatever   way suits you best.

The routes are broken down into manageable 'legs'. Each leg has a section to itself, beginning with an introduction and a simplified map. The page number for each such section is shown on this master map.

Always use the simplified maps in conjunction with detailed maps (suggestions are given on the introductory pages).

On the simplified maps:

RED *marks key sights and centres, not to be missed.*

BLUE *marks important places, certainly worth a visit.*

GREEN *places are for those who aren't in a hurry and want to experience the region in some depth.*

The *Thailand Overall* section is ideal for:

■ Planning, and undertaking, tours of the whole country, or parts.

■ Making the journey to or from your eventual destination as interesting and as rewarding as possible.

■ Linking the in-depth explorations of localities provided by the Local Explorations section, pages 156-253.

The Local Explorations
- *master map*

The Local Explorations – strategies for exploring all the interesting localities of Thailand – complement the overall routes, pages 8-9. **They are designed to be used in these different ways:**

1 *Ignore the marked route entirely*: simply use the alphabetically arranged Gazetteer of Sights & Places of Interest, and the map at the start of each Local Exploration, as a guide to what to see and do in the area, not forgetting the hotel and restaurant recommendations.

2 Use the marked route to make a tour by public transport (see the transport box), ferry, or by car. You can do sections of the route, or all of it. (In the introduction it tells you how long you might take to cover everything the quickest way, by car.)

If you are driving, you can generally follow the tour in any direction; usually, the route as marked is an attractive and convenient way to link the places of interest; you may well find other ways to drive it. Always use our map in conjunction with a detailed road map (suggestions are given on each introductory page).

Bangkok has a section of its own pages 134-55.

Contents

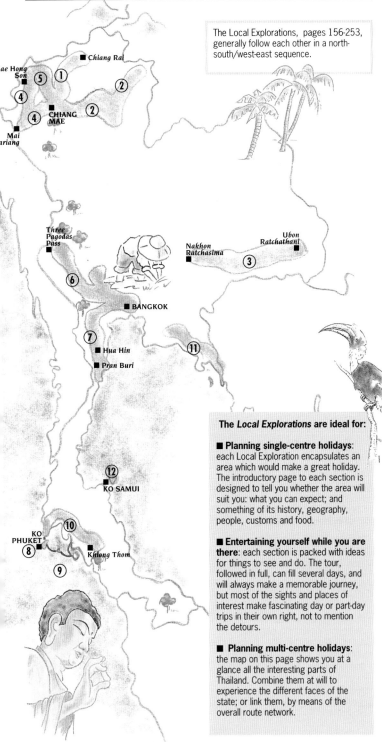

The Local Explorations, pages 156-253, generally follow each other in a north-south/west-east sequence.

■ Chiang Rai

Mae Hong Son ⑤ ①

④

④ ■ CHIANG MAI ②

②

Mai ariang

Three Pagodas Pass ■

⑥

Nakhon Ratchasima ■   Ubon Ratchathani ■

③

■ BANGKOK

⑦

■ Hua Hin
■ Pran Buri

⑪

⑫
KO SAMUI

⑩
KO PHUKET ■
⑧ ■ Khlong Thom

⑨

The *Local Explorations* are ideal for:

■ **Planning single-centre holidays**: each Local Exploration encapsulates an area which would make a great holiday. The introductory page to each section is designed to tell you whether the area will suit you: what you can expect; and something of its history, geography, people, customs and food.

■ **Entertaining yourself while you are there**: each section is packed with ideas for things to see and do. The tour, followed in full, can fill several days, and will always make a memorable journey, but most of the sights and places of interest make fascinating day or part-day trips in their own right, not to mention the detours.

■ **Planning multi-centre holidays**: the map on this page shows you at a glance all the interesting parts of Thailand. Combine them at will to experience the different faces of the state; or link them, by means of the overall route network.

11

A single *baht* sign – **B** – or several *baht* signs, such as **BBB**, in a hotel or restaurant entry, denotes a price band. Its object is to give an indication of what you can expect to pay. Bear in mind that accommodation offered at any one place may span two or more price bands.

Hotels

For a double room (one night) at high season (November to February) rate:

B	Less than 300 *baht*
BB	300-700 *baht*
BBB	700-1,000 *baht*
BBBB	More than 1,000 *baht*

Restaurants

For a one-course meal for one (Thai or Western style), excluding alcoholic drinks:

B	Less than 30 *baht*
BB	30-70 *baht*
BBB	More than 700 *baht*

Opening times -
hotels and restaurants

Hotels are open year-round unless specifically stated. The recommended **restaurants** are open every day, all year, unless noted, but many out-of-Bangkok restaurants close relatively early in the evening, around 9 pm. Open-air night market stalls tend to start work around dusk and may continue operating until about 9.30 pm (or until they run out of supplies). Street stalls selling breakfast snacks start before the sun rises.

Opening times -
museums and tourist attractions

Most museums follow government office hours, opening from 8.30 am to noon, 1 to 4.30 pm, but instead of closing at weekends most shut on Monday or Tuesday (sometimes Friday as well). Opening times are noted where appropriate in the text but it's always sensible to check with the local tourist office beforehand in case there have been recent changes. Official public holidays may not necessarily make any difference to their opening hours, since most tourist-related businesses continue operating on these days: only government offices and banks will definitely close on public holidays.

Important temples (wats) will usually open from 8 or 9 am to 5 pm daily (including Buddhist holy days) but some close after morning prayers or during lunch (11.30 am to 1 pm), some small or special wats are only open on request and others are open for visitors and devotees at any time. To be sure of finding a temple open, your best bet is to go first thing in the morning or in the early evening, but if you do find a

---

Symbols

⌫ after a heading in **Sights and Places of Interest** means that there is an accomodation suggestion (or suggestions) for that place in **Recommended Hotels**.

✕ after a heading in **Sights and Places of Interest** means that there is a suggestion (or suggestions) for that place in **Recommended Restaurants.**

↗ after a place name on a map means that the sight or place of interest is covered in detail in another part of the book: look up the place in the **Sights & Places of Interest** gazetteer which follows the map: a cross-reference is given in every case.

♣ on a map represents a National Park.

Transliteration

The transliteration of Thai into Roman script is either fraught with problems or delightfully capricious, depending on how you look at it. The problems arise because there's no consistent method of transliteration, so you'll often find several different spellings for one word. Place or street names are especially bewildering for the visitor: Phetburi, for instance, can be Phetchaburi; Rachdamri sometimes transforms into Ratchadamri; Ayutthaya into Ayudhia. Officially, there's a Royal Thai General System of Transcription but local variations always crop up. In this guide we've used the spellings you're most likely to find, but bear in mind that as with so much else in Thailand, almost anything goes. Think of it as a little linguistic teaser, Thai-(Tai)-style.

wat closed, just ask one of the resident monks if it can be opened: they're usually happy to help visitors. On Buddhist holy days, temples may be packed with devotees, making sightseeing difficult, though the festival itself may well be worth watching.

Addresses
Especially in Bangkok, addresses can often consist of a confusing list of numbers, for example, 23/1-5 Soi 10 Sukhumvit Road. A *soi* literally means a lane, though it can actually be a road of some size. In this example, Soi 10 is the tenth 'lane' off Sukhumvit Road; 23 is the lot number and 1-5 is where you'll find the lot on the *soi*.

Mileages for routes and tours
Are approximate. They represent the shortest distances you could expect to travel, almost always the 'red' option.

Credit cards
Expensive hotels and restaurants in Bangkok, large cities and major resorts accept the major cards – but see page 23. The further you go outside these centres, the less likely you'll be able to use plastic money. For this reason, hotel and restaurant entries in this guide do not list credit cards accepted.

Religious architectural terms
– Such as prang and prasat are explained on page 177.

Something for everyone
Getting the most from your guide

Here is a *small* selection of ideas for enjoying Thailand opened up by this guide, aimed at a range of needs and tastes. The list is just a start: the guide offers many, many more ideas for what really matters: suiting yourself.

Classic tour of Thailand: new and old, with some hill country thrills and a day trip to Burma
Thailand Overall: 1 *and Local Explorations*: 12, 14.

Fun in the sun: beaches and islands
Thailand Overall: 6, 7 *and Local Explorations*: 2, 3, 4, 5, 6, 7, 8.

Meandering by the Mekong River, at the border with Laos
Thailand Overall: 3, 4.

The Golden Triangle: trekking, rafting and elephant riding
Thailand Overall: 2 *and Local Explorations*: 10, 11, 12, 13.

Under ground and under the sea: best spots for diving and caving
Thailand Overall: 7 *and Local Explorations*: 3, 4, 5, 6, 7, 11.

Adventure on the Burmese border
Thailand Overall: 5 *and Local Explorations*: 1, 12.

Thailand's traditional hinterland and silk-weaving country
Thailand Overall: 3.

The deep south: a very different Thailand
Thailand Overall: 8.

Temple tour of Khmer architectural gems
Local Explorations: 9.

Birds, flowers, waterfalls and elephants: some of the best national parks
Thailand Overall: 4 *and Local Explorations*: 1, 2, 12.

Thailand:
an Introduction

Fifteen years ago, when I first visited Thailand, my friends in Europe thought of the country as almost impossibly exotic: a once-in-a-lifetime trip. Now they're on their second or third visits, and telling me about island getaways or remote jungle treks that I've scarcely caught up with myself. For them, and probably for many of the five million other visitors a year, Thailand is now more familiar and more enticing than anywhere else in Asia.

Sun and sand, shopping and nightlife, glittering temples in a 'Land of Smiles' – these are the kingdom's most famous attractions. But with a little curiosity and sense of adventure you can discover much, much more. This guide aims to point you in the right direction, on routes that have given me my own best discoveries and that can take you into the wildest corners of the land – or the most pampered place in the sun.

The choice of travel here is extraordinary. Within an area the size of France (413,120 square km) there's a wonderful variety of landscapes, from the untamed jungles and hills of the Golden Triangle in the north, to the tranquil coral-rich islands of the south. There are striking contrasts in lifestyles, too, reflecting the country's rapid but uneven development in the last decade. The choking sprawl of Bangkok with its five-star hotels and high-rises is a world away from the dirt-poor villages of drought-ravaged Isaan province in the north-east; the sophisticated island resort of Phuket a far cry from the hill-tribe villages on the Burmese border. The glue that keeps it all together – even, at times, the government itself – is an intense respect for monarchy and for Buddhism.

More than 90 per cent of the country's 58 million people are practising Theravada Buddhists. You'll find the evidence everywhere, not just in thousands of temples and saffron-robed monks, but in small daily acts of worship and compassion which thread effortlessly into both modern and traditional life.

King Bhumibol Adulyadej, too, has an influence far deeper than most of the world's monarchs and certainly than any of his predecessors. Since he inherited the throne in 1946, this multilingual, multi-talented king (among other things he's an accomplished jazz saxophonist and yachtsman) has travelled all over the country to support or initiate welfare development projects. Photographs of him and his queen, Sirikit, adorn almost every office, every home. To understand the reverence the Thais have for him is to understand what helps bind this diverse country together.

Pride in the kingdom's historical independence is an important facet of Thailand and the Thai character, too. Unlike its neighbours in South-East Asia, Thailand (known as Siam until the 1940s) has never been colonized. To you and me, Thailand may be the Land of Smiles. But to the Thais, it's *Muang Thai,* the Land of the Free.

Freedom to roam this land is one of the great joys for visitors. Apart from a few dodgy border areas (parts of the Cambodian border to the south-east, and the Burmese border to the north-west), and occasional trickery by thieves, Thailand is one of the safest and easiest places to travel in Asia. It's also quite cheap, allowing you to indulge in luxury often out of reach back home, or to travel for weeks on a budget that would scarcely blow the foam off a *cappucino* or two in Paris or Rome.

Not everywhere is delightful: rampant deforestation and environmental destruction have accompanied the country's economic boom; the sex industry has established its tenacious, seedy grip on many beach resorts and back streets; and Bangkok's traffic and pollution are a nightmare. But this is all part of the fabric: the shadow under the smile.

To make the most of a visit to Thailand, the adaptable traveller will weave all this together in an itinerary that encompasses the highs and lows, the glitter of the best tourist resorts with the thatched bamboo hut of a village that rarely sees a foreigner. Public transport can get you to most places; and even the most remote village mentioned in this guide can be reached on foot (or by boat, hired motorbike or *samlor*) within a few hours. Whatever you do, wherever you go, if you live as the Thais do, with smiles and *sanuk (joie de vivre),* you'll find the true spirit and the best discoveries that Thailand can offer.

Julia Wilkinson
Hong Kong

BEFORE YOU GO

Climate: when and where to go

If you hate feeling cold, you've chosen the right country: Thailand is hot and humid all year round, with average temperatures seldom falling below 24°C. However, there are a few variations which are worth taking into account when planning your trip.

In most of the country there are three main seasons: November-February is dry and (relatively) cool, with temperatures ranging from 18°C to 32°C; March -May is very hot, with temperatures soaring to 40°C at times (especially in the northeast); while June-October, the rainy season, is cooler but wetter, with the southwest monsoon sweeping through the country.

Obviously, most visitors opt for the cool, dry season (December is the peak tourist month) but if you're keen to get away from the crowds (and take advantage of off-season hotel rates) the monsoon season isn't nearly as bad as it sounds: sunny days are merely interrupted by short sharp downpours. August and September are the rainiest months for central and northern Thailand (but floods in Bangkok in October aren't unusual, either).

Southern Thailand, however, has more rain than elsewhere in the country since it gets hit by two monsoons: the north-east monsoon lasts roughly from November to February, and affects the south-east coast (including such popular resorts as Ko Samui and Ko Phangan); while the south-west monsoon, from May to October, affects the west coast (including Phuket, Krabi and Ko Phi Phi). No problem: just hop across the peninsula if it rains on one side and you'll find the sun again.

So does it ever get cold in Thailand? Yes, if you visit the north during the cool season (November to February). Temperatures in Chiang Mai can drop to as low as 13°C at night during this time, or even a chilling 7°C in Mae Hong Son, though they can just as easily climb back into the 20s later during the same day. Be prepared for hot and cold weather if you're combining a north and south holiday at this time.

Clothing

Cool, casual and cotton – if you stick to these guidelines you won't go far wrong. In addition, a sweater is recommended for cool-season visits to the north, an umbrella for the rainy season and a sun-hat at all times.

Other essentials include comfortable walking shoes and slip-on sandals – especially useful for visiting temples (where you have to take off your shoes). Sarongs make loyal companions, too, as beachwear, sheet and shawl. Wait to buy one in Thailand – there's plenty of choice and prices are rock bottom.

If you're staying in a smart hotel, however, or planning to dine out in up-market restaurants, bring something reasonably formal; wearing T-shirt, shorts and plastic sandals in your five-star hotel will not win you the legendary Thai smile.

Documentation

Many nationalities (including citizens of the U.K., U.S.A., Australia and of major European countries) may enter Thailand without a visa for stays of up to 30 days as long as they have a valid passport. A few nationalities (including those from the Netherlands, New Zealand and Scandinavia) get inexplicably special treatment: a 90-day stay without the need of a visa.

If you're planning on staying longer, you'll need to apply for a tourist visa (valid for 60 days), or a non-immigrant visa (valid for 90 days) from a Thai embassy or consulate. Tourist visas can usually be extended for a fee of B500 by applying at the Immigration Department in Bangkok (Soi Suan Phlu, Sathorn Thai Road, tel. 02 286 9176) or at immigration offices in other major cities. Beware of lingering beyond your visa limit: you'll get fined B100 a day.

Import duty

Your duty-free allowance into Thailand is 250 grams of tobacco or cigars, 200 cigarettes and one litre each of wine or spirits. Strictly prohibited are all kinds of narcotics, obscene literature and firearms (unless you have a permit from the Police Department).

Immunization

No inoculations are officially required unless you come from a contaminated area but it makes sense to have a tetanus booster as well as an injection against hepatitis A.

If you plan to travel to remote areas (especially high-risk ones such as Ko Chang) you should take anti-malarial tablets (see Medical matters, pages 25-6).

Medical and travel insurance

I used to scoff at medical insurance. Then I broke my neck hitting a rock as I dived into the South China Sea and realized that my 14-week stint in hospital might have broken the bank, too, had it not been for the last-minute insurance I'd taken out under parental pressure.

Most travel agencies can arrange or recommend a suitable insurance, but be sure it includes provision for loss of money and passport, and for repatriation in case of a medical emergency. If you do have to see a doctor during your stay, or if valuables are stolen, do insist on receipts or paperwork to show the insurance company back home.

Money

Travellers' cheques are the safest form of money to bring to Thailand as well as giving the best rate of exchange. Most major currencies can be exchanged, although U.S. dollars are the most widely accepted (preferably those issued by American Express or Thomas Cook). You'll find the best exchange rates at banks and legal money-changers (not in hotels). There's a commission charge of B13 per cheque cashed. Payment by credit cards, especially Visa, are increasingly accepted in all the major centres, but see page 23 for some important warnings.

Banks are open from 8.30 am to 3.30 pm from Monday to Friday, but in Bangkok you'll find many of the banks have foreign exchange services open until at least 9 pm every day, and in popular resorts such as Pattaya and Phuket until at least 7.30 pm.

The **baht** is the unit of Thai currency. There are 100 *satang* in one *baht*, with 25-*satang* and 50-*satang* coins. More commonly used coins are the 1B, 5B and 10B denominations; and just to confuse you, there are old and new 1B and 5B coins of three different sizes in circulation (the new coins have both Thai and Western numerals). Notes are easier to recognize, printed with both Thai and Western numerals, in increasing sizes according to value and differently coloured: 10B is brown; 20B green; 50B blue; 100B red; 500B purple and 1,000B beige. Large notes can be hard to change in small towns and markets, so always ask for some small notes when you change money.

Planted drugs

When you're ready to close your suitcase and head off to the airport (at home or in Bangkok), make double sure that your case is locked. And don't accept anything from a stranger *en route* or at the airport: slipping drugs into suitcases or planting them on foreigners is a favourite drug-smuggler's trick, and penalties for possession of drugs are extremely harsh in Thailand.

Tourist information

The Tourist Authority of Thailand (TAT) publishes stacks of colourful literature about the country, as well as lists of accommodation and a useful calendar of festivals and events.

Contact one of their overseas offices for information and advice:

Australia 12th Floor, Exchange Building, 56 Pitt St, Sydney, NSW 2000; tel. 02 247 7549.
France 90 Avenue des Champs Elysées, 75008 Paris; tel. 1 4562 8656.
Germany Bethmann Str. 58-60311 Frankfurt/Main 1; tel. 069 295 704.
Italy Via Barberini 50, 00187 Rome; tel. 06 487 3479.
United Kingdom 49 Albemarle Street, London WIX 3FE; tel. 0171 499 7679.
U.S.A. 5 World Trade Center, Suite No. 3443, New York, NY 10048, tel. 212 432 0433; 3440 Wilshire Blvd, Suite 1100, Los Angeles, CA 90010, tel. 213 382 2353; and 303 East Wacker Drive, Suite 400, Chicago IL 60601, tel. 312 819 3990.

Local customs: what to expect, how to behave

Thanks to the success of Thailand's tourism campaigns, foreigners know one thing at least they can expect in the country: smiles. And yes, it's true, the Thais seem to have an extraordinary ability to smile even in the worst situations. Criticize the monarchy or Buddhism, however, and you'll produce anything but smiles (at worst you could find yourself in jail: *lèse majesté* is still an imprisonable offence). In public, you should show respect for the monarchy as the Thais do: in towns beyond Bangkok, many people still stand respectfully when the National Anthem is broadcast at 8 am and 6 pm, and in cinemas everywhere the audience will stand when the anthem

17

is played before the films begin.

As for temple etiquette, the most important rule is to take off your shoes at the entrance to the temple. Neat appearance is another must (no shorts or sleeveless shirts), and respect for the Buddha images (no clambering over statues for that perfect picture). Women aren't supposed to come into contact with monks (though some young monks I've encountered obviously had different ideas), not even handing them anything directly. Above all, never point your feet at a Buddha image: feet are considered the lowest part of the body spiritually. If you sit on the floor, be sure to tuck your legs to the side or sit in a lotus position.

In fact, pointing your feet at anyone (for instance, when you sit opposite someone and cross your legs) is considered very offensive almost as bad as touching an adult on the head (considered the most sacred part of the body). Public shows of affection aren't greatly appreciated, either, nor nude bathing, though women bathing topless is increasingly accepted in the large tourist resorts. Casual (the Thais would say scruffy) clothing is also accepted in these resorts, but if you're dining with Thai friends it would be respectful to dress up a little. Another easy way to show respect, especially to someone older, is to give a greeting the Thai way, with a *wai*: hold your hands, palms together, at around chest height. Handshakes are rarely used except by Westernized Thais or business executives.

The Thais are usually very tolerant of the behaviour of *farangs* (foreigners), but the surest way to get on their bad side is to lose your temper. Whatever the situation: keep cool, keep smiling.

The times when your patience will be tested most are likely to be when you first arrive at a bus or railway station and get pounced on by a horde of touts trying to lure you away to their hotel or shop. In popular resorts you may be approached by young men or beautiful girls offering you incredible bargains or seeking friendship or 'English practice'. Sometimes they may be genuine. More often they're not. The best advice is to be wary and use your common sense.

And sexual harrassment? It's probably more of a problem for men than for women, especially in the major tourist resorts such as Pattaya or Phuket where single men are a target for touts and pimps (in Pattaya, watch out for the gorgeous – and unrecognizable – *ka-toeys* or transvestites). Women will find Thailand a relief compared with travelling in, say, India or Indonesia, but that doesn't mean you're totally free of unwanted attention. As anywhere in Asia, modest clothing helps you to avoid hassle (especially in the Muslim south). Always remember to lock your hotel door at night. And don't tempt fate by travelling alone at night in remote areas.

GETTING THERE

By air: from Europe

Direct flights to Bangkok's Don Muang airport are available from most major European cities. You'll get some of the best deals from London's 'bucket shop' travel agents which can offer fares from as little as £400 return (low season). With non-stop flights lasting around 12 hours you may want to stick to the guaranteed comforts of airlines such as Thai International, Qantas or British Airways (which all offer daily scheduled flights) but for bargain prices check out smaller airlines such as Eva Airways of Taiwan or Tarom Romanian Air Transport which have regular indirect flights to Bangkok.

Flights to the northern city of Chiang Mai and the southern resort of Phuket are also available from a few European cities such as Frankfurt, Amsterdam or Vienna.

Be sure to book well ahead for high-season flights (notably in July, August, December and January). For short trips, package deals, combining flight and accommodation, can be worthwhile: Thai International have a tempting range of Royal Orchid Holidays and there are also some excellent specialist tour operators in the U.K. such as Explore Worldwide (tel. 01252 319448) and Travel Bag (tel. 01420 80828) offering adventure tours or tailor-made holidays.

From the U.S.A.

The widest choice of flights and fares is from America's West Coast, especially, of course, from San Francisco and Los Angeles. Discount agencies here can offer fares from as low as $800 return. The main airlines flying to Bangkok from the West coast (with a flight time of around 18 hours and one or two stops) are United, Japan Airlines and Thai International, but if you're shopping around for bargain or 'Super-Apex' fares, it's worth asking about Asian carriers such as Korean Airlines and China Airlines. Some of these airlines also fly from the East Coast, though it may work out cheaper to fly to London and pick up a bargain flight from there. Round-the-world tickets are definitely worth considering if you're planning on visiting other countries in Asia as well.

From Australia/New Zealand
There are flights to Bangkok (around 9 hours' flight time from Sydney or Melbourne) on a number of airlines, most frequently with Qantas and Thai International, or from New Zealand with Air New Zealand. Off-season discounted fares offer the most attractive deals: a low-season excursion ticket from Sydney to Bangkok return costs around A$1,000.

From Asia
If you've got the time it's worth considering a combination of destinations in Asia to make the most of your Far East trip. Hong Kong, Singapore, or Malaysia's Kuala Lumpur or Penang are standard additions to a Thailand trip, while Vietnam, Cambodia and Myanmar (Burma) are increasingly popular. Flight connections are easy between Bangkok and these destinations: if you haven't already booked flights in advance (round-the-world tickets are worth considering), bucket shop fares are readily available from Bangkok and Hong Kong (be sure to book your flight out of Bangkok well in advance during high season).

Overland
The most popular way to enter Thailand overland is by train or bus from Malaysia (or from Singapore, via Malaysia). Air-conditioned coaches make the run from Singapore to Thailand's southern town of Hat Yai in about 14 hours (from where it is another 14 hours to Bangkok). The train is more tedious, taking about 16 hours to Butterworth (the station for Penang), where you have to change from Malaysian-run trains to the State Railway of Thailand trains. It is another two hours or so to the border. The smoothest choice of all is the super-deluxe Eastern & Oriental (E&O) Express, which runs once a week between Singapore and Bangkok and is the ultimate in nostalgic Asian train trav-el – for details contact E&O in London on 0171 928 6000; or in the U.S.A., on 800 524 2420.

The newest and most exotic overland (and over-water) route is across the Mekong River from Laos, usually to Nong Khai via the Friendship Bridge which opened in April 1994. Budget travellers from Vietnam often use this cheap route to get to Thailand, stopping at Vientiane *in transit.*

GETTING AROUND

By air
Thai International (89 Vibhavadi Rangsit Road, Bangkok, tel. 02 513 0121, or book through any local office or travel agent) fly to all the major destinations within the country, from Chiang Rai in the north to Narathiwat in the south. Other domestic airlines include Bangkok Airways (tel. 02 229 3456/3434), which flies to tourist destinations such as Ko Samui, Phuket, Hua Hin and Pattaya.

By train
Anyone who has travelled by train in India or China is in for a delightful surprise: the state-run trains in Thailand are comfortable, clean and punctual (well, nearly always). They're also relatively cheap and a good deal safer than buses. Not surprisingly, therefore, the train is first choice for most independent travellers touring the country (if you go third class you'll find it's the cheapest choice for long distances, too).

There are four main routes operated by the State Railway of Thailand (SRT), spanning out from Bangkok's main Hualamphong Station and covering some 4,500 km. That's plenty of railway, but unfortunately it doesn't go everywhere: expect to combine your comfortable train trips with the occasional bus ride to get you into more remote areas.

The fastest trains are the express (*rot duan*), special express (*rot duan phiset*), and rapid (*rot raew*). To travel on these you have to pay a surcharge. Not all trains carry all three classes of seats (express trains don't have a third class, while rapid trains don't have a first class) and the standard of classes can also vary between trains. But generally you'll find first class means an air-conditioned cabin with bunks and a small wash basin; second class means reclining padded seats or padded benches converting into sleepers; and third class means padded or wooden bench seats.

Tickets for first and second-class seats or sleepers should be booked in advance – at least a week ahead in high season or Thai holiday times. Trains for popular destinations such as Chiang Mai or Hat Yai fill up especially quickly. Timetables are available at Bangkok's Hualamphong Station and most major T.A.T. tourist offices. Train addicts might want to consider buying a tourist rail pass: a Blue Pass (B1,100 adults, B550 children) gives you 20 days' travel on second- or third-class trains (excluding supplementary charges); the Red Pass (B2,000 adults, B1,000 children) includes supplementary charges.

By bus

You have four choices when it comes to bus transport:

Government-run ordinary buses (*rot thamadaa*), are the cheapest and slowest, stopping wherever someone wants to get off or when someone flags them down (bus stops are superfluous).

Government-run air-conditioned buses (*rot ae* or *rot duan*) are still relatively cheap but usually faster and definitely more comfortable (first-class versions of both government and private air-conditioned buses even feature W.C.s, while VIP buses have reclining seats and stewardess service). Their drawbacks: they don't leave so frequently as ordinary buses and will often only stop at the bus terminals (not *en route* to the terminal).

The third choice is the increasingly popular private air-conditioned 'tour' bus (*rot tua*) or mini bus (rot tuu). These are the fastest and the most expensive of all, but often the least safe.

And the fourth choice? Once you've experienced the hair-raising driving techniques of most Thai bus drivers, the ear-splitting videos shown on board and the knee-cramping conditions, you may well choose to avoid the buses altogether.

But realistically, since you can't go everywhere by train (besides, the schedules are often inconvenient for short hops), you are bound to end up depending on buses at some point in your travels. Try to stick to the relatively reliable government-run buses (called *Baw Khaw Saw*): there's usually a BKS terminal in every town. And be prepared to practise patience, especially on ordinary buses,

which often take forever to move a few kilometres. Timetables for these buses exist in theory only: they leave when they are full, or when the driver has finished his noodles. By contrast, air-conditioned buses follow set timetables.

Most bus departures take place in the period 6-10 am, tailing off in the late afternoon. Unless you are miles from a population centre, you should be able to get a bus to your destination within an hour or so at any time of the day. The local tourist office can give you an idea of the frequency of service to your destination.

Tickets for air-conditioned buses and minibuses can be bought in advance (for private buses, go to the downtown office). However, this is not essential unless you want a popular route, for instance Chiang Mai to Bangkok. For ordinary buses you pay on board.

A few tips for safer and more comfortable bus travel: lock your luggage and keep all valuables with you; never accept a drink, snack or cigarette from a stranger, especially if you're travelling between Surat Thani and Phuket (a favourite route for robbers trying to drug passengers); and to preserve your sanity through those hours of shattering videos, take ear plugs.

By car

If you want to brave Thailand's roads you will need better-than-usual reserves of courage and patience to cope with the local driving habits, notably, a tendency to drive too fast, and little regard for traffic law. Officially, Thais drive on the left-hand side of the road and are supposed to stick to a speed limit of 60 km/hour within city limits and 80 km/hour on highways. Unofficially, anything goes. Among the unwritten laws, the main one to remember is that the biggest vehicle has the right of way even when overtaking in the face of an oncoming vehicle. Also, foreigners are likely to get the blame (and the bill) for any accident they're involved in. Note, too, that if you crash the car, rental operators may charge you for every day the vehicle is out of service being repaired.

However, I know people who drive regularly in Thailand and say it's no big problem – as long as you don't drive in Bangkok or at night. Roads are generally in acceptable condition, petrol stations plentiful on main roads and fuel, at around B10 a litre, relatively cheap and widely available. If you think you're up to the challenge, you'll find most of the big-name car rental firms at Bangkok's airport or downtown, including Hertz (tel. 02 390 0341/711 0574/251 7575) and Avis (tel. 02 255 5300/243 1234). Both these agencies also have offices in other major towns and resorts. Jeep hire is becoming increasingly popular at the resorts. Although jeeps look like plenty of fun, they can be hazardous: be particularly careful at sharp corners or you could find yourself upside-down in a paddy field.

It costs about B1,000 a day to hire a car from an international firm (a deposit of B2,000 is also usually required). Local firms are cheaper, but be sure to check the price includes insurance cover. If you're on a Royal Orchid Holiday with Thai International you can obtain a 20 per cent discount with Avis on self-drive or chauffeur-driven car hire. An international driver's licence is legally necessary for any car hire.

Assistance for the motorist

When you hire your car, make sure the company provides you with all their regional office telephone numbers, especially if you are planning a long trip. Ask also for a 24-hour emergency contact number and a photocopy of the insurance documents. In case of an accident, you should contact the police immediately (see Emergencies, pages 23-4), but be aware that Thais tend to settle damages between themselves without calling the police.

The best driving map is the bilingual *Thailand Highway Map* (1:1,000,000), published by the Roads Association of Thailand and available at major bookshops such as the DK Book House in Siam Square, Bangkok.

Motorbike

The risks of driving a motorbike in Thailand are probably even greater than for driving a car. However, it's an increasingly popular option among tourists, especially for short local explorations in the north and in resorts such as Phuket and Ko Samui.

You'll find it easy to rent a bike in these places (for about B80-150 a day for a 100cc Honda Dream scooter or B400 a day for a 250 cc off-road machine) but beware of unscrupulous hirers: some may refuse to return your deposit until you have paid for a few previously unnoticed scratches. The 'deposit' required is usually your passport, but if you're uneasy about this you could try offering your airline ticket instead. Note, too, that insurance cover is rarely provided for motorbikes: 'you crash, you pay' is the rule. Although hirers rarely ask to see your driving licence, be sure to have it with you: there can be major problems if you are involved in an accident and cannot produce it.

Choose your bike carefully – maintenance can often be shoddy. Wear a helmet (and proper clothing), even though many Thais don't (but then many Thais die from bike accidents). In remote areas, never ride alone or at night – attacks on foreigners have been known.

If you are riding in northern Thailand, get a copy of David Unkovich's *General Touring Information* or the more detailed *A Pocket Guide for Motorcycle Touring in North Thailand* (both available in Chiang Mai bookshops). These offer tips on repairs and breakdowns, weather and roads, as well as suggested tours. And see also Local Explorations: 12, page 249, for further information on motorbike touring.

Taxis, tuk-tuks, samlors and songthaews

Taxis are widely available in Bangkok (though less so elsewhere). Most now have meters (and air-conditioning) but if you come across a die-hard meterless taxi, be sure to bargain a price before getting in. It's an expensive way to get around Bangkok (especially in rush hour when everything comes to a standstill). Motorbike taxis are increasingly popular, not only in Bangkok (where they're the fastest and most lethal thing on wheels) but in the remotest corners of the land where they're invaluable for getting you to out-of-the-way places. Their drivers are easily spotted by their coloured, numbered waistcoats. You'll find, too, that they often hang around street corners and bus stops.

A popular alternative are tuk-tuks – the excruciatingly noisy three-wheeler scooters of the samlor ('three wheels') family. In Bangkok they can weave through the traffic much faster than taxis, but you may collapse from the fumes by the time you arrive. Again, you have to bargain a

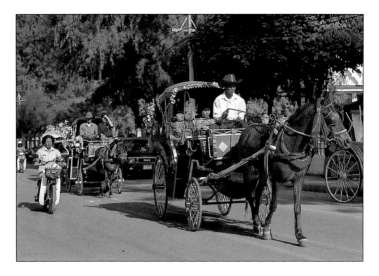

• *Taxi, Lampang.*

price before boarding (some knowledge of Thai is useful: few tuk-tuk drivers speak much English).

Pedal-powered samlors or trishaws are much more enjoyable (only available outside Bangkok). Some of my best small-town experiences have been thanks to a friendly samlor driver. Sadly, however, they are a dying breed, rapidly being replaced by the younger generation on their motorbike taxis. When you see them thronging around bus and train stations, be aware that many are paid commissions for taking visitors to certain hotels or guesthouses. Insist on your chosen destination and bargain the fare.

Songthaews ('two rows') are small (but sometimes large) pick-up trucks with a couple of benches in the back. They're widely used for short bus runs and are often crammed with passengers (during rush-hour boys hang off the back or climb on to the roof). In popular tourist spots, drivers may try to persuade you to rent the whole vehicle – not a bad idea if you're in a group and want to organize your own outing.

Long-tail boats
Some of your most exciting rides will be in these ridiculously noisy craft with the propeller mounted on a long shaft trailing the stern. Some, which are fitted with outsize engines possibly adapted from motor cars, reach amazing speeds.

Bangkok's waterways are full of long-tail boats (you can even hire one for a private trip) but they are also to be found on all the country's major waterways. Be prepared to get wet.

ESSENTIAL PRACTICAL INFORMATION

Accommodation
Thailand has accommodation to suit every taste and budget, from no-frills beach bungalows at a mere B50 a night to sumptious five-star suites for B5,000 or more. Between these two extremes you can find excellent value for money, especially off-season when prices drop considerably: the highest rates are in December and January.

Note that many hotels (and some guesthouses) have a variety of rooms, some with air-conditioning or fan, with hot water or attached bathroom. Unless you ask for an ordinary room (*hawng thammadaa*) you may well be offered the most expensive, complete with TV, fridge and other extras.

In major tourist areas the most popular form of accommodation for backpackers and budget independent travellers is the humble guesthouse, where room rates range from B80-300 a night (for a room with fan, no air-conditioning, and often communal bathrooms with simple showers and squat W.C.s). Catering for Western tastes and often providing tour and motorbike rental services, the guesthouse can be a friendly refuge and useful source of travel information, or – at worst – a heavily Westernized ghetto, with nightly videos.

Moving out of the backpackers' bracket, you'll find a range of Thai or Chinese hotels providing simple but clean accommodation for around B200-700 a night (usually with attached bathrooms and a choice of fan or air-conditioning). If you need a few more luxuries (like a swimming pool, room service, business centre and choice of restaurants) you'll be looking at a room rate of around B1,000-3,000 a night. Once you're at this level of accommodation, and in all the big international luxury hotels, expect to pay an additional service charge of 10 per cent and VAT of 7 per cent. Breakfast is not necessarily included in the room price.

Airport tax
For international flights there's an airport tax (payable when you check in) of B200; for domestic flights, it's B20.

Breakdowns
If you break down in your rented car or jeep, first call the rental agency for advice on a reliable nearby repair station: most local garages can fix simple problems. If it's serious, ask the agency how long it will take for them to provide a replacement vehicle: it may be simpler and quicker to take public transport to their nearest office and pick up a replacement there. See Assistance for the motorist (page 21) for further information.

Credit cards
In Bangkok and the popular tourist resorts, most major cards, especially Visa and MasterCard, are widely accepted in major stores, hotels and restaurants (Diners Club and American Express are less popular). The further afield you go, however, the less likely you'll be able to use them.

There are two main problems with using cards in Thailand: first, in most shops and restaurants you'll invariably be charged the 3 per cent (or sometimes more) bank surcharge which the vendor should actually pay. Without a great deal of hassle there isn't much you can do about this. Secondly, there's a risk that your card may be stolen or misused: never leave it in your guesthouse or hotel 'safe' while you go off on an excursion or trek; and never let a vendor take your card out of your sight when you're making a credit-card purchase: months later you may find yourself billed for vast amounts of unknown purchases, your signature faked on extra receipts.

Electricity
Thailand's electricity supply is 220 volts. Sockets are nearly always two-pronged, so bring an adaptor if necessary.

Embassies
The consular sections of these embassies in Bangkok can offer assistance to visiting nationals. If dialling from within Bangkok omit the capital's code, 02.

Australia 37 Sathon Tai Rd; tel. 02 287 2680.
Canada Boonmitre Building, 138 Silom Rd; tel. 02 238 4452.
Denmark 10 Soi Attakanprasit, Sathon Tai Rd; tel. 02 213 2021.
France 35 Customs House Lane, Charoen Krung Rd; tel. 02 266 8250; consular section for visas 29 Sathon Tai Rd; tel. 02 285 6104.
Germany 9 Sathon Tai Rd; tel. 02 213 2331.
Greece 412/8-9 Siam Square Soi 6; tel. 02 251 5111.
Italy 399 Nang Linchi Rd; tel. 02 285 4090.
Netherlands 106 Witthayu (Wireless) Rd; tel. 02 254 7701.
New Zealand 93 Witthayu (Wireless) Rd; tel. 02 251 8165.
South Africa Park Place, 231 Soi Sarasin, Rachdamri Rd; tel. 02 253 8473.
Spain 93 Witthayu (Wireless) Rd; tel. 02 252 6112.
U.K. 1031 Ploenchit Rd; tel. 02 253 0191.
U.S.A. 95 Witthayu (Wireless) Rd; 02 252 5040.

Emergencies
If you need the police, call the English-speaking Tourist Police. In Bangkok, their 500 officers patrol major tourist areas and are easily recognized by the TP markings on their cars and kiosks and by the blue and yellow badges on their uniforms.

Tourist Police Headquarters, Bangkok 509 Worachak Rd; tel. 02 221 6206 to 6210.

You can also call the **Tourist Assistance Center** in Bangkok on 02 281 5051 or 282 8129.

Out of Bangkok, Tourist Police can be found in the following places: **Chiang Mai**, tel. 053 248 974; **Hat Yai**, tel. 074 246 733; **Kanchanaburi**, tel. 034 512 795; **Pattaya**, tel. 038 429 371; **Phuket**, tel. 076 212 213; **Surat Thani**, tel. 077 421 281.

Where there is no Tourist Police, the emergency police number to call is 191 or 123. For fire, call 199.

Export of art and antiques

No Buddha images, Bodhisattva images 'or fragments thereof' are allowed to be taken out of Thailand, unless they are for worship by Buddhists or for cultural exchanges or study. To take such art objects or antiques out of the country (whether they are original or reproduction) you're supposed to have a licence from the National Museum of Bangkok, tel. 02 224 1370; Chiang Mai tel. 053 221 308; or Songkhla tel. 074 311 728. Allow five days for processing.

In practice, of course, the system isn't quite so strict, though officials do make spot checks. I was once stopped at Bangkok's airport when officials noticed a seated Buddha image (a modern, cheap reproduction) wrapped in my luggage. I protested my ignorance of the rules and the poor value of the product and they let me go, but it was a close shave: I wouldn't want to risk losing a more expensive purchase.

The durian

No other fruit in the world has been the subject of such insults and praise, such passion and disgust as the ugly durian. This football-sized fruit, covered with huge spikes, has an unforgettably foul odour – but its golden-yellow flesh ('like carrion in custard', according to a former British governor of Singapore) is considered by many Asians to be delectable. It's available from May to August, but out of season you can always introduce your tastebuds to durian-flavoured ice cream or chewing gum.

• *Omelet, Thai style.*

Food and drink

You never have to go hungry in Thailand. The Thais are incorrigible snackers, preferring frequent snacks to a few large meals, and you'll find street stalls, market stalls and noodle shops operating virtually round the clock. What's more, the food on offer is so varied that you're bound to find something you fancy.

It helps if you like spicy flavours: chillies are widely used, especially the tiny green chilli bombs called, literally, mouse-shit peppers, *phrik khii nuu*. (If you need relief, have a few mouthfuls of rice, which is far more effective than water.) Other distinctive ingredients of Thai *cuisine* are lemon grass, garlic, lime juice, ginger, coconut milk and fresh coriander – all indications of the range of international influences on Thai cooking, notably Chinese and Indian. If you can't take hot food, choose some of the blander Chinese-style dishes, or ask for dishes that aren't hot (*mai phet*).

Rice is a staple with most meals and two condiments are considered essential: *naam plaa* (a fish sauce used to provide a salty flavour) and *naam phrik* (a fiery, tangy sauce). Ingredients are nearly always fresh – the turnover is too fast for food to hang around.

That's one reason why eating at street or market stalls is generally safe. You can also see for yourself how the food is cooked – usually at wok-hot heat levels that would kill the most persistent bacteria. These food stalls, often congregating in open-air night markets, offer some of the tastiest (and cheapest) food of all. If you don't know what or how to order, just point politely to another customer's bowl or to the mix of ingredients you want.

In small restaurants, where there are often no menus, you can ask what's special – *Mii a-rai phi-set?* Unless you're in a totally Chinese restaurant, spoons and forks are the utensils provided (you eat with the spoon).

Of course, there are plenty of places where you can stick to tame Western fare, too. But you shouldn't leave Thailand without trying at least one uniquely Thai dish such as *tom yam kung* (a piquant prawn and lemon grass soup with mushrooms); *kaeng phet kai* (chicken curry); *plaa priaw waan* (sweet and sour fish) and *laap neua* (spicy beef salad). For desserts, you can't beat Thailand's wonderful fresh fruits, from mangoes, papayas and water melons to the less familiar rambutans and durians (see page 24).

The abundance of fruit makes fresh fruit drinks an ideal way to quench your thirst in Thailand. Never drink tap water – bottled or purified water and Western-brand drinks are available everywhere, as well as coffee and tea: iced water or weak Chinese tea is usually served automatically in restaurants. Beer is popular (though expensive due to a heavy government tax), especially the strong local Singha brew, closely rivalled by the lighter Kloster. Most Thais prefer the cheaper Mekong rice whisky, which is sweet and powerful, with an alcoholic content of 35 per cent.

Language

Like Chinese, the Thai language is tonal, with five tones (high, rising, falling, middle and low). This means that a syllable can have five different meanings, depending on the tone used. There are also regional dialects, quite distinct from Bangkok Thai. No wonder most *farang* visitors are scared of learning the language. But don't be put off: with a little practice (and some close listening) you can at least pick up a few essential phrases – and beyond Bangkok and the major tourist resorts you're going to have to, since English is by no means spoken everywhere (when desperate, look for a student since he or she will certainly have learnt some English at school).

The good news is that verbs have no tenses and most words are monosyllabic. To be polite, remember to end your sentences or phrases with *khrap* (if you're a man) or *kha* (for a woman). The word for I/me is *phom* (for a man) and *dii-chan* (for a woman), while the most respectful word for you is *khun*.

Maps and tourist information

The best country maps of Thailand are those published by Bartholomew and Nelles (both 1: 1,500,000), available overseas as well as in Bangkok bookshops. The detailed bilingual *Highway Map* (1:1,000,000) published by The Roads Association of Thailand and available in Bangkok bookshops is especially useful if you intend to cover much ground by hired car or motorbike.

The amazingly detailed maps of Bangkok and Chiang Mai by Nancy Chandler are great fun, packed with lively information on markets, shops and a range of oddities.

The Tourism Authority of Thailand (TAT) also publishes stacks of literature on the various regions of the country. In Bangkok, their temporary head office is at 372 Bamrung Muang Rd (tel. 02 226 0060/0072/0085). TAT has local offices at 18 destinations throughout the country (their addresses are listed under the appropriate towns in the text), which can help with information on accommodation, transport and sightseeing. Opening hours are from 8.30 am to 4.30 pm every day.

Medical matters

The complaint you're most likely to suffer from in Thailand is the age-old traveller's bugbear: stomach upset. Diarrhoea is usually caused by contaminated food or water, but your stomach may also simply grumble at the change in diet and climate. You can reduce the risks by sticking to bland foods for the first few days until you acclimatize to Thai cuisine. Don't eat unpeeled fruit, uncooked fish or unwashed salads. And never drink tap water (boiled or bottled water is available everywhere). Some visitors try to avoid ice altogether, though this is probably an unnecessary precaution and in any case difficult to achieve since drinks are nearly always served with ice.

Above all, drink plenty of fluids: it's easy to become dehydrated in Thailand's hot climate. Fluids and salt replacement are the essential treatment for diarrhoea, too. For severe diarrhoea, you should take oral rehydration sugar-and-salt solutions (readily available in Bangkok pharmacies). If the symptoms continue for more than three days, you must seek medical help.

Malaria is a growing problem throughout South-East Asia, with many strains increasingly drug-resistant. Thailand is no exception: even the nasty strain of *falciparum* malaria is becoming drug-resistant here. There are two schools of thought concerning preventative drugs: one says it's essential to take these prophylactics in order to secure at least some protection; the other says that the little protection they may offer is counteracted by possible unpleasant side-effects and a certain increase in drug-resistant strains.

If you are only intending to visit major cities, you are far less likely to be at risk than if you visit remote areas such as Ko Chang or northern Kanchanaburi Province. If you do decide to take prophylactics, contact a specialist hospital or doctor for advice on the latest recommended drug.

Simple precautions could be your best protection: always use a mosquito net and if you're outside at peak mosquito-biting hours (dusk and dawn), cover yourself with clothes and repellent. If you do develop symptoms (chills, headache and high fever), seek medical help immediately: malaria can be quickly treated and cured if caught early enough. Any hospital or clinic in Thailand should be able to provide assistance.

AIDS is another hazard which you should take very seriously indeed. Despite government AIDS-prevention campaigns since 1988 and intensive education and public awareness programmes (the most progressive in South-East Asia), AIDS is on the increase in Thailand, particularly among female prostitutes, many of whom are now reported to be HIV-positive. The message is obvious: if you come into sexual contact with a Thai prostitute, always use a condom. And avoid the use of unsterilized needles – the next highest-risk method of contracting the AIDS virus. The hospital blood supply is screened for HIV, so blood transfusions should carry little risk.

If you have a medical emergency you should try to reach a hospital in Bangkok or Chiang Mai. These are the best equipped, and include: Bangkok Adventist Hospital, tel. 02 281 1422; McCormick Hospital in Chiang Mai, tel. 053 240 823; or the less-crowded Chang Puek Hospital, Chiang Mai, tel. 220 022; or even contact your consulate for help in getting flown home. For further advice, consult *Staying Healthy in Asia, Africa & Latin America* by Dirk Schroeder, or *The Tropical Traveller*, by John Hatt.

Personal safety

The most likely danger in Thailand is robbery, usually by stealth, but very occasionally by force. On arrival at Bangkok's airport, avoid touts and unofficial taxi drivers who have been known to rob newcomers. During your stay, you should also take simple precautions such as locking bags and hotel rooms, and leaving valuables (carefully itemized) in hotel safes when you go trekking (see also Credit cards, page 23). An old trick among Thai thieves is to rob a victim after giving a drugged drink, snack or cigarette. It's safest to refuse such gifts from friendly strangers, especially when travelling on trains and buses in the south. What about risks to women travellers? I've travelled alone all over Thailand, without any problem (I've had far more hassle in Italy). But I dress conservatively, and I never travel alone at night or in very remote areas. However alluring the idea of night-time strolls in the wild might be, it's worth noting that there have been several nasty night-time attacks by robbers on solo foreigners (men and women).

The most dangerous area of Thailand for travel is probably the Thai-Cambodian border, especially around Aranyaprathet, where there are land mines and occasional Khmer Rouge activity. You should also avoid wandering into remote areas along the Thai-Burmese border north of Mae Hong Son and Chiang Rai where there's active and aggressive opium trading. Along the Burmese border to the west, near Three Pagodas Pass and Mae Sot, there are occasional outbursts of fighting between the rebel Karens and Burmese armies.

Lastly, don't even think about using drugs in Thailand: if you're caught in possession of marijuana you could face up to five years' imprisonment; smuggling marijuana will land you in jail for up to 15 years; smuggling heroin gets you life.

Post, telephone and fax services

Thailand's postal service is very efficient. Bangkok's GPO on Charoen Krung Road (including *poste restante* service) is open from 8 am to 8 pm weekdays, and from 8 am to 1 pm on weekends and public holidays. Provincial post offices are open from 8.30 am to 4.30 pm on weekdays and often from 9 am to noon on Saturday as well. Nearly all post offices have fax, telex and telegram services as well as a *poste restante* service (at Bangkok's GPO the *poste restante* service operates until 8 pm on weekdays). Be sure that your correspondents address letters with your surname in capitals, to avoid confusion.

In Bangkok, the 24-hour international phone, fax, telex and telegram office (behind the main GPO building) is the cheapest place to make overseas calls (hotels and private telephone offices will add a surcharge); to many countries there is direct dialling as well as the Home Direct collect-call service. Beyond Bangkok, you'll find similar government telephone offices in or near the town's GPO. They're usually open daily from 8 am to 8 pm (longer in large cities). Large hotels offer all these telecom-munications services, too, often in fully-equipped business centres.

Public telephones come in two colours: red for local city calls and blue for long-distance calls within Thailand. You'll need a 1B coin to operate them – though it's a toss-up whether the phone accepts the old-size or new-size lB coin (or even the size in-between). Card phones are increasingly common, with cards for sale at telephone offices, shops and even some bus terminals. For international operator assistance, dial 100; or 101 for domestic long distance service. The international code is 001.

Public holidays and festivals

In addition to the following public holidays (when all government offices and banks close), there are dozens of festivals all over the country throughout the year. For exact details and dates (some depend on lunar calendar timings) contact TAT for their annually updated *Major Events and Festivals* booklet:

New Year's Day (January 1); Magha Puja, commemorating Buddha's preaching to over a thousand people (February full moon); Chakri Day, celebrating the founding of the present Chakri Dynasty (April 6); Songkran, the beginning of the Buddhist New Year (April); Labour Day (May 1); Coronation Day (May 5); Visakha Puja, celebrating the birth, enlightenment and death of Buddha (May full moon); Asanha Puja, commemorating Buddha's first sermon (July full moon); Khao Pansaa, Buddhist Lent (July); The Queen's Birthday (August 12); Chulalongkorn Day, in commemoration of King Chulalongkorn (October 23); The King's Birthday (December 5); Constitution Day (December 10); New Year's Eve (December 31). Although Chinese New Year (usually late January/early February) is not an official public holiday, many shops close for a few days during this period.

Sales tax

There's a 7 per cent value-added tax (VAT) on certain goods and services, and on many tourist hotel bills.

Shopping and business hours

Government offices are open from 8.30 am to midday, and from 1 to 4.30 pm Monday-Friday. That gives civil servants plenty of time to go shopping: many stores in Bangkok, Chiang Mai and other major cities stay open until 7 or 8 pm daily (when the night markets take over). The department stores make up for their late nights by opening around 10 am. Smaller shops get a head start by opening around 8 am.

Shopping

Thailand is one of the best places in Asia for shopping, both for value and for variety. Bangkok and Chiang Mai are obviously the major shopping centres, with everything from street markets selling fake designer goods at rock-bottom prices, to air-conditioned malls and department stores with quality souvenirs. Wherever you go you'll find a wide choice of local handicrafts, particularly textiles. Tailor-made and ready-made clothes are also good buys. Bargaining is accepted everywhere except in the large department stores. But beware of touts offering you special bargains (especially in gems): at best, they're simply out to get a commission from whatever you buy; at worst, you'll be conned into parting with large sums for fake goods. Look for the TAT emblem or the gem trade's gold ring emblem to be sure of reliable merchants. Be particularly wary, too, when buying 'antiques': it's amazing how old fakes can be made to appear (see also Export of art and antiques, page 24). If you do have trouble, you should contact the Tourist Police (see Emergencies, pages 23-4).

Time
Thailand is seven hours ahead of GMT. It's also 543 years ahead of the rest of the world: Thais calculate their official calendar from 543 BC when Buddha is believed to have attained enlightenment. So while we're still waiting for the year 2000 to hit, Thailand is already looking ahead at 3000 BE (Buddhist Era).

Tipping and bargaining
Tipping isn't usually necessary, or expected, though most up-market hotels and restaurants now add a 10 per cent service charge. Hotel porters may also expect a tip (B5 or B10 is sufficient). Bargaining, on the other hand, is practised everywhere except in fixed-price department stores and shops selling daily commodities. It needs practice. If you're too aggressive, you'll never win. If you smile and enjoy the challenge, like the Thais do, you'll probably get at least a 10 per cent discount, and up to 50 per

Best buys
Textiles are Thailand's number one best buy, especially the shimmering, many-hued silk and quality cotton, widely available in Bangkok or in the north-east, where many of these textiles are made. Hill tribe handicrafts, from hand-woven shoulder bags to intricate jewellery, make unbeatable souvenirs, impossible to resist in the shops and markets of Chiang Mai. Burmese-style lacquerware and engraved silver inlaid with niello (a black alloy) are also excellent buys, as are sapphires, jade and rubies (as long as you can tell you're not being fobbed off with a fake). Short-sighted tourists have a special reason to splash out: Bangkok has probably the best bargains in the world for spectacles.

cent if you succeed in really charming the vendor. You can bargain for anything, from a bunch of bananas in the market to a room in a beach resort. But it's rarely worth haggling over a few *baht*. Remember the favourite Thai phrase, *mai pen rai* (never mind) and save your energy: you'll need it.

Religion
More than 90 per cent of Thais are Buddhists of the Theravada (also called Hinayana) school. This early form of Buddhism probably arrived in Thailand from India and Sri Lanka around the 3rdC BC and is now the dominant religion in Cambodia, Laos and Burma as well as Thailand. It differs from the later Mahayana tradition (followed in Vietnam, China and the Himalayan countries) by concentrating on individual enlightenment while Mahayana Buddhism aims to assist everyone in their search for nirvana.

Buddhism – or rather, the amalgam of philosophy, faith, morality and superstition that has evolved over the centuries – affects every aspect of daily life in Thailand and has strongly influenced the character and attitudes of the Thai people. Much of the activity you'll notice – giving alms to monks,

offerings at temples, releasing birds from captivity – is done to acquire merit, which Thais believe will help improve their chances of a better life in the cycle of rebirths. Grander merit-making donations go towards the building of new temples. There are now over 30,000 temples throughout the country, and some 200,000 monks. Every Thai man is expected to become a monk for a short period at some point during his lifetime.

If you're interested in delving deeper into Buddhism during your stay, you'll find many temples, forest *wats* and study centres where foreigners can take courses in Buddhism and in *vipassana* ('insight') meditation. For more information, consult the headquarters of the World Fellowship of Buddhists (33 Sukhumvit Rd, Bangkok) which also holds meditation classes in English every Wednesday, from 5 to 8 pm.

Prehistory, pre-Thai

In 1966, a young American anthropology student, Stephen Young, stumbled on some old potsherds in a field in north-eastern Thailand, and turned the theories of South-East Asia's prehistory upside down: the fragments from this burial site at Ban Chiang were dated to around 4600 BC, with subsequent bronzeware discoveries dated to 3600 BC – some 500 years older than anything found in the Middle East and 1,600 years older than China's earliest bronzeware.

Suddenly, Thailand had evidence that it wasn't just a cultural backwater, with technology trickling through from China and elsewhere, but an ancient civilization in its own right with a people who had not only mastered the art of agriculture (including rice cultivation) at least as early as 4000 BC, but also the arts of pottery by 3500 BC and metallurgy by 2500 BC.

Although the finds of Ban Chiang and other north-eastern sites are still being debated, they have thrown into question another long-held belief, that the Thai people originated in southern China and migrated south some 2,000 years ago. In fact, a linguistic group of Austro-Thais were scattered in river valleys all over Asia, including southern China. The Thais (sometimes spelt Tai to refer specifically to this large linguistic group also found in Burma, Laos and

• *Cave paintings, Ban Nong Pheu.*

southern China) emerged as the dominant race in Thailand in the 13thC when they established the first Thai kingdom. Only then was a written language formed – one of the reasons why earlier Thai history is so obscure.

In the years before the Thais ruled the scene there were several other kingdoms in the country, dominated by Mon and Khmer people. The Mon kingdom of Dvaravati was a thriving Buddhist civilization which flourished from the 6th to the 11thC AD, notably around Nakhon Pathom, while southern Thailand came under the sway of the Sumatra-based Srivijaya Empire in the 8thC, with Chaiya as its regional centre. But even during this time the invading Khmers from Cambodia had started exerting their power and influence: in the 10th and 11thC they built Khmer-style temples in north-eastern Thailand and established a base in Lopburi from where they controlled central Thailand. Meanwhile, the Thai people themselves were slowly migrating south from a state called Nan Chao (in what is now southern China), settling in northern Thailand and Laos. The Khmers employed some of these Thais as mercenaries, calling them Syams (probably a Sanskrit term meaning swarthy). Little did these tough soldiers guess that when the Khmer kingdom would

29

finally decline in the 13thC, they would promptly fill the power gap, and would eventually take the name Siam for their own domains.

Sukhothai: the first Thai kingdom
Kublai Khan was the spur the Thais needed to act: when he threatened to sweep down from southern China, several Thai princes united to establish a power base, capturing the Khmer town of Sukhothai in 1238 and declaring an independent kingdom.

At almost the same time, the Mons of northern Thailand were being defeated by a chieftain called Mengrai who first established a base in Chiang Rai in 1262 and then, in 1280, attacked the wealthy Mon kingdom of Haripunjaya. With the co-operation of King Ramkhamhaeng of Sukhothai and Ngam Muang of Phayao, King Mengrai founded his Lanna Thai Kingdom (Kingdom of a Million Rice Fields) in 1296, building his new capital at Chiang Mai.

In the event, Lanna was to last even longer than Sukhothai, finally falling to the Burmese in 1558. But Sukhothai's reign shone more brightly. Under its most famous king, Ramkhamhaeng, the new kingdom soon made its power felt, taking over from the Khmers and the declining Srivijaya Empire.

But this 'golden era' of Thai history is noted more for its benign and progressive ruler and its outstanding Buddhist art than for its military achievements: the remarkable Ramkhamhaeng established the first Thai written language (thereby uniting the various Thai tribes), codified the law and made Theravada Buddhism the state religion, endowing the city's temples with magnificent sculptures.

Compared with every government since, his rule sounds too good to be true: 'In the time of King Ramkhamhaeg,' an inscription from this period declares, 'this land of Sukhothai is thriving. There is fish in the water and rice in the fields... whoever wants to trade in elephants, does so; whoever wants to trade in horses, does so; whoever wants to trade in silver and gold, does so. [The King] has hung a bell in the opening of the gate over there: if any commoner has a grievance which sickens his belly and gripes his heart...he goes and strikes the bell...[and King Ramkhamhaeng] questions the man, examines the case, and decides it justly for him.'

The rise and fall of Ayutthaya
It couldn't last, of course. In 1351, Prince Utong (also known as King Ramathibodi) founded a rival kingdom in Ayutthaya, some 60 km north of modern Bangkok, which was to become one of the most powerful in the region, not only taking over Sukhothai in 1376 but also capturing the great Khmer city of Angkor in 1431. Khmer customs and rituals were adopted, including the concept of the king as *devaraja* (god-king) – a far less accessible status than the *dhammaraja* (dharma-king, one who rules according to Buddhist doctrine) style of Sukhothai's kings.

But Ayutthaya's rulers were progressive, too, introducing various civil and economic reforms and a new code of law. Benefitting from its strategic trading position, and the boom in trade between east and west, Ayutthaya became extremely wealthy, famous throughout the world. From the early 16th to the late 17thC, Western trading emissaries came calling. The Portuguese were the first to arrive, in 1511, followed in succession by the Dutch, Spanish, English, Danish and French.

But these brief flirtations on the international scene came to a dramatic end when the Burmese – who had continually pestered Ayutthaya with attacks, including a successful 20-year takeover in 1569 – finally got their way in 1767,

---

Farangs
When a Thai calls you a *farang* he's not being rude: the word simply means a foreigner of European descent. Some 300 years ago, the word then used, *farangset*, literally meant French. It was a dangerous time to be a Frenchman in Siam: the King's closest adviser was a Catholic Greek adventurer, Constantine Phaulkon, who showed increasingly strong French and Catholic sympathies. In 1688, his jealous enemies acted, expelling the French garrison from Bangkok and executing Phaulkon. It marked the end of close relations with the West for more than 100 years.

after a long seige. This time, the victorious Burmese slaughtered or enslaved the inhabitants and destroyed everything they could find: temples, buildings, sculptures, libraries. No other event has had such a devastating effect on Thai history and culture or impressed itself so darkly on the Thai psyche.

The new capitals: Thonburi and Bangkok

But the Thais weren't crushed for long: a young Thai general, Taksin, reorganized forces in the south-east and established a new capital at Thonburi (across the Chao Phraya River from present-day Bangkok), proclaiming himself king in 1768. Within just two years he had fought off the Burmese and succeeded in regaining the lands of Ayutthaya's kingdom.

The effort must have been too much: while his loyal general, Chao Phya Chakri, carried on fighting the Burmese and brought the Lanna, Cambodia and Lao kingdoms under Siam's control, King Taksin stayed in Thonburi and slowly went mad (among his most disturbing pursuits were torturing his wives and attempting to fly). On April 6, 1782, he was captured in a coup and General Chakri was asked to take the throne: the first of the Chakri Dynasty which still reigns today (King Bhumibol is the ninth of the line). Taksin's fate was one reserved solely for royalty: he was popped in a black velvet sack and beaten to death with a sandalwood club.

King Rama I, as Chao Phya Chakri was entitled, acted swiftly to secure his kingdom's safety from the Burmese, moving the capital across the river to Bangkok. Here he invested the new city not only with a Grand Palace and glittering monasteries (including a palace *wat* to house the Emerald Buddha which he had seized from Vientiane), but also with renewed confidence following the disastrous cultural losses at Ayutthaya and debilitating time with Taksin: he established new civil and religious laws, and set about recreating a literary heritage – himself writing at least part of the *Ramakien* (a version of the Indian *Ramayana* epic) which is now regarded as Thailand's literary masterpiece.

After a peaceful reign by his son,

Rama II, Thailand was again disturbed by skirmishes with Laos during the time of Rama III: in 1827 the invading Laotian army got within striking distance of Bangkok but were then roundly defeated and their capital, Vientiane, was sacked and destroyed. But it wasn't old neighbours such as Laos which posed the greatest threat to Thailand now: it was the new empire-grabbing foreigners from the West. But luck was on Siam's side: two enlightened kings were to save the country from being colonized in the 19thC.

Steps to modernization

The first, King Mongkut (Rama IV) had been a Buddhist monk for 27 years before taking the throne in 1851. During this time he had not only studied Sanskrit and Pali but also English, Latin and Western sciences. Recognizing that Thailand had no chance of defeating Western military might, he followed a skilful diplomatic path, signing the Bowring Treaty with the British in 1855 to allow certain trading rights, and balancing it with agreements with other Western powers. The first steps towards modernization were taken, including setting up a ship-building industry and reforming the education system. Mongkut himself studied Western medicine. Could this enlightened fellow possibly be the same King as portrayed by Yul Brynner in *The King and I*? Not according to the Thais, who find the film not only factually incorrect but also deeply offensive.

King Mongkut was succeeded in 1863 by his equally progressive son, Chulalongkorn, who succeeded when he was 15. Among his first steps were the abolition of slavery and the custom of prostrating before the King. Modernization surged ahead with the construction of roads and railways and the establishment of a civil service, though a revolt by the old guard in 1874 meant reforms had to slow down for a while. Like his father, Mongkut had the educational and diplomatic skills to deal with foreign pressure – he employed hundreds of foreigners (mostly British) to help with technological developments but at the same time guarded Thailand's independence from creeping colonialism. It was only when faced with direct military threats – as in 1893, when the French demanded Laos by

• *Tribute to the King, Bangkok.*

sending gunboats up the river to Bangkok – that Thailand had to give way.

Chulalongkorn's son, the British-educated Vajiravudh (Rama VI) never lived up to his father's record, though he did introduce compulsory education. But his extravagant lifestyle and opposition to any moves towards a constitutional monarchy were increasingly at odds with the trend to modernization. Soon after his brother, Prajadhipok, succeeded him in 1925, a small élite of Western-educated Thais decided it was time for change: the country was suffering badly from the Great Depression of the 1930s, and the government was floundering.

On June 24 1932, a peaceful *coup d'état* was staged by a group of army officers and civilians. The King, writing from his seaside palace in Hua Hin, immediately agreed to relinquish absolute monarchy, and three years later abdicated completely in favour of his ten-year-old nephew, Ananda.

Pre- and post-World War Thailand

This coup did not bring the parliamentary democracy, with a constitutional monarch, which some had hoped for. Instead, a pattern of military dictatorship was established, with countless coups and counter-coups over the years to come. At first, two names dominated the scene: Phibun Songkhram (an army major) and Pridi Phanomyong (a lawyer), both leaders of the 1932 coup. The ultra-nationalist, anti-Chinese Phibun initially took control; in addition to several discriminatory measures against the Chinese he also introduced, in 1939, a new name for Siam – Thailand, emphasizing that the country belonged to Thai (Tai)-speakers.

When the Second World War broke out, occupying the attentions of the Western powers, Phibun took it as an opportunity for further nationalism and grabbed back some territory in Laos and Cambodia that France had seized in the 19thC. But in December 1941, Thailand faced new encroachment from Japan and ended up signing a military alliance with them. As allies of Japan, the Thai government even issued a declaration of war against the U.S.A. and Britain, though Seni Pramoj, the Thai ambassador in Washington, refused to deliver it.

Meanwhile, Pridi was working behind the scenes with a resistance movement, Thai Seri. Following Japan's defeat, Phibun was forced to resign and after Seni Pramoj briefly held the post of Prime Minister, Pridi took over. But murky goings-on in the royal household soon unseated Pridi, too: in 1946, just six months after Ananda was at last officially enthroned, the new King was found assassinated. The murder was never solved, but suspicion surrounded anti-royalist Pridi and he was forced to resign. Quick as a flash, back came Phibun. See-saw politics were becoming a Thai trademark.

With his fervent anti-communist sentiments, Phibun was the man for the moment: the U.S.A. poured funds into Thailand to support its resistance to the region's sweeping communist movements. General Sarit Thanarat, who wrestled power from Phibun in 1957, brought the monarchy, under King Bhumibol (Rama IX), back into the limelight and encouraged economic development, but at the same time tightened the noose around any attempt at political reform and was notoriously brutal and corrupt. His successor, General Thanom, was equally uncompromising: his attentions focused on the increasing communist threat posed by the Vietnam War. American forces were allowed to operate air bases from Thailand for their bombing raids in Laos and North Vietnam, with tens of thousands of Americans based on Thai soil.

But the Communist Party of Thailand was gaining support among the poor and disillusioned of the north-east. And when Thanom instituted martial law, after a brief flirtation with democratic elections in 1969, he alienated students and the intelligentsia, too. In 1973, hundreds of students were killed during massive demonstrations at Thammasat University in support of a new constitution. Lacking support from the army, Thanom and his deputy Praphat were forced into exile.

If the students thought they'd won, they had little time to celebrate: in 1976, protesting against Thanom's return as a monk, Thammasat University students were again brutally repressed and the military installed the heavy-handed Thanin Kraivichien as prime minister. His successor, the more moderate General Kriangsak Chomanand, started to woo back the disillusioned Thais who had joined the ranks of the Communist Party of Thailand (CPT) after the 1973 riots. But it was General Prem Tinsulanond, taking over the premiership in 1980, who achieved the first real period of post-War stability.

Thailand in the 80s and 90s

With Prem's skilful carrot-and-stick approach (amnesties and attacks), the CPT gradually disintegrated. Economic and political advances followed, with a general election in 1983 which returned Prem to legitimate power, and foreign investment which provided rapid economic growth. Greater freedom of expression was also allowed. Even Prem's departure was unusually democratic: in 1988 he simply resigned, so that a truly elected representative could take over in general elections.

Chatichai Choonhaven, a former military man but a long-time civilian, introduced a period of great economic growth, supported by his cabinet, who were nearly all former businessmen. It worked wonders for Thailand's GNP and international reputation, but waiting in the wings, and growing increasingly upset by their marginalized role (especially in foreign policy) were certain diehard conservative soldiers.

On February 23 1991, General Suchinda Kraprayoon staged a bloodless coup (Thailand's 17th *coup d'état* since 1932), citing the previous government's corruption. In order to appease critics, Suchinda installed a civilian diplomat, Ananda Panyarachun, as prime minister. All went surprisingly well under Ananda's premiership until the promised 'elections' in March 1992 when Suchinda booted out the winner, Narong Wongwan (who was admittedly tainted by allegations of drug dealing), and took the post of premier himself.

This was one step too far for the long-suffering Thais: in May 1992, huge demonstrations in Bangkok and elsewhere demanded Suchinda's resignation. Predecessors in similar circumstances had fled into exile or stepped down, but Suchinda ordered a brutal crackdown. The confrontation between the military and the demonstrators resulted in at least 50 deaths and hundreds of injured. If he thought he'd get away with it, he had forgotten one thing: the monarchy. King Bhumibol, an increasingly influential figure in public affairs, publicly castigated Suchinda on television, and this was enough to force his resignation.

Ananda was reinstated as prime minister until elections were held again in September 1992. This brought a five-party coalition to power, with Chuan Leekpai, the civilian leader of the Democrat Party, as premier. Chuan's 'Mr Clean' reputation helped to keep him in power for a record two years and seven months – making him the longest-serving elected PM in Thai history. But his government was finally brought down in June 1995 by a land reform scandal. The following month a new coalition government was elected, led by the main opposition party, Chart Thai, under Banharn Silipa-archa, a traditionalist politician from the rural heartland. Few expected the result to usher in calmer, less corrupt times. Reflecting the country's mood, the prominent newspaper publisher Suthichai Yoon warned, 'Fasten your seat belt.'

<u>Northern Thailand</u>

Between Bangkok and Chiang Mai
The Road to Chiang Mai

700 km; map Nelles 1:1,500,000

This is the classic journey through Thailand, from Bangkok north to Chiang Mai, the country's second largest city and the jumping-off point for treks into hill-tribe country further north and west. You can fly or take the train direct to Chiang Mai, or you can dally on the way, as this itinerary suggests. Hopping between places *en route* is easily done by train or bus. (But, as with all the itineraries in this guide, you don't have to 'do' it at all: simply use the sightseeing, accommodation and eating information as and when you need it.)

Stopping at Ayutthaya, Lopburi and Sukhothai will introduce you to the historic and cultural heartland of the kingdom: at Ayutthaya, Thailand's illustrious former capital (and recently declared a UNESCO World Heritage Site), you can see some of the finest temple ruins in the country, dating from the 14th to the 18thC. Lopburi, 93 km to the north, goes back even further, to the 6thC Dvaravati civilization, though it's the 12thC Khmer ruins, an impressive museum and the town's horde of monkeys which lure the tourists these days.

Sukhothai is a must: the cradle of the Thai history, this former capital dating from the 13th and 14thC represents the golden age of Thai civilization, especially in art and sculpture. The well-restored ruins of the ancient city, now an historical park, are an easy day trip from the new town. From here you can also make excursions to two other less-visited and even more evocative ruined cities nearby, Si Satchanalai and Kamphaeng Phet.

Allowing for a day in each place, you could spend at least five days *en route* to Chiang Mai: a pleasantly relaxing pace before hitting this busy city, famous for its handicrafts, shopping and temples. Many people find the place too crowded for comfort these days: if you feel like escaping quickly, just flick to Thailand Overall: 2 for the Golden Triangle, or Local Explorations: 4, 5, 1 or 2 for a range of other adventurous options in the area.

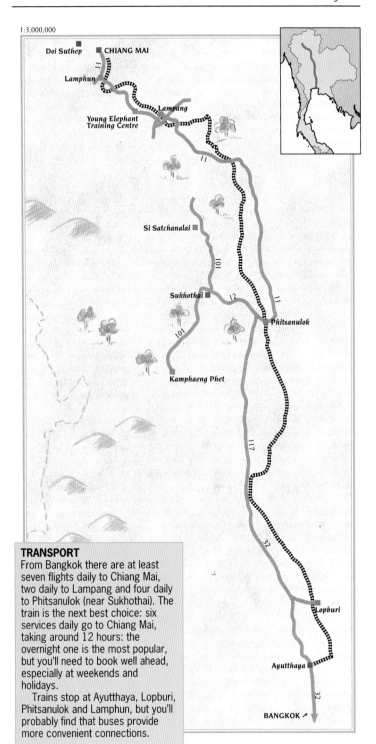

1:3,000,000

Doi Suthep   ■ CHIANG MAI

Lamphun

Lampang

Young Elephant
Training Centre

11

Si Satchanalai ■

101

Sukhothai ■   12   11

101   Phitsanulok ■

Kamphaeng Phet ■

117

32

TRANSPORT
From Bangkok there are at least
seven flights daily to Chiang Mai,
two daily to Lampang and four daily
to Phitsanulok (near Sukhothai). The
train is the next best choice: six
services daily go to Chiang Mai,
taking around 12 hours: the
overnight one is the most popular,
but you'll need to book well ahead,
especially at weekends and
holidays.
   Trains stop at Ayutthaya, Lopburi,
Phitsanulok and Lamphun, but you'll
probably find that buses provide
more convenient connections.

Lopburi ■

Ayutthaya ■

32

BANGKOK ↗

SIGHTS & PLACES OF INTEREST

AYUTTHAYA
See Bangkok, pages 152-3.

CHIANG MAI ⇌ ✕
Some 700 km N of Bangkok. Getting your bearings is the first challenge: the old city surrounded by moats lies to the west of the new town which effectively begins at Tha Phae Gate and spreads east across the Ping River. The railway station lies this way, a couple of kilometres east of Tha Phae Gate, while the main Arcade bus station lies 3 km to the north-east. Songthaews and tuk-tuks are the quickest way into and around town, but be sure to bargain: the drivers here know all the tricks (including so-called city tours which mostly feature shops where the drivers are able to collect commissions on your purchases).

The TAT office at 105/1 Chiang Mai-Lamphun Road (tel. 053 248604) is a useful first stop, especially if you want recommendations on trekking agencies – they keep a list of accredited operations. There's also a branch of the Tourist Police here (tel. 053 248974), which should be your first port of call if you have any trouble (for example, with unscrupulous dealers).

History
Founded in 1296 by King Mengrai as the capital of his rapidly expanding Lanna Thai ('million Thai rice fields') kingdom, Chiang Mai is still the north's most important city and the country's second largest. Frequently billed as 'The Rose of the North', it's not smelling quite so sweet these days: heavy traffic and pollution, over-development and business greed are taking their toll of Chiang Mai's charm. But its 300 temples, its excellent handicraft shopping and tourist facilities and its well-organized trekking industry make it an indispensable part of any visit to Thailand.

There's something else that persuades people to stay longer than they might: Chiang Mai and its people are intangibly different. Much of this is down to history. After the city enjoyed its golden age of civilization in the 15thC, it fell under Burmese control and remained a vassal state for 200 years. Even after it was liberated, it remained somehow aloof from the rest of Thailand, culturally set apart by its history and different races, geographically separated by the mountains. Before a railway was built here in the late 1920s it took several weeks of travel by boat and elephant to reach Bangkok. Politically, too, Chiang Mai retained a cloak of independence, with a prince who was nominally in power right up to 1939.

Even the Chiang Mai dialect is different – a strain that has evolved from the languages of eastern Burma and southern China, as different from central Thai as modern English is to Chaucerian. Here, in the furthest reaches of the country, something of the frontier atmosphere has never gone away. True, you're unlikely to see an elephant 'stalking down the market amidst a crowd of Karens, Shans, and Kamuks from across the Mekong', as a British surveyor observed in the 1890s. Nor will you find polo being played at the Chiengmai Gymkhana Club. But you still see Akha tribeswomen selling handicrafts in the bazaar, and expats at the Club coolly watching cricket.

Sights - the temples
A suitable place to start your temple tour is at the oldest wat, **Wat Chiang Man**, off Ratchaphakhinai Road in the north-eastern corner of the old city. Founded the same year as Chiang Mai itself, it's mostly famous today for two sacred Buddha images which you'll find (with some difficulty – they're almost hidden behind rows of bars) in the *viharn* to the right of the main hall. The **Phra Sila** ('Stone Buddha') is believed to have been made in India some 2,500 years ago, and brought to Thailand via Ceylon (Sri Lanka). The tiny (10-cm-high) **Phra Setangamani** ('Crystal Buddha'), probably originated in Lopburi several centuries later.

Heading south down Ratchaphakhinai Road, then west along Ratchadamnoen, you'll catch sight of the huge 15thC chedi of **Wat Chedi Luang**, which lost its top in a 16thC earthquake and is now being restored – though not with the original metal plates and gold leaf which once splendidly covered it. At that time, the Emerald Buddha itself (now in Bangkok) is said to have graced its eastern niche. Now its most important possessions are the **lak meuang** (city pillar), found inside the unceremonious small building by the entrance; and a huge **eucalyptus tree draped in silk** which legend says will keep growing for as long as the city thrives. A short stroll west along Ratchadamnoen Road brings you to the city's most impressive temple complex, **Wat Phra Singh**. Its loveliest building (behind the large modern *viharn* at the entrance) is a typical Lanna-style *viharn* dating from around 1400, which is ornately gilded and carved. Inside is a sacred **Phra Singh Buddha bronze image** from the 15thC – one of three identical images (the other two are in Nakhon Si Thammarat and Bangkok). Each one is claimed to be the original Ceylonese image.

Far more eye-catching, though, are the magnificent **18thC murals** covering the walls, which reveal fascinating scenes from village and court life. There's an elegant little 14thC library near the entrance, too, with detailed wooden carvings.

A short trip north-west of the city, just off the superhighway, is another important and rather curious temple, **Wat Jet Yot**, built in 1455. The seven spires of its chedi represent the seven weeks the Buddha stayed at Bodhgaya, India, following his enlightenment – a design believed to have been roughly copied from Bodhgaya's own Mahabodhi Temple. The exquisite stucco figures of celestial beings around the base of the chedi are worth a close look.

While you're here, you may as well pop into the nearby **National Museum** (open Wednesday to Sunday, 9 am to 4 pm). Its grand building houses a particularly fine collection of Buddha images of different styles from Chiang Mai's 15th and 16thC golden era. Among the ceramics on display there are some lovely pieces from the famous Si Satchanalai area (known as Sawankhalok in its Ayutthayan heyday). The most valuable museum for learning about local hill tribe culture is the **Tribal Research Centre** (open week-

---

SHOPPING IN CHIANG MAI

Even if you hate shopping, you'll undoubtedly weaken in Chiang Mai: textiles and handicrafts here are among the best in the country, both for variety and value-for-money. The **night market** on Chang Klan Road is a must (go early, around 6 pm, if you want to avoid the crowds or later if you want the full buzz). Hundreds of stalls here, both inside a covered arcade and on the streets, sell everything from bargain-priced cotton clothes and boot-leg cassette tapes to intricately embroidered hill tribe garments (often sold by the hill tribe people themselves), popular *yaam* shoulder bags, wooden carvings, fake antiques, silver jewellery, lacquerware and ceramics. There's even a post office in the depths of the market which operates a packing and shipping service (as well as overseas telephone booths so you can phone home for more money).

The older **Warorot Market** on Chang Moi Kao Road also has some excellent fabrics.

The other major area for textiles – especially silk – is **San**

Kamphaeng, 13 km east of town (hop on a bus on Charoen Muang Road, east of Ping River, to get here). One of the longest-established operations is Piankusol: its store 5 km from town has a display of silk-weaving out front, though most of its weavers still work at home to maintain the quality. Up until recently, the strictly Buddhist family which runs it even imported the silk threads to avoid killing the worms.

En route to San Kamphaeng, you can stop at the famous umbrella village of **Baw Sang**, a very tourist-oriented complex of workshops and stores selling the familiar painted umbrellas (made of silk, cotton or paper) as well as other souvenirs.

Some of the best-quality outlets for hill tribe products are the non-profit organizations that channel proceeds back to the artisans. You won't necessarily find bargains here, but you will be directly supporting the hill tribes. **The Hill Tribe Products Foundation** (near Wat Suan Dok on Suthep Road) and **Thai Tribal Crafts** (208 Bamrungrat Road) both sell a high-quality range of clothes and other items.

• Doi Suthep, Chiang Mai.

days only from 8.30 am to 4.30 pm) in Chiang Mai University (follow the super-highway south from the National Museum and then turn right along Huai Kaeo Road). As well as providing basic information on the major hill tribes, with displays of their distinctive clothing, it also has maps showing areas where they live. It's worth coming here before setting off on your trek.

Continuing south, off Suthep Road (about 4 km south-west from the town centre) you'll reach **Wat Umong**, Chiang Mai's weird and wonderful forest wat. Following an avenue of trees labelled with popular didactic messages ('those with good eyes are inclined to fall into deep wells'; 'when money speaks truth is silent') you'll come to an entrance hall of garish paintings by resident monks before reaching the historic heart of the compound: 14thC brick tunnels (*umong*) supposedly built specially for a famously mad monk to meditate in rural peace.

Above the tunnels (which still have vestiges of paintings) is a ruined chedi and a gruesome statue of the fasting Buddha, looking more skeleton than man. But it's the shady tranquillity of Wat Umong which I remember best: this is the place to run to when the city gets too much. Sometimes you can hear the gibbons calling.

On your way back into town, stop off at **Wat Suan Dok** ('flower garden'), just south of Suthep Road, for a picturesque view of Doi Suthep framing the wat's brilliantly white chedis in the foreground. These 14thC chedis contain the ashes of Chiang Mai's royal family, while the huge central whitewashed chedi contains a precious Buddha relic which is said to have split into two segments, giving off a supernatural glow, when it was being placed inside. The new relic was carried by a white elephant which finally stopped and died on Doi Suthep – the site thereby chosen for the Wat Phra That Doi Suthep (see below).

DOI SUTHEP

This 1,600-m-high hill, 16 km NW of Chiang Mai, is the site of the sacred **Wat Phra That Doi Suthep**, a dazzling hilltop temple founded by King Keu Na in 1383. Although one of the most popular tourist spots in the vicinity of Chiang Mai, its panoramic position and its religious importance make it a worthwhile excursion – especially if you go early to avoid the crowds and continue with a visit to the winter palace and surrounding national park. Songthaews go regularly to Doi Suthep from opposite Chang Pheuak Gate, on Mani Nopharat Road, though you may have to wait for them to fill up with passengers.

The legend behind the temple's

• *Local talent,*
Chiang Mai.

founding is suitably dramatic: it's said that King Keu Na placed part of the sacred relic from Wat Suan Dok on the back of a white elephant which trumpeted three times and headed for Doi Suthep. The holy animal climbed the hill, turned round three times, knelt down and promptly died. King Keu Na reacted to the obvious significance of the event by having the temple built on the very spot where it occurred.

A steep naga stairway (or a funicular for the weak) leads to the temple's two terraces, the upper one a dazzling array of gold: golden ceremonial umbrellas surround the sacred gilded chedi, a 16thC version of the original. The views over Chiang Mai are especially dramatic at sunset.

Continuing another 4 km up Doi Suthep will bring you to the royal family's **Phuping Palace** whose gardens are open weekends 8 am to 4 pm when no one is at home. You can forget the exploited **Hmong village** 3 km beyond the palace unless it's your only chance of seeing a hill tribe. But if you've still got time, the **national park** is a delightful and surprisingly close city escape, though you'll need your own transport to reach the park accommodation (the checkpoint before you reach the temple can provide maps).

Another, rarely-visited gem of tranquillity is the little-known **Wat Palad**, hidden on the slopes of the hill just 6 km before you reach the temple. Practically abandoned, its ancient chedi no longer visible beneath a tangle of undergrowth, this Shan Burmese forest wat is, to me, the most magical spot in Chiang Mai. Nine seated Buddhas are tucked on a rocky ledge above a trickling stream; and just before you reach the stream there are stone seats scattered in a circle of dappled sunlight. I met a foreigner here once, searching for seeds. He called

39

DETOUR – **YOUNG ELEPHANT TRAINING CENTRE**

This set-up (also called the Thai Elephant Conservation Centre) 37 *km* NW *of Lampang on the way to Chiang Mai*, is one of the best places in the country to see how elephants are trained. (You can ride and feed the elephants, too.) The set daily shows usually take place at 9 am and/or 11 am (except from March to May) and demonstrate how the young elephants push, pull and stack logs. It takes about 90 minutes by bus to get here from Lampang, so you'll need to leave early to arrive in time for the 9 am show.

them black pearls, claiming that if you rub them, they glow, like charms.

KAMPHAENG PHET

See Thailand Overall: 5, page 90.

LAMPANG ⋈ ✕

Some 100 km SE of Chiang Mai. Train and bus stations lie SW of town - from Chiang Mai, the bus service is the most frequent.
An ideal excursion from Chiang Mai or a relaxing stop-over *en route*, the historic city of Lampang, founded in the 9thC, has some beautiful Burmese temples – the legacy of Burmese teak merchants and loggers who came here at the end of the 19thC. Among Thais, the city is almost equally renowned for its horse-drawn carriages which now linger on as tourist attractions, their drivers in fetching stetson hats. (Songthaews and samlors are a better way to get around, however, especially on arrival.)

The town centre, around Boonyawat Road, just south of the River Wang, is a wonderful clutter of busy streets with heavy Chinese influence (especially in its many gold shops). The main temples are all on the quieter outskirts.

The most important is **Wat Phra Kaew Don Tao**, a couple of kilometres to the north-east of the town centre. Built in the 15thC, its main claim to fame is that it housed the Emerald Buddha (now in Bangkok) for 32 years. These days, it's the turn-of-the-century Burmese *mondop* which grabs all the attention: like some extravagant doll's house perched before the gold-tipped

chedi, its interior is a palatial excess of gold and glitter with columns of swirling golden patterns, a ceiling of podgy cherubs dangling from squares of enamel and coloured glass and coloured baubles everywhere. The more restrained carved wooden panelling on the outside is the most impressive piece of craftmanship. To the right of the mondop, in a modern building, you'll find a small museum of Lanna artifacts, with a hotch-potch of wood-carved panels, a stuffed crocodile and cabinets of Buddha figurines.

Wat Si Chum was once one of Lampang's loveliest Burmese temples, but a fire in January 1992 destroyed practically everything. Now only the fabulously ornate carved porches stand in the ashes, a horrifying testament to the vulnerability of old wooden temples.

All the more reason to be grateful for the **Wat Phra That Lampang Luang**, the most impressive complex of Lanna-style temple architecture in northern Thailand. Located 18 km south-west of Lampang (catch a songthaew to Ko Kha, then a motorbike taxi for the last 5 km), this temple complex was originally built as a fortress and is still enclosed by walls and cloisters.

The first building to greet you, at the top of a naga stairway and through a fantastically decorated gateway, is the late 15th to early 16thC **Viharn Luang**, triple-roofed and open on all sides in traditional Lanna style. A gilded and stuccoed *mondop* inside houses a sacred 16thC Buddha image, surrounded by faded 19thC jataka murals of battle scenes on wooden panels hanging from the *viharn's* eaves.

The faint remains of murals 300 years older than these can still be traced in the old wooden **Viharn Naam Taem** to the right further back: note the outlines of rich-looking women, with chunky earrings and elaborate hair-dos; and a mythical beast with huge eyes and crocodile jaws. The *viharn* itself is beautifully simple, with a sloping roof and plain interior. The 15thC **Viharn Ton Kaew**, just in front, cannot match its neighbour's style.

But don't miss the smaller **Viharn Phra Phut**, to the left of the main *viharn*. Perhaps the oldest of all in the complex, with a lovely carved wooden façade, it certainly receives the most attention from devotees since it houses several important Buddha images.

The devotees then visit the adjacent **15thC chedi**, its bronze surface now patterned and coloured with muted golds and greys. On one of the bars in the bronze balustrade surrounding the chedi you'll see a notice: 'This is the hole of a bullet which Nan Tip Chang shot' – a reference to an 18thC hero who killed a Burmese general during an attempted invasion.

Follow the devotees further and you'll step through a gate in the wall to the left past a fantastically huge bodhi tree, its hanging roots supported by dozens of poles. The focus of the pilgrims' attention lies in a building to the right: a tiny and much-revered **Emerald Buddha**, said to have been carved from the same block as the Emerald Buddha in Bangkok, can just be made out amidst a clutter of other Buddha images and guarded behind thick bars. The room also contains a bizarre collection of other bits and pieces, ranging from Buddhist scripture boxes and elephant tusks to a century-old lacquer hat, and a collection of old coins.

TREKKING
For full details on the possibilities near Chiang Mai and in the region, see Local Explorations: 10, 11 and 12.

LAMPHUN
This nondescript provincial capital 26 *km (and 45 minutes by bus) S of Chiang Mai* is only worth visiting for its two historic temples. These hark back to Lamphun's golden era, the 9thC, when princess Chama Thewi (daughter of Lopburi's Dvaravati-kingdom ruler) founded the Haripunchai state here. It remained an independent principality until 1281 when King Mengrai finally brought it to heel within his Lanna kingdom.

THE LAST OF THAILAND'S ELEPHANTS
Just under a century ago, as many as 100,000 domestic elephants were used for logging and transport in Thailand. Now there are only about 4,000 and probably half that number of wild elephants. Their natural habitat is being destroyed and – since the ban on logging in Thailand – their working role is fast disappearing, too.

But an elephant is an expensive beast to keep idle at home: an average elephant consumes 20 per cent of its own body weight each day, along with hundreds of litres of water. And it can live for at least 80 years. No wonder, then, that villagers from the poor north-east often bring their elephants into town to find free food and water and some income for themselves – even if it means travelling hundreds of miles by foot or by truck. Once at their destination, the mahouts lead the elephants about the streets, where people offer fruit and vegetables and often pay to duck under the elephant's belly three times for good luck. Other members of the group may sell handicraft trinkets to passers-by.

During 1995, there were about 30 elephants led by their mahouts to roam the polluted, noisy streets of Bangkok in search of food. They stayed in temporary camps on empty land for a couple of months before returning home. As the Thailand Elephant Lovers Foundation admits, this street life is a pitiful and unhealthy existence, but at least the animals are fed.

However, even this method of survival may soon be impossible. The Bangkok Metropolitan Administration issued an order in 1995 banning elephants from the city. Other cities may follow suit. The Foundation is hoping to create elephant centres around the country instead, where visitors can come and ride the animals and see how they're trained. The elephant may have disappeared from Thailand's national flag, but it has an honoured place in Thai culture and few want to see it disappear altogether.

• Wat Si Chum, Sukhothai.

Wat Phra That Haripunchai, first founded in the 9thC, is on the town centre's main road and is dominated by a 51-m-high 15thC chedi, shielded by a gold umbrella. Two other chedis stand in the grounds: the one to the north, built like a tiered pyramid in Dvaravati style, still has some stucco decoration visible; the other is built in Chiang Saen-style. The *viharn* (rebuilt in 1925) has some fine carved woodwork and interior murals. To the left is a graceful library building with gilded roof; to the right, a pavilion sheltering a huge bronze gong – reputedly the biggest in existence.

Wat Kukut is 1 km west of town and houses two important chedis, dating back to the 8th-10thC. The smaller one nearest the entrance is an octagonal brick structure decorated with niches housing eight standing Buddhas. The second, 21-m-high chedi is the more outstanding, built as a five-tiered pyramid with three terracotta standing Buddhas of Dvaravati style in niches on all four sides. Nowhere else in Thailand can you see such a fine example of the religious architecture of this period.

LOPBURI ⌘ ✕

Relaxed and tourist-friendly, this provincial capital 147 *km* (*and about three hours by bus or train*) N *of Bangkok* makes an enjoyable stop-over on your way north. The major sights here are several Khmer ruins; the palatial remains of the town's 17thC heyday under King Narai, and an impressive national museum in the king's former palace buildings, which houses evidence of Lopburi's 1,400 years of history.

First called Lavo in its Dvaravati heyday (6th-10thC), Lopburi has maintained a prestigious role ever since. It was a major centre during the 10th-13thC Khmer period, and even more important in the 17thC when it was used as a second capital by King Narai. Tumbling over its central historic sites today are the town's horde of spoilt monkeys, which have almost usurped the Khmer ruins in popularity with day-trippers. They scamper along the telephone wires, sit on the traffic lights and run along the railway track with complete abandon: if you want to see the frenzy at feeding time, wait by the tracks around 4.30 pm, opposite the shrine-cum-monkey playground at San Phra Kan.

The main sights are all within easy walking distance in the old part of town east of the Lopburi River, west of the railway station.

The most impressive is just opposite the station: **Wat Phra Si Ratana Mahathat** is a peaceful grassy compound of partly-restored Khmer prangs and Ayutthaya-style chedis. The tallest 12thC prang in the centre still shows some impressive details of stucco carving while a topless chedi in the northwest corner has a tantalizing frieze of five headless stucco Buddhas. The most recent addition is the large roofless *viharn* added by King Narai, now in atmospheric ruins.

Just a few minutes' walk to the northwest, you'll come to the king's palace (**Phra Narai Ratchaniwet**) built in the late 17thC and restored by King Rama IV (Mongkut) in the 19thC. Its outer courtyard is now a shady, relaxing park dotted with ruins of outhouses. Western influence is clearly seen in the imposing fortress walls and arches. Even in the very Thai-style **Chanthara Phisan Pavilion** in the central courtyard, there once hung a portrait of Louis XIV and French mirrors on the walls. The exhibit now displayed here is a fascinating account of Western influences and attitudes during King Narai's time, including accounts of how the Jesuits introduced the king to astronomy and amusing portraits of French nobles in Siamese dress.

The **Dusit Sawan Hall,** the other side of the museum, illustrates a similar cultural dichotomy, even though it's in ruins: formerly an audience hall for foreign VIPs, one half has distinctly Western-styled arched windows, the other blatantly Thai. Between the two is the raised platform for the king's throne. The king himself had his private residence in the area to the south-west of this, but now only the ruins of the **Suttha Sawan** hall remain.

The central buildings in the main courtyard contain the **National Museum** (open Wednesday to Sunday, 8.30 am to noon, 1 pm to 4 pm). One of the best in the kingdom, its display covers Lopburi's entire history, from prehistoric pottery on the ground floor to memorabilia of King Mongkut on the top floor. Highlights not to be missed on the ground floor are the endearing 7thC carved heads of deities: small smiling faces, each one different; and fascinating terracotta sculptures from the same period revealing a belief in occultism. Upstairs, there's an excellent display of the various Thai art styles as illustrated by its Buddha figures, which leads you through each period. Among the interesting Khmer artifacts look out for an especially lovely lintel of Shiva and Uma dating from the 11thC.

A small **folk museum** behind the main building has a well-displayed collection of farm implements, pottery and weaving as well as a typical rural bamboo house.

Walking north along Rue de France you'll pass **Wat Sao Thong Thong**, which started life as a Christian chapel for foreign ambassadors (hence its Gothic-style windows) and was later converted to a Buddhist sanctuary. The

Lopburi-style Buddhas in the wall niches have great serenity.

The road ends in the ruined residential complex of the former ambassadors, an enclave called **Ban Wichayen**. The most famous ambassador to live here was the influential Greek, Constantine Phaulkon (known as Chao Phraya Wichayen) who was King Narai's prime minister. Only the shells of the chapel and residences for Phaulkon, the Jesuit priests and French ambassador remain, but you can still make out Thai-Western decorations on the chapel walls.

Follow Wichayen Road to the east and you'll reach the town's central Khmer ruin (and the one most popular with the monkeys): **Prang Sam Yot** consists of three large laterite prangs which were originally Hindu, then Buddhist shrines. Some excavation and restoration work is going on here, so it's not as photogenic a site as it used to be. But it is still a pleasant place to sit and watch the monkeys performing trapeze acts along the surrounding telephone wires.

PHITSANULOK ✉ ✕

Some 390 km N of Bangkok, just over halfway to Chiang Mai. Arriving by train you'll find yourself right in the centre; the bus terminal is a couple of kilometres to the east. Surprisingly, there are few motorbike taxis, but plenty of samlors and songthaews for getting around. The TAT office is at 209/7-8 Borom Trailokanat Road (tel. 055 252742) and has heaps of information on the area..

Nicknamed 'Phi-lok', this sprawling city beside the Nan River has a couple of worthwhile places to visit but is mostly popular as a base for day trips to Sukhothai and Kamphaeng Phet.

The town's number-one attraction is the **Wat Phra Si Ratana Mahathat** in the north of town, beside the river. This 14thC temple houses one of Thailand's most revered Buddha images, the **Phra Buddha Chinnarat**, a glowing bronze image in late Sukhothai style, with an unique flame-like halo curling from the head down either side of the torso to end in upturned naga heads. Thousands of pilgrims pour daily into the ornate little *viharn* to pay homage to the image; the *viharn* complements its precious possession with its rich interior decoration of black-and-gilt columns, a red-and-gilt ceiling and doors inlaid

with mother-of-pearl. Outside, there's almost a fairground atmosphere, with devotees crowding round the dozens of stalls selling religious knick-knacks and souvenirs.

Phi-lok's other major place of interest – **The Folk Museum** on Wisut Kasat Road – is across town, to the south. One of the best of its kind in Thailand (open 8.30 am to noon, I pm to 4.30 pm daily), it was founded by a Sergeant Major Dr Thawee Buranakhet who has been collecting artifacts and rural implements from northern Thailand for decades. You'll be taken on a tour of the exhibits (housed in attractive Thai-style pavilions) by a guide who will patiently explain the uses of the more bizarre-looking items. Every aspect of traditional rural life is represented, from baskets and looms and children's games to musical instruments and superstitious practices (crab-shell wind chimes are believed to provide protection against ghosts, while a woman giving birth traditionally placed a branch of a gardenia tree below her house to guard her newborn child against evil spirits). Don't miss the fascinating hardwood massage tools (different shapes for men and women), a whole spectrum of old lamps, and the collection of ingenious animal, bird, snake and even cockroach traps.

Across the road (where the 65-year-old Dr Tawee is often working) you'll find his **Buddha-Casting Foundry** where all sizes of Buddhas are made. Visitors are welcome to walk around and watch the process. There's no guided tour, but you'll find a very helpful photographic display in English by the entrance.

SI SATCHANALAI HISTORICAL PARK

The partly restored ruins of this Sukhothai-era town (now a historical park), lie *57 km to the north of old Sukhothai* and make a delightful day trip: the park (open daily 8.30 am to 4.30 pm) is far less tourist-oriented than Sukhothai's and far more peaceful, with an attractive setting of hills and the nearby Yom River.

Buses leave new Sukhothai regularly for new Si Satchanalai, 11 km north of the ruins: ask for *meuang kao* (the old town) and you'll be dropped after an hour or so at one of three entrances to the ruins – the first two pass bicycle rental shops which are well worth considering if you also want to take in the ruins at Chaliang (a former Khmer site) a couple of kilometres south-east of the park (directly accessible from the first two entrances); or the Sawankhalok pottery kilns a couple of kilometres north-west of the park.

Chaliang's highlight is the **Wat Phra Si Ratana Mahathat**, a 15thC complex (considerably restored in the 18thC) consisting of a large central chedi with ruined *viharns* either side. The eastern one is the more notable, containing a typical Sukhothai-style seated Buddha and an outstanding example of the elegant trade-mark of Sukhothai Buddhist art: a walking, smiling Buddha, here in stucco relief. As you step into the *viharn* under a low gateway, be sure to check out the lintel of four smiling faces either representing Brahmin or Avalokitesvara and strikingly reminiscent of Angkor Thom's Bayon temple.

Heading west along the riverside track, past the Khmer-style prang of **Wat Chao Chan**, you'll soon reach the site of the old city of Si Satchanalai, surrounded by a 12-m wide moat. You can reach the major ruins in the park by bike or on foot or even by elephant – rides are (appropriately) available from outside **Wat Chang Lom**, whose huge chedi has a pedestal of 39 standing elephants – many missing their trunks, making them look like strange, long-legged dogs.

Wat Chedi Jet Thaew, opposite, is very impressive, with seven rows of chedis. One is a copy of Wat Mahathat's lotus-bed chedi at Sukhothai. To the south is **Wat Nang Phaya**, renowned for the fine stucco reliefs on its laterite *viharn*. Looking over the whole site is **Wat Khao Phanom Phloeng** on a hilltop just north of Wat Chang Lom. The ruins of the chedi here and of **Wat Khao Suwan Khiri** on the slightly higher hill to the north-west aren't among Si Satchanalai's best, but the panorama (especially at dusk) is undeniably atmospheric.

Si Satchanalai in its 14th to 15thC heyday (when it was called Sawankhalok) was as famous for pottery as for temples: the area's excellent clay led to hundreds of kilns being established. At the **Centre for Study & Preservation of Sangkalok Kilns** a couple of kilometres upstream from the Historical Park you can see a couple that have been excavated, together with a small collection of the famous ceramics. Any 'Sawankhalok ware' that you're offered by hawkers *en route* should be viewed with caution: antique fakes are perennial favourites with local entrepreneurs.

SUKHOTHAI ⌷ ✕

The ruins of old Sukhothai are 58 km NW of Phitsanulok and 11 km W of new Sukhothai, a small town which makes an ideal base for day trips both to Sukhothai and Si Satchanalai. Regular songthaews to old Sukhothai, journey time around 30 minutes.

Thailand's first capital, Sukhothai ('dawn of happiness') is considered the cradle of Thai civilization: from 1238 to 1376 (when it was annexed by the upstart Kingdom of Ayutthaya) Sukhothai presided over a golden age of art and architecture, peace and prosperity, law and order. Under the most brilliant of its rulers, Ramkhamhaeng, Theravada Buddhism was established (supplanting the Khmer's Hinduism), free trade encouraged, and a modern Thai script developed. Ramkhamhaeng's famous account of the state, inscribed in stone, extols his benevolent rule, and though obviously a masterpiece of propaganda, it's still honoured as Thailand's first real work of literature, epitomizing the Sukhothai civilization.

The ruins of old Sukhothai – extensively restored and declared a Historical Park in 1988 – are spread over a large area; unless you're a keen walker the best way to get around the site is by bicycle (available near the entrance). Just the central city area, which contains 21 historical sites including the most famous temples, covers three square kilometres; while the 70 sites beyond are scattered up to 5 km away in four different 'zones'. The central zone is the most visited and most sanitized, with neat paths, a few snack stalls and even a bus tour service. But in the zones beyond you can quickly get away from the tour groups and find some ancient Sukhothai atmosphere.

The **Ramkhamhaeng National Museum** (open Wednesday to Sunday, 9 am to 4 pm) by the entrance to the

central zone is worth just a brief visit to see a copy of Ramkhamhaeng's famous stone inscription (the original is in Bangkok). But grabbing your attention more dramatically nearby is **Wat Mahathat**, the religious heart of the Sukhothai kingdom and as such, the largest and most important site in the

• *The revered Phra Buddha Chinnarat, Wat Phra Si Ratana Mahathat, Phitsanulok.*

city. Dating from the 13thC, with additions by later kings, it is surrounded by walls and moats and contains hundreds of monuments, including ten *viharns* and nearly 200 chedis. The centrepiece

is a large chedi in typical Sukhothai lotus-bud style, surrounded by eight smaller chedis. Around the base of the whole ensemble is a stucco relief of walking monks – one of Sukhothai's most memorable pieces of artistry.

To the south is **Wat Si Sawai**, originally a Hindu shrine built by the Khmers and later converted into a Buddhist site. Its three corn-cob-shaped prangs are distinctively Khmer in style. **Wat Trapang Thong** (Golden Pond) and **Wat Trapang Ngoen** (Silver Pond) flank Wat Mahathat to the east and west and are named after their surrounding lotus ponds (two of many in the old city). Even more beautifully situated over water is **Wat Sa Si**, north of Wat Trapang Ngoen. Its Ceylonese-style chedi, columned sanctuary and large seated Buddha have an exceptionally pleasing and confident elegance.

Venturing north from here, just outside the central zone, you'll come to the large 12thC complex of **Wat Phra Pai Luang**, which was probably the centre of the Khmer town that existed before the foundation of the Sukhothai kingdom. The three Khmer-style prangs which remain from this early period still show some stucco evidence of Hindu figures as well as later Buddha images. To the west is one of Sukhothai's most photographed sites, **Wat Si Chum**. Its colossal seated Buddha, 15 m high, is squeezed inside a narrow *mondop*, which emphasizes its extraordinarily daunting size.

• *Wat Phra Si Ratana Mahathat.*

If you want to see one of Sukhothai's most remote and untamed temples, make the effort to go to the hill-top **Wat Saphan Hin**, several kilometres west of the central walled city. It is best seen when the sun is low. There is a steep climb along the 'stone bridge' steps after which the wat is named, but when you get to the top you'll share the view of the plain below with a large standing Buddha, flanked by laterite columns. If you can linger until dusk, this is one of

---

LOY KRATHONG FESTIVAL

One of Thailand's most popular festivals, the Loy Krathong is said to have originated in Sukhothai some 700 years ago when one of the king's concubines designed her own style of homage to the water goddess by placing a candle and offerings in a tiny banana-leaf container (*krathong*) and setting it afloat on a lotus pond.

Today, millions of *krathong* are set afloat on rivers and lakes all over the country on the full moon night of the 12th lunar month (usually November). But nowhere is the sight more enchanting than at Sukhothai where the festival continues for three nights, highlighted by magnificent *son et lumière* shows and a grand firework display.

RECOMMENDED HOTELS

CHIANG MAI

Eagle Guest House, B; 16 *Changmoi Kao Soi 3; tel. and fax 053 235387.*

Run by Pon and his Irish wife Annette, this popular little place has a range of basic rooms (all with bathrooms) and a pleasant, shady sitting-out area. Super-efficient Annette has information on practically everything. She and Pon pride themselves on their 'clean' treks (no drugs, no rubbish).

Pao Come Guest House, B; 9 *Chiangmoi Kao Soi 3; tel. 053 252377.*

Much more low-key than Eagle, with friendly 'Ae' at the helm, this has clean rooms and a quiet atmosphere (except for Ae's dog).

Gap's Guest House, B-BB; 3 *Ratchadamnoen Soi 4; tel. 053 278140.*

This should be the perfect budget hideaway: a delightful tangle of a garden wraps around individual bungalows and wooden buildings, with generous scatterings of pots, plants and wood carvings.

Galare Guest House, BB; 7 *Charoen Prathet Road; tel. 053 273885; fax 053 279088; cards, MC, V.*

A smart riverside hotel with a small garden. All rooms have air-conditioning and simple but pleasant decoration.

Top North Guest House, BB; 15 *Moonmuang Road, Soi 2; tel. 053 278900; fax 053 278485.*

At the quiet end of a *soi* of bars, with good-value air-conditioned rooms and even a small swimming pool.

River View Lodge, BBBB; 25 *Charoen Prathet, Soi 2; tel. 053 271109; fax 053 279019; cards, MC, V.*

Very stylish hotel with an open-air riverside restaurant and swimming pool. All rooms are decorated in traditional Northern Thai style with tasteful antiques and artifacts. Book ahead.

LAMPANG

No. 4 Guesthouse, B; 54 *Pamai Road.*

A rambling old teak house with lofty rooms and vast garden. Mattresses are plonked on the floor – but what a floor,

all gleaming wood. There's a trendy little bar-restaurant outside.

Asia Lampang Hotel, BB; 229 *Boonyawat Road; tel. 054 227844; cards, MC, V.*

More up-market than most in this road, with air-conditioned rooms and a pleasant street-side restaurant. You could give its Sweety Music Room a miss.

LOPBURI

Nett Hotel, B-BB; 17/1-2 *Ratchadamnoen Road; tel. 036 411738.*

Clean and central, with fan or air-conditioned rooms and the cheery Khun Narumol at reception.

Asia Lopburi, B-BB; 1/7 *Surasak Road; tel. 036 411892.*

A popular place, right opposite King Narai's palace, though street rooms can be noisy.

PHITSANULOK

Phitsanulok Youth Hostel, B; 38 *Sanam Bin Road; tel. 055 242060.*

This must be one of the most aesthetically pleasing hostels in Thailand. You enter through a jungly garden, fragrant with jasmine adorned with old pots and carts to find a huge teak *sala* – used as a sitting and dining area. Antique beds and lamps furnish the simple rooms. The only drawback is the location, beside a main road.

Rajapruk Guest House, BB; 89/9 *Phra Ong Dam Road; tel. 055 259203; cards, V.*

Dull and indifferent compared to the youth hostel, but the large clean rooms (with hot water showers) are peaceful and fairly priced.

SUKHOTHAI

Yupa Guesthouse, B; 44/10 *Pravet Nakhon Road; tel. 055 612578.*

My favourite of the several welcoming guesthouses along this riverside road. The rooms in the modern house are fairly basic, but Yupa and her daughter Tuk make solo travellers feel at home.

Ban Thai Guesthouse, B; 38 *Pravet Nakhon Road; tel. 055 610163.*

Attractive and new with seven bungalows around a pretty garden. Winai and his English-speaking staff can also arrange day trips to nearby sites.

Sawatdiphong Hotel, B-BB; 56/2-5 Singhawat Road; tel. 055 611567.

A cheap choice if you need air-conditioning, though there are simple fan rooms too.

RECOMMENDED RESTAURANTS

CHIANG MAI
New Lamdoun Faharm Kao Soi, B; 352/22 Charoenrat Road.

The place to try the north's famous *khao soi* noodles, a Burmese-influenced spicy chicken broth. King Bhumibol has eaten here.

Thanom Restaurant, B-BB; Chaiyaphum Road, near Daret's.

Small, prim and proper (no alcohol served, closes at 8 pm) you can get delicious food here at reasonable prices: try the melt-in-the-mouth sweet green chicken curry.

Aroon Rai, BB; 43 Kotchasan Road.

I have fond memories of this relaxing open-air restaurant, thanks to its delicious fried grasshoppers. Plenty of less daunting northern dishes, too.

Antique House, BB-BBB; 71 Charoenprathet Road; tel. 053 276810.

If you like rooting around in junk shops you'll love eating here: this renovated 19thC teakwood mansion is stuffed with antiques and curiosities. You can even buy the chairs you sit on. The extensive menu ranges from hot dogs to *filet mignon* (Thai dishes, too).

Tha Nam (Riverside) Restaurant, BB-BBB; 43/3 Moo 2 Changklan Road; tel. 053 275125.

Attractive teak riverside pavilion, stuffed with carvings, antiques and Lanna-style artifacts. Dine on Thai specialities to the sound of traditional music and the croaking of frogs.

LAMPANG
The Riverside Restaurant, B-BB; 328 Thipchang Road; tel. 054 221851; cards, MC, V.

Not a particularly charming stretch of river and the live band can be dismal, but this old riverside building makes a relaxing spot for a candlelit drink or dinner.

LOPBURI
Julathip Hotel Restaurant, B-BB; Na Phra Kan Road; name not given in English.

You'll recognize this place from the crowds of early evening diners: no-frills, no English, but hearty fare and a great spot for people-watching: the night market is across the street.

PHITSANULOK
Night Bazaar, B; Phuttha Bucha Road (near junction with Naresuan Road).

The silliest culinary spectacle in Thailand takes place here when a couple of the riverside restaurant stalls perform their 'flying vegetable' act for the tour groups: unsuspecting tourists don aprons and hats draped in vegetables, climb to the roof of a van and try to catch a wok-full of morning glory tossed to them by the cook. You can eat better at stalls elsewhere, but it's worth a look and a laugh.

Butter Home, B-BB; 175/4-5 Ekathotsarot Road (sign in English announcing `Food & Drinks'); tel. 055 258287.

A spic-and-span bakery-cum-restaurant, run by a friendly Khun Vipaisin, with cheap Thai favourites and Western snacks.

SUKHOTHAI
Dream Cafe, B-BB; Singhawat Road (opposite Bangkok Bank).

If you're suffering from 'ache all over the body', or need your blood, brain or sexual desire nourished – or if you simply like an environment of tasteful antiques – this is the place to come. Owner Chaba Suwatmekin has created a nostalgic den of loot from the past in which to serve more than 200 imaginative menu items, including whisky-based 'stamina drinks' that will apparently cure all ills. A smaller, simpler branch is opposite Win Tour on Ramkhamhaeng Road.

Chinnawat Hotel, B-BB; 1-3 Nikhon Kasem Road; tel. 055 611385.

This long-established budget favourite (its rooms are now a little seedy) has a restaurant where *farangs* feel comfortable: the menu includes standard Thai and Chinese fare, and sandwiches.

<u>Northern Thailand</u>

Between Chiang Rai and Chiang Khong
The Golden Triangle

290 km; map Nelles 1:1,500,000; and Guide Map of Chiang Rai by V. Hongsombud, with detailed maps of various scales

The infamous Golden Triangle refers to a vast area around the junction of the Laotian, Thai and Burmese borders. Since the 1960s it has been a major producer of opium poppies bringing golden rewards to its drug barons, and now accounts for nearly 80 per cent of the world's heroin supplies. But in Thailand's corner of the Golden Triangle – the border area north of Chiang Rai – it's not convoys of opium-carrying mules you'll encounter on the roads these days but lines of air-conditioned tour buses. The Thai government's efforts to tame the region, and its on-going campaign to persuade hill-tribe people to substitute opium poppies for alternative cash crops, has shifted the centre of opium activity across the border to the ethnic Shan state of north-east Burma. Here, the world's biggest drug warlord, Khun Sa, uses profits from the drug trade to finance his fight for independence from the Burmese government.

This itinerary gives you the thrill of being on Khun Sa's doorstep and never more than a glance away from Burma or Laos: at the heavily commercialized village of Sop Ruak where the borders meet, you can even see both countries at the same time. Further south down the Mekhong River, at Chiang Saen and at nearby Chiang Khong (an official border crossing for Laos), the convoy of tour buses thins to a trickle and you can soak up the riverside frontier atmosphere in your own way, your own time.

You can spend anything from three to ten days on this trip, depending on whether you include a trek in the area around Mae Salong north-west of Chiang Rai, or venture across the Burmese border at Mae Sai to Keng-tung. If you're the lingering sort, you'll find Mae Salong and Chiang Khong especially seductive.

TRANSPORT

Flying to Chiang Rai is your quickest route into the Golden Triangle: there are at least three flights daily to Chiang Rai from Bangkok and two daily from Chiang Mai. Buses from Chiang Mai take about four hours (12 hours from Bangkok or 13 hours on VIP buses direct to Mae Sai). Or you can take a long-tail boat from Tha Ton (see Local Explorations: 1).

Once at Chiang Rai you can hop on one of the frequent buses to Mae Sai (taking 90 minutes), and from there pick up less frequent songthaews or buses for Sop Ruak, Chiang Saen and Chiang Khong. Buses leave frequently from Chiang Khong for the three-hour ride back to Chiang Rai.

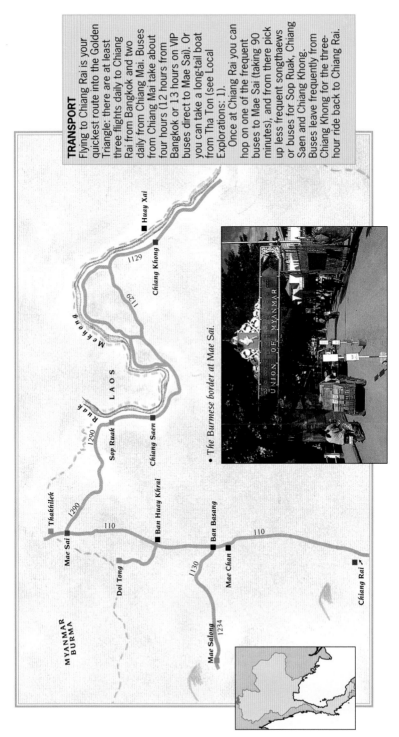

• *The Burmese border at Mae Sai.*

SIGHTS & PLACES OF INTEREST

BAN BASANG
See Mae Salong, page 55-8.

CHIANG KHONG ⇌
On Route 1129, 52 km by road E from Chiang Saen. The journey from Chiang Saen to Chiang Khong is one of the most spectacular in the area, with the road climbing past hill-tribe villages and orchards of lychee, mango and oranges to reach a grand viewpoint over the Mekhong valley below and the hills of Laos to the east. It's worth coming here for the ride alone, though bus and songthaew connections are infrequent along this riverside stretch. You'll find it easier (though far less attractive) to get to Chiang Khong from Chiang Rai: buses leave regularly throughout the day from here for the three-hour journey.

Chiang Khong itself is an important trading town strung out beside the river. At the southern end is the main market and bus terminal while at the northern edge of town, 2 km away, is the pier where passenger ferries cross to the Laotian town of Huay Xai. If you have a visa for Laos you can cross here, too (and continue to Luang Prabang on a long-tail boat, around six hours). There are several agencies in Chiang Khong which can arrange 15-day visas for Laos within 24 hours: unlike the border crossings with Burma, casual day trips to Laos are not possible at the time of writing.

Following the 1994 opening of the Friendship Bridge from Nong Khai in Thailand to Vientiane in Laos, a second bridge across the Mekhong has been proposed here to link roads all the way across Laos to China's Yunnan province. But as yet nothing has been confirmed and Chiang Khong remains a wonderfully low-key place to rest at for a few days, especially if you stay in one of its riverside guesthouses.

Among the few attractions are a couple of excellent **handicraft shops** at the northern end of town which sell local hand-woven cloth and clothes by the Thai Lu ethnic minority (if you've been to China's southern Xishuangbanna province, where the Thai Lu originated, you'll recognize the similarities in design immediately).

And if you're around from mid-April to May you may be able to witness Chiang Khong's main claim to fame – the **giant catfish** (*plaa beuk*). Probably the world's largest freshwater fish, it can measure up to 3 m in length and weigh as much as 300 kg. It's found only in the Mekhong, and especially in the stretch of river near Chiang Khong. **Ban Hat Khrai**, 1 km south of town, is the fishing port from where the boats set off each morning during the catfish season and where you'll have the chance of seeing the famous fish when the boats return.

CHIANG RAI
See Local Explorations: 1, pages 158-9.

CHIANG SAEN ⇌ ✕
This historic old town *on the banks of the Mekhong, 60 km (and about one hour by bus) north-east of Chiang Rai*, is a delightful escape from the commercialization of Sop Ruak (the designated official centre of the Golden Triangle; see pages 58-9) 14 km to the north. The ruins you'll find scattered around this relaxing and slow-moving town mostly date back to the 14thC when Chiang Saen was founded by Saenphu, the successor to King Mengrai of Chiang Mai. Later falling into the hands of the Burmese, Chiang Saen was only recaptured by the Thais in 1803 who then destroyed it to keep the Burmese at bay. The present town dates from the 1880s and has built up around the ruins of the original walled city, whose ramparts are still visible in the undergrowth.

If you stay overnight in one of the guesthouses (mostly found along the north-south riverside road) you can rent a bicycle from the guesthouse for touring the ruins; otherwise you might want to hop on a samlor or songthaew for those sites a few kilometres away.

Heading west from the river along the main Phahonyothin Road you'll pass a couple of ruined chedis standing incongruously among shops and houses before reaching the important **Wat Prathat Chedi Luang** which was probably built in 1331 as the city's main temple. Its huge octagonal chedi is girdled with saffron cloth and surrounded by other ruins, some of which now house small shrines. The **National Museum** next door (open Wednesday to Sunday, 9 am to 4 pm) houses some of the more notable relics of the area, including some lovely Lanna-style Buddha images.

Across the road, in the grounds of the ruined **Wat Mahathat**, there's the office of the 'Restoration and Conservation Chiang Saen Historical City' and a small tourist information bureau, with a model of the town showing the staggering number of temples that once existed here. Now the hundreds of ancient wats are mostly ruined or abandoned.

Passing through a gap in the chunky ramparts to the west you'll reach Chiang Saen's loveliest complex of ruins, **Wat Paa Sak**, now a historical park. Its name (Forest of Teak Wat) refers to the many teak trees originally planted here in the 14thC to surround and protect the chedi that was built on the site in 1340. The chedi is still the most impressive of the seven monuments in the leafy grounds, combining a hotchpotch of artistic influences from various places including Pagan (Burma), Sukhothai and Dvaravati. Above the standing Buddha images around the base there's some fantastically detailed stucco work including a host of nagas and bug-eyed beasts.

A couple of kilometres north, at the end of a quiet rural road, the hilltop **Wat Phra That Chom Kitti** makes a pleasant goal at dusk. The golden-tipped chedi is believed to have been built a couple of centuries earlier than Chiang Saen's founding. Today visitors here tend to turn their backs on the chedi and lean on the surrounding wall to gaze at the addictive view below of the town and the river, and the endless, empty hills of Laos disappearing into the eastern haze.

DOI TUNG

An ideal day-trip from Mae Sai, Doi Tung is the 1,322-m-high wooded peak *about 45 km SW of Mai Sai*, right on the Burmese border. A popular pilgrimage site because of its ancient wat, Doi Tung makes for an exciting journey: Route 1149 which leads to the peak from Ban Huay Khrai on Highway 110, climbs a winding route for 18 km past Ahka, Lahu and Shan villages, and plantations of teak and pine to end in a spectacular view of the plains below.

The **Wat Phra That Doi Tung** gave the peak its name when King Achutarat

THE LONG AND WINDING ROAD TO CHINA

As a long-established market town on the Mekhong River border with Laos, Chiang Khong is the kind of place you'd expect to be busily engaged in cross-border trade – not all of it perhaps entirely legal. But one of its more extraordinary and lucrative trading activities these days is in second-hand German luxury sedans destined for the booming China market.

According to a report in the *Far Eastern Economic Report* in 1995, many of the cars start their journey from the Gulf states (where they're relatively cheap). They are then shipped to Bangkok, driven all the way through Thailand to Chiang Khong, ferried across the Mekhong to the Laotian town of Huay Xai and driven on the rough road to Boten, the northern Laotian town on the Chinese border.

Even with all the 'handling charges', Chinese import duties and other cross-border 'fees', the profits on the sale of the cars in China are still considerable. 'A successful merchant can ship 60 cars a month, for an annual profit of around U.S. $3.6 million', noted the FEER report.

of Chiang Saen ordered a mammoth flag (*tung*) to be flown from the peak to mark the completion of two chedis enshrining Buddha relics (reputedly part of the Buddha's left collarbone).

That was more than a thousand years ago, in 911, and the chedis are still here, although renovated this century. Receiving more attention these days are the temple bells which devotees enthusiastically bash for merit, and a fat Chinese Buddha statue whose huge belly-button serves as a receptacle for donations.

A summer palace for the Queen Mother was built on the slopes of the peak in 1988 to indicate royal support for efforts to help villagers switch from slash-and-burn agriculture and opium poppy production to cash crops such as strawberries, cabbages and cucumbers. This whole area was once very volatile, with frequent clashes between factions controlling the drug trade. Now

it's largely peaceful, although with Khun Sa still clashing with Burmese forces just over the border, it's still no place to go wandering off the main route, and certainly never after dusk. If you're on a bike, don't even consider tackling the rugged mountainous back road from Doi Tung to Mae Sai which skirts the sensitive Burmese border unless you're an experienced rider and travel during daylight hours in the company other people.

• *Marking the Golden Triangle.*

HUAY XAI

See Chiang Khong, page 52.

MAE SAI ⇔ ×

Travel as far north in Thailand as you can and you'll end up in Mae Sai on the Burmese border, *846 km N of Bangkok and 61 km (90 minutes by bus) from Chiang Rai.* Once you get here, it seems everyone else has arrived at the same time: Phahahonyothin Road, the busy broad street leading to the border, is full of buses, tour buses, minibuses, songthaews and samlors.

Mae Sai's **border crossing** with Myanmar (Burma) is the reason why everyone comes here. Crowds of mostly Thai day-trippers stream over the bridge crossing the Sai River to the Burmese town of Thakhilek (also spelt Tachilek) to buy cheap Chinese products and Burmese souvenirs,

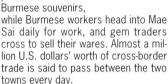

•*Akha hill tribe head gear.*

while Burmese workers head into Mae Sai daily for work, and gem traders cross to sell their wares. Almost a million U.S. dollars' worth of cross-border trade is said to pass between the two towns every day.

A large and controversial gambling den which opened in Thakhilek in February 1995 is the latest lure. Reportedly a joint venture between Thai investors and members of the Red Wa ethnic minority (with the tacit permission of Burma's junta) it has caused concern among Thai authorities (gambling is illegal in Thailand) and been hotly denied by the Burmese. Not surprisingly, it has so far maintained a very low profile.

As at the other official land crossing in Thailand – the quieter Three Pagodas Pass – foreigners are also allowed to enter Burma here, not just for the day (as at Three Pagodas Pass) but for up to four days to visit Kengtung, 163 km from the border (see box, page 56). The border is open from 6 am to 6 pm weekdays and until 9 pm on weekends.

This isn't always the safest spot in Thailand: opium warlord Khun Sa and his Muang Tai Army (MTA) have frequently clashed with Burmese Government troops in the Thakhilek area. As recently as May 1994, a couple of shells landed near Mae Sai during an outbreak of fighting. And in March 1995, at the start of a government dry season offensive against Khun Sa, a small group of guerillas from the MTA launched a counter-attack on a Burmese army barracks within Thakhilek itself, causing a flood of refugees into Mae Sai and the closure of the bridge for a day.

If tripping into Burma doesn't appeal even when times are quiet, you can simply take advantage of Mae Sai's central location as a base for day trips to Doi Tung and Sop Ruak. It's also a nifty place for **shopping**: the stores along the main road to the bridge are stuffed with gold jewellery and gems, Burmese lacquerware and handicrafts, hill-tribe clothes, bags and ornaments. Not all of it is genuine, of course, but some of the loot is intriguing: check out shop number 432 on Phahonyothin Road for Akha hill-tribe wares; number 384 for classy jewellery and handicrafts; and the shop near the bridge for Burmese 'antiques' and junk – everything from Burmese puppets and sequinned hangings to old telephones, fans and wireless sets.

At dusk, a walk up to **Wat Phra That Doi Wao** just west of the main road gives you the best view of the surrounding area, including Thakhilek. Another intriguing peephole across the border is from the Maesai Guest House which is right by the river, merely a paddle from the dingy backstreets of Thakhilek.

MAE SALONG ✉ ✕
You don't get villages more curiously alluring than this: Mae Salong is a fascinating little quirk of history, a Chinese enclave high in the hills in the wild west borderland *67 km NW of Chiang Rai*. When the communists swept into power in China in 1949, a sizeable group of Nationalist Kuomintang fled south into Myanmar and northern Thailand. Many ended up in Mae Salong.

They soon turned their energies to the opium trade together with drug warlord Khun Sa, who made his base in nearby Ban Hin Taek, but after a major battle in 1983 between the Thai forces and Khun Sa's Shan United Army, Khun Sa had to flee across the border. The Thai authorities subsequently began to make progress towards 'pacifying' the area around Mae Salong and encouraging the hill-tribe people to switch from opium to other cash crops.

These days, Mae Salong – officially renamed Santikhiri (Hill of Peace) as part of the pacifying process, though the name hasn't stuck – is making its money from tourism, tea and herbs. Minivans of Thai and Taiwanese tourists now hurtle up the dramatically winding mountain road from Ban Basang, the junction on Highway 110, 32 km north of Chiang Rai (you can pick up songthaews for the one-hour, 36-km ride from Ban Basang). They come to buy locally-grown herbal tea, fruit wines, Chinese herbs and strong liquors sold in the various shops that line the village's main road.

But the first inkling I had that this place was something different was at the noodle stall by the bus-stop: Mae Salong's *khanom jiin naam ngiaw* is a delicious Yunnanese speciality, a rich chicken curry broth with peanuts and wild mushrooms thrown in for good measure. As I slurped the noodles in local fashion I heard villagers speaking Yunnanese, and looked up to see Chinese faces among a crowd of Akha and Lisu women.

It's this cultural mix that makes Mae Salong so fascinating: there are Chinese shop signs and Akha women smoking cheroots; posters of the former Nationalist leader Chiang Kai-shek alongside posters of the King of Thailand; Lisu girls in sky-blue bodices bar-

OVERLAND TRIPS TO BURMA

At the time of writing, non-Thais can cross overland into Myanmar (Burma) from Thailand at two official points: the Three Pagodas Pass in Kanchanaburi province (currently open only for day trips), and Mae Sai, 61 km north of Chiang Rai, which lies across the Sai River from the Burmese town of Thakilhek. Mae Sot, in north-west Tak province, is another important crossing for border trade, likely to open up fully to tourist traffic once the Thai-Burmese Friendship Bridge being built across the border's Moei River is completed.

For a day visit into Burma from Mae Sai or Three Pagodas Pass you don't need a visa: you simply leave your passport at the Thai immigration post and pay a fee of U.S. $5 at the Burmese checkpoint. You collect your passport when you return. Mae Sai-Thakilhek is the livelier and more important of the two border crossings, though it's arguable whether there's enough to see or do in Thakilhek to justify the visa fee ("It's not worth it", a Thai border guard whispered to me. "And the money goes to buy arms.")

But if you want to delve deeper into Burma you may want to consider paying U.S. $18 for a three-night, four-day permit (plus the U.S. $100 mandatory payment for Foreign Exchange Certificates). This gives you time to reach the far more interesting town of Kengtung (also spelt Cheng Tung), 163 km from Mae Sai and an arduous six-hour ride by jeep. There are ambitious plans to open up this route to tourism and trade by improving the road all the way to the Chinese border – another 100 km beyond Kengtung – thereby opening up overland access to China's southern districts of Xishuangbanna and Yunnan. The Asian Development Bank sees this as an important part of a vast infrastructure linking the economies of Indochina, Burma, Thailand and southern China – the 'Greater Mekhong Subregion'. As a first step, Mae Sai is likely to become a permanent, international border point in the near future.

Several tour agencies in Mae Sai can arrange the Kengtung trip, including the town's only *farang* tour operator, an enterprising American called Joe St Esparza (nicknamed 'Kobra' Joe), who runs the King Kobra Maesai Guest House and travel agency at 135/5 Sailomjoi Road (tel./fax 053 733055). Married to a Wa woman from Kengtung, Joe can also arrange eight-day overland return trips across the Chinese border to Xishuangbanna's capital, Jinghong.

HILL TRIBES

The hill-tribe people of northern Thailand (known as *chao khao* or mountain people in Thai) number about 550,000 and belong to at least ten very different tribes, with several distinct sub-groups. Each tribe has its own language, customs, beliefs and style of dress.

The hill-tribes originated from Tibet, Myanmar (Burma), China and Laos, mostly migrating to Thailand over the past two centuries. Like other semi-nomadic people, they don't really belong to any one nation, recognizing instead their own cultural and linguistic differences as 'borders'. In recent years, the Thai government has increasingly tried to assimilate them into the Thai state and modern Thai life. They have also tried to change their slash-and-burn farming methods and reduce their economic dependency on opium poppies, a vital (and easy-to-grow) cash crop for many hill-tribes. The increase in tourism and hill-tribe trekking is also having wide-ranging effects on the tribes' traditional culture.

The tribe people you meet on your trek may already show signs of the changing times: some may wear Western clothes, others sell made-for-tourists trinkets. But for many, the basic tribal beliefs and customs still remain intact.

The **Akha** are perhaps the most traditional, easily distinguished by the women's ornate head-dresses of silver beads, coins and ornaments, short black skirts and heavily embroidered black jackets. Originating in Tibet, they migrated to Thailand from Yunnan at the turn of the 20thC. They are among the poorest of Thailand's hill-tribes and still grow opium for their own consumption.

The **Karen** (comprising four distinct sub-groups) are the most numerous – about 285,000 now live mostly in the Mae Hong Son area. In Burma, they have been at the forefront of the ethnic minorities' fight for independence from military rule and thousands are now in refugee camps along the Thai border. Where they have settled elsewhere (often in lowland valleys) they practise an 'ecological' system of crop rotation rather than slash-and-burn agriculture. The women (who are prolific and skilled weavers) wear V-necked tunics (coloured white for unmarried girls) and the men wear baggy blue trousers.

The **Hmong** or Meo are the second largest tribal group (numbering around 87,000, comprising two sub-groups) and are scattered widely throughout Northern Thailand. Fiercely independent, they live at high altitudes and still produce much opium (about 30 per cent of their menfolk are believed to be addicted) although many are now turning to other cash crops. Their chunky silverware and intricately embroidered, brightly coloured, pleated skirts are among the most popular hill-tribe handicrafts on the tourist market. The **Lahu**, meanwhile, are famous for their ornately woven shoulder bags (*yaam*). Originating from southern China, they migrated into Thailand from Burma and are still mostly found along the Burmese border. About a third of the 58,000 Lahu have been converted to Christianity.

The **Mien** or Yao also originated from China and have maintained many Chinese cultural traditions including a similar written language and an ancient Taoist form of religion. Numbering about 38,000 in Thailand, they make exquisite embroidery and silverwork: the women's trousers in particular are intricately embroidered. The **Lisu** are one of the smaller and more recent tribes to migrate here: they started arriving in the 1920s from Tibet and now number around 25,000, living mostly west of Chiang Mai. Unique among the hill-tribes, patrilineal clans have authority over the villages – there's no village headman or shaman. They wear colourful clothing: the women in long (often bright blue) tunics and knee-length blue or green trousers; the men in blue or green trousers and a blue or black jacket.

These are just the six main hill-tribes. You can find more detailed information during your travels at the Tribal Research Centre in Chiang Mai (see pages 37-8) or the Hill-Tribe Museum and Education Centre in Chiang Rai (see pages 158-9).

• *Top, Karaoke bar, village near Mae Salong; above, hill-tribe girl, Mae Sai.*

gaining over steamed buns with Chinese hawkers. Go to the morning market and you'll see and hear it all; or walk along the poinsettia-adorned roads past the karaoke bars, where the young men hang out during the day playing snooker, and you'll catch a flavour of the new influences which are now seeping into Mae Salong.

Once you've soaked up the local atmosphere you might well be tempted to do some day-long walks to several different hill tribe villages in the area – Akha, Hmong, Lisu, Mien or Lisu. Some of the guesthouses also offer longer guided treks near the Burmese border (not recommended for solo explorations). Another Mae Salong speciality are six-hour horse-riding excursions (ask at the Shin Sane Guest House), though they tend to be too tame for real riders.

SOP RUAK ✍

The goal of all Golden Triangle tour coaches, this village 14 *km* N *of Chiang Saen* (one hour by songthaew east of Mae Sai) is the official centre of the Triangle where the tag is most easily packaged and presented for tourists: at the confluence here of the Ruak and Mekhong Rivers, the borders of Thailand, Laos and Myanmar (Burma) meet. You can choose from several Golden Triangle signposts along the riverside road for your snapshot of the river-border (the girls posing in hill tribe dress cost extra).

The most impressive viewpoint is actually above the road, at Wat Phra That Phu Khao. The only development scarring the unspoilt landscape across the river is the huge and controversial Golden Triangle Paradise Resort being built by a wealthy Thai businessman on a spit of Burmese land leased from the Myanmar government. A luxurious casino is reported to be part of the complex another borderline attempt, in more ways than one, to cash in on the Sino-Thai's love of gambling (see Mae Sai, page 55).

Sop Ruak itself is little more than a strip of souvenir stalls along the river, though the **House of Opium** museum (open 7 am to 6 pm daily) at the southern end of the road is well worth a visit. It provides an informative display on the history of the region's opium production, with exhibits on all the various accoutrements used in making, selling and smoking opium, including opium scales with tiny animal-shaped bronze weights; and enchanting violin-shaped boxes for carrying the scales.

If you want to say you've crossed into Laos at the Golden Triangle you can take one of the half-hour **boat** **tours** (available at several of the riverside stalls and restaurants) which circuit an island in the Mekhong belonging to Laos. More worthwhile are the boat trips down river to Chiang Saen or even to Chiang Khong, though they're not cheap and you may have to wait for a full party of passengers before the boat leaves.

THAKILEK

See Mae Sai, *page* 55.

TIPS ON TREKKING

For many travellers, the main reason for coming to Chiang Mai and Northern Thailand is to go on a hill tribe trek. Chiang Mai, the centre of the trekking business, now has more than a hundred registered companies organizing expeditions. Most take place in areas north and west of Chiang Mai, last three to four days and include an elephant ride and river rafting. Nearly all companies now claim to offer 'non-touristic' treks to 'monopoly' areas, for a 'real jungle experience.' But with so many other tourists out there (and the jungle largely decimated), how can you choose a reliable and honest trekking company?

First, pick up the list of registered trekking companies issued by TAT (all guides and companies should be government-licensed). Ask other travellers for their recommendations. Then check out some companies carefully: how many people go on their treks? More than ten is too many. Can they guarantee no other group will join you? And do their guides speak English and the language of the tribes you'll be visiting? If possible, try and meet the guides. Explanations about the hilltribes' culture and customs (and advice about what to do or not to do) is essential if you want to be more than just a voyeur and to avoid causing offence.

Also ask for details about the itinerary: some 'treks' spend more time on buses getting there and back than actually walking.

Since you'll be heading high into the hills to visit most villages, the trekking can be quite demanding. And sleeping conditions in the villages will be Spartan. Be sure to bring stout walking shoes or boots, sunhat and suncream, insect repellent and a first aid kit. Food is usually brought along by the company and cooked by the guide, but don't expect *haute cuisine*. Sleeping bags should be provided by the company if it's the cool season (October to February) – the best time to go trekking.

And what about safety? Armed robbery is rare, but it does happen, although regular police patrols in the area have ensured greater protection. If you're unlucky enough to have an encounter with bandits, hand over your money and don't resist. Leave your valuables and credit cards behind (preferably in a bank safe deposit box).

Most people I've met have hugely enjoyed their trekking experience – even if it's with an insensitive company that rushes them through the villages. But it's worth considering what the experience of having camera-clicking *farangs* on their doorsteps does for the hill tribe people themselves. To try and reduce the cultural impact, be sure to dress modestly, ask permission before taking photos (don't even touch religious shrines), and don't hand out gifts – if you want to give something, a donation or materials for the village school is best. Lastly, resist the 'exotic' attraction of participating in opium smoking if it's offered by your guide: it does nothing to help villagers kick the habit. Indeed, there's growing evidence that trekkers' involvement serves to increase addiction among the hilltribe villagers.

RECOMMENDED HOTELS

CHIANG KHONG

Ta-mi-la Guesthouse, B-BB; 113 *Soi 1, Ban Wiang Kaew, N end of town; tel./fax 053 791234.*

Nine bungalows of various standards (the cheapest with communal bathrooms) set amidst a tumbling hillside garden in an enchanting riverside setting. The views across to Laos are so dreamy that you can get stuck here for days.

The owner, Khun Watchala can also arrange visas for Laos.

Reuan Thai Sophapham, B-BB; *Soi 1, Ban Wiang Kaew; tel. 053 791023.*

Next door to Ta-mi-la, this is a smarter operation with similar room rates but with rather less of a Bohemian atmosphere.

CHIANG SAEN

Chiang Saen Guest House, B; *on the Sop Ruak Road, just N of the turning to Chiang Rai.*

Cheap and central, although it's the wrong side of the river road to be completely restful. The best among its range of rooms are the new bungalows with attached bathrooms.

Gin Guest House, B-BB; *on the Sop Ruak road in the N part of town.*

Take your pick here from dormitory beds to comfy bungalows or rooms with private bathrooms.

MAE SAI

Chad's House, B; *52/1 Soi Wiengpan, at the S end of town, about 1 km before the bridge; tel. 053 732054.*

Bangkok-educated motorbike enthusiast Chad opened his guesthouse here in 1984 and it's been a favourite with travellers ever since: casual and friendly with a collection of rooms at various prices (the ones in the pretty clapboard house are pleasant). Chad can tell you everything about motorbike jaunts in the area and can also organize trips to Kengtung (in Burma).

Maesai Guest House, B-BB; *688 Wiengpangkam Road; tel. 053 732021.*

The best in the bunch of riverside guesthouses, at the end of the riverside track. There are some 20 bungalows here – the most attractive with their own patios so you can sit and watch all the goings-on in back-street Thakhilek across the river. The guesthouse also arranges daily tours to Mae Salong, Doi Tung and Sop Ruak.

Mae Sai Plaza Guest House, B; *386/3 Sawlomchong Road; tel. 053 732230.*

Funkiest place in town, a vast wood and bamboo complex which looks like some oriental Gothic castle. Popular with Thais, many of its rooms (some with balconies) overlook the river. There's only one drawback: the towels are minuscule. Buy one from the market if you want a decent wraparound.

Top North Hotel, BB; *306 Phahonyothin Road; tel. 053 731955.*

A useful choice for those needing air-conditioning and private bathrooms with hot water; and it's located conveniently close to the bridge and all its activity.

MAE SALONG

Shin Sane Guest House, B; *32 Mu 3; tel. 053 765026.*

The budget choice, with Spartan rooms in an old wooden building at the centre of the village. Twelve new bungalows at the back now provide a few extra comforts, with attached bathrooms and hot water (though they haven't got around to buying beds, yet: you'll find your mattress on the floor).

Mae Salong Villa, BB; *on the left, just before the village; tel. 053 713444.*

An attractive medium-range choice. Pick one of the bungalows with a balcony and sit back to look out at the Burmese hills.

SOP RUAK

Le Meridien Baan Boran Hotel, BBBB; *1 km N of Sop Ruak, en route to Mae Sai; tel. 053 716678; Bangkok reservations, 02-254-8147.*

Incongruous luxury at the heart of the Golden Triangle, making the most of the river views in surroundings of rich Lanna-style decoration.

RECOMMENDED RESTAURANTS

CHIANG SAEN
Rimkhong Resort and Sala Thai Restaurant, B-BB; *on the riverside Rimkhong Road, just S of the junction to Chiang Rai; tel. 053 77702.*

A relaxing tourist-friendly haunt, pleasantly decorated with plants and antique fans and lamps. The catfish fried in fresh chilli paste is a mouthwarming way to sample the local speciality.

MAE SAI
Rabieng Kaew Restaurant, BB; *356/1 Phahonyothin Road; tel. 053 7311172.*

Mae Sai's swankiest town-centre restaurant, as you can tell from the fussy decoration and abundance of Lanna artifacts. Choose from the excellent northern Thai specialties included on the extensive Thai and Chinese menu.

Restaurant '25', B; *383 Phahonyothin Road, near the turn-off to Chad's Guest House.*

Named after its '25-hour' opening hours, this is a local favourite for its fast service and cheap dishes. There's no English menu and only one waitress speaks a few English words, but what you get (even if it isn't what you wanted) is always extremely tasty.

Jojo Coffeeshop, B; *Phahonyothin Road, opposite Sri Wattana Hotel.*

A great little haunt when you're dying for a coffee or an ice-cream. It also serves Thai dishes and vegetarian fare.

MAE SALONG
The restaurants at **Mae Salong Resort** and **Mae Salong Villa** are the best (though also the most expensive) places to eat at in the village. Be sure to try the delicious Yunnanese dishes which feature wild mushrooms.

KHUN SA AND THE OPIUM WAR

He's sometimes called Chang Chi-Fu or Sao Mong Khawn, but worldwide he's known as Khun Sa, the opium warlord and world's biggest drug trafficker. In 1989 he was declared a wanted criminal by the U.S. for his drug-running operations and has been labelled a terrorist by Burma's ruling military junta, the State Law and Order Restoration Council (Slorc) who have recently stepped up their efforts to capture him and defeat his 10,000-strong Muang Tai Army in order to win international (and particularly American) favour.

But Khun Sa (who is half Chinese and half Shan) is also viewed sympathetically in some quarters as a freedom fighter – one of the last left in Burma – fighting against Slorc's hated rule by means of the profits from the drug trade. This image of a champion of ethnic rebel forces was reinforced in 1993 when he declared the Shan state in northeastern Burma where he operates to be an independent nation. Not that his opium warlord reputation has diminished: he is the man largely responsible for the steadily increasing production of opium in the Golden Triangle, and its conversion into heroin. Burma is now the world's largest international source of heroin, producing up to 2,500 tonnes of opium a year and supplying 60 to 70 per cent of the entire United States market.

Slorc claims to have launched its own programme to wipe out the opium production by trying to introduce alternative cash crops, but narcotics officers are sceptical: there's plenty of evidence that Burmese security forces, too, are heavily involved in the drug trade. Slorc's offensive against Khun Sa is not so much an attempt to stop the opium production, they say, as an increasingly determined attempt to stamp out one of the few remaining pockets of ethnic rebellion.

North-Eastern Thailand

Nakhon Ratchasima (Khorat) – Ubon Ratchathani – That Phanom – Nong Khai - Nakhon Ratchasima

Isaan: the North-Eastern Hinterland

1,378 km; map Nelles 1:1,500,000

This is one of the longest itineraries in the guide, covering the vast north-east, an area known as Isaan (the name comes from a Sanskrit word for the region's ancient Mon-Khmer kingdom). The region, almost a third of the country, receives fewer tourists than anywhere else in Thailand. That's partly because its major places of interest are few and far apart, but also because Isaan has long been regarded as the country's backward hinterland. Poor and drought-stricken, it has none of the glitz or glamour of Thailand's seaside resorts. Only Surin, with its Elephant Round-Up in November, is on the regular tourist trail.

Travelling in Isaan takes you back to an older, poorer, more traditional Thailand, one that feels very different from the rest of the country. Bordered by Laos to the north and east, and Cambodia to the south, Isaan demonstrates strong Lao and Khmer influences in its language (many people still speak a Lao dialect), in its spicy cuisine, and in a culture with distinctive folk music and some of the finest silk and cotton fabrics in the land.

Above all, there are hundreds of architectural masterpieces left by the Khmers: Hindu-Buddhist temple complexes dating from the 10th to 13thC, some predating even Angkor Wat. The best have been restored and are now the region's biggest attraction for tourists. Several are featured in this section, but others are covered in greater depth by Local Explorations: 3.

If you tackle the whole of the marked route (allow about ten days) you'll need to have a stomach for long bus rides, a tolerance for large, charmless cities and an affinity for slow meanderings along the Mekhong. Stick to the smaller towns and villages wherever possible: it's here you'll find the real Isaan – arguably the real Thailand. You can always short-circuit the route (though it's less interesting away from the border), deviating westwards towards Sukhothai, or concentrate on the Mekhong by linking this journey with Thailand Overall: 4.

Travellers to or from Laos will also find this itinerary ideal for entering or exiting at the various border points along the river, most obviously, Nong Khai.

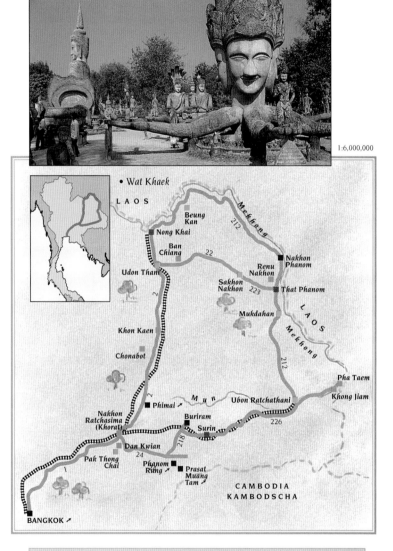

1:6,000,000

TRANSPORT

Your quickest way to Isaan from Bangkok is by plane: Thai Airways flies to Nakhon Ratchasima (Khorat), Ubon Ratchathani, Khon Kaen, Udon Thani and Sakon Nakhon via Nakhon Phanom. The next least painful method is by train: regular services go to Ubon Ratchathani (via Khorat and Surin) and Nong Khai (via Khon Kaen and Udon Thani). If you're going direct to Nong Khai (11 hours), or Ubon Ratchathani (ten hours) try to get a sleeper on one of the overnight trains which arrive at a civilized hour – in time for breakfast.

Between towns, buses usually work out to be more convenient than trains, leaving frequently throughout the day. The further you get into the remote corners of Isaan, however, the more evasive timetables and buses become. Be prepared to go slow, or to rent a motorbike.

SIGHTS & PLACES OF INTEREST

BAN CHIANG
See Udon Thani, page 72.

BANGKOK
See pages 134-55.

BEUNG KAN
137 km E of Nong Khai. The only reason you'd want to stop in this dull and dusty town is because you've dawdled so long by this remote stretch of the Mekhong that you've run out of time to go on. Once you're here, though, you might as well detour to Wat Phu Thawk, an extraordinary meditation wat built among the caves and cliffs of a huge sandstone outcrop about 40 km south-east of town. Awkward public transport deters the casual visitor and makes an overnight stay practically essential if you want to climb all the mountain wat's seven levels. First take a songthaew to Ban Siwilai on Route 222, then wait for a songthaew, a truck or a lift with Thai pilgrims for the next 25-km stretch. There's no charge for staying overnight, but a donation should be offered.

CHONABOT
See Khon Kaen, below.

KHON KAEN 🚏 ✕
At the junction of Highway 2 which goes N to Nong Khai (193 km) and S to Bangkok (450 km) with Highway 12 running west to Phitsanulok (323 km). Arriving by train you'll be a short samlor ride away from the town centre; the bus stations are more centrally located near the hotels and museum. The TAT office is at 15/5 Prachasamosorn Road, tel. 043 244498.

Khon Kaen is one of those places that the traveller in northern Thailand bumps into, rather than seeks out. Major highways cross here from all directions, and it is one of the biggest commercial and university cities in Isaan: no place for peaceful reveries.

However, there are two sights – the National Museum and the nearby silk-weaving village of Chonabot – that make a stopover more worthwhile than just a change of buses.

The National Museum (open Wednesday to Sunday, 9 am to noon, l pm to

> **MAT-MII**
> Similar to Indonesian *ikat*, where the cloth is patterned by tie-dyeing the threads before weaving, *mat-mii* is one of Isaan's most famous handicrafts. Made of either silk or cotton, the cloth often reflects Lao influences in its design. The *mat-mii* cottage industry was in decline until the 1970s when Queen Sirikit encouraged its revival (though natural dyes are now rarely used). Increasingly popular as a fashion material, cotton *mat-mii* is also often used to cover the traditional Isaan triangular-shaped pillows, now favourite tourist souvenirs.

5 pm) on Lang Sunratchakan Road is famous for its Bronze Age pots and jewellery from Ban Chiang (see page 72). Once you've seen the treasures here you hardly need trek to Ban Chiang itself. Don't miss the folk art display, either: a typical trove of curiosities and clever fish and animal traps.

Chonabot, 57 km and an hour's songthaew ride south-west of Khon Kaen, is a must if you're into textiles: the *mat-mii* cotton and silk woven here are nationally renowned. Even if you're not interested in fabrics, it's fascinating to see the cottage industry process in action, with traditional looms under almost every stilted house. The easiest place both to see and to buy the cloth is at the official handicraft centre, which is open daily.

KHONG JIAM
See Pha Taem, page 71.

KHORAT 🚏 ✕
See Nakhon Ratchasima, pages 65-6.

PRASAT MUANG TAM
See Local Explorations: 3, pages 110-21.

MUKDAHAN
About 50 km S of That Phanom on the Mekhong. Travellers rarely bother to stop here, but if you have the time, try to visit on a weekend when Mukdahan's ' Indochina Market' is at its best. Mukdahan thrives because of its riverside position right opposite Savannakhet, Laos' busy trading town, which is a major conduit for goods from Thailand

and Vietnam. The market, spreading around Wat Si Mongkon Tai near the pier, is popular with Thais for its cheap Chinese and Vietnamese goods, but there's plenty to tempt visitors, too, including Isaan handicrafts and Vietnamese lacquerware and ceramics.

NAKHON PHANOM

About 312 km SE of Nong Khai. This is the first sizeable town you reach travelling from Nong Kai on the remote, river-hugging Route 212. Thailand seems a long way away here: the town looks east, to Laos, boasting one of the best river views along this stretch, with the hazy Annamite mountains forming a dramatic backdrop to the Mekhong. Enjoying this dreamy setting over a meal of Mekhong catfish is the best thing to do here. In fact, to be honest, it's the only thing.

NAKHON RATCHASIMA (KHORAT) ⌷ ×

About 250 km NE of Bangkok on Highway 2. The city sprawls westwards from the old city moat, with the railway station in the western part and the main bus terminal to the north-west, both a short taxi ride away from most hotels and shops. The TAT office, though informative, is inconveniently located on the far western edge of town, at 2102-4 Mittraphap Road (tel. 044 213666). Buses 1, 2, and 3 will eventually get you there, though there are also plenty of tuk-tuks for getting around cheaply.

It's unfortunate that many visitors' only impression of Isaan comes from this unattractive city: used as a base for visiting the area's most famous Khmer temple ruins – Phimai and Phanom Rung (see pages 174-8) – it's often as far as people bother to go in the north-east.

As one of the largest cities in Thailand, and relatively close to Bangkok, it has more in common with the capital than with outback Isaan, notably traffic-jammed roads with accompanying pollution, and a throbbing nightlife of discos and massage parlours – a legacy from its days as a U.S. air base during the Vietnam War.

Still, it's undeniably convenient for transport connections: to and from Bangkok there are daily flights (taking 40 minutes), and numerous buses and trains (four to five hours), as well as air-conditioned buses direct to the south-

DETOUR - **PAK THONG CHAI**

This famous silk-weaving village 30 km south of Khorat (buses leave frequently from town, taking about an hour) produces some of Thailand's best-quality silk. You can see how the silk is made at the official Silk & Cultural Centre but don't expect prices to be any lower here than in town: the weavers have become as skilled at making money as they are at weaving cloth.

eastern resorts of Pattaya and Rayong (three to four hours) and even all the way north to Chiang Mai (eight hours). If you are only interested in quick visits to Phimai and Phanom Rung, it makes sense to stay here. The city's most interesting cultural sight, bagging the best position right by the Chumphon Gate (the western entrance to downtown Khorat), is the **Thao Suranari Memorial**. Thao Suranari, the wife of a governor of Khorat, was responsible for the defeat of the invading Laotians in 1826 whether by seductive trickery or brazen show of bravery isn't quite clear. At any rate, she's been honoured ever since and her statue and shrine are the focus of daily offerings from the townsfolk who now consider her their most effective protection against any mishap. The annual festival which is

DETOUR - **DAN KWIAN**

You'll find it quickest to get here by bus: it's half an hour from Khorat's southern city gate.

In the old days, when merchants were travelling to Khorat market with their bullock carts of goods, they used this village, 15 km south-east of Khorat, as a convenient resting place. Now, Dan Kwian (literally ' bullock cart station') is more famous for pots than carts: dozens of stalls along the roadside display the highly sought-after Dan Kwian ceramics, with their distinctive unglazed bronzen hue and geometric designs.

Behind the pottery workshops you'll also find a memorial to the bullock cart – an open-air museum of carts of all sizes as well as traditional agricultural implements.

• *Wat Pho Chai, Nong Khai.*

held in her honour in late March is great fun, with all kinds of parades and Thai entertainments.

If you're kicking your heels, you could pop in to the **Mahawirawong National Museum** (open Wednesday to Sunday, 9 am to noon, I pm to 4 pm) in the grounds of Wat Sutchinda, Ratchadamnoen Road. Its most notable collections are the Khmer door lintels and the 6th to 13thC Buddha statues. Otherwise, the most interesting things happen at night. The night market on

Manat Road is great for typical Isaan food as well as cheap clothes and souvenirs (however for local silk you're better off at the specialist shops in Chumphon and Ratchadamnoen Roads); while the Veterans of Foreign Wars (VFW) Cafeteria on Phoklang Road is a Vietnam War relic that still hosts a knot of resident ex-GIs. Even the food here is genuine: greasy American fare.

NONG KHAI ⋈ ✕

At the end of Highway 2, 620 km N of Bangkok. Arriving at the train station, a couple of km W of town, take a tuk-tuk or samlor to the centre. The bus terminals are closer, just S of Prajak Road, one of the town's two main roads that run parallel to the river for several km.

The other main thoroughfare, Meechai Road, is where you'll find the downtown bustle of shops and restaurants, though on its eastern edge there are still several old colonial-style houses, with beautiful pastel-coloured façades and stucco decorations. At Nong Khai I used to watch the little Laotian ferries trundling passengers across the Mekhong to and from Laos, and dreamt of the day when visa restrictions would ease to allow me to make the journey too, not on an organized tour from Bangkok, but solo, like the local Thais.

Now it's come true: anyone can go to Laos on their own (once they pay the exorbitant visa fee), and Nong Khai, only 23 km from Laos' capital, Vientiane, has become the busiest border point along the Mekhong. In April 1994, the first bridge to breach the lower Mekong – the Australian-funded **Friendship Bridge** – opened just a few kilometres west of town. I was lucky: I managed a couple of crossings by the old-fashioned ferries before the regulations changed, diverting foreigners to boring bus transport via the bridge.

But this is the last place to feel nostalgic about the slow old days. Nong Khai, once a quaint backwater, is now booming: flash new hotels and office blocks are going up along the highway by-pass south of town and the funky old French-Laotian shophouses are coming down. There are still eddies of charming atmosphere in the bustling market area around the old pier and further east along the shady riverside, but with a new promenade under construction

• *Wat Khaek, near Nong Khai.*

here, even these may soon disappear. Nevertheless, Nong Khai is still an ideal and addictive Mekhong River base: transport from Bangkok is easy (the 11-hour overnight train is best); there are frequent bus connections to other towns; and nearby sights – including one very weird and one very revered temple – are worth at least a couple of days' stay.

The best place to get a feel for old Nong Khai, though, is around the **Tha Sadet** pier on Rimkhong Road. This is where foreign travellers of the 1980s – when Laos first inched open the door to modern tourism – were greeted with a sign prohibiting entry to those whose dress styles identified them as an 'alien with hippy characteristics'. You were unwelcome if you were 'a person who wears just a singlet or waistcoat without underwear', or 'a person who wears silk pants that do not look respectable'. The last time I looked, the sign, though faded and completely ignored, was still there.

Stretching east from the pier along a narrow lane is the tightly-packed **clothes and souvenir market** which keeps traders on both sides of the river busy. Thai day-trippers love to come here to buy cheap Chinese products – everything from plastic toys and silk pyjamas to stereos and clocks. Foreigners pick up curiosities such as old-fashioned Burmese and Laotian slateboards, wooden back-scratchers and collapsible stools, as well as local silk and cotton clothes.

Moving further east you'll come to the town's most prominent temple, **Wat Pho Chai**, off Prajak Road. It's famous for its gleaming, solid-gold seated Buddha statue, set on a throne of yellow flowers and bright lights. On the walls of the Lao-style *viharn* are modern murals depicting the story of the statue's dra-

67

matic arrival in Nong Khai (spot the *farang* spectator in the crowds). Legend has it that it was looted from Vientiane by the future Rama I, only to sink to the bottom of the Mekhong during the crossing to Thailand and rest there for 20-odd years before eventually being recovered.

Another religious item that's still in the river – and sinking deeper into the middle every year – is the **Phra That Nong Khai**, an ancient chedi that started slipping into the water in the 1840s. You can only see it when the river is low, during the dry season: follow Meechai Road eastwards until the asphalt runs out and then turn down one of the *sois* to the river. When the Mekhong drops so low that you can see the top of the chedi, it looks temptingly easy to swim (or even walk) across to Laos. But it's not recommended: currents here are deceptively strong and there's an old tale that the river needs annual victims to ensure a bountiful harvest. (That obviously didn't deter the young German I met recently who boasted he'd swum across three times: once, admittedly, he was caught – it was the day the new bridge opened and police were thick on land and sea – but twice he succeeded, although in such a state of drunken dare-devilry that he can barely remember the feat. He has yet to use the bridge.)

Sunset boat rides are the usual way of enjoying the Mekhong. The boats leave at 5.30 pm daily from the western end of Rimkhong Road, and chug along for an hour. At only B20 a trip, this is the best bargain in Nong Khai.

The weirdest experience hereabouts is undoubtedly a visit to **Wat Sala Kaew Ku**, more commonly called **Wat Khaek**, 5 km south-east of town. This garden of Hindu-Buddhist concrete figures is an Alice-in-Wonderland phantasmagoria inspired by the mystic Luang Puu Bunleua Surirat, whose life story is as bizarre as his creation. He is said to have fallen into the lap (literally) of a Hindu guru who lived in an underground cave in Vietnam (some say Laos). After several years of instruction on Buddha and the underworld, Luang Puu emerged to build the first of his sculpture gardens across the river in Laos. When the communists threw him out he settled in Nong Khai, winning a wide following of devotees. His garden here is

> **MYSTERIES OF THE MEKHONG**
> A curious phenomenon takes place every October full moon along the Mekhong River between Nong Khai and Beung Kan: coloured lights, locally called ' dragon rockets', shoot up from beneath the waters into the sky. There are said to be scientific explanations for the spectacle, but locals can concoct far better stories if you ask them.
> **Ban Ahong**, 23 km west of Beung Kan, and **Phon Phisai**, 45 km east of Nong Khai, are the most famous sites for catching a glimpse of these curious natural fireworks.

even more flamboyant than the one in Laos. Using the material of modern Asia – low-budget concrete – Luang Puu's hundred-odd volunteers have constructed figures not only from Buddhist and Hindu mythology but also from popular Thai proverbs. Many of them tower dozens of metres high, bearing an enigmatic smile. To the sound of Luang Puu's favourite pop music, visitors wander through this exhibition of fantastic figures with bemused astonishment. Luang Puu himself is rarely seen these days, but it's as well to bring your own water supply: his charisma is said to be so powerful that if you drink water offered by him you will immediately hand over all your possessions.

After Wat Khaek, any other temple seems tame, but **Wat Phra That Bang Phuan**, 22 km south-west of Nong Khai (Sangkhom-bound buses pass right by) is serious competition, drawing busloads of pilgrims. The most revered monument at this wat is an ancient Indian-style chedi – possibly 2,000 years old and said to contain chest bones of the Buddha. It's now hidden beneath more modern versions: a 16thC Lao-style chedi, built by a merit-seeking King of Vientiane, which was in turn restored in the 1970s by the Fine Arts Department. More atmospheric are the other 16thC chedis in the compound, unrestored and gracefully crumbling.

PHANOM RUNG
See *Local Explorations*: 3, pages 176-8.

PHIMAI
See *Local Explorations*: 3, pages 174-6.

SAKHON NAKHON

About 224 km SE of Nong Khai. This dull provincial capital is only worth a stop if you're a fan of Lao-style chedis and Khmer prangs (towers). **Pra That Choeng Chum**, just west of the Nong Han Lake, is considered one of the most sacred in the country. Underneath the 24 m-high white chedi is an 11thC Khmer prang which you can see clearly if you enter the chedi through the *viharn* next door.

Another important 11thC Khmer prang, **Wat Phra That Narai Jeng Weng**, lies about 5 km north-west of town (songthaews to the airport can drop you at the turn-off to the wat). The restored laterite prang has some wonderful carvings, including one of a dancing Shiva.

For a little light relief, the town's large **Nong Han Lake** makes a pleasant outing, with boats for hire and plenty of jolly Thai families at weekends.

SURIN ⬑ ✕

About 450 km NE of Bangkok. Both train and bus stations are walking distance from the centre. Elephants have put this provincial capital firmly on the tourist map. The **Elephant Round-Up**, held in the third week of November, is Isaan's most famous festival: a celebration of the skills of both elephants and their trainers, with over a hundred elephants taking part in tug-of-war contests and log-pulling demonstrations.

The **mahouts** are from the local Suay tribe, renowned for centuries as elephant-catchers and trainers: the Round-Up was initiated as a way to preserve those skills when domestic elephants were no longer needed for transport or in the logging industry. The heart of the Suay's elephant-training area is at their village of **Ta Klang**, about 50 km north of Surin. It's best to visit just before the Round-Up to see the training in progress. For the rest of the year, Surin sinks back into typically slow Isaan gear. It makes a delightful first stop from Bangkok: numerous buses take about eight hours, or seven by train (book seats well in advance for the Round-Up).

Apart from a very small **museum** (open Monday to Friday, 8.30 am to 4.30 pm) on Chitramboong Road in the southern part of town, whose highlight is a collection of sacred elephant-catch-

DETOUR - **RENU NAKHON**

This traditional weaving village 15 km north-west of That Phanom makes an enjoyable day trip, especially on a Saturday when market stalls cluster round the **Wat Phra That Renu Nakhon** (a smaller version of That Phanom's famous chedi), selling local and Lao cotton and silk cloth. You can pick up other Isaan handicrafts here, too, including the popular triangular-shaped pillows. On other days you'll find shops selling similar items near the wat. Or you can buy direct from the weavers: expect to pay at least B200 for a cotton sarong length, or up to several thousand *baht* for silk.

ing ropes, there's nothing much to see in Surin itself. However, it makes an excellent base for visiting some of the lesser-known Khmer ruins on the Cambodian border about 70 km to the south, as well as the more famous **Prasat Phanom Rung**, about 75 km to the south-west. These are described in detail in Local Explorations: 3, pages 176-8.

THAT PHANOM ⬑

About 90 km SE of Sakhon Nakhon, at junction of Routes 223 and 212. Buses stop just W of town on Highway 2121, near Wat Phra That Phanom. It's a long way to come some 700 km from Bangkok – but if you go nowhere else in Isaan, you should really come here. This small

THE CANDLE FESTIVAL

The Khao Phansa Festival in July marks the start of the three-month Buddhist Rains Retreat when monks customarily stay inside their monasteries to study and meditate. It's a public holiday and celebrated throughout Thailand but nowhere so flamboyantly as in Ubon Ratchathani. Here, floats carrying huge beeswax candles carved into all kinds of shapes and figures are paraded through the town. The five-day festival also features music, beauty contests and local entertainment, but it's the candles that take the cake.

• Wat Phra That Bang Phuan, near Nong Khai.

haggling over their last hens in a cacphany of shouts and laughter. Once I remember seeing an elderly Westerner amongst the traders, selling second-hand clothes on the pavement. He glared at me when I asked where he was from. "I stay here. I live everywhere. I have no home, I stay here 15 years. I stop writing letters five years ago. Now I go to markets to sell clothes. It is all the same everywhere: rich and poor and broke." He refused to say any more and by the time the Laotians had left, he too had disappeared. I often wonder what has happened to him.

Walking from the river and under the arch (an imitation of the one in Vientiane, though smaller) is the most dramatic way to approach the **Wat Phra That Phanom**. The white and gold chedi, over 50 m high, is believed to have been built either in the 6th or 9thC by five local rulers to enshrine relics of the Buddha. It has been restored seven times since (most recently in 1977 after heavy rains in 1975 caused it to collapse, an event considered ominous by the Laotians who indeed then faced a turbulent year with the communist Pathet Lao taking over the country). With a solid gold spire and decorations, and a brilliant white platform, the chedi makes a dazzling impression. Around the base are restored 10thC carvings relating the story of the wat's founders.

town on the banks of the Mekhong hosts the most highly revered temple in Isaan, the Lao-style chedi Wat Phra That Phanom. Equally respected by the Laotians, it ranks second in importance to Laotians after the Wat That Luang in Vientiane. But it's not just the chedi that makes That Phanom a special place. The village, spreading beside the river beyond a crusty old Laotian arch of victory, is more seductive than anywhere else in Isaan – a combination of old-fashioned charm and tantalizing Lao-French-Chinese influences, with old wooden shophouses and hotels that have kept the concrete builders at bay for decades.

On the Monday and Thursday **market days**, Laotian villagers breach the Mekong boundary in their long, leaky boats to trade their wriggling pigs and herbal medicines, their fish and hens and woven cloth for plastic kitchenware and bags of rice, sweets, fruit and clothing. Towards noon they rush to finish trading before the border closes,

The most enthralling time to visit That Phanom (although the most difficult for accommodation) is during the mid-February ' homage-paying' festival. Thousands of Thai and Lao devotees crowd round the wat, making offerings and covering the surrounding Buddha statues with gold leaf. The town devotes itself to merry-making for a whole week: a grand opportunity to see and hear traditional Isaan music, dance and entertainment.

UBON RATCHATHANI

Just over 300 km E of Khorat and 557 km NE of Bangkok. Frequent air, train and bus connections. Trains and buses from Bangkok take around ten hours, and under five from Khorat. Arriving by train will put you S of town, across the Mun River (hop on a bus number 2 or 7 to get to the centre, or take a samlor). Bus terminals are scattered all over the place, depending on where you've come from, but air-conditioned buses generally

• Wat Phra That Nong Bua, Ubon Ratchathani.

stop around the town centre. The TAT office is conveniently central, too, at 264/1 Kheuan Thani Road (tel. 045 243770).

A former U.S. airforce base, Ubon (no-one usually bothers with the Ratchathani) is a typically huge Isaan city with little appeal. It does, however, make a logical stop-over before going on to explore more remote parts of the Emerald Triangle – the forested and tantalizingly 'undiscovered' corner of Thailand bordered by Cambodia and Laos. An informative museum and a couple of interesting wats are the only real diversions in the city itself, though its **Candle Festival** in late July is definitely worth seeing if you're in the area at the time (see page 70).

Near the TAT office is the **Ubon National Museum** (open Wednesday to Sunday, 9 am to noon, 1 pm to 4.30 pm) which provides an excellent introduction to the area with its well-labelled displays on Khmer carvings, Isaan textiles and musical instruments and a reproduction of the Pha Taem rock

---

DETOUR – PHA TAEM

Not many foreign tourists make it this far, to the eastern edge of the Emerald Triangle bordered by Laos to the east and Cambodia to the south. But it's worth it if only to see the prehistoric rock paintings of Pha Taem, 95 km north-east of Ubon, one of the most extraordinary sights in Isaan.

Believed to be at least 3,000 years old, the reddish paintings cover a stretch of cliff almost 200 m long, and feature animals and huge fish, geometric designs and dozens of eery hand prints.

Pha Taem, just north of the confluence of the Mun and Mekhong Rivers, isn't easy to get to if you don't have your own transport: the nearest village (with some simple accommodation) is Khong Jiam, 18 km down-river and accessible by bus from Ubon. You can hire tuk-tuks here to get to the cliff, or walk 5 km from the turn-off on Route 2112 passed by the Ubon-Khong Jiam bus.

paintings. One of its rarest items is a Dong Son bronze drum, similar to those in the museum at Nakhon Si Thammarat. Of the city's many wats, the two most notable are **Wat Thung Si Meuang** and **Wat Phra That Nong Bua**. The former, dating from the mid-19thC, has a beautiful teak library, built on stilts above water (a common ploy to preserve manuscripts from insects). The nearby bot has well-preserved murals which are a fascinating revelation of 19thC life.

Wat Phra That Nong Bua, on the northern outskirts of town, couldn't be more different: a copy of India's Bodhgaya stupa, it has some striking carved reliefs of scenes from the *Jataka* (life-stories of the Buddha).

UDON THANI

Regular bus and train links with Bangkok, 560 km S and with Nong Khai, 56 km N. Yet another of Isaan's former U.S. military bases (during the Vietnam War, the U.S. ran bombing raids on Vietnam and Laos from seven air bases in Thailand), Udon Thani still shows lingering American influences, recently revived when a Voice of America transmitter was established nearby. Now a major commercial and industrial centre and important transport hub, it has nothing to detain you unless you need a U.S. consulate or a fix of *farang* food.

Somewhat ironically, one of the most important cultural sites in Thailand happens to be 50 km to the east: the Bronze Age settlement of **Ban Chiang**. In 1966, an American anthropology student literally stumbled on Bronze Age potsherds in Ban Chiang's fields. Later excavations also unearthed bronzeware, dated to at least 2,000 BC, and indicating that Thailand, not China, possessed the earliest bronze technology in South-East Asia.

Ban Chiang's **National Museum** (open Wednesday to Sunday, 9 am to 4 pm) is now the best place to see the treasures from this remarkable era, especially the attractive and well-known ochre-coloured pottery with swirling designs. Souvenirs and fakes abound in the village stalls. Forget about stumbling on your own discovery: the fields were looted as soon as the American student revealed his find. What the villagers themselves didn't take, the archaeologists did.

RECOMMENDED HOTELS

KHON KAEN

The Klang Meuang Road area has dozens of hotels, though they're often noisy. This one is a little more appealing than most:

Muang Inn, BB; 41/1-6 Na Muang Road; tel. 043 238667.

Small new place with 37 spic-and-span air-conditioned rooms.

NAKHON RATCHASIMA (KHORAT)

Plenty of middle- and upper-range hotels, with the **Sima Thani Hotel, BBBB;** Mittaphap Road; tel. 044-243812 at the top of the heap.

For budget travellers, here's something special:

Doctor's House, B; 78 Soi 4, Seup Siri Road, near TAT on the western edge of town; tel. 044 255846.

The ideal guesthouse: quiet location, friendly and informative staff and a homely garden area. There's nothing else like it in Khorat – pity there's only a handful of rooms.

NONG KHAI

Mut-Mee Guesthouse, B; 1111/4 Kaeworawut Road.

' No phone, no TV, no bothers'. With its shady riverside garden, range of rooms in various houses and huts and excellent menu, Mut-Mee is justifiably popular. Now efficiently run by Englishman Julian Wright (maybe too efficiently for some old hands) it's still a quintessential Mekhong hang-out.

Sawasdee Guesthouse, B-BB; 402 Meechai Road; tel. 042 412502; fax 042 420259.

Rooms are small and simple but you can't fault the setting: a converted shophouse with an antique-filled lobby.

Phanthavy Hotel, B-BB; 1049 Haisoke Road; tel. 042 411568; fax 042 421106.

Decent, if dull, central hotel, with neat rooms around a paved courtyard.

Holiday Inn Mekong Royal, BBBB; 222 Joammanee Beach, by the new bridge; 042 420024; fax 042 421280; credit cards, MC, V.

Newest and smartest hotel in town, isolated from all the interesting hubbub, though the rooms do look across the river to Laos.

SURIN
Hotels are booked solid (and rates soar) during the Elephant Round-Up: be sure to book weeks in advance.

Pirom's House, B; 242 *Krung Si Nai Road; tel.* 044 515140.

Unbeatable, largely thanks to Pirom himself, who suggests fascinating day-tours to remote Khmer temple ruins.

Petchkasem Hotel, BB-BBB; 104 *Jit-bamrung Road; tel.* 044 511274; *fax* 044 511041.

Not as smart as the Tarin Hotel (on Sirirat Road), but not a bad runner-up. All rooms are air-conditioned.

THAT PHANOM
Unless you book well in advance you won't get a room here during the That Phanom Festival in mid-February. Even hotels in nearby Nakhon Phanom are often full. At other times of year, try:

Niyana Guest House, B; *Soi Withi Sawrachon.*

A welcoming travellers' haunt, close to the river, which organizes boat trips.

Saeng Thong Hotel, B; *Phanom Phanarak Road.*

A creaky old wooden hotel oozing with character (forget comfort).

RECOMMENDED RESTAURANTS

If you try nothing else in Isaan, be sure to sample the famous specialities: *kai yang* (grilled chicken) and *somtam* (spicy papaya salad), accompanied by *khao niaw* (sticky rice: roll it up and eat with your hand). You might want to leave another speciality, fried grasshoppers, until you are really hungry.

KHON KAEN
Khrua Weh, B-BB; 1/1 *Klang Muang Road.*

For a change from Thai fare, try some Vietnamese specialities (the fresh spring rolls are delicious) in this attractive restaurant in an old wooden building.

Night Market, B; *Lang Meuang Road, next to terminal for air-conditioned buses.*

As usual, the best place for a bargain feast: look out for Khon Kaen's famous spicy sausages.

NAKHON RATCHASIMA (KHORAT)
Veterans of Foreign Wars (VFW) Café, B-BB; *Phoklang Road.*

Pizzas, chips, ice cream and ex-GIs make this a famous *farang* hang-out.

Thai Phochana, B-BB; 142 *Jomsurangy-at Road.*

A locals' favourite. Don't miss the frog salad.

NONG KHAI
Naem Meuang, B-BB; 1062/1 *Banthoengjit Road.*

The place to come at lunchtimes, to savour the house specialty: do-it-yourself spring rolls, including Vietnamese-style pork sausage (*naem meuang*) wrapped up with slices of cucumber, star-fruit, garlic, chillies, mint, plus cold white noodles and sweet peanut sauce.

Thai Thai Phochana, B-BB; 257/1 *Banthoengjit Road; tel.* 042 420373.

Cheap and delicious Thai and Chinese favourites, in a barn-like restaurant.

Nong Naen, B; *Rimkhong Road, in the thick of the market alley, behind Wat Srimeuang: look for the fish and chicken being grilled outside.*

This simple shack of a restaurant serves a great *kai yang* (there's no menu: just point). Get here early to occupy one of the few river-view tables.

SURIN
Country Roads Restaurant & Bar, B-BB; 165/1 *Sirirat Road.*

Run by Ron, a retired Texan, and his Thai wife, this open-air restaurant is pleasant for a drink and simple meal.

Phaw Kin, B-BB; *Lak Meuang Road.*

Nothing flash, but a local favourite for good-value Isaan specialities.

Night Market, B; *Krung Si Nai Road.*

A chance to choose from a wide variety of Isaan fare at bargain prices.

North-Eastern Thailand
Between Nong Khai, Loei and Nakhon Ratchasima
The Northern Mekhong Border

556 km; map Nelles 1:1,500,000

I f you're the kind of person who likes to dawdle, this section is for you: a lovely, lazy journey in the northern part of the north-east, following the Mekhong River west of Nong Khai, and then slowly dropping south towards Bangkok. Or you could do it in reverse. As with all the itineraries suggested by this guide, it's not something you *have* to to do: it's a framework for discovery, and you can just as well use the section as a general guide to the area – all the key points are covered, on and off the marked route.

It's a part of Thailand rarely visited by the average tourist since there's nothing much to do but potter about the countryside on short excursions or sit back and watch the sun set over the river from a chain of simple riverside guesthouses. Nong Khai, the furthest point from Bangkok (and the main border crossing for Laos), is easily accessible by train from the capital, and buses make all the connections you need between towns though they're increasingly irregular and erratic the further west you go. If you're planning to explore a little, and then return to Nong Khai, hiring a car or motorbike at the start of your trip would make life much easier.

You'll need at least two nights for the 180-km journey on Highway 211 between Nong Khai and Chiang Khan, though that's rushing it: four nights gives you more of a taste for lazy Mekhong moods. When you're ready for some action, you can dart out on a day-trip to the little-visited border area to the west of Chiang Khan – a string of deceptively quiet riverside villages heavily involved in cross-border trade with Laos. Heading south on Highway 201 brings you to Loei, within striking distance of one of the best national parks in the area, Phu Kradung, where you can spend all your stored-up energy by climbing to the top of its 1,360-m high mountain. Allow at least a day and a night here.

If you're heading towards Sukhothai and Chiang Mai, you can cut west at this point on Highway 12 and link up with Thailand Overall: 1. Alternatively, continuing south brings you to Khorat via Chaiyaphum and its nearby silk-making and silk-weaving village. Thailand Overall: 3 and Local Explorations: 3 give details of the impressive Khmer temple sites to be seen in the Khorat area.

TRANSPORT

The most comfortable way of travelling between Nong Khai and Bangkok is by train – assuming you can get a sleeper or reclining seat, the overnight ones are best (around 11 hours). If you don't fancy that, there are also daily flights to Udon Thani, just 56 km south of Nong Khai. Buses, songthaews or passenger trucks connect towns and villages *en route*, less reliably the further off the beaten track you go. Heading south from Loei there are buses direct to Bangkok (about ten hours); from Chaiyaphum it's six hours to Bangkok or two to Nakhon Ratchasima (Khorat).

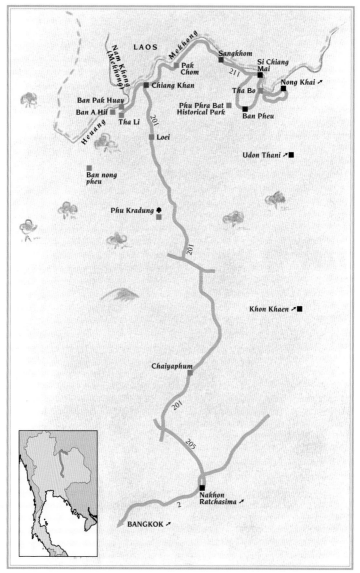

1:3,000,000

SIGHTS & PLACES OF INTEREST

BAN A HII AND BAN NONG PHEU
See Detour - Ban Pak Huay, page 78.

BAN KHWAO
See Chaiyaphum, below.

CHAIYAPHUM 🖼 ✕
On Route 201, 118 km N of Khorat. Out in the sticks of western Isaan, Chaiyaphum is usually by-passed by travellers zooming along Highway 2 between Bangkok and Nong Khai. But if you're on your way south from Loei (217 km away) or heading north from Khorat, this small, laid-back town is a pleasant place to stop on the alternative north-south Route 201. And it does have one major attraction: the nearby silk-making and silk-weaving village of **Ban Khwao**, which lies 15 km west of town.

Reasonably-priced tours to Ban Khwao and other silk-making villages in the area are organized by Chaiyaphum's guesthouses and are worth taking if you've never seen the silk process from start to finish: millions of silkworms munching on mulberry leaves is an unforgettable sight (and sound). You can buy silk in the village, too, at prices often cheaper than in Chaiyaphum or Khorat. Getting to Ban Khwao on your own is no problem: songthaews leave regularly from the junction of Tantawan and Non Muang Roads.

Within Chaiyaphum itself, there are a couple of historical sites which put the place in context: **Prang Ku** is a Khmer temple ruin dating from the late 12thC, situated a couple of kilometres east of the town centre on Bannakan Road. Originally built as one of several resting places *en route* between Angkor, Phimai and Si Thep (about 140 km north-west of Phimai), only the main laterite tower now stands, with remains of lintels on the ground and a laterite surrounding wall. Inside the tower is a seated stone Buddha from the Dvaravati period (6th to 10thC), though the head is a copy (the original was stolen). The sanctuary still holds a powerful appeal: locals come here frequently to make offerings. Also on Bannakan Road, but in a prominent position at the town centre's main roundabout, is a statue of Chaiyaphum's early 19thC Laotian ruler, **Jao Phraya Lae**, known in Thai as Phraya Phakdi

Chumphon. Lao people from Vientiane had first come to the area a century before and had re-established a settlement in Chaiyaphum, long abandoned by the Khmers. Phraya Phakdi Chumphon became something of a local hero when he lost his life in battle against his invading countrymen in 1806. A festival is held in his honour every mid-January, when Chaiyaphum folk let their hair down with a week of celebrations.

CHIANG KHAN 🖼 ✕
On the Mekhong, 48 km N of Loei. One of the most delightful small towns along the Mekhong River, Chiang Khan has somehow managed to keep progress at bay: its riverside backstreet still features mostly wooden shophouses and its modest guesthouses still like to emphasize relaxation rather than refined comforts. That said, when the sun goes down, Chiang Khan's nightlife starts swinging: hostesses in mini-skirts loiter at several restaurant doors and the disco music at the central Chalalai Restaurant gets so loud you can hear it several kilometres up river. Not to be outdone, young Laotians across the river frequently party to a high-decibel din. If you can handle this (and there are some nights when the discos don't operate), it's worth lingering here at least a couple of days to take advantage of organized boat trips on the river, and day trips you can do yourself by bicycle or motorbike. The best sources of information on where to go are the detailed files on the area put together by Frenchman Pascal who runs the **Rimkhong Pub**; and those by Englishman Robert of **Nong Sam Guesthouse**.

Zen Guesthouse operates the most varied river trips, as well as offering herbal steam baths and traditional Thai massage. Take advantage of it all while you can, because you won't find anything else like it for miles around. The most popular boat trip is the 50-km, three-hour jaunt up-river to the **confluence** of the Mekhong (which curves north into Laos at this point) and its western tributary, the Heuang River (in Thai, Mae Nam Heuang).

Other river favourites are the one-hour sunset trips and the two-hour down-river excursions to the **rapids of Kaeng Khut Khu**. The 'rapids' here are actually very mild, but the picturesque hillside setting has made it a popular place with Thai picnickers who come here to feast on Isaan specialities sold at various stalls (there's a proper restaurant here, too). On foot, or by bike, it's a pleasant 4-km trip from town. On the way, you can call in at **Wat Tha Khaek**, a 600-year-old temple set in attractive, tranquil and shady grounds. The Buddha image in the bot is considered very sacred.

Simply wandering around Chiang Khan brings its own pleasures, too, especially if you follow the riverside Chai Khong Road eastwards to the outskirts of town, a route which gives you frequent glimpses of Laos across the river. Just before reaching the ferry pier near Soi 21, you'll pass the pretty **Wat Thakhok** which has an ornate little Laotian-style *viharn* with yellow stucco decorations on the outside. The town centre's oldest and most important wat is the 17thC **Wat Mahathat**, near Soi 14. A candle-lit procession takes place here every February full moon to commemorate the **Magha Puja** religious festival. It's an enchanting occasion, full of chatter and laughter and generosity. Villagers share out their candles, flowers and incense to any *farang* spectators, and before you know it you're part of the procession, slowly walking round the bot to the sound of chanting prayers and the deep, rhythmic beat of a gong. Once everyone has completed the obligatory three rounds of the bot, they disperse in a flurry and roar of motorbikes, leaving their candles flickering at outdoor shrines.

Not to be missed on your daytime wanderings is a visit to Chiang Khan's **cotton factory** beside the market on Soi 10. Cotton has long been a major part of Chiang Khan's trade: Laotian raw cotton passes through on the way to the factories of Loei, and Chiang Khan's own factory produces locally-famous cotton quilts. Here you can see every step of the process, from the plucked cotton puffs being sorted and cleaned, to the finished cotton quilts being packed up ready for sale (they're available at several shops along the riverside Chai Khong and main Chiang Khan Roads). No one minds if you just walk into the factory and wander around. The **market** next door is best in the morning when chubby women sell buckets of eels and piles of plump tomatoes.

LOEI ✍ ✕

Just 48 km S of Chiang Khan, and 147 km W of Udon Thani, Loei is a hot, concrete town of little interest, saved by its friendly folk. An important transport hub for the surrounding villages, it's also the most convenient base if you want to visit Phu Kradung National Park, 80 km to the south (see pages 80-1).

The only notable attraction within Loei itself is its fine-quality cotton goods: Loei is a major cotton centre so there's plenty of it around, made up into quilts, triangular 'axe' cushions or clothes. Two recommended sources are **Chaosakul** at 4 Ua Ari (also spelt Are-Ree) Road, which sells quality locally-made clothes under the auspices of the Loei Handicraft Industrial Association; and the more tourist-oriented **Chao Dork** which sells a wider variety of cotton souvenirs at 138/2 Charoenrat Road.

If you're around in early February, you'll also be able to enjoy Loei's event of the year, organized, of course, around cotton: the **Cotton Blossom Festival** is, as you can imagine, very pretty and rather silly, with processions of cotton-decorated floats and Cotton Beauty Queens. Another big annual event packing considerably more punch is the **Rocket Festival** (see box, page 80) held in May.

NONG KHAI

See Thailand Overall: 3, pages 67-8.

PAK CHOM

This riverside town *40 km down river from Chiang Khan* was put on the map when the huge Ban Winai refugee camp was established nearby in 1975. This housed Hmong refugees from Laos who, as Royalist supporters, had to flee from communist Pathet Lao rule. At its most crowded, some 30,000 people lived in the camp, in a complex of huts that sprawled over the hillsides. When I sneaked in once during the early 1980s (the camp wasn't officially open to visitors) I found many of the women already busy making their now-famous cotton embroidery pieces and quilts – despite appallingly cramped and primitive living conditions. Now the camp is closing down, with the tribespeople either being transferred to camps elsewhere, or returning to a more peaceful Laos. Other than a few shops selling the **Hmong embroidery** and some attrac-

lawlessness a joint venture: **Ban Pak Huay** is one of several border villages thriving on mostly illegal trade with Laos.

Ban Nong Pheu, several kilometres to the east of Ban Pak Huay, and **Ban A Hii**, 5 km to the west, both have lively markets where lorry loads of goods change hands: mostly cotton, liquor and lumber from Laos in exchange for mechanical or medical goods. Cheap clothes, bedding and cigarettes from China also make their way south through Laos to the Thai markets. Ban Pak Huay is quieter, though certainly no less discreet. But the *frisson* of

• *Ban Nong Pheu.*

DETOUR – **BAN PAK HUAY**

Not many people explore the wild west area around Ban Pak Huay, the riverside border village 50 km west of Chiang Khan on Route 2195 – and I can give you one reason why not: there's no public transport to get you here, other than via Loei, 50 km to the south and then via Tha Li, 50 km north-west of Loei. When I made the journey this way, it took me four hours one way, thanks to a very infrequent songthaew service. If you want to make this trip, rent a motorbike. And go warily: the area was the scene of border skirmishes with Laos as recently as 1987 and it's still considered sensitive and rather lawless. Current amicable relations with Laos have made

watching the trading isn't the only reason to come here. A traditional way of life still permeates the village: old men weave baskets, women card cotton, and farmers spread tobacco out to dry on rattan trays. The sight of a *farang* in the village still causes a stir.

If you like the mood of the place, you can even find somewhere to stay: Ban Pak Huay has the most off-the-beaten-track guesthouse in the area, the **OTS Guesthouse**. Run by the daughter of extrovert 'Mama', Sangkhom's TXK Guesthouse owner, OTS is as introvert a guesthouse as you can get: just three Spartan huts perched on the river bank at the southern end of the village (follow the signs to find it). If you want to get away from it all, you can't do much better than this.

• *Mekhong sunset, near Nong Khai.*

THE MEKHONG RIVER

Westerners have always referred to it as the Mekong (or Mekhong) River. But strictly speaking, we should call it the Khong River, like the Thais do: their name for this mighty waterway is Mae Nam Khong (*mae nam* actually means river, or 'mother water'), while the Lao call it the Nam Khong. But while the names may differ there's no confusion about its importance as the twelfth longest river in the world: from its source in Tibet to its mouth in the Mekhong Delta of Vietnam – a distance of some 4,500 km – the Mekhong irrigates vast stretches of land in Burma, Laos, Thailand, Cambodia and Vietnam as well as providing an important means of transport.

Increasingly, too, its power is being channelled into giant hydro-electric projects, built either on the Mekhong itself or on tributaries. One of the first, Laos' Nam Ngum Dam north of Vientiane, has been so successful that the Laotian government now plans at least a dozen more hydro-electric schemes, raising the country's hydro-electric capacity to 3,000 megawatts of electricity by the beginning of the 21stC (half of which would be bought by Thailand). China, too, plans major dams in the upper Mekhong reaches – an alarming prospect for both environmentalists and countries in the lower basin of the Mekhong.

Concerned about such developments, these countries have finally re-activated the Mekhong Secretariat with a set of new agreements on sharing the river's resources and protecting it from environmental damage. The first agreement was made in 1957, but subsequent decades of war in Vietnam, Laos and Cambodia and squabbles over the use of the Mekhong for irrigation frequently brought efforts at co-ordination to a halt. However, at a November 1994 meeting, officials from Thailand, Cambodia, Laos and Vietnam (significantly, China and Burma were absent) pledged to co-ordinate their use of the Mekhong's resources for purposes such as irrigation, flood control, hydro-electric power, recreation, tourism and fishing. This was followed by a discussion in February 1995 on measures to protect the environment in the lower river basin during the following three years.

It's a hopeful start, but without agreement from all concerned – notably China – environmentalists fear the worst as commercial exploitation of the Mekhong River rapidly increases.

tive river views, Pak Chom itself has little to offer. You'll find Sangkhom, 63 km further east, a far better place to stay (see page 81).

PHU KRADUNG NATIONAL PARK

About 84 km S of Loei. One of Thailand's oldest national parks, established in 1966, Phu Kradung ('Bell Mountain') features a 1,360-m-high mountain crowned by a 60-sq.-km plateau of pine forests and waterfalls. It's most easily reached from Loei: buses leave every half hour for Phu Kradung town, from where songthaews make the last 7 km hop to the visitor centre. If you catch the first 6 am bus and don't mind six hours of walking in one day, you can visit the park on a day trip from Loei (last bus back from Phu Kradung is at 6 pm). But most people prefer to stay at least one night to enjoy the cool mountain climate and walk some of the many well-marked trails, several offering fantastic panoramas of the surrounding lowlands and Phetchabun mountains.

The main trail to the plateau at the top (6 km) takes at least three hours (with rest stops and food stalls on the way). In another 3 km you'll reach the park headquarters, passing meadows of rhododendrons (in bloom during March and April), violets and orchids, and well-hidden carnivorous pitcher plants. One of the most dramatic walks you can make once you're at the top is a 12-km **trail along the plateau's precipitous southern edge**, but even the 2-km **trail to Pha Nok An** on the eastern edge affords breathtaking views – if you're staying overnight be sure to come here for the sunrise. Another popular spot, and the focus of many pilgrimages, is the Buddha statue on a hill near park headquarters.

If you're lucky during your walks, you may spot some of the park's wildlife such as gibbons, barking deer and macaques and the tiny eastern mole. Other inhabitants, such as elephants, Asian wild pigs, yellow-throated martens, sambar and serow, rarely appear near the main trails. In the evergreen forests, watch for some of the park's bird species which include brown hornbill, silver-breasted broadbill, maroon oriole and slaty-backed forktail. There are several less common Thai residents, too, such as jay, sultan tit and snowy-browed flycatcher. The park can get surprisingly cold during the winter months, when temperatures drop to near freezing. Be sure to bring plenty of woollens. One extra layer is useful at any time of the year for the chill nights and mornings (blankets can be hired if you're staying overnight).

At weekends and during school holidays the park is often crowded with parties of students: the best time to visit would be midweek just after the rainy season (early October) when the waterfalls are at their best. During the rainy season itself (from mid July to early

---

ROCKETS, GODS AND SEX

So what's the connection? In Isaan, the three are inseparable around the end of the dry season (early to mid-May) when **Rocket Festivals** (*bun bang fai*) take place all over the north-east to encourage the gods to provide rain for the parched land. Heavy with obvious sexual symbolism, this was originally an animist fertility and rain-making rite; now it has Buddhist merit-making overtones. In fact, not so long ago, it was the Buddhist monks themselves who made the rockets. It's a free-for-all in more ways than one. Giant rockets, often made by experts, and elaborately decorated, are fired from bamboo platforms to the accompaniment of loud cheering (or lewd jeering if the rockets flop miserably after only a few feet or fail completely to get up). Drunkenness, gambling and flirtation are part and parcel of the event, most notably in **Yasothon**. This otherwise forgettable town in central Isaan is famous only for its Rocket Festival which has developed into a major event, the magnificent firework display as much an attraction as the splendidly-decorated rockets. In other places, such as Loei in northern Isaan, you can still find less tourist-oriented versions, though the blatant phallic overtones which were once a feature of the festivals (men used to parade through the streets wearing phallic symbols) have now been prudishly dropped.

October) the park is closed because of the treacherously muddy trails.

SANGKHOM ✕

On the Mekhong, some 83 km W of Nong Khai. If you've wondered why you have met so few travellers on the road west of Nong Khai or east of Chiang Khan, you'll find out why when you reach Sangkhom: travellers get stuck here for weeks and sometimes months on end. The reason? Sangkhom has some of the most relaxing riverside guesthouses on this stretch of the Mekhong, and is a base for easy day trips that don't demand too much brain or muscle power. Life is slow and simple, the river views soothing, the food delicious, the nights peaceful. What more could a weary traveller want?

The village itself sets the mood: ducks and hens wander beside the main street where stalls sell candied bananas and home-made dishes. At dusk it's like a Women's Institute gathering, with villagers bringing their specialities to sell as take-aways. It's hard to tear yourself away from the seductively slow rhythm of life here, not least because no one seems to know (or care) exactly when the next bus is due to arrive. The only departure that's reliable is the 7.30 am bus to Nong Khai, and that's because it stays in Sangkhom overnight.

When you need a little gentle activity, you can drift downriver lolling in an inner tube, or even get on a bicycle and tour the area. **River Huts** and **Bouy Guest-houses** both have rough sketch maps showing places of interest (they also provide a massage service or herbal sauna for soothing aching bones when you get back).

One of the most popular day trips is to the **Than Thip Waterfall**, about 10 km west of Sangkhom, just off Route 211 (the easiest way to get here is by motorbike). The waterfall has several levels – the second one with a rock pool where you can swim.

SI CHIANGMAI ⇌

About 40 km W of Nong Khai on Route 211. As you approach this unexpectedly large town, set in a rural landscape of fields of tomatoes, tobacco and maize, you'll start to notice hundreds of circular spring roll wrappers drying on long bamboo racks at the side of the road. These are Si Chiangmai's international claim to

---

DETOUR – WAT HIN MAAK PENG
In a beautiful shady location above the River Mekhong, this temple is famous for the strict and ascetic lifestyle of its monks: they eat only once a day, wear rough, simple robes and spend much of their time in meditation. The main halls are surprisingly large modern buildings but the tranquil riverside setting is what attracts many visitors. If you clamber down to the rocky beach below the wat you can see a Laotian forest wat – very small and modest by comparison – across the river. Wat Hin Maak Peng is just off Route 211, about 19 km east of Sangkhom: you can get here on a day trip from Nong Khai, Si Chiangmai or Sangkhom by songthaew or bus.

---

fame: from here, the wrappers are exported all over the world. Most of the people who make the wrappers are Vietnamese and Lao who fled their countries in the wake of war or revolution. There's not much reason actually to stop here, unless you want to see a slice of Vientiane across the river (don't get excited, it doesn't look at all exotic) or watch the ferry traffic going to and fro. You could also use the town as an overnight base for day trips to nearby Wat Phra That Bang Phuan or the Phu Phra Bat Historical Park, although these are more usually visited from Nong Khai.

TOPIARY TRENDS
As you travel Route 211 along the Mekhong to or from Nong Khai, keep an eye out for the fantastic topiary creations that pop up along the roadside. These range from everyday elephants or deer to imaginative displays of fighting cockerels or trees full of playing monkeys – each tree-clipping masterpiece obviously trying to outdo the next. The source of the inspiration and escalating fashion seems to be a large topiary garden approximately 8 km west of Tha Bo where gardeners have gone to town creating a zoo of leafy animals and birds.

• *North-eastern instrument and musician.*

THE KHAEN: PIPE MUSIC OF ISAAN

Of all the north-east's many distinctive folk instruments, none is more ubiquitous than the *khaen*, a reed instrument originating from Laos. It consists of rows of reed pipes strung together around a central wooden sound box.

The best-made *khaen* are said to come from central Isaan, especially Roi Et and surrounding villages, but you'll find them for sale throughout Isaan at any handicraft or souvenir shop.

THA BO

About 20 km W of Nong Khai. An important market town surrounded by fertile agricultural land, Tha Bo's biggest claims to fame are its tomatoes and its Laotian-style temple, **Wat Nam Mong**, 3 km west of town. Also called Want Ong Teu after its highly-revered 300-year-old bronze image, the wat receives many Lao devotees.

DETOUR – PHU PHRA BAT HISTORICAL PARK

About 70 km SW of Nong Khai. This is one of the most extraordinary and sacred places in the region, a remote cluster of bizarre rocky outcrops that have intrigued man since earliest times. From prehistoric cave paintings to 7thC Buddha images and 20thC temples, the area has a long history of spiritual significance. Even today, pilgrims flock here to lay offerings at the outline of a Buddha footprint housed in a modern stupa.

Now officially called the Phu Phra Bat Historical Park (open 8.30 am to 5 pm daily), it offers a trail (allow at least three hours) connecting the most interesting formations, wats and precariously balanced boulders. The largest of the park's three wats, **Phra That Phra Phuttabat Bua Bok,** is near the entrance and features a modern copy of That Phanom's white *that* (tower), housing the Buddha footprint. The charming bas-reliefs around the doorways are actually more interesting than the legendary footprint. Other highlights are the prehistoric paintings of three ochre bulls (Tham Wua) and eight black stick figures (Tham Khon) under a rocky overhang: evidence that human habitation here dates back at least 6,000 years.

In the bizarre rock shelter of **Wat Po Tha** (The Father's Temple), you can also see evidence of habitation from the Dvaravati period (7th to 10thC), with Dvaravati bas-reliefs of both seated and standing Buddhas.

The Father's Temple gets its name from a local legend which has managed to weave many of the unusual rock formations and hanging boulders into the story: long ago, so it's said, a local king sent his daughter Ussa to this remote spot to be taught by a hermit living in one of the caves. By the time she was 16 the princess was desperate to escape and sent a message

• *Phra That Phra Phuttabat Bua Bok.*

floating down a tributary of the Mekhong. A certain Prince Barot came to her rescue and married her, much to the king's fury who challenged his son-in-law to a duel of merit-making: whoever would finish building a temple last would be beheaded. The arrogant king was the loser.

Getting to the park is easiest if you have your own transport (motor bikes can be rented in Nong Khai). Otherwise, take a bus or songthaew from Nong Khai (or Udon Thani)

direct to the nearby village of Ban Pheu (13 km east of the park) or a sequence of buses to Ban Ngoi on Highway 2 and then another bus west to Ban Pheu. From Ban Pheu it's quickest by motorbike taxi; the only alternative is to hitch or take a songthaew to the next village, Ban Tiu, a 2-km walk from the park entrance. Try and leave early for this trip: it takes a couple of hours just to get here.

RECOMMENDED HOTELS

CHAIYAPHUM

Yin's Guest House, B; *off Niwetrat Road, 300 m north of the main bus terminal.*

Run by a friendly Norwegian and his Thai wife, this is a simple backpacker's favourite. Bikes and silk-weaving tours are available from here, too.

Lert Nimitra, B-BB; *1/447 Niwetrat Road; tel. 044 811522; fax 044 822335.*

Closer to the bus station than Yin's and a good deal more up-market, with a choice of fan or air-conditioned rooms. It's popular with Thai business-men, but nothing special.

CHIANG KHAN

Nong Sam Guest House, B; *407 Chiang Khan Road; tel. 042 821457.*

Nong Sam was Chiang Khan's first guesthouse; this reincarnation (the original was located in town) enjoys a shady riverside setting a couple of kilometres to the west. Run by Noi, the Thai wife of Englishman Robert (a biologist working with Thailand's World Wide Fund for Nature), the guest house has eight spacious rooms in sturdy new bungalow units. It's the most peaceful place to stay in the vicinity.

A pet pony and guinea fowl add a touch of rural atmosphere. Robert has compiled very detailed files of information on the area which are worth dipping into for day trip ideas.

Souksomboon Hotel, B; *243/3 Chai Khong Road; tel. 042 821064.*

A traditionally cavernous old wooden hotel overlooking the river and run by a *troika* of genial but assertive women. Rooms (with very thin walls) are so-so, but it's worth visiting the terrace restaurant to toast the sunset.

LOEI

Moeng Loei Guest House No. 2, B; *103/72 Soi Aw Daw Rouamchai Road; tel. 042 832839.*

Now that Moeng Loei No. 1 has closed, this is the only budget guest house in town, run by the efficient English-speaking Somdy (her husband takes any overflow of guests at the smaller No. 3 Moeng Loei nearby). The eight lino-floored rooms are adequate but poky.

Somdy has plenty of regional travel information and can provide Thai, European and even Israeli dishes in her ground-floor café.

Thai Udom Hotel, B-BB; *122/1 Charoenrat Road; tel. 042 811763; fax 042 830187.*

Central and friendly with plain but comfortable fan or air-conditioned rooms.

Cotton Inn, B-BB; *191/1-9 Charoenrat Road; tel. 042 811302.*

Smarter than most, with 63 fan or air-conditioned rooms just south of the town centre (near the GPO).

SANGKHOM

There's a generous handful of budget guesthouses here, with the two most outstanding described below.

Bouy Guest House, B; *60/4 Rimkhong Road; tel. 042 441065.*

Run by the lively and jovial husband-and-wife team, Toy & Toy (Bouy is their son), this is one of the most seductive guesthouses along the Mekhong, with 15 well-spaced-out riverside huts, five of them on their own little spit of land accessible by a plank walkway. Try and get hut no. 14 for the prime river-view spot. Husband Toy often works overseas but if he's at home you're in for a treat: he's an audacious story-teller (ask to hear the one about Sangkhom's very own Lorena Bobbett).

The restaurant here adds its own alluring flavours, in huge helpings: try the jungle curry or the speciality sandwiches on French bread. Guesthouse facilities also include bicycle and motorbike rental, boat trips, massage, and overseas telephone.

River Huts, B; *Rimkhong Road, next to Bouy Guesthouse.*

En route to Sankghom you're bound to hear rave recommendations about River Huts, run by an assertive American owner, Igalle, and his Thai wife, Lupette. But to be frank, I found their complex of huts very cramped compared to Bouy's. There are no complaints when it comes to the restaurant, however, which is justifiably popular.

SI CHIANGMAI

Tim Guest House, B; *Rimkhong Road, beside the river (follow the signs down Soi 17).*

The one and only guesthouse in town and luckily it's a welcoming place, efficiently run by a Swiss-Frenchman who can arrange everything from herbal saunas to boat trips.

RECOMMENDED RESTAURANTS

CHAIYAPHUM

Phaibun Restaurant, B-BB; *Ratchathan Road, near the Non Muang Road intersection.*

Standard dishes in a typically casual eat-and-go Thai-Chinese restaurant.

Night Market, B; *Taksin Road.*

Your best bet for local flavours, both culinary and ethnic. Look for the always-reliable Isaan specialities such as grilled chicken and spicy salad.

CHIANG KHAN

Lomluk Restaurant, B-BB; *304 Soi 9, opposite Phoonsawad Hotel; tel.* 042 821251.

You know a restaurant is reliable when it's full of locals. Here they queue up outside for take-aways, assured of fast service and honest home cooking. Try the delicious local version of *phat thai* (fried rice noodles with bean sprouts, eggs and pork). A bevy of cooks operates from the open-air kitchen on the street outside: great for people-watching while you're waiting.

Rimkhong Pub, B-BB; *297/2 Chai Khong Road.*

Run by Frenchman Pascal, this is a favourite travellers' haunt – especially at night when the music is bopping and at breakfast-time when you can get real French coffee, bread and jam. While you're here, be sure to look at Pascal's detailed files of information on places all along the Mekhong, including suggestions for day trips. He also organizes boating expeditions from Chiang Khan (including a trek to a nearby cave); and sells great little cotton caps made locally.

LOEI

Chuan Lee Bakery & Restaurant, B-BB; *131 Charoenrat Road; open 6 am to 9 pm.*

This is an old-fashioned family-run place, with an easy-to-choose display of dishes and a delicious bakery selection. The next-door Savita is similar, but trendier, and a notch less welcoming than friendly Chuan Lee.

Nawng Neung Restaurant, B; *8/22 Ruamjai Road, near Moeng Loei Guest House No. 2.*

A simple lunchtime place popular for its excellent *khao man kai*, slices of chicken, hard-boiled egg and savoury sausage, served with rice.

Isaan, B-BB; *Nok Kaew Road.*

As the name implies, this no-frills restaurant specializes in spicy north-eastern fare, at reasonable prices.

SANGKHOM

Most travellers eat at their guesthouses, but the restaurants at River Huts and Bouy Guesthouse (see pages 84-5 and 84) are particularly worth visiting if you're not staying here. The excellent range of *farang* and Thai dishes comes in huge helpings, at reasonable prices.

For something more local, wander out on to the main road around dusk and you'll find local women selling home-made take-aways from roadside stalls.

Northern Thailand

Between Mae Hong Son and Mae Sot
The Burmese Border

610 km; map Nelles 1:1, 500,000

The road running south along the Burmese border from the north-west town of Mae Hong Son to Mae Sot in central west Thailand has always been a rough and rather risky route. Ethnic rebel groups, concentrated along the border, have been fighting successive Burmese governments for greater autonomy ever since 1948. In particular, the Karens – Burma's largest ethnic minority – have been the most tenacious in struggling for an independent state in the area across from the border's Salawin River. Not so long ago, if you were prepared to face the rigours of travelling for hours in the back of a pick-up truck on unpaved roads you could sneak across the border at certain unofficial trading points and into the heart of a Karen camp.

Now the road south from Mae Hong Son is finally paved all the way, and the situation is very different: ceasefires have been negotiated with many rebel groups, and in early 1995, Burmese forces finally captured the Karen National Union's almost impregnable headquarters at Maner-plaw, upriver from Mae Sot, breaking the back of the Karens' insurgency. The main fighting may be over but this is still a journey for the adventurous traveller: the border is a major smuggling area (especially between Mae Sot and Tha Song Yang) which sees only a trickle of tourists and makes few concessions to tourist comforts. Only Mae Sot itself – a fascinating black-market border town – is firmly on the travellers' trail and serves as a useful base for treks in one of Thailand's last great wilderness areas, Umphang.

If you decide to follow this itinerary all the way from Mae Hong Son, you'll need to break the ten-hour bus ride half-way at Mae Sariang. From Mae Sot, transport connections to the east are far easier (and more comfortable), bringing you quickly back into a calmer part of the country.

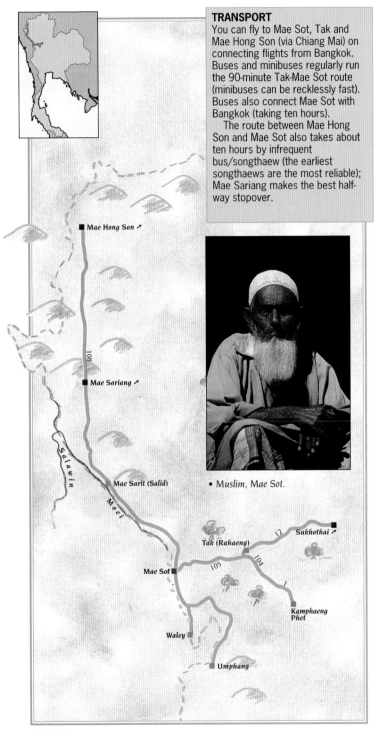

TRANSPORT
You can fly to Mae Sot, Tak and Mae Hong Son (via Chiang Mai) on connecting flights from Bangkok. Buses and minibuses regularly run the 90-minute Tak-Mae Sot route (minibuses can be recklessly fast). Buses also connect Mae Sot with Bangkok (taking ten hours).

The route between Mae Hong Son and Mae Sot also takes about ten hours by infrequent bus/songthaew (the earliest songthaews are the most reliable); Mae Sariang makes the best half-way stopover.

• Muslim, Mae Sot.

1:3,000,000

SIGHTS & PLACES OF INTEREST

MAE HONG SON
See Local Explorations: 4, pages 184-7.

MAE SARIANG
See Local Explorations: 4, page 188.

MAE SARIT (OR SALID)
This small border village 118 km north of Mae Sot is a mid-way stop-over if you're tackling the six-hour Mae Sariang to Mae Sot route. There's basic accommodation in the village and even better bungalows nearby (ask for **Chai Doi House**). If the area takes your fancy, you can base yourself here for a day or two for treks to nearby villages.

MAE SOT ⚑ ✕
At the end of Highway 105 and only 6 km from the Burmese border, Mae Sot is a fascinating frontier town. If you think the journey from Tak, 80 km to the east, is impressive (winding mountain roads which are positively hair-raising if you're

---

THE THAI-BURMA FRIENDSHIP BRIDGE AT MAE SOT

For years, the Thai and Burmese governments discussed the possibility of building an international bridge across the River Moei border between Mae Sot and Myawaddy to develop trade and tourism between the two countries. The U.S. $3.2 million highway bridge is now quickly becoming a reality, with completion scheduled for mid-1996.

This isn't just a simple cross-border convenience, however. The bridge is part of an ambitious plan to link Asia with Europe overland by a 65,000-km Pan-Asian Highway connecting Indochina, Thailand, Burma and West Asia with Turkey and Azerbaijan. The particular little link in the chain at Mae Sot will also entail building a 400-km, four-lane highway from the new bridge to Rangoon (Yangon) via Moulmein. Discussions are already underway with the Economic and Social Commission for Asia and the Pacific (ESCAP) about funding for this particular project.

---

in a minibus) you should try the journey from Mae Sariang, which is 226 km to the north.

As long as you don't mind five to six hours in an open-sided songthaew truck, this is an incredible trip, along the occasionally crumbling Highway 1085 which winds through sparsely-populated hills and along the broad, lush Moei valley. En route, all kinds of passengers crowd on board, from neatly-dressed Karens fingering rosaries to bright-eyed old Hmong women chewing betel and farmers clutching machetes. Even more villagers are picked up just beyond Mae Salid where long-tail boats speed across the river on cross-border trading runs.

Mae Sot itself is a master at black-market trade (especially in gem, jade and teak). This, and its startling ethnic mix – Chinese and Indian traders, Burmese Muslims, Karen refugees, Thai businessmen and Hmong hill tribe villagers – provide a rich cocktail of atmosphere, unlike any other place in the whole of Thailand.

It's a small place with little actually to do in town, but this atmosphere, plus several welcoming guesthouses, make it easy and tempting to hang out here for days. The **market**, behind the Siam Hotel, off Prasat Withi Road, is a great spot for tuning into the place (and for picking up cheap Burmese cloth and Indian food). Along Prasat Withi Road itself you'll find Indian and Burmese traders hanging outside the gem shops in secretive little clusters – especially during the early afternoon.

And at the western end of Prasat Withi you can pick up songthaews for the ten-minute hop to the **border at Rim Moei** (the Moei River). When I first came here, ten years ago, there was nothing more than a row of huts selling Burmese souvenirs, and a plank bridge leading to a mid-stream island where you could stare at the Burmese village of Myawaddy on the opposite bank. Thai and Burmese villagers could cross the border but not farangs.

The only thing that's the same now is the restriction on farang travel – though even that is likely to change once the Friendship Bridge currently under construction is finished (see box, above). The row of huts has been supplanted by a huge complex of stalls the other side of the bridge where minibuses disgorge Thai day-trippers to shop for Burmese clothing, carvings, sarongs and gems, and cheap Chinese plastic goods. One stall that appeals particularly to *farang* tastes sells violins and big old clocks.

More up-market stores and restaurants now line the busy broad road leading to the bridge (a scene that's rapidly becoming identical to the border town of Mae Sai (Thailand Overall:2, pages 54-5). Among the shops worth checking out here is the store next to Jintana Jewellery selling antiques from Burma, including English-style silver, chinaware, lacquerware and yet more clocks.

If you're dependent on songthaews

THE RISE AND FALL OF BURMA'S KAREN REBELS

After Burma's independence from Britain in 1948, the five-million-strong ethnic Karen minority (many of whom had supported Britain during the Second World War) saw their promised chance of autonomy disappearing under Burman domination. They took up arms and have been fighting for their independent state of Kawthoolei (or Kawtulay) ever since, joining a number of other ethnic minorities in a loose alliance against the Burmese authorities.

The rebel forces dug in at various camps along the Thai border, north and south of Mae Sot, and though there were regular offensives by the Burmese forces, the Karen National Union's headquarters at Manerplaw seemed impregnable. The 10,000-strong KNU rebels – and their international image – were considerably boosted by a new wave of mostly student sympathizers and exiled politicians after the slaughter of thousands of pro-democracy protesters in a 1988 uprising against the military regime and the subsequent elections in 1990 (a landslide for the opposition), which the ruling Law and Order Restoration Council (Slorc) blatantly failed to honour. The opposition's leader, Nobel Peace Prize Winner, Aung San Suu Kyi, remained under house arrest and Slorc remained in power.

Keen to improve their badly-tarnished international reputation and open up border areas for logging and other economic developments, Slorc declared a universal ceasefire with the insurgents in 1992 and opened peace talks with five of the guerrilla movements. Thailand, in particular, stood to benefit from the suppression of the insurgency, not only from logging concessions but also by electricity from proposed hydro-electric dams in the Salawin Valley and gas from a pipeline crossing Burma from the oilfields in the Gulf of Martaban. The KNU – once tolerated by the Thais who saw them as a useful buffer – saw the writing on the wall.

By January 1995, 13 rebel groups had struck ceasefire deals with the ruling military junta. Negotiations with the KNU had got nowhere. The chink in the KNU armour finally appeared when a serious rift developed between the Buddhist and Christian communities of its own ranks. Helped by the new splinter group, the Democratic Kayin Buddhist Organization (DKBO), the Burmese forces finally captured Manerplaw at the end of January 1995. The rebels' last main stronghold of Kawmoora fell just a month later.

The Burmese government victory has, however, back-fired on Thailand. Some 10,000 KNU refugees fled across the border following the fall of Manerplaw, adding to a Karen refugee population of 80,000 already based in over 30 refugee camps along the border. Hot on their heels came members of the DKBO who abducted several KNU leaders and then raided and set fire to five of the rebels' refugee camps. Stung by criticisms about the suspiciously slack border control, Thai authorities stepped up their patrols and promised retaliation against any incursions. The authorities were very careful, however, to confirm that their policy of 'constructive engagement' with Burma remained unchanged.

• *Above, border trading, Mae Sot; right, Mae Sot.*

to return to Mae Sot, don't linger too long: the last one leaves at 6 pm. Note, too, that this border is still quite sensitive: during past skirmishes between the Karen rebels and Burmese troops the border crossing was often closed when fighting got too close for comfort. Most recently, it closed again in March 1995 after prickly exchanges between the Thai and Burmese governments over border incursions by Burmese troops.

TAK 🏪

Situated *on the* E *bank of the* River Ping, this small provincial capital with ugly concrete shophouses only features on the traveller's itinerary as a stop-over *en route* to or from Mae Sot, 80 km to the west. If you've got time to kill while waiting for onward bus connections, you can hop on a songthaew into town from the bus terminal which is a couple of kilometres east of the centre.

A more interesting detour would be to **Lansang National Park**, 18 km south-west of town, just off Highway 105. A favourite recreation spot for locals, the 104-sq.-km-park covers a mountainous area of the Tenasserim Range. The main attractions are four **waterfalls**, easily accessible from a trail starting near the park bungalows. From the last waterfall, **Phathe**, a rougher trail, often crossing the Lansang river, leads to a **hill tribe centre** (more conveniently reached directly from Highway 105). On the way, keep your eyes open for barking deer, macaques and gibbons and a wide variety of birdlife.

WALEY

In the early 1980s, when I first came to this blackmarket border crossing, 60 km S *of* Mae Sot, the camp on the oppo-site side was in Karen hands. Since 1989, the Burmese government forces have been in control. It's still an impor-tant smuggling point, though, especial-ly for Burmese teak. Visitors aren't offi-cially allowed to cross the border here, but you can always ask at the check-point if you might be able to nip over for a quick visit.

En route to Waley, off Route 1206, is a large Karen refugee camp at **Mawk-er**, housing about 7,000 people. Dona-tions of clothes or other goods are always welcome. Mae Sot's No. 4 Guesthouse has more details.

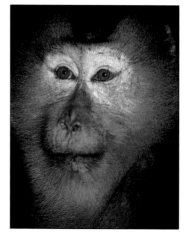

• *Lansang National Park.*

DETOUR – **KAMPHAENG PHET** ⌂ ✕

Lying *on the* E *bank of the* River Ping, Kamphaeng Phet (Diamond Wall) was established in the 14thC as a defensive garrison town by the rulers of Sukhothai, 77 km to the north. The partly restored ruins of the old city – now a historical park (open 8.30 am to 4.30 pm daily) – can easily be visited on a day trip either from Sukhothai or from Tak, 65 km to the north-west.

Within the well-preserved 6-m-high old city walls you'll find the city's most important temple, **Wat Phra Kaew**, a laterite complex with three chedis in different styles and many weathered Buddha images, so faded, thin and pitted that they are now often compared with Giacometti sculptures.

To the south-east is **Wat Phra That,** which features a central Ceylonese-style chedi surrounded by laterite columns and flanked by two smaller chedis. The nearby **Kamphaeng Phet National Museum** (open Wednesday to Sunday 8.30 am to 4 pm) has an extensive display of Sukhothai and Ayutthaya-era artifacts from the area on the second floor and a more general exhibition downstairs. Worth a long, lingering look here is the outstanding bronze statue of Shiva which was crafted in the early 16thC in typical Khmer Bayon style.

Even more interesting and atmospheric ruins lie in the wooded area to the north-east of the old city walls (hire a samlor or bicycle to get here), where Buddhists built their temples and monasteries to meditate in peace. **Wat Phra Non**, the first that you'll reach along the track, once contained a huge reclining Buddha, though only bits of it are now left. More impressive are the fine laterite columns that supported the *viharn.*

Next is **Wat Phra Si Ariyabot,** whose main feature is its four colossal stucco Buddha statues – standing, walking, sitting, reclining (hence the name of the wat, which means four postures). The seated and reclining images are hardly distinguishable now, but the two others give a clear idea of the former grandeur of the temple.

Wat Chang Rob ('temple surrounded by elephants') lies on a small incline another 0.5 km down the track. Like its namesake temples in Sukhothai and Si Satchanalai, it features a Ceylonese-style chedi (here, just the remains) on a high square base surrounded by 68 laterite elephant buttresses covered with stucco. Those on the south side are the best preserved: you can still make out faint vestiges of elegant decoration and the stucco plaques which were once interspersed between the elephants, featuring demons and sacred trees.

DETOUR – **UMPHANG** ✍

One of Thailand's largest and richest evergreen forest areas, the **Umphang Wildlife Sanctuary** and adjoining **Thung Yai-Huai Kha Khaeng Wildlife Sanctuary** (a World Heritage Site), lies about 150 km south of Mae Sot. In the old days, you'd risk your life getting here: a dirt road cut across the border into a jungle of bandits and insurgents. Even when a new road was built in 1988 on the Thai side of the border it was nicknamed Death Highway because of the continuing guerilla activity: over 400 people were killed by sniper fire during the road's construction.

Now the area has quietened down, Umphang is one of the most rewarding areas for adventure tourism, with the chance of white-water rafting and trekking deep into the jungle. Its most easily accessible and popular attraction, however, is the spectacular **Thilawsu Falls** which now draw more than 20,000 visitors a year, mostly Thais. Only discovered in 1987 by a helicopter flying low over the jungle, these are the largest falls in Thailand, with 98 cascades. The most popular way to reach the falls is by rafting down the Mae Klong River, followed by a four-hour trek or elephant ride. Add two days of trekking to nearby Karen villages and you have one of the most enjoyable (and as yet unspoilt) three-day treks in Thailand.

More challenging white-water rafting and trekking activities are also possible, including a rigorous six-day trek south to Sangkhlaburi. For further details, contact agencies in Mae Sot such as Maesot Conservation Tour, 415/17 Tangkimchiang Road (tel./fax 055 532818); BL Tour in Umphang (tel. 055 561021); white-water rafting specialists, Thai Adventures, run by Guy Gorias, 13 Moo 4 Rangiyanon Road, Pai (tel./fax 053 699111); or Nature Traveller Tour, which is run by local guide and guesthouse owner, Duangdao Suwanrangsri, at House of Cool Water, 495 Gankheha Soi 19, Sukaphiban 1 Road, Bangkapi, Bangkok (tel./fax 02 377 7959).

RECOMMENDED HOTELS

KAMPHAENG PHET
Ratchadamnoen Hotel, B;
Ratchadamnoen Road; tel. 055 711029.

A reasonable mid-range choice in the new part of town, with fan or air-conditioned rooms.

Cha Kang Rao, BB-BBB; 123/1 Thesa Road; tel. 055 711315.

The best in Kamphaeng Phet (which doesn't mean much): all rooms are air-conditioned.

MAE SOT
Mae Sot Guesthouse No. 2, B;
208/4 Intharakhiri Road; tel. 055 532745.

A popular travellers' hang-out, with half-a-dozen cheap rooms and half-a-dozen air-conditioned ones in a concrete row. There's a spacious sitting area where it's easy to relax, and a laid-back staff of Karens and Burmese. The owner, Khun Too, can arrange a three-day trek to Umphang.

No. 4 Guest House, B; 736 Intharakhiri Road.

The other backpackers' favourite: a big old house set back from the road at the western end of town, with both dormitory accommodation and simple rooms.

Porn Thep Hotel, B-BB; 25/4 Soi Srivieng (Si Wiang), Prasat Within Road; tel. 055 532590.

Right in the thick of town, with the market on the doorstep. Adequate rooms (with fan or air-conditioning) and friendly reception.

Central Mae Sot Hill Hotel, BBBB; Highway 1085, just outside town; tel. 055 532601.

Incongruously posh (obviously there's more money in Mae Sot than meets the eye) with all the frills city-slickers expect (swimming pool, disco, cocktail lounge and so on).

TAK
Sa-Nguan Thai, B; *619 Taksin Road; tel. 055 511265.*

Nothing special about the rooms, but the hotel is centrally located. For others in this price range, try the nearby Mahat Thai Bamrung Road.

Wiang Tak, BB; *25/3 Mahat Thai Bamrung Road; tel. 055 511910.*

A decent choice if you need a few more comforts (such as air-conditioning). It's a big, business-like hotel with another branch on the river.

UMPHANG
Since it's mostly Thais who visit this area, you are advised to avoid weekends or holidays when accommodation can get crowded.

Garden Huts/Resort, B; *beside the Huay Umphang stream.*

Reasonably comfortable thatched-roof huts in a pleasant position with a genial owner.

House of Cool Water, B-BB; *2 km beyond the village, beside the Huay Nam Yen River; Bangkok reservations, tel. 02 377 7959.*

Three atmospheric teak buildings, furnished in typical rural Thai style (plenty of bamboo, rattan and axe pillows). The owner, Khun Duang Dao, was one of the first people to find an overland route to the Thilawsu Waterfall and to photograph it. She still leads treks in the area.

RECOMMENDED RESTAURANTS

KAMPHAENG PHET
Malai, B-BB; *77 Thesa Road.*

Get out your phrase book for this no-English-menu restaurant serving fine north-eastern fare (if you're stuck, choose the old stand-bys: *kai yang* – grilled chicken; and *khao niaw* – sticky rice).

Night Market, B; *Wijit Road in the new town.*

The always-reliable choice for delicious, budget fare. Part of this market is open during the day, too.

THAILAND'S BURMESE RESIDENTS
When you visit Rim Moei, the border crossing just outside Mae Sot, don't be surprised if you're approached by a young Burmese asking if you'd like to buy cigarettes or foreign whisky at bargain prices. It's all part of the daily small-time smuggling that helps migrant Burmese workers earn some extra pocket money.

Nearly half of the 80,000-strong population in Mae Sot district are Burmese immigrants. Many cross the border for the day to work in the construction business, including the building of the Thai-Burmese Friendship Bridge.

But they're not the only Burmese in the country: some 50,000 who fled from the fighting in Burma between 1984 and 1991 are officially classified as 'clandestine refugees' and are housed in restricted camps along the border. There are also 80,000 'displaced' Burmese (those who arrived before 1984) living in different parts of the country, and an estimated 150,000 illegal Burmese immigrants.

MAE SOT
Pim Hut Restaurant, B-BB; *415/17 Tangkimchiang Road; tel. 055 532818.*

A pleasant place, run by Khun Boon and his wife Boon (at least you won't forget her name), this is popular with travellers hankering after pizzas, fish and chips and burgers. There's Thai food, too (including 'flog fried with garlic') and a pleasant, lazy atmosphere. (Boon also runs tours and treks to Umphang.)

Kwangtung Restaurant, B-BB; *2/1 Soi Sriphanich, near Porn Thep Hotel.*

For all your Chinese (especially Cantonese) favourites, this surprisingly low-key eaterie is the best place in town.

Burmese/Muslim food stalls, B; *opposite and near the mosque, S of Prasat Withi Road.*

Explore this area if you want to find some excellent Burmese-style curries, flat breads, and curried noodles, all at rock-bottom prices.

Eastern Thailand
Between Bangkok and Ko Samet
The East Coast

210 km; map Nelles 1: 1,500,000

This is the easiest, quickest seaside trip from Bangkok. Within a few hours, heading out along the east coast, you can be at the country's liveliest (and most notorious) resort, Pattaya, or at one of two quieter budget destinations, the island of Ko Si Chang or Ko Samet. None of them is more than four hours from Bangkok and each could serve very well as a holiday base for several days or more. Getting there by public transport is simple: buses leave frequently from Bangkok's eastern bus terminal for Si Racha (jumping-off point for Ko Si Chang), Pattaya and Ban Phe (for Ko Samet), with songthaews or local buses shuttling along the coastal Highway 3 throughout the day. The islands are accessible, too, with a regular ferry service taking 30 to 40 minutes from the mainland.

Which seaside spot you choose depends on what you want: for nightlife, watersports, sex and sin, raunchy Pattaya is the number one choice for millions of package tourists, watersports enthusiasts and middle-aged Western males. Polluted waters and an over-developed coast hardly make it the prettiest place in Thailand, but the watersports facilities and deluxe resort hotels (not to mention the transvestite shows) are undoubtedly among the best in the country. You can avoid the sex scene altogether if you stick to resorts in the smarter outskirts of Pattaya (Jomtien in the south or Naklua in the north).

But for cheaper, simpler and more innocent fun you'll probably be happier in Ko Samet or the overlooked little island of Ko Si Chang. Try to avoid visiting any of these destinations on a weekend or public holiday when they get flooded by Bangkok expats and Thai families. If you have time to continue round the eastern seaboard a little further – or fancy a slightly more remote island, see Local Explorations: 11, which takes you on to the remarkably unspoilt island of Ko Si Chang.

TRANSPORT

The most convenient way to reach the east coast resorts is by bus. Air-conditioned buses depart from Bangkok's eastern bus terminal (at Sukhumvit Road, Soi 40) throughout the day for Si Racha (leaving every 40 minutes, taking two hours); Pattaya (every 30 minutes, taking two-and-a-half hours); and Ban Phe (every two hours, taking three hours).

Boats to Ko Si Chang leave from Si Racha's pier on Jermjompol Road at least four times a day, taking about 40 minutes. For Ko Samet you should head for the pier at Ban Phe where boats leave frequently throughout the day (until about 7 pm), taking about 30 minutes.

There are several different operators at Ban Phe going to the various Ko Samet beaches: if you're unsure which one you want, take any regular boat going to the main pier at Na Dan from where you can walk or get a songthaew to the beaches.

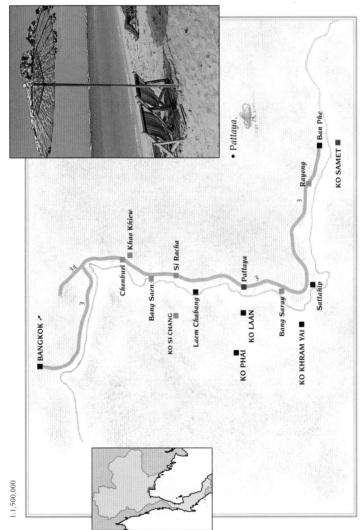

Pattaya.

1:1,500,000

SIGHTS & PLACES OF INTEREST

BANG SAEN

In the days before Pattaya rose to fame, this little town 50 km N of Pattaya (98 km SE of Bangkok) was the most popular seaside resort along the eastern coastline, especially among middle-class Thais escaping from Bangkok for the weekend. It still attracts the city folk, who come to picnic or to paddle along the narrow sandy beach, but it has inevitably been overshadowed by brash Pattaya to the south.

You're not likely to want to come here for the swimming (the sea isn't much cleaner than Pattaya's) but if you've got kids in tow you should head for the **Ocean World Amusement Park** on Beach Road, with its water slides and swimming pools. Another aquatic sight worth visiting is the **Scientific Marine Centre** (closed Mondays) in Sinakarinwirot University, which is one of the largest aquariums in the region.

BANG SARAY

On Route 3, some 20 km S of Pattaya, this former fishing village is rapidly being transformed into another major resort area for Bangkok Thais, with up-market hotels and restaurants. On weekends, prices escalate in many of the resorts and the beaches are often crowded, but come here on a weekday and you'll be able to make the most of the facilities: windsurfing and game

GENERAL TAKSIN: CHONBURI'S HERO

Chonburi is famous for two things: buffaloes and battles. The buffalo races, held every October, are a fairly new attraction. But the battles date back to the 18thC when the Burmese swept through the country and destroyed the Thai capital, Ayutthaya. A Thai general, Phaya Taksin, regrouped the scattered Thai army at Chonburi and managed to re-assert power, establishing a new capital at Thonburi. He was crowned king in 1768 and then gradually managed to win a huge new empire for the kingdom.

His later days, however, were rather less glorious: he grew more and more irrational and dangerous, and was finally executed according to royal etiquette – stuffed into a velvet sack and beaten to death with a sandalwood club.

fishing outings are available from several of the resorts (try the Ban Saray Fishing Lodge or Sea Sand Club), and there are some excellent seafood restaurants, too, which can put on a far more authentic Thai seafood meal than most places in Pattaya.

CHONBURI

There's no reason to stop in this dull provincial town 80 km SE of Bangkok unless it's for the annual Buffalo Races, held every October. This was one of the first festivals I witnessed in Thailand, and I'll never forget the bizarre procession of beauty queens and drag queens, elderly farmers and young toughs with tattooes on their arms – not to mention the buffaloes with ribbons in their horns and garlands round their necks, ceremoniously pulling red carts through the street.

The races were a laugh: the beasts charging all over the place on an increasingly muddy race course, their riders hanging on desperately (and often falling off). Best of all, no one seemed to take any of it seriously. It was one of the jolliest examples of the Thai love of fun (sanuk) that I've ever witnessed. As for the town itself? Utterly forgettable.

DETOUR – KHAO KHIEW OPEN ZOO

This 480-hectare park, 14 km SE of Bang Saen, and 30 km N of Pattaya, is home to about 130 bird species and more than 30 mammal species, including deer, gaur and sambar, which wander freely throughout the grounds. Separated on their own islands are Malayan sun bears and gibbons. Best of all is the walk-in aviary, one of the largest in Thailand. The park is near the Bang Phra Golf Course, on Route 3144. If you haven't got your own transport, the easiest way to get here is to charter a songthaew or hire a taxi from either Pattaya, Bang Saen or Si Racha.

KO KHRAM YAI, KO LUAM, KO PHAI AND KO RIN

See Pattaya's Diving, page 100.

KO LAAN

See Detour - Around Pattaya, page 101.

KO SAMET ⇌ ✕

Island just three hours SE from Bangkok (and 90 minutes from Pattaya). Ko Samet is one of the closest island escapes from the capital. You would have thought that the east coast's stunning white sand beaches (stretching practically the entire 6-km length of the island) would have been totally ruined by resort developers catering for hordes of Bangkokians. But although there's far more development than there should be for a national park (Ko Samet and a number of nearby islands were made a marine national park in 1981), it's only really the northern **Hat Sai Kaew** beach and central **Ao Wong Deuan** bay where development is rampant.

Elsewhere, particularly if you go to the far south of the island, you can still find remarkably quiet little coves with simple bungalow accommodation. Different boat operators at the mainland **Ban Phe** pier go to the various beaches (most frequently to the northern **Na Dan** pier and **Hat Sai Kaew**) or you can walk or take a songthaew from Na Dan: vehicles can go as far south as Ao Wong Deuan. Beyond that you'll have to resort to walking along rocky headland trails or along the beach to the more remote clusters of bungalows. The west coast, just 3 km across the other side at the island's widest point, has only one pleasant beach, **Hat Ao Phrao** in the north, and accessible by one daily boat from Ban Phe or by taxi from Na Dan. The interior is often impenetrable forest, home to lesser mouse deer and gibbons, hornbills and crab-eating macaques. Facilities aren't as sophisticated on Ko Samet as on more developed islands in the south: both water and electricity are rationed in some of the cheaper resorts, though if you stay in the most popular areas of Hat Sai Kaew or Ao Wong Deuan you're unlikely to face any shortages (and certainly not of videos). Be prepared, however, for mosquitoes: Ko Samet is still considered a slight malaria risk, so use plenty of repellent at dusk.

Arriving at the main pier and village of **Na Dan** on the north-eastern handle of the dagger-shaped island, you'll find a few shops, food stalls and travel agencies and a small health clinic *en route* south to the park entrance where you have to pay a B50 entrance fee. Other than the fee, the National Parks Division's presence is hardly noticeable. At the moment they seem to be keeping a low profile: a sharp contrast to 1990 when they made a big fuss about environmental damage, and closed the whole island to overnight visitors. It was a dramatic attempt to protect the park from further development, but inevitably it took only a month for the park authorities to back down in the face of fierce protests from resort developers. A system has now been introduced whereby operators pay monthly 'fines' to the Forestry Department for their 'forest encroachment' but there are still occasional clampdowns and restrictions on new developments.

Striking a balance between environmental protection and tourist facilities is a tricky problem which isn't just confined to Ko Samet (if you go to Ko Phi Phi, Local Explorations: 9, pages 230-2, you'll see an even more blatant example) but Ko Samet has become something of a test case: development has gone too far to stop overnight visitors (besides, some operators were here before the island even became a national park), but some controls are obviously needed to stop future damage. Just ten minutes' walk south of Na Dan you reach one of the areas caught up in the dispute, the over-developed **Hat Sai Kaew** or **Diamond Beach** (a reference to its kilometre of dazzling sands). It's the biggest and best beach on the island. But it's also the most crowded. Walk around a rocky promontory, with its mermaid statue (see box, page 99) and you'll come to **Ao Hin Khok**. It's instantly quieter here, and though the beach is smaller than Hat Sai Kaew, it's just as pretty.

Beyond it is the little palm-fringed bay of **Ao Phai** with a couple of efficient resorts. By scrambling over the headland you can then reach the more secluded **Ao Phutsa** (also called Ao Tub Tim), and the Bohemian enclave of **Ao Nuan**. For the most luxurious accommodation and facilities, the next

big bay, **Ao Wong Deuan** is the one to head for, though you're unlikely to find much peace and serenity what with the ferries, jet skis, crowds and beach resorts.

If you're after solitude, keep heading south: just ten minutes' walk away is **Ao Thian (Candlelight Beach)** which has a couple of simple bungalow operations among its rocky coves. Beyond this are the even more remote **Ao Kiu** and **Ao Karang**: at the last clutch of bungalows here, life becomes utterly simple (no water supplies, no electricity) and you'll know you've reached the ultimate retreat on Ko Samet. (If the idea of such environmentally-friendly simplicity appeals, you can always camp on any of the beaches on the island.)

To reach the west coast's **Ao Phrao**, follow the trail inland from Ao Phai or Ao Phutsa. Alternatively, you can get a songthaew taxi from Na Dan or the direct daily boat from Ban Phe. Walking to Ao Phrao from your east coast base makes a pleasant excursion, but I wouldn't recommend staying here: the accommodation is mediocre and the setting less inviting than else-

• Ko Samet

where on the island.

Activities on Ko Samet are mostly limited to swimming or windsurfing by day, and video-watching by night. But one outing well worth doing is the day snorkelling trip to some of the park's other islands, notably **Ko Thalu** and **Ko Kuti** to the north-east, which have some fine coral reefs. Most of the larger bungalow operations offer this trip, though less frequently during the monsoon season (May to October) when the seas are too rough for snorkelling.

KO SI CHANG

This rocky little island, 40 *minutes from the mainland town of* Si Racha (a two-hour bus ride from Bangkok) was once the site of a **summer palace** for King Chulalongkorn until the French invaded the place in 1893 during their brash assault on Bangkok to demand suzerainty over Laos. Now it's a half-forgotten little bolt-hole, sparsely inhabited (mainly with fisherfolk) and with a couple of attractive beaches along the southern and south-western coastlines.

The easiest way to get around the island is by motorbike taxi – dozens hang around near the pier in the island's only town on the north-east coast. A ring road connects the town with the south-eastern end of the island.

Beyond the road you can follow trails or scramble over headlands to get to some of the prettiest and quietest spots. The most interesting area is in the south-west, about 2 km from the pier: at the end of the ring road past a marine research centre you'll come to a popular public beach, **Hat Tha Wang**. There are better places for swimming, but Thais love to picnic here. Up above the beach you can find the eery ruins of **King Rama V's summer palace**. The best part, built of golden teak, was moved to Bangkok in 1910. Called Vimanmek Palace, it became a favourite residence of the king and his concubines. There's little of the rest of the palace left on Ko Si Chang except for the half-ruined **Wat**

• K*o Si Chang.*

Atsadangnimit and chedi at the top of the hill where the king used to spend time in meditation.

For swimming, your best bet on the island is at **Hat Sai Kaew,** over the hill from the palace. It's a pleasantly protected spot, popular at weekends but practically deserted midweek. Even more secluded is rocky **Hat Tham Pang** on the west coast, though it's not

---

POETRY ON KO SAMET

If Ko Samet moves you to write verse, you won't be the first: during the early 19thC, a prominent young poet, Sunthorn Phu, who was born close to the nearby coastal town of Klang in 1786, used Ko Samet (known then as Ko Kaew Phitsadan, or 'Island with Sand like Crushed Crystal') as the backdrop for part of his epic poem, *Phra Aphaimani*: the mermaid on Ko Samet's Ao Hin Khok promontory refers to the mermaid in Sunthorn's much-loved poem who helps a mythical prince (Phra Aphaimani) escape to Ko Samet from the amorous clutches of a female sea giant. By playing a magic flute, the prince defeats the giant, and later marries the mermaid.

Sunthorn himself had first-hand knowledge of capture and escape (and amorous entanglements) during his lifetime: born into an ordinary rural family, his skill as a poet drew him to the attention of King Rama II, but the glamorous courtly life led to an indiscreet affair with a young princess and a subsequent spell in jail during the reign of King Rama III. He regained fame and honour during the next king's reign when he was given a position equivalent to Poet Laureate.

In addition to putting the Royal Chronicles into verse and writing epic poems such as Phra Aphaimani, Sunthorn was also a peace-loving philosopher and proponent of Thai culture. It is these aspects of his personality, as much as his poetry, which UNESCO honoured on his bicentennial in 1986 by designating him an 'eminent classical poet'. An annual festival, held on June 26 in Ban Kram village, near Klang, commemorates the poet's birthday with puppet shows, poetry recitals and folk entertainment.

so suitable for swimming as Hat Sai Kaew. In the north-west of the island the headland of **Khao Khat** is another popular weekend destination, especially with Sunday fishermen from Bangkok and lovers gazing at the sunset.

But for the best sea views, it's worth staggering up to the **Chinese temple** in the north of town, which has an intriguing variety of shrines and caves. Don't try and come here during Chinese New Year, though: the temple is packed with thousands of Chinese devotees from the mainland. You'd be lucky if you even managed to squeeze your way up the steps.

PATTAYA ⚓ ✕

About 100 km S of Bangkok on Highway 3. Buses from Bangkok terminate in North Pattaya, on North Pattaya Road, near the intersection with Sukhumvit Road. The helpful TAT office is at 246/1 Moo 9 Beach Road in Central Pattaya, tel. 038 428750.

Affectionately nicknamed Sodom and Gomorrah by the Sea, Pattaya is everything you love to hate about sinful seaside resorts: its go-go bars and discos are outrageous; its polluted beaches appalling; its decadence shocking. You don't come here for an innocent holiday snoozing on the beach. If you are a middle-aged Western male on your own, everyone knows what you are here for: sex, and more sex, in any and every

GOLF ON PATTAYA

Pattaya has long been a favoured spot for golfers. There are now nine courses within 50 km of town. Among the best (and closest, just 20 minutes' away) is **Siam Country Club**, with an 18-hole championship, par 72 layout on a hilly location. A popular course for competitions, including several past Thailand Open championships, it also features a clubhouse with adjacent swimming pool.

A relatively new course is the **Panya Resort Country Club**, 45 minutes north of Pattaya. Designed by Ronald Fream it offers a mixture of American and British styles of fairways set in a delightfully aquatic landscape.

For organized outings to these or other courses, contact Cherry Tree Golf Tours in South Pattaya, tel. 038 422385.

variety. That said, not all Pattaya's visitors are sex-mad, and not all of Pattaya is awful. Nor was it always like this. It's hard to believe now, but Pattaya was once just a modest little fishing village. Even after it had been transformed during the 1960s into a resort for U.S. servicemen on R & R from the Vietnam War

PATTAYA'S DIVING

Forget the sleaze. If you want to learn to dive, Pattaya is the place. Not only are the operators experienced (many are foreigners with wide professional expertise), and the costs reasonable, but the area's shallow reefs provide ideal conditions for beginners. In addition, you can dive here year-round (unlike Phuket which is affected by the south-west monsoon).

There are a dozen or so dive operators in Pattaya, including one PADI 5-star facility (Seafari Sports Center on Beach Road, South Pattaya). Most of the others offer PADI, NAUI or BSAC courses, at prices ranging from around B2,000 for a two-day course (including equipment and lunch) to at least B7,000 for a four-day Open Water course. Be sure to shop around, not

necessarily for the best price, but for a safety-conscious operator with reliable equipment.

Most open-water qualifying dives take place near a group of islands close to the coast: the visibility isn't great, but there's plenty of small-scale reef action. Better visibility – and the chance of seeing sharks, rays or barracudas – is available a couple of hours' boat-ride away from Pattaya, around the islands of **Ko Phai, Ko Rin, Ko Khram and Ko Luam**.

Reputable operators include Dave's Divers' Den, 1/1 Pattaya-Naklua Road, North Pattaya (tel. 038 221860); Mermaid's Dive School, Soi Mermaid, Jomtien Beach (tel. 038 330272) and Steven's Dive Shop, 579 Soi 4, Beach Road (tel. 038 428392).

(there was a U.S. base at nearby Sattahip) it had a brief spell in the 70s as a trendy, jet-setting resort. But as up-and-coming Phuket appeared on the scene, so Pattaya's old sleaze reputation rose to the competition.

The most notorious part of town, known as **The Village**, or **The Strip**, is in the southern end of Central Pattaya. At night this is where Pattaya shows off and strips off, in the glare of neon-lit gaudiness, with dozens of bars, discos and massage parlours and hundreds of prostitutes and transvestites (known as *ka-toeys*) cruising the streets. There's nothing quite like it anywhere else in Asia. However horrified you may or may not be, you have to give The Strip credit for unabashed *chuzpah*, if nothing else.

Central Pattaya is the busiest daytime scene, where you'll find most of the hotels and restaurants, tour agents and shops, while **North Pattaya** is quieter and more respectable, home to the deluxe and very up-market **Dusit Resort** (see Recommended Hotels, page 104).

The next bay north from here, **Naklua**, is a notch quieter still, and though its beach can't match Jomtien's in the south, its low-key atmosphere makes it a suitable place for families. Getting from one area of Pattaya to another is easy: songthaews zip up and down two main roads, Pattaya Beach Road and the parallel Pattaya 2 Road, which are linked to each other by a busy network of *sois*.

Pattaya's seaside scene is as varied as the town. The main bay hosts **Pattaya Beach,** which has to be the ugliest beach in Thailand: all high-rise hotels, bars and boats. Years of chucking raw sewage into the bay has also made the sea here very polluted, though the authorities have finally woken up to the problem and started to take action: water treatment plants are now in operation and fines are being slapped on hotels or businesses still releasing untreated sewage into the bay. But I still wouldn't recommend swimming here: a much better choice is the cleaner, shadier **Jomtien Beach** in the next bay south, 7 km from Central Pattaya. It's neither unspoilt nor pretty (condominiums and shopping arcades have reached here, too) but it's a great spot for watersports, espe-

PATTAYA'S TRANSVESTITE SHOWS

Not all of Pattaya's night-time entertainment scene consists of seedy go-go bars or discos. The transvestite cabarets are slick and sophisticated performances, geared for tour group and family audiences: all glitz and glamour (no sex, no smut). The costumes and stage-sets are fantastic, the dancers the most glamorous in Asia. Two theatres on Pattaya 2 Road put on shows nightly: **Tiffany's**, near Soi 1, and **Alcazar's**, opposite Soi 4.

DETOUR – **AROUND PATTAYA**

When the sun, sea and sex combination begins to tire, or the kids are crying out for an alternative to building sandcastles, your best option is to join an organized tour (or hire a car, or charter a songthaew) to see some of the nearby tourist attractions.

The most impressive attraction (especially, of course, for its orchids) is **Nong Nooch Orchid Wonderland**, 18 km south. Among the 550 acres of landscaped gardens are a zoo, a lake (with boats for hire) and twice-daily cultural shows of Thai dancing and Thai boxing, as well as elephant rides.

Mini Siam, 3 km north of town, is very twee: a cultural park of over 100 of Thailand's most historic sights, all in miniature. Another old favourite is the **Elephant Kraal** (located near the Siam Country Club, 30 minutes' drive north-east of town) where elephant shows take place daily.

The off-shore island of **Ko Laan** also makes a convenient day trip: organized tours in glass-bottomed boats usually include lunch and time to snorkel or scuba-dive. Or you can pay more to go in a Chinese-style junk. Alternatively, just hop on the regular ferry which leaves from Tangke Pier for the regular 45-minute boat service. There's a bungalow resort on the island (tel. 038 428422 in Pattaya for information), so you could even stay a few days if you felt tempted.

• Female monastery inmates, Ko Samet.

cially windsufing. And that's one major reason Pattaya still attracts so many visitors – including large numbers of families on package tours: the water-sports and other sports here are fantastic. Water ski-ing, windsurfing, para-sailing or scuba diving, tennis, golf and bowling – not only is it all available, but costs are reasonable too. Unfortunately, that's not so true of the restaurants or the accommodation: if you're on a tight budget you'd be better off coming to Pattaya on a day trip (an all-night trip would actually be more appropriate) or missing it altogether and heading for a nearby off-shore island such as **Ko Samet** (pages 97-98), or **Ko Si Chang** (pages 98-100).

RAYONG

Near the junctions of Highway 3 and 36, about 220 km SE of Bangkok and 70 km from Pattaya. TAT office at 300/77 Liang Muang Road, tel. 038 611228.

If you're on your way to Ko Samet or points further east, you might want to linger a while on the beaches around Rayong, but there's not much to keep you occupied in the town itself, though admirers of King Taksin (see box, page 96) like to pay a visit to his shrine at **Wat Lummahachai Chumpon**. This commemorates the hero's brief stay in

town while he was re-grouping his forces to seize power back from the invading Burmese.

Rayong is mainly famous among Thais as the capital of a province renowned for its durian and pineapple and spicy fish sauce (*naam plaa*). There's even an annual Fruit Fair held every May to celebrate the local orchards' abundance: as well as stalls piled high with pongy durians there are also processions of floats decorated with fruits and flowers, and fruit contests. If you can't stand the smell of durian, stay clear.

The province's best beaches are all about 20 km south-east of Rayong town, near **Ban Phe**, the jumping-off point for Ko Samet (see page 97). Thai tourists have been visiting these beaches for years, but most foreign visitors head straight for Ko Samet and never discover them. If you feel like dawdling a little first, try the beaches east of Ban Phe: **Suan Son** (which has a popular pine forested park) and **Suan Wang Kaew**.

As these are favourite picnic spots with Thais, you should find plenty of open-air seafood stalls here, too. Resort accommodation is popping up all along this strip of coastline and will

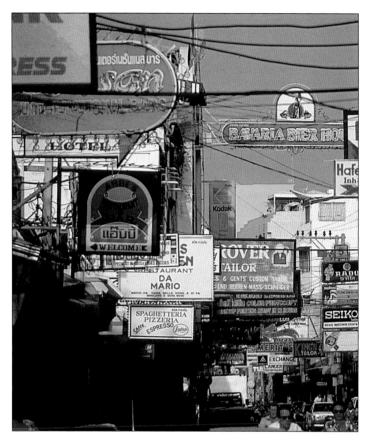

• Downtown Pattaya.

probably stretch right to Trat before very long.

SI RACHA ×

Just over 100 km and two hours by bus SE of Bangkok, this little coastal town is a curious oasis of eccentricity amidst burgeoning industrial development. In addition to an oil refinery just a few kilometres away, there's also the massive deep-water port of Laem Chabang under development 10 km south, while the off-shore waters are full of boats unloading goods on to lighters and barges for the trip up the Chao Phraya River to Bangkok.

Si Racha, however, is famous for none of this. It's known throughout Thailand for its spicy sauce – *naam phrik sii raachaa* – which is most often served with seafood. Naturally, eating seafood with *naam phrik* is the thing to do here, though some of the many seafood restaurants in town (especially

those on the jetties) charge exorbitant prices on the strength of the town's sauce fame.

If you haven't come here to eat, you've probably come to take the boat to Ko Si Chang (see pages 98-100). But it's worth leaving time to check out Si Racha's rather quaint atmosphere. The only cultural sight of note is a gaudy **Sino-Thai wat** on a rocky isle north of the pier and connected to the mainland by its own long jetty. The temple was apparently built in memory of a monk who spent many years living on the rock. But far more memorable are the town's huge, macho, motorized samlors, which dominate the town like a battalion of Roman chariots (they also roar round Ko Si Chang and Chonburi). Who needs sauce? It's well worth coming to Si Racha just for the thrill of a spin in a samlor.

RECOMMENDED HOTELS

KO SAMET
Saikaew, BB-BBBB; H*at Sai K*aew.
The most attractive of the six resorts on this beach, with some of the poshest bungalows. Expect prices to escalate at weekends.

Naga, B; A*o* H*in* K*hok; tel.* 013 210732.
A long-established favourite, run by Englishwoman Sue Wild who bakes delicious home-made bread. A no-frills place with a laid-back atmosphere.

Wong Duan Resort, BBB-BBBB; A*o Wong Deuan; tel.* 038 651777.
Typical of the up-market resorts on this popular beach, with air-conditioned or fan bungalows and even a swimming pool.

KO SI CHANG
Tiewpai Guest House, B-BB; *ten minutes' walk from the pier, on the way to* H*at* T*ha* W*ang beach; tel.* 038 216084.
A lively place with a variety of cheap accommodation (including dormitory beds) and a popular restaurant.

Benz Bungalows, BB; *near* H*at* T*ha* W*ang beach; tel.* 038 216091.
Attractive stone bungalows with a choice of fan or air-conditioning.

PATTAYA
As with everything else about Pattaya, rooms are in excess here: over 13,000 at the last count, more than anywhere else in Thailand outside Bangkok. There's little in the budget bracket, though you should be able to get discounts midweek and low season.
Avoid the southern part of Central Pattaya if you want peace and quiet.

PATTAYA - Naklua and North Pattaya
Dusit Resort, BBBB; 240/2 P*attaya* B*each* R*oad, tel.* 038 425611; *fax* 038 428239; *credit cards,* AE, MC, V.
Overlooking the bay (all rooms have their own balconies), plus two pools, tennis and squash courts, Pattaya's largest fitness centre and some excellent restaurants. Only the Royal Cliff Beach Resort in the south can beat this oasis of luxury.

Woodlands Resort, BBBB; 164/1 P*attaya-N*a*kula* R*oad; tel.* 038 421707; *fax* 038 425663; *credit cards,* AE, MC, V.
Plenty of greenery and landscaped gardens make this colonial-style place very pleasant.

Garden Lodge, BB; 170 M*u* 5, P*attaya-N*a*klua* R*oad; tel.* 038 429109; *fax* 038 421221.
Excellent value, with air-conditioned rooms, swimming pool and quiet garden setting.

PATTAYA - Central and South Pattaya
Diana Inn, BB; 216/6-9 P*attaya* 2 R*oad; tel.* 038 429675; *fax* 038 424566.
Surprisingly pleasant for this part of town: fan rooms are good value and there's even a swimming pool.

Ocean View Hotel, BBB-BBBB; 382 M*u* 10, B*each* R*oad; tel.* 038 428084; *fax* 038 428551.
Right in the centre of the bay, this old hotel is a little run-down, but the rooms are big and cosy, and you can't beat the position.

Siam Bayshore Resort, BBBB; 559 P*attaya* B*each* R*oad; tel.* 038 428678; *fax* 038 428730.
At the southern end of town, set in 20 acres of tropical gardens, with plenty of sports facilities.

PATTAYA - Cliff and Jomtien
Royal Cliff Beach Resort, BBBB; C*liff* R*oad; tel.* 038 421421; *fax* 038 428511; *credit cards,* AE, MC, V.
This is as smart as you can get: an exclusive complex on the headland between the town and Jomtien Bay, with every conceivable comfort and facility plus a private beach.

Sea Breeze, BB-BBB; 347 J*omtien* B*each; tel.* 038 231056; *fax* 038 231059.
Popular and efficient, with fairly priced air-conditioned rooms.

Marine Beach Hotel, BBB; 131/62 J*omtien* B*each; tel.* 038 231129.
Reasonable medium-range hotel

towards the southern end of the beach.

RECOMMENDED RESTAURANTS

KO SAMET
Most people eat in their bungalow resorts, but if you're nearby or fancy a night-time stroll along the beach, head in the direction of:

White Sands Restaurant, BB-BBB; Hat Sai Kaew; tel. 038 2127249.

Probably the best seafood restaurant on Ko Samet, though expect to dig deep in your pocket when the bill arrives.

PATTAYA
As you'd expect of a former U.S. R&R resort, and now a favourite with Western package tours, Pattaya is thick with *farang*-run eateries serving every kind of Western fare from pizzas and burgers to *bratwurst* and bacon. Don't expect to savour many Thai delicacies here, though you will find plenty of delicious seafood (at a price).

PIC Kitchen, BB-BBB; Soi 5, North Pattaya.

A rare exception to Pattaya's Western-dominated culinary scene, this restaurant emphasizes everything Thai, both in its setting (charming Thai-style teak pavilions with low wooden tables and cushions) and its delicious Thai food. There's often a Thai classical dance show, too.

El Toro Steakhouse, BB-BBB; 215 Pattaya 2 Road; tel. 038 426238.

The place in Pattaya for steaks. Get here early for dinner – the place fills up quickly.

Nang Nual, BB-BBB; 214/10 Beach Road, South Pattaya.

One of Pattaya's most famous seafood restaurants, right on the waterfront, and not as outrageously pricey as some of the others.

La Gritta, BB; Beach Road, past Soi 1; tel. 038 428161.

One of the most popular Italian restaurants in Pattaya. The seafood

---

NAAM PHRIK: THE ESSENTIAL SAUCE
There's *naam som phrik* and *naam plaa phrik* and, best of all, *naam phrik sii raachaa*. No Thai meal is complete without one of them. Literally 'pepper water', *naam phrik* is the basic chilli sauce that can set your mouth on fire. It's made from a concoction of pounded red chillies (the hottest variety available, literally called 'mouse shit peppers') and shrimp paste, together with pepper, garlic and onions, fermented fish, brine and lemon juice. The variations include chillies and vinegar (*naam som phrik*), chillies and fish sauce (*naam plaa phrik*), and the ultimate speciality – *naam phrik sii raachaa* – a fiery red chilli sauce made in the coastal town of Si Racha.

---

specialities (try the pasta with clams) are excellent.

Dolf Ricks, BB-BBB; Sri Nakorn Centre, North Pattaya; tel. 038 418269.

A long-established up-market favourite, specializing in Indonesian cuisine, especially the 18-dish *rijstafel*.

Vientiane Restaurant, BB-BBB; 485/18 Pattaya 2 Road; tel. 038 411298.

A refreshing change from Western fare, with Thai and Lao specialities.

SI RACHA
Some of the most atmospheric places to eat (and stay) in are the restaurants and hotels on Si Racha's piers overlooking the water. Seafood here can be pricey, but it's worth splashing out in this seafood-famous town (and don't forget to sample *naam phrik sii raachaa*, the famous spicy sauce).

Seaside Restaurant, BB-BBB; Soi 18, at the end of the pier.

An unbeatable location, friendly service, and mouth-watering menu make this a memorable spot.

Jarin, B-BB; Soi 14 pier.

A casual eatery with simple rice-and-seafood or noodle dishes. Travellers often hang out here while waiting for their boat to Ko Si Chang.

<u>Southern Thailand</u>
Between Bangkok and Surat Thani/Phuket
South from Bangkok -
Prachuap Khiri Khan and Chumphon
615/915 km; map Nelles 1:500,000

M any visitors to Thailand make straight for the famous island resorts of Ko Samui and Phuket as soon as they arrive and then find themselves trapped by the islands' seductive tropical delights, all plans for sightseeing elsewhere tossed to the coral-blue sea.

This itinerary forestalls that possibility with a little gentle sightseeing *en route* from Bangkok, with a choice of west or east coast travel south of Chumphon. If you're strong-willed, you can just as easily base yourself in Ko Samui or Phuket and tear yourself away for short excursions to some of the places suggested here. Those prepared to take things really slowly and to see the area in depth will find this trip combines perfectly with Local Explorations: 7. Phuket and Ko Samui are covered in sections of their own – Local Explorations: 8 and 12.

To or from Phuket, the route by road along the west coast is the easiest and most obvious, with the chance of cutting across the peninsula to Surat Thani, and on to Ko Samui. If Ko Samui is your base, or your goal, you have the option of a wonderful island-hopping trip via Ko Pha-Ngan and Ko Tao – though I make no guarantee that you'll ever want to regain the mainland afterwards (or that you'll even make it beyond the first island).

Either way, you'll probably want to spend at least a few days on the island of your choice, and a week *en route* – more if you fancy taking a guided trek or raft trip through the jungles and rainforest of the Khao Sok National Park, one of the most rewarding inland destinations of southern Thailand.

Note that the weather may decide which coastal route or island you choose: the north-east monsoon brings rain and choppy seas to the Ko Samui area from November to February while the south-west monsoon affects Phuket from May to October or November.

TRANSPORT

The most relaxing way to travel south is by train (air-conditioned buses are more frequent, though not much faster). From Bangkok's Hualamphong Station trains run to Surat Thani nine times daily, taking about 11 hours (five to Prachuab Khiri Khan; eight to Chumphon). If you're heading for Ko Samui or Ko Pha-Ngan, it's worth buying the combination train-bus-boat tickets for sale at Hualamphong Station.

From Chumphon there are daily midnight boats to Ko Pha-Ngan (taking six hours) or an 8 am speedboat service (two hours).

Heading south from Chumphon or across the peninsula, you'll find regular bus connections.

The most painless way south is by plane: Thai Airways flies several times daily from Bangkok to Surat Thani and/or Phuket in just over an hour.

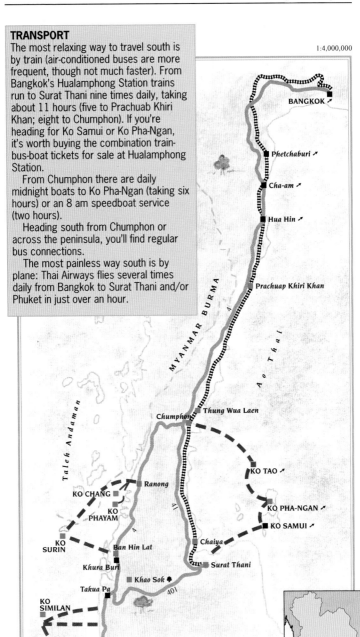

1:4,000,000

SIGHTS & PLACES OF INTEREST

BANGKOK
See pages 134-55.

BAN HIN LAT
See Ko Surin, page113.

CHA-AM
See Local Explorations: 7, page 210.

CHAIYA
About 25 km N of Surat Thani off Highway 41 and best visited as a day trip from there. You'd never guess that this nondescript little town was once an important provincial capital in the Srivijaya Empire, a powerful dynasty based in Sumatra that ruled much of Indonesia, Malaysia and southern Thailand from the 8th to the 13thC.

Today, it's just a quaint, old-fashioned town with rows of wooden shophouses that wouldn't look out of place in a cowboy movie, and a busy central market packed with produce. The small-town atmosphere makes for a pleasant meander, but the main reasons for coming to Chaiya are to see the last few relics of Srivijaya religious architecture, and to visit the famous modern forest wat of Suan Mokkhaphalaram (which is called Wat Suanmok for short).

• *Wat Suanmok, near Chaiya.*

Chaiya's most impressive Srivijaya monument is **Wat Phra Boromathat** (on the western edge of town, along the road that leads to Highway 41). Within a pretty little cloister, dotted with bougainvillea bushes and lined by gilded Buddha images, stands the 9thC white chedi, typically Javanese with its decoration of gilded lions and distinctive square tiers topped by miniature chedis. School parties pack the cloister at weekends, playing hide-and-seek around the bougainvillea plants and tossing good-luck coins into the chedi's algae-green moat.

The nearby **National Museum** (open Wednesday to Sunday, 8 am to 4 pm) mixes displays of local folk arts and handicrafts with pieces of ancient sculpture, though the best Srivijan artifacts from this area were long ago whisked off to Bangkok's National Museum.

A short walk or motorbike-taxi ride away (from Wat Phra Boromothat head for the town, and take the first turning on the right) is another Srivijan relic, a rarely-visited ruined stupa in the shady grounds of **Wat Kaeo**. The stupa oozes neglect, weeds sprouting from its cracks, grass growing at its feet. Headless Buddha images sit in a niche on the north side; on the west side is the hacked-about corpse of another image, victim of treasure-hunters. In the grounds, dogs yap, hens peck. And local devotees pass by, carrying their offerings into a barren building nearby, where a modern, gilded Buddha now receives all their attentions.

Wat Suanmok (Garden of Liberation) is an astonishing contrast, more like a Disneyesque religious theme park (visitors flock here at weekends) than the secluded forest retreat you may have expected. It's certainly not remote: 6 km south of Chaiya, right next to Highway 41 and easy to reach by motorbike taxi from Chaiya or Chumphon-bound bus from Surat Thani.

The wat was founded by Ajaan Buddhadasa Bhikkhu, one of Thailand's most famous monks, who was born in Chaiya in 1906, and died in 1993 (candid photos of his death and cremation are on display near the entrance). His eclectic brand of religious philosophy, incorporating Taoism, Zen Buddhism and Christianity, as well as standard Theravada Buddhism, has attracted many followers, including foreigners, many of whom come here for the meditation retreats held the first ten days of every month.

The 120 hectares of wooded grounds feature a weird collection of stone carvings and modern buildings, notably the huge **Theatre of Spiritual Enlightenment** which has a frieze of eye-catching bas-reliefs (copies of Indian Buddhist sculptures) on the outside, and dozens of moral and didactic paintings by resident monks inside.

Nearby is an ugly cement rendition of a boat ('metaphor for carrying living beings across the Sea of Suffering'), now looking a little green at the edges. But if you wander beyond the main complex you'll capture the traditional, peaceful essence of this forest wat: well-signposted paths lead deep into the dense woods buzzing with cicadas towards a **Sculpture Workshop** ('for those who have fallen into vices') and a **Meditation Hall**, then back past the **Solitary Coconut Pond** ('metaphor for nibbana').

Best of all is the **Golden Buddha Hill Shrine** at the top of the wooded hill near the Spiritual Theatre. A circular stone platform with a single Buddha image is surrounded by trees, like a secret stone circle: highly atmospheric.

TYPHOON GAY

Chumphon became a household name among Thais in 1989 when Typhoon Gay ripped through the province with unprecedented violence, killing more than 300 people, and causing widespread flooding and the destruction of acres of plantations. It followed a disaster the previous year in nearby Surat Thani province when floods brought tons of cut timber down deforested slopes, wiped out several villages and killed more than a hundred people. Typhoon Gay was yet another warning of the dire consequences of deforestation, and finally propelled the government into action: later the same year, logging was banned in Thailand, as well as the sale of timber felled in the country. It hasn't been good news for the country's domestic elephants, who are suddenly out of employment as log-pushers (see Thailand Overall: 1, page 41), but it has gone some way to help save the last of Thailand's forests.

If you're attracted to the idea of the ten-day retreat, all you have to do to enrol is arrive on the last day of the month (tel. 02 4682857 for further details). It's not for those who need creature comforts: a friend of mine once tried to stay here for two months but gave up after a fortnight. "I could cope with rising before dawn," he said, "and with the rule of silence, the simple meals and the long meditation sessions. What really finished me off was the lack of a comfortable bed."

CHUMPHON ⊯ ✕

Near the junction of Highway 4 and the newer Highway 41, about 500 km S of Bangkok. Chumphon is little more than a transport hub (its original Thai name actually means meeting place). There's no real reason for staying in this scruffy, noisy provincial capital unless you want to take advantage of boats leaving for **Ko Tao,** the little island north of Ko Samui which is rapidly surpassing Ko Pha-Ngan in popularity with backpackers – see Local Explorations: 12, page 253.

Slow boats leave Chumphon's port of Pak Nam for Ko Tao at midnight every day; or you can take the faster 8 am speedboat. If your eventual aim is Ko Samui, this could be the start of a delightful island-hopping itinerary via Ko Tao and Ko Pha-Ngan: there are daily boats, taking about three hours, between the three islands. Infinity Travel Service, at 68/2 Tha Tapao Road, Chumphon (tel. 077 501937), near the bus station, can provide transport and accommodation details.

Chumphon has one other lure: the **Thung Wua Laen Beach**, 12 km north-east (and easily reached from town by regular songthaew). Still relatively undeveled, this area boasts excellent off-shore diving during the February to October season (when west coast resorts such as Phuket suf-

• *Monk's forest dwelling, Wat Suanmok.*

fer from the south-west monsoon). Even out of diving season, the beach's best resort, the Chumphon Cabana, is a great spot to get away (as the resort brochure puts it) 'from the noisy, electricity life'.

HUA HIN
See Local Explorations: 7, pages 210-12.

KHAO SOK NATIONAL PARK ⌘
N of Highway 401, between Surat Thani and Takua Pa. Easy to reach: buses between Surat Thani and Takua Pa go right past the entrance (look for the Km 109 sign) taking two to three hours from Surat Thani, and an hour or so from Takua Pa.

This 646-sq.-km park is overlooked by most travellers intent on seeking their patch of sun and sand in Phuket or Ko Samui. But if you want a break from the sybaritic island life – a taste of Thai wilderness but without too much dis-

---

ECO-TOURISM: KHAO SOK LEADS THE WAY

Long before eco-tourism became the politically correct approach for developing the tourist industry, Thailand had been promoting its own form of eco-tourism with jungle tours and trekking, elephant rides or river rafting. True, many operators have simply cashed in on this growing trend without paying genuine attention to environmental concerns (few of them, for instance, bother to find alternatives for the styrofoam lunch-boxes and plastic water bottles that are used and then often dumped during the treks).

But with 79 national parks and more than 30 wildlife sanctuaries covering some 12 per cent of the country, Thailand undoubtedly has huge potential for developing the eco-tourism approach. Aware of the growing international interest (and concerned about its tarnished environmental reputation in overdeveloped tourist spots such as Pattaya and Ko Phi Phi), the Tourist Authority of Thailand has now decided to play the eco-tourist card by launching an Eco-Tourism Promotion Plan.

As part of the plan, TAT hired academics from Kasetsart University, headed by national park expert Dr Surachet Chettamart, to study possible sites in southern Thailand for eco-tourism promotion and development. They came up with 16 potential areas. Khao Sok National Park was at the top of the list. It was chosen as the best site for an eco-tourism pilot project because of its convenient location in the centre of the upper southern region, its healthy ecosystem, and its diversity of trees and animals. Stunning scenery, a reservoir on which tourists can take boat trips, plus accommodation, puts Khao Sok a step ahead in eco-tourism terms.

Environmentalists are watching TAT's moves with interest – and a certain amount of scepticism. Already, too many national park areas – notably Ko Samet and Ko Phi Phi – have fallen victim to rampant over-development and unchecked pollution in the race for the tourist dollar. Will Khao Sok and the other 15 sites on TAT's list now be threatened too? Optimists are keeping their fingers crossed, hoping the project will mark a new approach to sustainable tourism and help to save these sites from unscrupulous private developers.

comfort – you'll find Khao Sok the ideal place.

Its scenery is dramatic, featuring limestone cave-studded cliffs, jungle waterfalls and dense native rain forest, as well as the large Chiaw Lan Reservoir. There's plenty of attractive accommodation right by the park (at the last count, six different bungalow and resort operations of all standards).

Khao Sok caters to all levels of activity, from easy walks along park trails or a day's relaxing 'tubing' on the river (inner tyres are used as floats) to tough three-day guided hikes taking you deep into the jungle.

It's only on these longer treks that you may be lucky enough to see some of the park's more impressive wildlife – elephants and leopards, serow, gaur, bison and Malayan sun bears. But even along the main trails you'll be serenaded by hooting gibbons; and if you're around in January or February you may catch the flowering of one of the world's rarest flowers, the rafflesia. Locally known as *buah poot*, this huge, 80-cm-diameter flower is found in Thailand only here and in the adjoining Khlong Nanka Wildlife Sanctuary. It flowers once a year for just three or four days. When I arrived once in early February, I'd missed the grand occasion by 24 hours.

SURAT THANI'S SPECIAL LENT FESTIVAL

The end of Buddhist Lent, usually around mid-October, is celebrated all over Thailand with a one-month period when special offerings (such as new robes) are given to the monks. For Surat Thani folk, it marks the biggest and most exciting festival of their year – the one time the town really comes to life.

Called the **Chak Phra Festival** (literally, 'pulling the Buddha') it commemorates both the end of the monks' three-month retreat and the return to earth of the Buddha. A fleet of brightly-decorated rafts pull prized Buddha images on the River Tapi while a similar procession takes place on land. As in northern Nan province, among the most exciting features of the festival are the long-boat races held on the river.

DETOUR – **HALF-DAY TRIP TO BURMA'S VICTORIA POINT**

The Burmese border opposite Ranong has recently allowed foreign tourists through for short visits, a result of Burma's increasingly open-door foreign policy. The easiest way to hop across to Victoria Point is with a half-day tour organized by Ranong's Jansom Thara Hotel: it's not cheap, but avoids the hassles with border guards and bribe-greedy officials. An even simpler alternative is to go 10 km north of Ranong to Hat Charndamri, where you can watch the sun set over Victoria Point from the patio of the Jansom Thara Beach Resort.

Disappointed botanists can see photos of the specimen at the park's Visitor's Centre (open 8 am to 4.30 pm daily) whose only English-language display is on the rafflesia. Maps of the park trails are supposedly available here too, but often aren't – and anyway, they're practically useless. It's best to ask at your guesthouse for suggestions on where to go and then study the trail map board near the Visitor's Centre. The **main trail west** (a fairly easy walk for the first few hours) follows the Klong Sok River past a series of waterfalls – it would take you a full day to get to the last, Ton Sai Waterfall, and back.

The **northern trail** is shorter but damper and denser (watch out for leeches), ending at the Sip-et Chun Waterfall. Most of the guesthouses can organize outings to nearby caves as well as rafting trips on the Chiaw Lan Reservoir.

KO PHUKET
See Local Explorations: 8, pages 218-25.

KO SAMUI
Also Ko Pha-Ngan and Ko Tao, see Local Explorations: 12, pages 250-3.

KO SURIN
Five-island group, about 60 km north-west of Khura Buri. Here is some of the finest snorkelling in the Andaman Sea, particularly between the two main islands, Ko Surin Nua (north) and Ko Surin Tai (south). The group is a marine national

park, with simple accommodation available on Ko Surin Nua and a campsite on Ko Surin Tai. The drawback is the lack of a regular ferry service. Day trips are much easier, but don't give you much time to snorkel or dive (it takes four to five hours to get to the islands).

Trips are organized by Ranong's Jansom Thara Hotel (see Recommended Hotels, page 117) and by various Phuket diving centres. Or you can take a tourist boat (weekends only) from **Ban Hin Lat** pier, just off Highway 4 north of Khuraburi at Km 110. If you can get a group together (eight maximum for most boats) you could charter your own boat from here. Expect to pay around B5,000 for a round trip. The best diving and snorkelling season for this area is from December to April.

KO SIMILAN

Island group just 40 km off-shore from Thap Lamu, which is on Highway 4, 30 km S of Takua Pa. This is the closest point - a three-hour boat ride. There's no regular ferry service. Chartering your own boat is expensive, so the best option is to take one of the tours organized by diving centres in Thap Lamu, Hat Khao Lak (25 km S of Takua Pa) or Phuket's Patong Beach. Expect to pay around B2,500 to B3,500 per person per day including food and accommodation. There are also day-trips from Phuket on high-speed jetcats (Nov to Apr only).

Ask a diver for his dream destination in South-East Asia – or the world, for that matter – and the chances are that the Similan Islands will be top of the list. These nine islands boast spectacular waters with visibility of up to 30 m and a wealth of incredible marine life, from a rainbow array of coral fish to manta rays and tuna, whale sharks and barracuda.

Like the Surin Islands (pages 112-13), the Similans are a national park, with some dormitory and camping accommodation available on Koh Miang. *See also Local Explorations: 8, page 220.*

PHETCHABURI

See Local Explorations: 7, pages 213-15.

PRACHUAP KHIRI KHAN ⋈ ✕

About 290 km S of Bangkok on Highway 4. Municipal tourist information office on Salachip Road in the town centre, tel. 032 611491. This small provincial capital, about five hours from Bangkok by bus

or train, makes a pleasant overnight stop on your way south – especially if you like seafood, for which the town is famous. Thais swarm here at weekends just to eat.

There's not much else to see or to do, a fact which has helped to keep Prachuap Khiri Khan off the main tourist trail and preserved a relaxed local atmosphere in its streets of old-fashioned wooden shop-houses and beachfront restaurants.

Between seafood banquets you can drag yourself up the 395 steps of **Khao Chong Krajok** (Mirror Tunnel Mountain) in the north of town for a splendid view of the coastline and the hazy Burmese mountains, just 12 km to the west. At the top of the hill is **Wat Thammikaram** and a horde of monkeys who enjoy pestering visitors for hand-outs. The mountain's name comes from a hole in the rock face (accessible by a precarious metal ladder) which is supposed to mirror the sky. Beaches aren't the city's strong point: the best one, **Ao Manao**, is 5 km south of town, past an air force base where you have to sign your name. But a few km north of town there are several small traditional fishing villages which are worth a visit, and a secluded bay, **Ao Noi**, which has a couple of simple places at which you can stay.

RANONG ⋈ ✕

About 580 km S of Bangkok, on Highway 4 between Chumphon and Phuket. This small

---

DETOUR – **BOAT TRIPS TO KO CHANG AND KO PHAYAM**

These two little islands off the coast of Ranong, and just south of Burmese waters, are often nick-named the 'Cashew Islands' – the small resident population depends on cashew nut production as their only source of income. Visitors come here for the fine beaches and coral reefs, though accommodation is so sparse (and boat services rare) that day trips are only really feasible.

Jansom Thara Hotel organizes these for about B500 a person, but it's also worth checking with J & T ('Food & Ice') coffee shop at 259 Ruangrat Road which arranges occasional trips to Ko Chang.

provincial capital and important fishing port lies close to the Burmese Border, whose southernmost tip, **Victoria Point**, lies just across the Chan River from Ranong. Some 60 km north of town, at Kraburi, is the narrowest place in peninsular Thailand, the Isthmus of Kra: only about 50 km of land separates the Gulf of Thailand from the Andaman Sea at this point.

The other notable geographical feature of Ranong Province is its mountains, which cover 67 per cent of the total area. You wouldn't necessarily notice this if you were just passing through, but you might notice the rain: the mountains encourage rainfall, and Ranong is well known as the rainiest province in Thailand, often recording more than 5,000 mm a year.

Don't let that put you off. Ranong has a bustling, border-town atmosphere. Its Hokkien Chinese houses and coffee shops and its mix of Thai, Chinese, Malays and Burmese make it an intriguing place for an overnight stop-over if you're on the way to or from Phuket (six hours away by bus).

You're under no pressure to run around sight-seeing: there's little to do except take a soak in the town's famous **hot mineral spring waters**, conveniently piped into a large jacuzzi pool at the town's best hotel, the Jansom Thara, on Highway 4 (Phetkasem Road), a short songthaew ride from the town centre (non-residents must pay a small fee of B50 to use the pool).

The **hot springs** themselves are 1 km east at Wat Tapotharam, in the grounds of a little park. This is a popular picnic spot for locals who boil eggs in the three bubbling 65°C pools, named mother, father and daughter wells, or lounge around by cooler

• *Ao Manao Beach, Prachuap Khiri Kahn.*

streams eating snacks and getting drunk. If you can ignore the litter strewn everywhere it's quite a pleasant place to while away an hour or so.

Taking in the town's atmosphere is more rewarding: if you walk along the main Ruangrat Road you'll notice a number of gold and jewellery shops which testify to Ranong's prosperity as a trading centre for cross-border activities which aren't always legal; while old-fashioned coffee shops and cavernous shophouses, their owners lounging on Burmese-style long wooden chairs, recall the late 18thC when Hokkien Chinese (from the south-eastern region of China) first settled here to work in the nearby tin mines.

Keep heading north along the street, to the outer edges of town, and you'll eventually come to an old white wall enclosing a rambling, overgrown estate. This is **Nai Khai Ranong**, the former residence of a wealthy and influential Hokkien tin miner, Koh Su Chiang, who became governor of Ranong during the late 19thC reign of King Rama V. The only remaining original building on the estate – a clan house full of Chinese mahogany furniture, ancestral tablets and family portraits of stern, moustachioed Koh menfolk – has become a popular local shrine. Newlywed couples come here to seek a blessing on their marriage, and others come to pray for good luck in love and business.

To find the clan house, you have to walk behind the long wooden yellow building which faces the entrance. This is the home of Koh Sim Kong, the great-grandson of Koh Su Chiang. Now an elderly man, he can often be found watching television in an annexe at the back. He speaks excellent English and seems happy to have the occasional visitors to talk to. Nine of his ten children now live in Bangkok and though family members still own the other houses on the estate, the only time they all get together is at Ching Ming, the Chinese festival held to honour family ancestors and to clean their graves.

Ranong's **fishing port**, 8 km from town, is a fascinating hive of activity, especially in the mornings when Thai and Burmese fishing boats unload their catch. Burmese illegal immigrants (see box, this page) make up much of the local fishing fleet's workforce: without them, say those in the business, the fishing industry would suffer serious labour problems.

SURAT THANI ⌂ ✕

About 650 km S of Bangkok on Highway 41. If you've arrived by train (about 11 hours from Bangkok), you'll find yourself in a place called Phun Phin, 14 km W of town: during the day, shuttle buses run every ten minutes into town, some going straight to the pier. Long-distance buses terminate at fairly central locations, while the airport, 27 km S of town, has regular minibus connections. The TAT office is at 5 Talaat Mai Road (tel. 077 282828), at the SW end of town.

The only reason most tourists come to this busy port town and transport hub is to leave on the first boat out to nearby Ko Samui or Ko Pha-Ngan or to pick up connecting buses to destinations further south.

For new arrivals who've leap-frogged peninsular Thailand from central or northern Thailand, Surat Thani will seem distinctly southern, with women in Malaysian *batik* sarongs, Muslim men and swarthy fisherfolk and labourers around the piers and **port** (a great place to potter around if you're entranced by commercial boat activity – here mostly dealing in rubber and coconut exports). But unless you happen to be in Surat during the **Chak Phra Festival** (see box, page 112) there's little else to detain you from heading for your island in the Gulf.

THUNG WUA LAEN
See Chumphon, page 111.

VICTORIA POINT
See Ranong, page 114.

BURMESE ILLEGAL IMMIGRANTS

As the least populous province in Thailand – and with the closest coastal border to Burma (Myanmar) – it's not surprising to learn that in Ranong province Burmese migrant workers fill many of the local jobs, particularly in the fishing industry. But it's not just the labour shortage that prompts many employers to hire Burmese: only a fraction of these workers are in Thailand legally (they're officially allowed to work in ten coastal provinces, but only in the fishing industry and only if they have obtained a work permit). The rest – reportedly some 150,000 in Ranong province alone – are illegal immigrants.

They're welcomed by employers because they accept much lower wages than Thais (as little as half as much) and do work Thais are increasingly unwilling to tackle such as trawling, mining and construction. They're more docile, too: they daren't complain if they're badly treated by their bosses in case they're reported to the police and deported. And if they get caught? They lie low for a few days and sneak straight back. Despite the exploitation in Thailand, few want to stay in Burma. 'Life is hard there,' said one when interviewed in the *Bangkok Post*. 'I have nothing to eat and no means of living.'

One particularly unpleasant sideline to this business is the use of Burmese illegal immigrant women in local brothels. The *Bangkok Post* interviewed one girl who had arrived in Ranong through a Burmese job broker. 'I wanted to earn a living and decided to come to Thailand,' she said. 'The broker told me there were many job vacancies and I could get good pay. He took me to a place and left. The owner of the place told me that I was sold for 5,000 baht. I didn't know what to do, I could not see the police as I was an illegal immigrant.' As a prostitute, she earned B35 from the B100 each customer paid; but she was allowed to keep none of that until she repaid her 'boss' the B5,000 fee.

RECOMMENDED HOTELS

CHUMPHON

Tha Tapao Hotel, BB; 66/1 Tha Tapao Road, near the bus station; tel. 077 511748.

Conveniently located middle-range hotel, with decent rooms (choice of fan or air-conditioning).

Paradorn Inn, BB; *180/12 Paradorn Road; tel. 077 511598; credit cards, MC, V.*

Popular with Thai tourists and businessmen (maybe it's because of the pretty, welcoming girls at reception) and located on a side street away from the busy main road. All rooms are air-conditioned, and there's a swimming pool. I think this hotel is much better value (and has a friendlier staff) than the top-of-the-range Janson Chumphon.

Chumphon Cabana Resort, BB-BBB; *Thung Wua Laen Beach, 16 km N of town; tel. 077 501990; fax 077 504442; credit cards, AE, MC, V.*

This is undoubtedly the best of the five resorts on the beach, featuring a beautifully rustic design with wooden bungalows surrounded by flowering shrubs and coconut palms. The staff may not speak brilliant English, but they're all sweetness and light, especially the front office manager, Khun Ratchawan ("Call me Bee," she giggles). No wonder Bangkok expats flee here for weekend escapes.

For divers, this is the only place in Chumphon to consider: the diving centre offers NAUI and PADI open water and advanced courses during the February to October diving season as well as one-day diving packages to the nearby island of Ko Ngam. Midweek and out of diving season you may well find you've got the Cabana to yourself (there's a 20-30 per cent weekday discount, too).

KHAO SOK NATIONAL PARK

Bamboo House, B; *just off the main road to the park, and ten minutes' walk from the park entrance (follow the signs).*

Scruffiest, cheapest and liveliest of the six bungalow operations on the edge of the park, with 12 simple huts (some with attached bathrooms) in an orchard of limes, rambutan, durian and mangosteen. The energetic and ambitious 27-year-old who runs it, Sao Witaya, is the son of a park ranger who has lived here all his life and is dedicated to promoting environmentally-conscious tourism in the area (no styrofoam lunch boxes on his treks: you get your *khao pat* wrapped in banana leaves). It's very much a family place: dad pops by to watch the television, mum entertains her village friends with merry parties on Sao's river raft while brother Nung ('King of the Jungle') leads the treks, together with the legendary 'Tiger Pin' who can show you where the communists once hid out in the 1970s.

Our Jungle House, B-BB; *further down the same road as Bamboo House (above), about 1 km from the park; radio tel. 01 7230689*

The quietest and most secluded spot to stay (midweek it's almost spooky), with ten bungalows in the woods, two fabulous tree houses and two family bungalows right by the river, across from a towering limestone cliff. Jungle birds send you to sleep and gibbons wake you at dawn.

Khao Sok Rainforest Resort, BBB; *first left on the road to the park, before the Bamboo House turn-off; radio tel. 076 421155*

The gaudy signs put me off visiting this place at first, but I stumbled on it anyway on a walk back from the park. Obviously built with Bangkok or Phuket weekenders in mind, it's the smartest resort in Khao Sok, with just five stylish cottages discreetly tucked into the bamboo-dense hillside above the river and with a fantastic view of the karst (limestone) hills beyond. Try to get the cottage called Morning Mist – it has the best position.

PRACHUAP KHIRI KHAN

Thaed Saban Bungalows (also called Mirror Mountain Bungalows), B-BB; *Chai Thaleh Road, just S of Khao Chong Krajok, facing the bay.*

Modest but fair-value bungalows of various sizes, catering for up to eight people (ideal for families). There's a choice of fan or air-conditioning, and the bay is just a glance away.

Had Thong Hotel, BBB plus a B200 surcharge in the December to January peak season; 7, *Susuk Road, facing the bay near the town centre; tel.* 032 611960; *fax* 032 611033.

The best in town, with plush air-conditioned rooms and a choice of mountain or sea views.

RANONG
Jansom Thara Hotel, BBB-BBBB;
2/10 *Phetkasem Highway; tel.* 077 811511; *fax* 077 821821; *credit cards,* AE, DC, MC, V.

If you like lolling in jacuzzis, you'll love the two here: they're the largest public jacuzzis in South-East Asia with warm mineral waters piped in from the nearby hot springs (book a suite and you'll get your own jacuzzi). Other healthy attractions include a fitness centre, swimming pool and massage parlour (the degenerate can retire to the cocktail lounge and disco). Twenty per cent discount on weekdays.

SURAT THANI
Surat's budget hotels are generally seedy and noisy: you're better off heading straight to the islands. But if you want to visit Chaiya, or have arrived too late to go on, the following are worth paying a little extra for:

Seree Hotel, BB; 2/2-5 *Tonpor Road; tel.* 077 272279; *credit cards,* MC, V.

Quieter and cleaner than most in this price range, and conveniently close to the night market.

Wang Tai Hotel, BBB-BBBB; 1 *Talaat Mai Road; tel.* 077 283020; *fax* 077 281007; *credit cards,* MC, V.

Surat's number-one hotel, with all the usual frills, including a swimming pool and air-conditioning in all the rooms.

RECOMMENDED RESTAURANTS

CHUMPHON
Fai Thong Food Shop, B-BB;
188/130 *Komluang Chumphon Road, near the department store.*

This simple, open-fronted restaurant serves up a great grilled chicken and north-eastern style spicy green papaya salad. Service can be a little slack: the waitresses in pretty pink and blue outfits seem to be there to lure the customers inside, rather than do much serving.

Tiw Restaurant, B-BB; 174 *Sala Daeng Road, near the junction with Pracha Uthit Road.*

A popular travellers' haunt, with cheap, delicious dishes and useful snippets of travel information stuck on the board.

PRACHUAP KHIRI KHAN
Sai Thong Seafood Restaurant, BB-BBB; 39 *Susuk Road; tel.* 032 611293.

One of the best seafood restaurants in town, with prices that won't make you choke on your chilli sauce.

Pan Pochana, BB; 84/2-3 *Salachip Road; tel.* 032 611195.

Locals love this place for its fish curry, but you'll find plenty of other seafood dishes on the menu. It's worth asking for the seasonal speciality.

RANONG
Veetiang Restaurant, B-BB; 59 *Ruangrat Road; tel.* 077 811155.

Popular with middle-class townsfolk, this friendly little restaurant with giggling waitresses serves a delicious baked prawn in a clay pot. You can choose your fresh seafood from a display outside.

SURAT THANI
Liang Fa Mai, B-BB; 293 *Talaat Mai Road, near the local bus station; open 7 am to 5 pm only.*

Pop in here while waiting for your bus to sample the delicious local speciality: *khao kai op*, tender baked chicken on rice with a sweet sauce.

Southern Thailand

Between Surat Thani and Songkhla
The Far South

933 km; map Nelles 1:1,500,000

This section is for those who want something more from Thailand than the usual southern islands-northern hills combination, and is also ideal if you're planning to continue your travels into Malaysia. Not that islands are out of the picture: Ko Tarutao and tiny Ko Bulon Leh are among the most unspoilt and beautiful islands in the Andaman Sea. However, to reach them you'll need time and effort, and to leave them, willpower.

But the major interest of this itinerary lies in the cultural differences of the far south compared with the rest of the country. It was once under the sway of the Indonesian Srivijaya Empire, which ruled much of Malaysia and southern Thailand from the 8th to the 13thC. It still feels more Malay-Indonesian than Thai. Many of the inhabitants (called Thai pak tai, or southern Thais) are Muslim, and they all speak a fiendishly fast dialect that even has other Thais scratching their heads. In the towns there's a heavy Chinese presence, too, many of them originally drawn here to work in (and make money from) the important rubber and tin industries.

The easiest, and most interesting route to follow is along Highways 401 to Nakhon Si Thammarat and 408 (or 4) to Songkhla. Both these towns make useful bases for exploring the eastern coastline in more depth. Particularly rewarding are the two water bird sanctuaries of Thaleh Noi and Khukhut. At this point you can either cut across the peninsula to reach Ko Tarutao and the spectacular and little-visited west coast, or delve even further south, into the distinctly Malay-influenced areas of Pattani and Narathiwat.

My personal choice would be to combine the west coast highlights with a slow journey north to Krabi (see Local Explorations: 10 and 9) where I could easily get stuck for the rest of my holiday. Allow at least ten days for this all-inclusive round trip, or five for the quick hop south to Songkhla.

TRANSPORT – ISLAND CONNECTIONS

To reach the dreamy Andaman Sea islands of Ko Tarutao or Ko Bulon Leh, you first have to get to the west-coast village of Pak Bara (60 km north of Satun), where boats leave regularly. Buses or shared taxis from Satun, Trang or Hat Yai can get you to the inland town of La-Ngu, 10 km from Pak Bara. Use a songthaew for the last hop to the pier.

During the non-monsoon season (November to April), boats leave from Pak Bara for Ko Tarutao at 10.30 am and 3 pm daily; and for Ko Bulon Leh at 2 pm daily.

TRANSPORT

As the main transport hub of the region, Hat Yai is your best bet for quick access to the south: there are daily flights from Bangkok and Phuket as well as flights from Singapore and Penang. Trains leave for Hat Yai from Bangkok's Hualamphong Station four times daily, taking about 16 hours, while air-conditioned buses (a last resort) take around 14 hours (or 12 to Nakhon Si Thammarat).

From Surat Thani, trains for Hat Yai only leave around midnight (and at the crack of dawn for Nakhon): you're better off taking buses (around four hours to Hat Yai, two to Nakhon). Minibuses and shared taxis are also popular ways to get around the region.

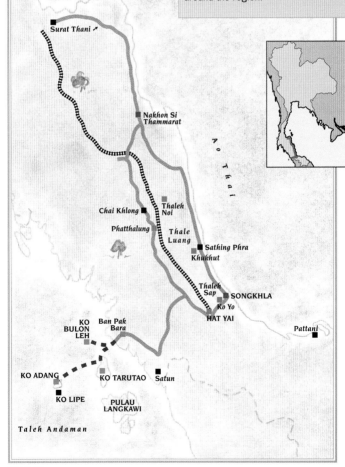

1:3,000,000

SIGHTS & PLACES OF INTEREST

HAT YAI 🚌 ✕

On Highway 4, 25 km SW of Songkhla. If you've arrived by train, you'll be eased into the melée from the western edge of town (at the end of Thamnoonvithi Road). Buses from Bangkok deposit you at a terminal south-east of the centre, while many local buses (and minibuses to and from Songkhla) stop at the northern end of town, on Phetkasem Road, in a chaotic turmoil of buses, songthaews and motorbike taxis. From the airport 12 km to the west, you can catch a taxi or Thai Airways minibus.

It's a pity this section has to start with Hat Yai: it's the least attractive place on the whole itinerary, little more than a crowded shopping centre and 'entertainment' dive for visiting Malays (the border is just 50 km away). Trouble is, you're bound to end up here one way or another (especially if you're travelling overland to or from Malaysia) since it's a major transport hub for the region, surpassing in importance the dozy provincial capital, Songkhla (see pages 129-31).

For most tourists, the first thing to decide once they arrive in Hat Yai is how to leave. But, to be fair, there are aspects you can enjoy while you're here. The town's daytime scene can be fun if you let yourself go with the flow: walking with the shoppers along the lively consumer-geared streets of

• The Muslim South.

Niphat Uthit 2 and 3 (not far from the train station) provides an intriguing insight to local (ie, Malay and southern Thai) tastes.

Batik and electronic gadgets are obviously as much in demand as dried shrimps, dates and cashews, while the dozens of gold shops reveal where the real money goes. In some of the curry restaurants in this area you could easily imagine you were already in Malaysia, while the night market on Montri 1 Road (near the local bus station) is one of the best in southern Thailand for its variety and quality of food, offering everything from unusual Muslim dishes to delicious seafood at bargain prices.

As for night-time entertainment, you won't have any difficulty finding bars or discos once you start trawling the streets around the central Thamnoonvithi Road. Indeed, Hat Yai is renowned for its quality hangovers: many a traveller, on his or her last day in Thailand before the visa runs out, has decided, after weeks of simple island living, to go out on the town – and woken up next day to find they've missed the bus to Malaysia.

For help or information, you'll find the TAT office at 1/1 Soi 2 Niphat Uthit 3 Road (tel. 074 243747).

KO ADANG AND KO LIPE

See Ko Tarutao, pages 121-4.

KO BULON LEH

Island just N of Ko Tarutao and a 20-km (45-minute boat ride) W from the peninsular coastal village of Pak Bara. Not many people know about tiny Ko Bulon Leh and even fewer bother to visit it, lured instead to the better-known islands of Ko Tarutao and, to the north, Ko Lanta and Ko Phi Phi. Indeed, I'm somewhat reluctant to reveal its presence, so quickly are 'unspoilt' islands in Thailand added to the travellers' information network and transformed into strips of bungalow resorts.

But I'm confident that if you're the kind of person who only wants some peace, a patch of sand or coral reef for the day and a bamboo hut for the night, you're also the kind of person to respect the low-key lifestyle of this simple, no-frills isle in the Andaman Sea. Snorkelling and diving in the fabulous coral-rich waters are the island's main attraction. There's little else to see or do, but the atmosphere is so relaxing that many visitors end up staying for weeks. However, you might also use it as a base for short excursions along the west coast to Krabi. A handful of bungalow operations provide adequate accommodation and food. At one of them you may well bump into a New Yorker (an avid diver) who has spent six months every year on Bulon Leh for the past seven years or so. I often wonder what happened to his New York girlfriend: when I met her in Songkhla (on her first-ever visit to Thailand) she was having some trouble adjusting to Bulon Leh's pace: after only a month she admitted she was already suffering from "island claustrophobia", and was taking a break by travelling around southern Thailand. Her boyfriend, needless to say, had stayed behind on Bulon Leh. Somehow, I think she knew she was beaten.

KO TARUTAO

Archipelago some 30 km (and 90 minute boat-ride) SW of the port of Pak Bara, with its main island, also called Ko Tarutao, just 5 km north of Langkawi, the booming Malaysian island resort.

The Ko Tarutao National Marine Park is one of the finest and best-protected archipelagos in the Andaman Sea, with many of its 51 hilly islands boasting dazzling beaches and unspoilt rainforest, marine-rich seas and coral reefs.

PRISONERS AND PIRATES ON KO TARUTAO

When a penal colony was built on Ko Tarutao in 1939 it looked like the perfect place of exile: so far from Bangkok (almost 1,000 km) that it was practically in Malaysia; and on islands so remote hardly anyone had heard of them. Surrounded by the Andaman Sea, escape was all but impossible. At first, food supplies were brought over by boat from the mainland, some 30 km away. But as the Second World War tightened its stranglehold on the area, supplies came less and less frequently. Both prisoners and guards began to starve and grow desperate.

Finally, there seemed to be only one way to survive: they teamed up to become pirates. As you can imagine, they did well. So well, in fact, that they would probably have carried on quite happily even after the war finished had it not been for the British Navy who were sent in to deal with them. Some 30 years later, in 1974, the islands were declared Thailand's first marine national park, and the prison left to fall into ruins.

Ko Tarutao, Ko Adang (43 km west) and tiny Ko Lipe, just south of Ko Adang, are the only islands in the group which are feasible to visit, with regular boat services from Pak Bara, and park accommodation (or camping facilities) available for visitors. It's advisable to book the park bungalows well in advance (tel. 02 579 0529) if you want to visit during the popular holiday and New Year periods. From June to October (the monsoon season) the park is officially closed.

Ko Tarutao (Tarutao is a Malay word meaning mysterious and primitive) couldn't be more different to that other marine national park in the Andaman Sea, Ko Phi Phi. While private development there has gone unchecked, with some appalling results, Ko Tarutao has so far managed to keep the resort and bungalow sharks at bay, though there are plenty of rumours about future tourism development plans (including ferry connections to nearby Langkawi).

• *Shadow puppets, in the making, and complete.*

Meanwhile, however, don't expect much in the way of tourist facilities, even on the main island: the attractions here are still entirely natural, including waterfalls and inland streams, limestone caves and mountains of rainforest, pockets of coral reefs and mangrove swamps. Wildlife is thick on the ground and in the seas: on Ko Tarutao, especially, keep an eye out for dusky langurs and crab-eating macaques, mouse deer and wild pig. From September to April four species of migratory sea turtle nest on several of the islands' beaches (especially on Ko Adang), while over one hundred bird species have been spotted, notably reef egrets, white-bellied sea eagles, hornbills and ospreys.

The simplest way to enjoy the main island, Ko Tarutao, is to follow some of the nature trails that have been established: from the park headquarters at **Ao Pante** (where the boats dock and where you'll also find the visitor's centre, park accommodation and cafés), a half-hour trail leads up the 114-m-high Toe-Boo Cliff to a grand panorama of the surrounding islands. You'll also see

• *Opposite: Wat Phra Mahathat, Nakhon Si Thammarat.*

two bays – Ao Jak and Ao San – which are the island's best camping sites.

One of the longest trails, a four-hour, 12-km trek through the forest, leads to the east coast bay of Talo Wao where convicts were imprisoned during the 1930s and 40s (political prisoners were holed up in a penal colony a little further south, at Ao Taloh Udang).

For a more unusual trip, you can hire a boat at park headquarters and follow the nearby Khlong Pante Malaka river a couple of swampy kilometres to Crocodile Cave, though there's nothing much to see inside except for stalagmites (the crocodiles have long since disappeared). Even better, if you've got your own sea kayak, you can discover pristine beaches where the rainforest reaches right down to the shore.

Getting to Ko Adang and Ko Lipe isn't so easy: a boat leaves Pak Bara only three times a week (currently Tuesday, Thursday and Saturday), taking about three hours to reach Ko Lipe before going on to Ko Adang.

Ko Adang's park office, accommodation and restaurant is on its southern tip, at Laem Son, where the boats also dock. As on Ko Tarutao, there are a number of trails you can follow to explore the island, including one a couple of kilometres from the park office to a west coast beach and an inland waterfall romantically called Pirate Waterfall after the island's most famous former visitors.

Just a couple of kilometres south of Ko Adang is the relatively crowded little island of **Ko Lipe**, where about 500 *chao naam* or sea gypsies make a living from fishing, farming and coconut-gathering. Some also rent out bungalows to visitors (mostly on the east coast near the main village) and boats for exploring nearby coral reefs.

NAKHON SI THAMMARAT ✉ ✕

At junction of Highways 403 and 408, 138 km SE of Surat Thani. Often overlooked by tourists racing for the Krabi coastline or islands in the Gulf, this is a delightful and fascinating town, well worth an overnight stop.

In fact, traders, tourists and pilgrims have been stopping here for centuries. Originally called Ligor, the prosperous capital of an ancient kingdom, it was a prominent religious centre for both Hinduism and Mahayana Buddhism during the 3rdC. It then became an important part of the 8thC Srivijaya Empire and increasingly attracted merchants from both China and southern India as well as Theravada Buddhists from Sri Lanka, particularly during the 13thC. It was due to the Buddhists' influence that the town was given a Pali-Sanskrit name, Nagara Sri Dhammaraja (City of the Sacred Dharma-King), transformed into Thai as Nakhon Si Thammarat and now often shortened to Nakhon.

Intermarriages between Indian merchants and locals resulted in a rich, lively culture, with the development of the *lakhon* or classical dance-drama and the *nang thalung* or shadow play, as well as the manufacture of a variety of fine handicrafts.

Nakhon today is still a cultured and religious place, with a number of important temples, a fine little museum, and shops selling exquisite **nielloware** (engraved silver inlaid with a black alloy – a technique originally introduced to Nakhon from India), and finely-woven basketware from the locally-grown *yaan lipao* vine. And though the *lakhon* dance drama is nowadays rarely performed, the *nang thalung* is still alive and well, thanks to Nakhon's master puppeteer, Suchart Subsin, whose workshop is open to visitors.

My own best memories of Nakhon are linked to its Bovorn Bazaar, a cultured enclave of old buildings that have been imaginatively and artistically converted into restaurants and coffee shops, replete with folk crafts and curious antiques.

The town is easy to get around, with songthaews zipping along the main Ratchadamnoen Road which links the modern town (and railway station) in the north with the older section and its historic sites to the south. Between the two, near the post office and police station, is the City Park, or Sanam Naa Meuang, an open grassy area where the townsfolk come to fly their kites or do a little after-work jogging. On the western side of the park, and backing on to the handicraft shopping street, Thachang Road, you'll find the TAT office (tel. 075 346516) which has a young, eager-to-please staff who can help with any queries. The best place to start a tour is at the **National Museum** (open Wednesday to Sunday, 9 am to noon, 1 pm to 4 pm) which is on Ratchadamnoen Road in the far south of town.

Take a look in the prehistory section at the largest bronze kettle drum ever found in Thailand, dating from the Dong Son culture of the 5thC, and topped by four little frogs (drums with multiple frogs indicated VIP ownership). Other exhibits reveal the town's overseas influences: many of the Ayutthaya-period Buddha images, for instance, are in the style of Phra Sihing, the revered Buddha image supposedly cast in Sri Lanka in the 2ndC and which found its way to Thailand in the 13thC. The original, or more likely a copy, now sits in the town's City Hall chapel. The Phra Sihing style – influenced in its turn by the Indian Pala style – gives the Buddha a round and rather flat face and a short, chubby body, but it became very popular in Thailand during the 16thC.

The museum's upstairs section shouldn't be missed: there's a seriously intricate nielloware panel which once graced the royal barge of King Rama V, and an amusing collection of folk crafts including curly walking sticks, a wonderful *yaan lipao* trilby hat, and the crudest coconut grater in town. (You can see more examples of these extraordinary carved wooden grater-seats at the Krua Nakhon Restaurant in Bovorn Bazaar, see Recommended Restaurants, page 133.)

A kilometre or so north of the museum, just off Ratchadamnoen Road, is one of the largest, oldest and most important religious sites in southern Thailand: **Wat Phra Mahathat** (open daily 8.30 am to 4.30 pm). You'll see the temple's huge and heavily-gilded 77-m-high chedi long before you reach it: distinctly Ceylonese in style, it was supposedly built 1,200 years ago to house relics of the Lord Buddha brought from Ceylon (Sri Lanka), but has been restored many times since (at the time of my visit, scaffolding covered it for yet another rescue mission).

Walk through the surrounding courtyard of smaller, blackened *chedis* and potted plants to reach Vihara Pra Ma, an enclosed stairs at the foot of the chedi. Inside, a huge standing Buddha faces an elaborately gilded doorway at the top of the stairs dating from the early Ayutthaya period, with lions and huge *naga* heads (plastered with gold leaf from devotees) at the foot of the stairs. In side chapels on either side you will see impressive stucco friezes of the Buddha's life.

Aggressive temple touts (trying to sell you squares of gold leaf or other offerings) will then direct you to the covered cloister at the base of the chedi which features a row of restored Buddha images interspersed by crudely-carved elephant heads (visitors squeeze under the trunks to ensure good luck).

More interesting is the fusty old **museum** across the courtyard (open daily 8.30 am to noon, I pm to 4.30 pm) which houses all kinds of artifacts from devotees. Most of the museum was closed during my latest visit, but even the one small room that was open was crammed with fascinating offer-

---

FESTIVALS IN THE CITY OF MONKS

Nakhon Si Thammarat, known as *muang phra* (city of monks), shows off its religious credentials with several notable festivals. The **Hae Phaa Khun That**, held in the third lunar month (usually February), is a spectacular three-day event which attracts devotees from all over southern Thailand to pay homage to the relics of the Buddha enshrined in Wat Mahathat's famous chedi. The highlight is a traditional merit-making procession in which a Phra Bot (a saffron cloth painting of the Buddha's life story) is carried around the chedi.

Even more colourful are the two festivals held in the tenth lunar month (usually October), both of which feature evening cultural performances (including the town's unique shadow plays). The **Tamboon Deuan Sip** is celebrated during the 15 nights of the waning moon period to pay homage to the souls of ancestors, while the **Chak Phra Pak Tai** (also celebrated in Songkhla and Surat Thani) is a form of merit-making in which Buddha images are paraded around the city to collect donations for the temples.

---

ings, from gold rings, amulets and alms bowls to miniature brass *bodhi* trees, votive tablets and tiny Buddha figures. In the outer cloister, to the north of the museum, you'll find another dusty, fusty relic: the skeleton of a whale.

The most beautiful building in the temple grounds lies in the shadow of the chedi, outside the cloister to the left: the **Viharn Luang** is an elegant Ayutthaya-period hall which looks more regal than religious, its tall pillars leaning slightly inwards, their pediments a mosaic of blue glass. If the hall is open, take the chance to see the intricately painted ceiling inside.

A ten-minute walk from Wat Mahathat you'll find the **home and workshop** of Nakhon's renowned shadow puppet master, Suchart Subsin (110/18 Soi 3, Si Thammasok Road: walk north from Wat Mahathat along Si Thammasok Road, which runs parallel to

DETOUR – **THALEH NOI WATER-BIRD SANCTUARY**

• *Thaleh Noi Waterbird Sanctuary.*

The day I visited Thaleh Noi – in fact, the very moment I stepped into the long-tail boat for a trip across the lagoon – the monsoon began. But it says something for the richness of the birdlife here and the dreamy quality of the landscape that even in the downpour, crouched under an umbrella and soaked to the skin, I was enchanted. This huge (475-sq.-km) marshy, freshwater lake hosts up to 200 species of water birds: during the migratory period (January to April), hundreds of thousands arrive from as far away as Siberia. Easy to spot are the *nok i kong* (a kind of long-legged peahen) and the soaring sea eagle, but there are dozens of different waterfowl, too, as well as kingfishers, terns and swallows. Pushing through the water vines, the *don kok* reeds and lotus flowers, the boat merges effortlessly into this bird world, leaving the hazy mainland far behind. It's worth the B150 just for the ride.

Songthaews from Phattalung take an hour to reach the park; or you can hire a motorbike taxi (B60 one way) from the Highway 41 turn-off for Ban Thaleh Noi, at Ban Chai Khlong.

The last bus back to Phattalung leaves around 5 pm.

Ratchadamnoen Road, and you'll soon see signs to the house). This rotund and cheerful 54-year-old, the son of a rubber tapper, is a self-taught puppeteer who has been in love with the art since he was a lad: he started making paper puppets when he was 12, selling them for a *baht* each. Now he is recognized as the leading *nang thalung* puppeteer in the country and has performed overseas as well as for the King (he'll proudly show you his albums of photos).

Being a puppeteer doesn't just mean performing, however: it also means making the puppets (see box, page 128), and Suchart is renowned for both. In his rustic house, decorated with buffalo horns and cages of cooing doves, you can see the master at work carving the figures from buffalo hide (some of his finished pieces are available for sale). For B50 Khun Suchart will put on a short performance, too, often aided by his teenage son, Wayatee, who plays some of the accompanying instruments.

Heading north towards town, you'll come to the small **City Hall chapel** (in the grounds of the provincial offices) which houses the **Phra Buddha Sihing**. This small, stocky Buddha image is said to have been magically created in Sri Lanka (*Sihing* means Sinhalese) nearly two millenia ago and shipped to Thailand in the 13thC. Bangkok and Chiang Mai also claim to have the original, but none of them are

• *Phattalung.*

actually Ceylonese in style, so their authenticity remains in doubt.

A little further north along Ratchadamnoen Road are two small 13th to 14thC Hindhu shrines: the **Hor Phra Narai** (usually closed), and the **Hor Phra Isuan** opposite (next to Wat Sema Muang). Distinguished by the small ritual swing in its grounds, the latter shrine has a phallic image of Shiva inside, the focus of offerings from women hoping to conceive.

In the city centre, among the gold and jewellery, electronics and motorbike retailers, you'll find the **Bovorn Bazaar** which caters to the trendy young set (as well as to tourists) with a fashionable emphasis on old local artifacts and folk crafts. The **Hao Coffee Shop**, in particular, is a treasure trove of antique oddities.

For a night-time ethnic Malay atmosphere, visit the lane leading to Bovorn Bazaar and the **night market** along Jamroenwithi Road. In both places you'll find excellent curry and *roti kluay* (banana *roti*) stalls: one in particular is run by a chubby mum, dad and daughter family who told me proudly and confidently that they serve the tastiest, freshest banana *rotis* in the south.

PHATTALUNG ⌂

At junction of Highways 41 and 4, 95 km N of Hat Yai. When I first arrived in Phattalung late one night it struck me as a

127 SHADOW PUPPETS

Before the days of TV, cinema and video, shadow puppets – called *nang* in Thailand – were the most popular form of entertainment in both villages and official ceremonies, with performances lasting for hours until long after midnight. Probably introduced into Thailand from Java in the early Ayutthaya period, *nang* (the name means hide, referring to the buffalo or cow hide from which the puppets are made) comes in two versions. *Nang yai* (large hide) puppets can be over 2 m tall and are reserved solely for performing the Indian Hindu classic, the *Ramayana*; while *nang thalung* (from the town name Phattalung) puppets are more closely related to the Javanese style, with the figures' arms and mouths often articulated by rods.

In both cases, the puppet master is the genius behind the screen, skilled not only in making the puppets but also in bringing them to life during performances and holding the attention of his audience with jokes, mimicry, music and, not least, a gripping yarn. Despite their latest attempts to modernise the art form with the introduction of new figures into the story line such as gun-wielding thugs, corrupt politicians and even camera-toting tourists, *nang thalung* puppeteers are fighting a losing battle against the video. The only place you're likely to see *nang thalung* performed in public today is in its stronghold, Nakhon Si Thammarat, during important festival times.

very strange place: its main streets, Ramet and Pracha Bamrung Roads, were flashing like Christmas trees, with coloured lights strung outside restaurants and some dark and dubious bars, their bored hostesses loitering outside. But hardly anyone seemed to be around. It took me half-an-hour to find out where the real action was: at the good old innocent night market, where motorcyclists were queuing up to collect their take-away meals. Obviously,

Hat Yai-style nightlife has yet to take off in this small provincial capital.

By day, the town is as traditional as a rural village: many shops and houses are decorated with cages of songbirds, while thick white mats of rubber are stacked by the roadsides, ready to be sent to nearby rubber factories. With only one notable temple in town, and a couple of interesting sites just outside, you can take in all there is to see in an hour or so. Its main purpose for tourists is to serve as an overnight stop on visits to the nearby Thaleh Noi Waterbird Sanctuary, 32 km away.

Phattalung is famous for one thing, though: it gave its name to the **nang thalung** shadow plays (*nang* means hide, the material the puppets are made from; and *thalung* is an abbreviation of the town name), though nowadays you have more chance of seeing *nang thalung* performances in Nakhon Si Thammarat.

Bordering the town to the west and east are two limestone peaks: **Khao Hau Taek** (Broken-Head Mountain) and **Khao Ok Thalu** (Punctured-Chest Mountain) whose names refer to a legendary fight the two female mountains had over a lover. You can climb to the top of Khao Hau Taek for a view of the town and surrounding rice paddies (Phattalung is one of the few rice-producing provinces in the south), and explore the temple cave of **Wat Kuha Sawan** at the foot of the hill: the cave itself isn't particularly interesting but it's a welcome cool spot at midday, and the shady temple grounds are a delight. Catch a songthaew by the railway track on Ramet Road and you can nip out of town for a half-hour ride to **Lam Pam**, a popular place to while away a few hours snacking on seafood and beer beside the banks of the Thale Luang lagoon, part of the inland sea of Thaleh Noi.

On the way, don't miss Phattalung's most interesting architectural and artistic sights: first is the lovely old 'palace temple' of **Wat Wang**, set within a white-walled cloister in quiet, sandy grounds surrounded by coconut palms. Some 200 years old, it used to be the site where people swore an oath of allegiance to the King during the early years of the Rattanakosin era. Only a ruined wall in the grounds – near an original old chedi – shows where a Thai prince's palace once stood. The outer windows of the wat, their frames of white stucco carvings, still show faint, pastel-coloured paintings, but it's the interior frescoes of the Buddha's life which are the most remarkable feature. Probably painted in the 18thC, they're still incredibly bright and lively. Note the distinctly Chinese-style houses in some of the scenes of everyday life.

A five-minute walk further down the road will bring you to **Wang Kao** and **Wang Mai**, the old and new courts of Phattalung's former governors. Beautifully restored by the Fine Arts Department and set in neatly-landscaped gardens beside the Lam Pam canal, the two buildings exemplify the best of 19thC southern Thai architecture. The first court is the oldest, built entirely of wood without the use of nails, while the second, dating from 1889, has polished wooden platforms around a central stone courtyard, all enclosed within a Chinese-style high white wall.

SONGKHLA ⊯ ✕

About 25 km NE of Hat Yai. Perched on the tip of a peninsula shaped like a pointing finger, between the inland sea of Thaleh Sap Songkhla and the Gulf of Thailand, Songkhla is one of the most delightful destinations in southern Thai-

> ### DETOUR – **KHU KHUT WATERBIRD SANCTUARY**
> This 520-sq.-km park, on the edge of the Thaleh Sap, is about 30 km north of Songkhla (take a Ranot-bound bus to Sathing Phra and then a motorbike taxi for the last 3 km). Like the Thaleh Noi Waterbird Sanctuary near Phattalung (see page 126) these wetlands are an important habitat for some 200 species of birds, both resident and migratory, including plovers and sandpipers, bitterns and fishing eagles (a book in the park office has detailed listings). A B150 jaunt in a long-tail boat is enough for most visitors (bring a hat as a sun-shade), but dedicated twitchers might want to splash out on a longer B300 trip which includes a visit to the birds' nest island of Ko Si Ko Ha.

land and an ideal base for short excursions in the area.

It's a provincial capital of 84,000 people but has nothing of the brashness and little of the commercialization of Hat Yai, which is linked to Songkhla by regular buses and minibuses depositing visitors right in the centre

> ### DETOUR – **KO YO**
> This is an easy half-day trip from Songkhla (or full day, if combined with Khu Khut Waterbird Sanctuary), with the attraction of seeing one of the best folklore museums in southern Thailand as well as some high-quality cotton-weaving.
>
> Ko Yo is a small island in the Thaleh Sap, half-an-hour west of Songkhla, with Route 4146 connecting it to the mainland north and south (take a songthaew from Songkhla or a Ranot-bound bus). On the northern slopes of the island is the **Southern Folklore Museum** (open daily 8 am to 6 pm), part of the Si Nakharinwirot University. Its complex of Thai-style buildings and pavilions spreads up a hillside of landscaped gardens with splendid views over the Thaleh Sap. The main display halls contain a fascinating array of folk crafts and artifacts:

don't miss pavilion no. 23 with its basketware and fiendishly clever fish traps; or no. 2 with its collection of amusing *lek kood* coconut-grater seats, carved into all sorts of bizarre and naughty shapes, from monkeys and tigers to beauty queens and phallic objects.

Back at the southern end of the island you can visit **Ban Nok**, the village of cotton-weavers just off the highway which has become a major tourist attraction. In fact, most tourists just stop at the stalls by the roadside which sell the finished products (as well as cheap batik clothes, durian cakes, dried fish and beef). But if you wander down the side road to the village you'll soon hear the clack-clack of the looms and see the women at work on the real thing. You can try bargaining, but expect to pay up to B200 a yard for the best-quality cloth.

• *Songkhla.*

of town.

During the Srivijaya period (8th to 13thC) Songkhla was situated across the Thaleh Sap from its present harbour and flourished as an important port. In the 17thC, a prominent Muslim trader brought Songkhla into the commercial limelight, though King Narai the Great then decided that the upstart trader deserved a lesson in humility and razed the town to the ground. The town got its greatest boost in the 18thC when a Chinese merchant, Yienghoa, was given permission to collect birds' nests from islands in the east of the province. He became so rich and influential that he was made the town's governor, the first in the Na Songkhla

dynasty of Chinese governors.

Soon afterwards, the town moved across the harbour and quickly started growing, helped by an influx of more Chinese who were attracted to the local tin mining industry.

Today, the town still has a predominantly Chinese atmosphere, particularly in the **old town** (south of Jana Road and west of Wat Machimawat) where decrepit Chinese shophouses with red-tiled roofs still stand among the occasional old Portuguese-style residences with their pastel-coloured stucco façades and wooden shutters. Samlors trundle through the area's most atmospheric trio of streets, **Nakhon Nawk, Nakhon Nai** and **Nang Ngam Roads**, where you'll find tailors, barbers and black, oily workshops next to traditional Chinese cafés and neat Chinese temples. The town's most important wat, the 19thC **Wat Machimawat**, is also in this area, on Saiburi Road, its buildings spread out in spacious, pleasant grounds. Its main bot is impressive inside and out, with Chinese-style lions and guardian figures at the entrance and beautifully carved, gilded shutters on every window. The Chinese stone bas-reliefs around the base of the bot are elegantly restrained compared to the scene inside: an exuberant display of gorgeously rich murals cover the walls, featuring everything from the previous lives of the Buddha and dramatic battle scenes to fascinating pictures of 19thC life, including the arrival of European visitors to Songkhla (note a charming European lady holding a parasol on the right side wall).

I can recommend arriving here in the early morning when the monks are chanting their prayers and the door is open just enough to glimpse this extraordinary backdrop of paintings. The monks are happy to open the shutters after their prayer session so you can see the murals more clearly.

In a building behind the bot is a strange little **museum** (open Wednesday to Sunday, 8.30 am to 4.30 pm) whose half-forgotten collection of odds and ends provides an eccentric contrast to the bot's splendour.

Among the dimly-lit, unlabelled cabinets of treasures and junk you'll find conch shells and neolithic stone axes, 19thC European ceramics and 14thC Sukhothai ware, as well as a 19thC typewriter and various skulls, stuffed snakes and dried sea-horses.

More impressive is the **National Museum** (open Wednesday to Sunday, 8.30 am to 4.30 pm) on the town centre's Jana Road. Actually, it's not the contents which are memorable but the building itself, a charming Sino-Thai mansion built in 1878 as the private residence of governor Phraya Sunthranuraksa. Its spacious garden is now dotted with various artifacts, including old cannon, anchors and stone *lingams*, while an annexe at the back houses an eclectic assortment of agricultural implements; krises (Malayan

daggers with wavy blades); rifles; a complete whale skeleton and some finely carved wooden panels from Wat Machimawat. In the museum itself, 5,000-year-old **Ban Chiang pottery** with swirling ochre designs is the highlight of the ground floor exhibits. Upstairs, in cool, wooden-floored rooms are Buddha images in Ayutthaya and U-thong styles as well as fabulous carved door panels and ornate Chinese gilded furniture that once belonged to the Na Songkhla governing family.

North of the museum, just before you reach Hat Simila beach, two hills pop up: **Khao Tung Kuan** and **Khao Noi**. The former is worth climbing for its breezy views over the town and fishing port. Concrete steps from Ratchadamnoen Road lead right up to a chedi and lighthouse at the top (there's little shade, so avoid midday) past a recently-restored royal pavilion, a bizarre Neo-classical red-brick affair. But for the best sea breezes, go to **Hat Simila**. Don't expect clean beaches or sea: this 8-km strip is the town's favourite picnic spot, with rubbish and plastic bags strewn among the seafood stalls which line the front under the shade of casuarina trees. At weekends, though, you can't beat the jolly atmosphere: families are out flying their kites, Muslim girls in their long blue dresses and white veils paddle tentatively in the sea while giggling lovers snap photos by the popular mermaid statue. If you can close your eyes to the litter, there's nothing more pleasant than to loll back in one of the deckchairs, drink in hand, and let the sounds of surf and laughter roll by.

In late afternoon, drag yourself to your feet, hop on a songthaew and head for **Kao Seng**, a Muslim fishing village a few kilometres south of town. It is famous for its beautifully-painted *kolae* fishing boats drawn up on the grubby beach where kids trail after you, hands out for *baht*. But I think that the lively **fish market** along the road is just as interesting – as much for the variety of fish as the people selling it: chubby Muslim women and boisterous men, who are distinctly Malay in looks and manners, a reminder of Songkhla's multi-cultural mix.

SURAT THANI

See Thailand Overall: 7, page 115.

RECOMMENDED HOTELS

HAT YAI

Cheap hotels in Hat Yai can be sleazy and grotty, like the town itself. If you've got to stay it's worth paying a little extra to avoid the brothel-hovels.

Laem Thong Hotel, B-BB; 44-46 Thamnoonvithi Road; tel. 074 352301; fax 074 237574.

A reasonable central choice, with either fan or air-conditioned rooms. Avoid the noisy street rooms if possible.

King's Hotel, B-BB; 126 Niphat Uthit Road; tel. 074 234140.

Cheaper and less flashy than the Laem Thong, above, with a distinctly Malay-Chinese atmosphere (and clientèle).

New World Hotel, BBB; 144-158 Niphat Uthit 2 Road; tel. 074 230100; fax 074 230105; credit cards, AE, MC, V.

A friendly reception, fairly central location and a little bit of luxury (satellite TV and swimming pool) make this an easy temptation in the upper price bracket.

NAKHON SI THAMMARAT

Bua Luang Hotel, B; 1487/19 Soi Luang Muang, Jamroenwithi Road; tel. 075 341518.

I'll never forget my first visit to this hotel: as I stepped out of the samlor at the entrance, I looked up into the trunk of an elephant. Its mahout was leading it on a food-begging round of the nearby market and hotel guests were feeding it bananas. The rooms were dull by comparison, but at least they were clean and reasonably quiet.

Thai Hotel, B-BB; 1357 Ratchadam-noen Road; tel. 075-356505.

An easy-going, friendly place, close to the train station and Bovorn Bazaar, with dull but decent rooms (fan and air-conditioned).

PHATTALUNG

Thai Hotel, B; 14/1-5 Disara-Nakarin Road; tel. 074 611636.

Nothing special, and the staff are sultry, but it has a fairly peaceful location behind the Bangkok Bank and the rooms are large and clean.

SONGKHLA

Narai Hotel, B; 14 Chai Khao Road; tel. 074311078.

This rambling old wooden hotel has definitely seen better days (it's been around for 50 years) but it's still the best budget choice if you want somewhere with character (ie, dicey plumbing, hard beds and huge spartan rooms). Glamorous English-speaking Tip Kiripat (whose family clutter fills the downstairs room) tries to keep the place together. Avoid the noisy street-facing and pokey annexe rooms. Bikes are for rent here, but they're almost as decrepit as the house.

Suksoomboon 2, B-BB; 18 Saiburi Road; tel. 074 311149 for old wing; 074 323808 for new wing.

Not to be confused with Suksoomboon 1 on Phetchakiri Road (which is a much lower standard) this version has two wings: a typically Chinese old wing with rows of simple but spacious rooms; and a flashy new wing, all air-conditioned.

Lake Inn Hotel, BB; 301-3 Nakhorn Nawk Road; tel.-fax 074 321044; credit cards, AE, MC, V.

The best in town, especially if you splash out for the lake-view rooms. All have air-conditioning, TV and refrigerator.

RECOMMENDED RESTAURANTS

HAT YAI

Muslim O-Cha, B-BB; 117 Niphat Uthit 1, opposite King's Hotel.

A tiny, long-established favourite with ethnic Malays, serving not-too-hot curries all day long. It closes around 9 pm and is often packed, so go for an early lunch to be sure of a table.

Nakorn Nai, B-BB; 166/7 Niphat Uthit 2; tel. 074 236301.

A pleasantly decorated place, open to the street, serving all your home favourites: American breakfasts, burgers, pizzas and pastas. Shame about the intrusive video screen.

Tang Ha Heng Restaurant, B-BB;
83 Niphat Uthit 2 Road; tel. 074 243310.

One of Hat Yai's typical Chinese seafood restaurants, with the usual mouth-watering selection on display outside – squid, crab, prawns (and frogs).

NAKHON SI THAMMARAT
Bovorn Bazaar, **B**, across from the Thai Hotel on Ratchadamnoen Road. An unusual artistic haven, with three attractive eateries perfect for breakfast, lunch and/or dinner.

Hao Coffee, B; tel. 075 346563.
More than just a coffee shop serving Hokkien-style ('Hao') and 17 other international coffees: this is also a treasure trove of antiques and curiosities – wall clocks and wireless sets, old jewellery and pen-knives, scissors, locks and lanterns. Waitresses in white caps and aprons lend a quaint Victorian air.

Ban Lakhon Restaurant, B-BB; tel.
075 345910; credit cards, V.

An old wooden house built around an Indian rubber tree which grows through the middle. Best to come here for dinner, when lights in the tree make the upstairs, open-air tables the most romantic spot in town. The menu is stimulating: 'piquant cocks' salad', sour hot fried catfish and charcoal-grilled mother crabs (among other delicacies).

Krua Nakhon, B-BB; tel. 075
317197; open 7 am to 3.30 pm only.

Packed at lunchtime, and with good reason: this blue-and-white pavilion is the place to savour local *cuisine*, especially *khanom jin* (white noodles served with a curry or fish sauce and a variety of raw vegetables). It's also an extraordinary little museum, stuffed with local artifacts and folk crafts (including a wall full of coconut-grater seats, some of them wonderfully lewd). The manageress, Suparp Wongprot, maintains a distinct touch of elegance.

SNAKE BLOOD NECTAR
If you need a pick-me-up, Hat Yai has the answer. Down Thanon Nguu (Snake Street – Soi 2, Channiwet Road) you'll find the serpents of your choice – a banded krait, perhaps, or little cobra. Those in dire need should go for a King Cobra, though they're expensive – B2,000 and up.

Preparing the beverage is simple: a live snake is slit lengthwise, its blood collected and mixed with honey or rice wine. The effects, according to Chinese belief, are extremely beneficial, not only improving stamina but boosting longevity and libido. One gulp is probably not enough for the best results.

SONGKHLA
Raan Aahaan Tae, B-BB; 85 Nang Ngam Road, tel. 074 311505.

Locals love this plain old-fashioned place in the heart of Chinatown: the select menu (no prices – be sure to ask) specializes in seafood as well as delicacies such as 'fried battered century egg' and 'stirfried chicken with herbal leaves.' Go early for dinner: it closes around 8 pm.

Mae Sawang, B; 56 Nakhorn Nai
Road.

Start the day the Chinese way, with a breakfast of savoury *dim sum* morsels. No one speaks English here but there's no menu anyway: you just choose from items on display out front and they're steamed on the spot for you.

Buakaew Seafood Restaurant,
BB; Samila Beach; tel. 074 311341; credit cards, MC, V.

Typical of the fancy seafood restaurants in this area, and popular with wedding parties. Get a group together to make the most of their delicious seafood banquets. There's only one bar to having a riotous party here: no alcohol is served.

Bangkok: *introduction*

Bangkok is a city of contrasts, where the Thai gift for mimicry of things Western collides with their stubborn adherence to their ancient customs. It's a place where secretaries go to work in Anne Klein tailored business suits, then remove their shoes and pad around the office in bare feet. It's a city where a thousand new cars are sold each day, and share the roads with pedicabs and elephants. It's a place where the famous Thai capacity for *sanuk* (fun) is displayed everywhere and the phrase *Mai pen rai* (`It's nothing') is the answer to any problem; where you can buy the latest computer software from a street vendor for pennies but where an overseas telephone call is a bigger drama than *Othello*. It's a place almost guaranteed to confuse, and perhaps infuriate, the newly-arrived Western observer.

It has never been possible to do an accurate census in Bangkok, but most estimates put it at somewhere around ten million souls, all of them living in a rat's maze of tiny streets, major thoroughfares and stagnant canals that reflect a jaunty disregard for planning and logic that many old Asia hands describe as `typically Thai'. The air of Bangkok is so polluted you can taste the lead in it, the roads are jammed with traffic from dawn to dusk (even when they are flooded hip deep, as they are four months every year) and prices are sky-high compared to Thailand's outer provinces.

But for the adventurous and hearty traveller, a short stay in Bangkok can have its rewards. There is a multitude of places to go shopping, from the massive Chattuchak weekend market to modern multi-level malls, though for imported items such as electronics and designer clothing, duties and taxes imposed by the Customs Department make Hong Kong or Singapore more attractive.

There are the temples, notably the Temple of The Dawn, Temple of the Golden Buddha and Temple of the Emerald Buddha, and the Grand Palace, each a stunning example of traditional Thai architecture and art beautifully preserved by a caring people who still revere their gods and kings in a way which was lost in the West centuries ago.

There are modern discos packed every night with the children of the new middle class, casual bistros and cafés filled with world travellers and the business people attracted by Thailand's annual double-digit economic growth, and a few notorious red light districts peopled by a sad and distinctive type of 'sex-tourist', though successive Thai governments have been united in their resolve to eliminate this aspect of their society. There is the grand old Chao Phraya River, sprawling Lumpini Park, several major universities and libraries and two famous Thai boxing stadiums. There are two English-language daily newspapers, uncensored satellite TV, several expatriate clubs, dozens of movie theatres, bowling alleys, equestrian clubs and even an ice-skating rink. But for the tourist, the best thing that can be said about Bangkok is that this is where you enter Thailand, and where you leave it. While the city can boast some of the most elegant hotels in Asia, some of the most beautiful temples and some of the best food, in this reporter's opinion the best thing a tourist can do upon arrival is book an immediate flight out.

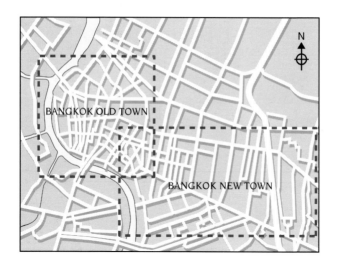

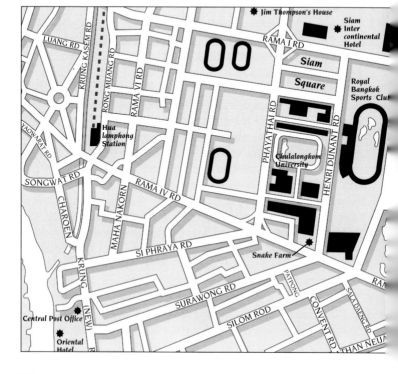

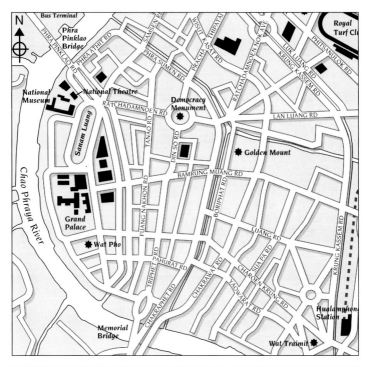

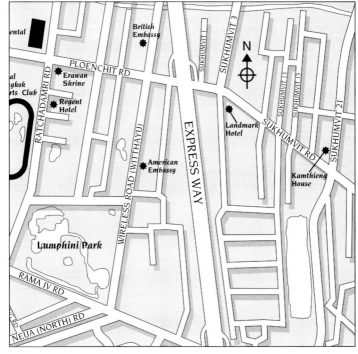

IN THIS SECTION

General information on coping with Bangkok is given on this page and page 139. Sights and places of interest within Bangkok and Thonburi start on page 139, arranged alphabetically. Sights outside Bangkok begin on page 152, with the exception of the floating market at Damnoen Saduak, which is featured on page 142. Recommended hotels are on page 153 and recommended restaurants on page 155.

Walking is not a comfortable way to see the city, and we have not recommended any walking routes, as in other titles in this series.

Please bear in mind that prices in Bangkok are higher than elsewhere in the country, so that you will find relatively few places mentioned in our lower price bands; also that where specific prices are quoted, these were accurate at the time of writing and may rise by the time you come to use this guide. Finally, please remember that *Versatile Guide* editorial policy is to use authors with minds of their own. Steve Rosse, who contributed the Bangkok section, has some personal (but by no means uncommon) views on Bangkok which we believe add both depth and interest to our coverage of Thailand's capital. Don't let the occasional negative remark put you off a visit to Bangkok, which, organized properly, can be a great experience.

ARRIVING

Your introduction to Bangkok will, more than likely not, be Don Muang Airport. The name means 'a hill in the city' and reflects the fact that the original airport was built on this spot because it was the one place on the whole vast delta that didn't flood with the annual monsoons. The current facility is a major hub for air traffic in Asia, and as busy as any major airport in Europe or America.

Upon arrival you'll find the airport to be modern, clean and efficient, an impression that will leave you the minute you drag your baggage outside the gate. At that point you'll be faced with an army of touts, dressed in uniforms that would make you believe that they work for the government, who will try to steer you to a taxi service or hotel. There's nothing wrong with using their services, except that you'll pay twice as much as you would if you choose your own. At least in Bangkok touts tend to take a polite 'No' for an answer, unlike in Jamaica or Bali.

Once you walk out of the doors of the airport you'll also run head-on into a wall of hot, humid and polluted air filled with the thunder of traffic on the highway that runs directly in front of the airport. Depending on that traffic, a taxi will cost anywhere from B250 to B400 into the centre of Bangkok. There are buses that serve the airport, but finding the right one, unless you speak fluent Thai, and getting your luggage aboard, is a Herculean task best left alone.

There are three main bus stations and a train station in Bangkok, but if you're arriving by rail or road you've already experienced Thai bus and train stations and you don't need me to warn you about the questionable food served there and the downright menacing touts who inhabit these places; they are to the ones at the airport as Rottweilers to Pekinese.

Bangkok also boasts a huge port, called Klong Toey, but no tourists have arrived in Bangkok by boat since Somerset Maugham.

ORIENTATION

For the visitor, Bangkok can be divided into two simple parts. Crammed willy-nilly between a curve in the Chao Phraya River and Hua Lumphang Railway Station is the **Old Town**, with its temples, ethnic neighbourhoods and the Grand Palace. East of the Railway Station is **New Town**, with most of the modern shopping districts, hotels, embassies and offices.

Within these two broad areas, there are sub-divisions which may or may not be significant to the visitor.

The **river** itself can be said to 'host' several luxury hotels and several major sights, such as the Grand Palace, Wat Arun, Wat Po and Wat Phra Kaew; it's also the departure point for boat trips.

Banglamphu, the neighbourhood bordered by the river, Ratchadamnoen Klang Road and Phrasumen Road is the area for bottom-end accommodation and alternative lifestyles.

Chinatown is around the Railway Station.

Silom Square, Siam Square and Sukhumvit Road are the main shopping districts (see box, page 141). And the infamous (and unattractive) Bangkok nightlife (see box, page 144) is concentrated on **Patpong Road**, on **Soi Cowboy** and in the **Nana Entertainment Plaza**.

PUBLIC TRANSPORT

The public bus system in Bangkok is cheap, with rides going from B2 to B15. But because of the current madcap road construction in the capital and the daily traffic jams, bus routes change frequently on the whims of the bus drivers. With 10 per cent of Thailand's population living in Bangkok, and almost all of them with a job to go to, the buses are always crammed to bursting, and pick-pockets are becoming commoner every day.

But for the budget traveller with democratic sensibilities, bus schedules are easily purchased at the book stores, and if you're going to be stuck in traffic, it is often more interesting to do so with fifty locals of all ages and classes than alone in the back of a taxi. Thai buses have conductors, like on a train, who will pass down the aisles, collecting fares and issuing tickets. Often these conductors will be asleep, or unable to move in the crowd, and your ride will be free. The 'Bankok Bus Map', showing bus routes, is the best general map of the city and widely available.

Metered taxis are an innovation in Bangkok, but drivers tend to be better about turning on the meters than in other Asian capitals, probably because they know the meter will continue to run if they get stuck in traffic, which is almost a certainty. The advantage of metered taxis are privacy, air conditioning and professional drivers who know the streets, factors of some importance in a crowded, disorganized tropical city.

And finally, the most emblematic public transportation in Thailand are the tuk-tuks, named for the noise they make: small, open, three-wheeled, two cylinder un-muffled go-karts that zoom in and out of traffic at break-neck pace and are helmed by uneducated country boys who rarely know more than the major thoroughfares of Bangkok. Prices are negotiated with the driver, and the choice of route left to the passenger, making tuk-tuks the preferred mode of transport for the resident expatriate and local alike, prized for their mobility and economy, if for nothing else. Motorbike taxis are also becoming increasingly common, though not recommended for the faint-hearted. See also Getting Around, pages 21-2.

ACCOMMODATION GUIDELINES

The range of accommodation available to tourists in Bangkok is staggering, from the Oriental Hotel (page 154) to the seedy and dangerous flop-houses of Khao San Road in the Banglamphu neighbourhood, where, as some say, out of every three travellers you meet, one will be a drug dealer and one an undercover cop.

The range of prices for a bed and roof over your head go from B30 for a flea-ridden cot in a dorm full of shaven-headed back-packers to B3,000 and upwards at the Oriental, Peninsula or Dusit Thani. See Recommended Hotels, pages 153-4, for further details, also Using this Section, page 138.

NEIGHBOURHOODS TO AVOID

Bangkok can still claim to be one of the safest capitals in Asia, though for how much longer remains to be seen. It is part of the Thai character that to gain a stranger's money by guile or deception carries greater 'face' than to have it by force; thus safety is more a matter of avoiding certain people than certain places (see Personal safety, page 26). Perhaps the greatest concentrations of con-men in Bangkok are where there are most tourists, especially around Wat Phra Kaew and Khao San Road.

That said, the list of bad and doubtful neighbourhoods in Bangkok, as in New York or Paris, is too long to give in full. The best approach is to avoid areas that are dimly lit at night or rarely visited by foreigners. Women travelling alone should take extra precautions. And when shopping, remember that if a deal seems too good to be true, it undoubtedly is. (See also Emergencies, page 23).

SIGHTS & PLACES OF INTEREST

CHAO PHRAYA RIVER

Bangkok was originally built around countless canals that fed a giant S-curve in the Chao Phraya River. The entire life of the city was centred on the water, and though the canals have long since been turned into roads, the river still holds a special place in the hearts and minds of the Thai people.

HISTORY

Bangkok was established by the first king of the Chakri Dynasty, Rama I, after the ancient Siamese capital of Ayutthaya was sacked by the Burmese in 1782. Scholarly tomes on Thai history, written by foreigners, will tell you that the name Bangkok means 'Village of the Olive Trees', though olives are not indigenous to Thailand and any Thai you ask will deny that the word has any literal translation at all.

The official name of the city is: Khrungthepmahanakhornbowornratta nakosinmahintarayuth ay amahadilokpopnopparatratchathanibu riromudo mratchaniwetmahasathan, which *The Guiness Book of Records* says is the longest place name in the world. Luckily, it is referred to most of the time in its abbreviated form: *Khrung Thep* or City of the Angels.

Bangkok used to be referred to by Western romantics as The Venice of the East due to its huge system of canals, or *klong*. The city is built on a vast flood plain of the Chao Phraya River, and until the 20thC all transport was by boat. New Road, which is in fact the oldest paved road in the city, was built in the first decade of the 20thC by King Chulalongkorn, Rama V, at the urging of Western diplomats and businessmen who wanted a place to show off their new motor cars.

During the Second World War Thailand signed a pact with the Japanese and declared war on the Allies, which saved the country from the devastation suffered by her neighbours, but bought her massive bombing raids by General Hap Arnold's B-19s towards the war's end. Since the country had few deposits of granite, it had been illegal to build anything but temples and palaces from stone. Thus most of the city was wood and suffered tremendous damage in a relatively short period of hostile bombardment.

After the war the city was rebuilt with brick and cement, and most of the canals were filled in and paved over to make roads. This had the unfortunate side effect of producing tremendous flooding in the annual monsoons, from July to October, and of removing most of the romantic, water-based culture of the city.

In recent years, amazing economic growth, coupled with chaotic and usually unenforced building codes, has resulted in a city with world-famous traffic jams, crowded slums, massive, uninhabited high-rise condominiums, no distinctive architectural style and a truly unimpressive skyline.

The reason that Bangkok is the capital, and virtually the only major city in Thailand, is because the monarchy resides here. Thai society has always been based on proximity to the monarchy, with power and prestige radiating out in concentric rings from the Grand Palace. The Thai people hold their kings in a type of reverence that Westerners may find hard to fathom. Respect for the king is what unites the rich urban Thai with the poor rural Thai, the Muslim Thai with the Buddhist Thai, the Thai of Chinese descent with the Thai of Indian descent, the Thai who speaks the northern dialect with the ones who speak the central or southern dialects.

Despite the disturbing aspects of Bangkok's development, its anarchic qualities, its pollution and corruption, its spiralling cost of living and embarrassing overseas reputation as one huge red light district, the people have tended to retain the light-hearted, optimistic and genuinely friendly Thai-ness that has made this country one of the world's most popular vacation destinations.

Visitors to Bangkok will undoubtedly meet the occasional con-man or price-gouging merchant, the periodic rude taxi driver or strident tout, but those with an open mind and ready smile will meet countless more genuinely open, honest and friendly people in Bangkok than they would in a city of equal size almost anywhere else in the world. Amid the temples, the markets, the canals and the hotels, it is this Thai-ness that most surely characterizes Bangkok, and which is its only hope to avoid the urban nightmare that now seems ever more likely to become reality.

The words Chao Phraya refer to a title of nobility bestowed by a king, and carry with them a code of respect and obeisance which has sadly been ignored in recent history, rendering the once-verdant river nearly lifeless with pollution. Still, most of the interesting sites in Bangkok are to be found along the river, and a trip on one of the ubiquitous (and loud) long-tail boats is a must for visitors to the city.

The Chao Phraya begins its life with the convergence of the Ping and Yom rivers in the farming province of Nakhon Sawan, then snakes a short but meandering 365 km past the ancient capital of Ayutthaya, then through the modern capital at Bangkok before emptying its burden of silt and industrial waste into the Gulf of Thailand at Pak Nam.

On its way through Bangkok, the river hosts countless homes built on stilts over the water, a staggering amount of boat traffic from mighty ocean-going oil tankers to chains of barges laden with rice, to tiny sampans packed with the produce of thousands of kitchen gardens. Water taxis take children to school and monks on their alms rounds, while modern executives by-pass Bangkok's traffic jams by speeding to work on powerful motor launches.

The Chao Phraya River is the heart and soul of Bangkok, and with any luck, future governments will continue to ignore a plan to line both banks with multi-lane highways, thus cutting the river off from the city completely.

CHINATOWN AND PAHURAT

Off Yaowarat and Ratchawong Roads. Like the Chinatowns of New York, London or Los Angeles, this was once an ethnic ghetto but is now one of the most successful neighbourhoods of the metropolis because of the energy, thrift and cleverness of its inhabitants.

Some of the best restaurants in Bangkok, some of the best shopping and some of the best photo opportunities are here, crammed within a few blocks of narrow, meandering streets. Unlike its counterparts in other parts of the world, there is less of a sense of separation here. Historically, all Thais are of Chinese descent, and the waves of modern immigrants during the reign of King Rama IV were limited exclusively to males, so assimilation through inter-marriage has been fairly thorough.

SHOPPING

Although the obvious places to start a shopping trip in Bangkok are the modern shopping centres along Sukhumvit and Silom Roads, the ridiculously large duties imposed on imports make them the worst places in Asia to buy designer labels or electronic goods. Gem stones are worth looking into, but only if you know enough about them to make a wise purchase. Silk is probably still one of the best buys in the city, and Jim Thompson's company (see page 144) is still one of the best places to purchase the fabric.

Handcrafts make good mementoes, and even if you pay twice what you should for a teak elephant or hill tribe embroidered vest, it will still be a third of what you'd pay for the same item in New York or Rome, assuming you could find it there. The Chattuchak Market or Weekend Market (pages 150-1) is one place to look for these ethnic products, as are the floating markets (below). But prices won't be noticeably cheaper than in any small souvenir stall. The vendors who set up their stands at night on Silom Road have low overheads and thus lower prices, and they can be bargained with, especially as the evening wears on.

Buddha images: exporting them is illegal (see page 24); but there is also a point of principle at stake if you buy. They are religious ikons, intended to be displayed with proper respect. Buddhists don't like them to be used for any other purpose than worshipping the Buddha - and that includes using them as *objets d'art*.

Around the intersection of Pahurat and Chakraphet Roads is a small but vibrant community of Indian immigrants, who, though less completely assimilated than the Chinese, are nonetheless just as successful materially. The shopping here is excellent, especially for fabrics, and the food unique: Indian recipes done with Thai spices and produce.

FLOATING MARKETS

These markets, made up of dozens, or indeed hundreds, of tiny canoes, each

• *Khlong Dao Kanong.*

with a woman or two at the paddle, buying and selling everything from vegetables to roller skates, are probably the last remains of the once-widespread water culture of Thailand. Unfortunately, Thai shopping habits have in recent years replaced the floating markets of Bangkok with shopping malls and department stores. The water-borne emporiums are only to be found on the few remaining canals on the Thonburi side of the Chao Phraya, and even they have become almost completely irrelevant commercially, except as tourist attractions.

However, they are still worth a visit, if only to see the way things used to be. One snag: you have to rise as early as 5 am to make it to the site for the action at 7 am. This tends to daunt the casual tourist, but if you're a hearty early riser, there are three main floating markets from which to choose:

The market at **Khlong Dao Kanong** in Thonburi is the largest and most popular with Bangkok visitors. It is easiest, and cheapest, to take one of the Floating Market Tours that leave each morning from the pier behind the Oriental Hotel, though you can still rent your own boat at that same pier. Renting your own

boat has the advantage of allowing you to choose which vendor boats you'll stop at, though this is rarely a consideration because most tourists go to take pictures rather than to shop. (Ten kilos of peanuts, or a bushel of un-husked rice don't make ideal souvenirs.) Most tours start at around B50. But the cheaper ones give you less than half an hour at the market.

The market on **Khlong Damnoen Saduak** in Rajburi Province, 100 *km south of Bangkok*, is more traditional and less of a spectacle for tourists. Getting there means leaving the Southern Bus Terminal in Thonburi by 5 am. You really have to want to shop at a floating market to do that; but if you want to see the real thing, it's the way to go.

There is also a tiny, neighbourhood floating market at **Khlong Bang Khu Wiang** in Thonburi between 4 and 7 am each day. You'll only find a few boats, but they will be authentic, there to sell produce and not to have their picture taken. To get there, take a boat from Tha Chang pier near Wat Phra Kaew any morning at about 6 am.

JIM THOMPSON'S HOUSE

Soi Kasem San 2, Rama 1 Road. An interesting place to visit: though the reason why this beautiful but unassuming residential house has become a tourist distraction will probably strike many as somewhat eerie.

Jim Thompson was an American who came to Thailand in mid life, stayed 20 years without ever learning to speak the language and almost single-handedly restored the almost-dead Thai silk industry. During his stay Thompson built his little house and furnished it with an astonishing array of Asian art, and the result is a wonder for amateur and professional decorators, architects and art collectors alike. It costs B100 to tour the house, and the proceeds go to the Bangkok School for the Blind.

But wandering the house can be unsettling because everything in it has been preserved, like a bizarre museum exhibit, exactly as it was on a particular day in 1967 - the day Jim Thompson went for an afternoon walk with friends in the Cameron Highlands of central Malaysia, never to be seen again.

Trekking in the jungle was one of the attractions of the resort at which he stayed, and the trails were well main-

'CULTURAL' ENTERTAINMENTS

Most hotels and all tour agents offer **Khan Toke** dinners, a traditional 'dinner-theatre' at which diners are entertained with scenes from the *Ramakien* performed by well-trained and beautifully costumed actor-dancers. The *Ramakien* is the Thai version of the ancient Indian epic, the *Ramayana*, which formed the basis of almost all South-East Asian pictorial and performance art for almost three thousand years.

A wonderful experience, for those interested, is to tour Wat Po by day taking in the intricate and ancient bas-relief murals on the stone temple walls, then to see the same scenes performed by living artists over dinner that evening.

There are several forms of **Thai dance**, ranging from the Khmer-influenced palace dances to the simple and quaint country styles of the provinces. Since almost all of these forms have disappeared from Thai culture except as show-pieces performed for tourists, they are now most often presented in revue, with several snippets from each style done by the same dancers.

Whether this undermines the integrity of the art form is a question for the Thais themselves, but it is probably a boon for the tourist. Most Westerners could not sit through a complete performance of unfamiliar dance, with its atonal, unmetered accompaniment. The half-hour revue gives a taste of each style without overwhelming the senses. Again, almost any hotel or tour agent can arrange tickets.

• T*hai dance.*

Meanwhile, **western culture** is flourishing in Bangkok. In a recent interview, the producer who won an Academy award for his production of *Cyrano de Bergerac* in 1990 told a local newspaper that he felt 'Bangkok is now the centre of European intellectualism.' He may have been exaggerating, but organizations such as the Alliance Français, the Goethe Institute and the American University Alumni Association do attract international talent to their film seasons, art exhibitions and concerts. Bangkok has two creditable symphony orchestras and a ballet company, plus dozens of world-class art galleries. These may not attract tourists, but they are well attended by the growing Thai upper classes and by the large number of expatriates now living in Thailand's capital.

NIGHTLIFE

The Thais are a convivial race, and Bangkok has a wealth of restaurants, night clubs, concert halls, art galleries and museums that can provide an evening's entertainment to suit almost any taste or budget. The Bangkok Post and The Nation devote space to advertising and reviews which will tell you what's on during your visit.

The current economic boom has given rise to many European-style dance clubs that fill up at weekends with well-to-do, trendy Thais. At the time of writing, Spasso and Rome Club are the hot tickets, though as in any cosmopolitan setting, fashion is fleeting and the scene may have moved on by the time you visit. Look in the latest issue of Thailand Tatler if you want to know which are the latest 'in' places.

As is well known, Bangkok has a much more notorious nightlife scene. The authorities have historically been lenient about enforcing prostitution laws, and in a few well-defined districts dozens of bars, lounges and clubs stand cheek-by-jowl offering almost any kind of sexual commodity. Recent governments have been increasingly strident in trying to curtail, or at least to subdue, the so-called special services industry. See the cautions on page 26.

tained and clearly marked. The weather was clear, it was daylight, and no large predators were known to be in the area, nor were there bandits. Thompson was more than 60 years old, but he was an experienced trekker and knew the trails. No trace of him - not a body, nor a footprint, nor a scrap of clothing was found. What happened to him on that stroll in the woods has remained a mystery from that day to this, though various theories have been advanced, from the plausible to the paranoid.

The best of the several books written about Thompson is The Legendary American by William Warren, who knew Thompson well and writes with authority. Warren is himself perhaps the most distinguished ex-pat writer living in Thailand. The book is sold at the house in a special edition published by the Jim Thompson Thai Silk Company.

PASTEUR INSTITUTE SNAKE FARM

Rama IV Road. All over Thailand you'll find snake farms with dare-devil handlers putting drugged and harmless snakes into their mouths and down their shirts and trousers. This place has, however, a purpose beyond parting tourists with their money. The handlers are zoologists, and the snakes are truly deadly, milked daily for the venom, which is made into antidotes and distributed to areas where snake attacks are common. Since snakes eat rodents, and rodents eat rice plants, this means virtually every farming community in Asia.

While the snake handling displays here may not be as exciting as those in straightforward tourist traps, they are much more authentic. Feeding time is 3 pm daily. However, it takes a snake an hour to swallow a small mouse.

SIAM SOCIETY

131, Soi Asoke, Sukhumvit 21. This is my favourite place in Bangkok after the departure lounge at Don Muang Airport. Sponsored by the Royal Family, the Siam Society has for generations chronicled and preserved classical Thai culture, from brass buttons to erotic floral symbolism in Romantic poetry. With the notable exception of anything even vaguely political, a vast amount of written information and a staggering variety of artifacts (considering the limited space), is filed, categorized and recorded under the watch of knowledgeable and helpful librarians and curators.

The cool and peaceful atmosphere of the library, coupled with a sense of kindred spirit among the visitors (you know that if someone is using the archives it is because they have a love for, or at least an interest in, the country that goes beyond the beaches and the major temples) creates an atmosphere of calm and reflection and an impression that one has had a brief but meaningful glimpse into a rich and varied culture: which is what travel should be all about.

In the grounds, Kamthieng House contains a so-so ethnological museum. For further information, telephone 02 258 3491.

WAT ARUN (TEMPLE OF DAWN)

In Thonburi, across the river from Wat Pho;

RIVER TRIPS

The **Chao Phraya River Express Boats** (tel. 02 222 5330) run from the Tha Wat Ratchasingkhon pier, just north of the Khrung Thep bridge to Nonthaburi every 20 minutes from 6 am until 6 pm daily. The round trip, giving a pleasant view of the city from the river, where it all began, takes about one-and-a-half hours and only costs B10.

You can take shorter tours by catching the boat at Tha Phayap or Tha Phra Athit in Banglamphu. The boats are fairly comfortable, except for the obese or the physically impaired who may have trouble boarding or disembarking. This trip is not recommended during the mnsoon season (June to September), but in fine weather it has the advantage of showing how the river is still a vital part of the city's life.

The Chao Phraya Express Boat Company also runs day-long cruises, including stops at the **Bang Pa In Palace** in Ayutthaya and the **Wat Pailom Bird Sanctuary**. The boats leave from Tha Maharat at 8 am and return at 5.30 pm and the price is B150 not including lunch.

More than a dozen companies run **dinner cruises** up the Chao Phraya with prices ranging from B50 to B1,000 depending on distance covered and food served. Most luxurious is the Oriental Hotel's (tel. 02 236 0400), with a modern and safe air-conditioned boat and some of the finest food you'll find on the water anywhere. Departure is from the Oriental's pier and the trip cost B800 at time of writing.

One of the most interesting river cruises, especially for families, is offered by the Chao Phraya River Barge Programmes (tel. 02 439 4740). An off-shoot of the Chao Phraya River Club, organized to help revitalise the river and its place in Thai culture, the CPRBP takes groups of students from local international schools, or groups of visiting families, on extended trips up-river on a converted antique rice barge from Bangkok to Ayutthaya and back. There are stops at temples, villages, markets and jungles along the way, where accredited teachers give lectures and demonstrations on cultural and environmental themes. This is a trip for the visitor who has an in-depth interest in Thailand: if that's you, you may well find it the most valuable three days you spend in the country.

---

catch a ferry from Tha Tien at Thai Wang Road on the Bangkok side.

The 82-m tall prang of Wat Arun is visible for miles around, and is one of the most recognizable Bangkok landmarks, though technically it's in Thonburi.

The prang was built during the first half of the 19thC, work beginning in the reign of Rama II and reaching completion during the reign of King Rama III. Made of brick and plaster, as are most religious buildings in Thailand, the prang is covered with a mosaic of broken Chinese porcelain. (This is typical of the early Ratanakosin period, when Chinese ships, ballasted with tons of broken porcelain, called at Bangkok.) The tower can be climbed, to about half its height, by means of an exterior stairway; the view of Bangkok will make you wish that the city had a skyline.

The interior has an impressive mural, probably dating from the reign of King Rama V, showing Prince Siddartha contemplating scenarios of birth, sickness, old age and death outside his palace walls. Buddhists believe that seeing these things caused Siddartha to turn his back on worldly life. The principal Buddha image may have been designed by King Rama II, and his ashes are interred in its base.

Wat Arun was the last resting place of the Emerald Buddha before it was taken finally to Wat Phra Kaew. This ensures Wat Arun a place in Thai history. Apart from that, the best thing about the place is its peace and quiet. Thai people practise meditation the way the Chinese practise Tai Chi: at all ages, at all times of day, and often in public places. The grounds of Wat Arun are always dotted with people meditating: school kids in uniform, senior citizens, businessmen and women, all seated on the grass or stone steps, with their eyes shut and hands in their laps.

Wat Arun is the place to go if you want to dispel some of Bangkok's manic energy from your system.

WAT BENCHAMABOPHIT

At junction of Ayutthaya and Rama V Roads. Known by tourists and tour guides as the Marble Temple, this striking complex was built from white Carrara marble, imported at enormous expense by King Chulalongkorn (Rama V) at the turn of the century.

The largest building, or bot, is a beautiful example of modern Thai religious architecture, and in a courtyard behind the bot are 53 Buddha images, copied from various Thai periods and even from other Buddhist countries (somewhat similar to a smaller version of the Wat Phra Kaew galleries); also a condensed history of Buddhist iconography.

WAT BOVORNIVES

Phra Sumon Road. This is the home of Thailand's second Buddhist university, and the national centre for the minority Thammayut monastic sect, distinguished by their bare feet, brown robes and adherence to an especially rigid and orthodox brand of the faith.

The Thammayut, or 'lesser vehicle' sect, was founded by King Mongkut, Rama IV (the one played as a clown by Yul Brynner) in the mid 1800s. He was a monk here for 17 years, some say to avoid assassination by other aspirants to the throne, before becoming king and taking the traditional multitude of wives and producing an awe-inspiring number of children.

The 'lesser vehicle' is a more personal, less populist form of Buddhism than

• Wat Pho – page 147.

the mainstream faith, centred on individual spiritual growth and a more serious withdrawal from public affairs. Like Wat Mahathat, Wat Bovornives offers English language instruction in the *dharma*, or teachings of the Buddha.

Since Wat Phra Kaew, in the palace grounds, is the only temple in Thailand without a resident community of monks, Wat Bovornives is where the Royal Family do most of their worshipping, and where all the kings since Rama IV have spent a few months as a monk – a rite of passage which they are obliged to make in common with every other Thai male.

WAT MAHATHAT

Across Sanam Luang from Wat Phra Kaew. This is a very old monastery, the home of Thailand's Mahanikai sect. One of Thailand's two Buddhist universities is here, and the foreign visitor is almost certain to be approached by groups of young, very earnest monks, hoping to practise their English. Most men who attend the Buddhist universities intend to go back into secular life after graduation, so don't be surprised if a young monk asks you questions about economics or political theory.

The architecture of this wat is nothing special, but there is an open-air market most days, specializing in old herbal medicines. There are also English-language classes in *vipassana*, or Buddhist theology.

WAT PHO

On Maharaj Rd, opposite the Grand Palace.
If it weren't for its proximity to the Grand Palace and Wat Phra Kaew, this temple would probably be better known than it is. Most tourists plan to visit both sites in a single day, then become exhausted walking around the palace grounds and leave without ever enjoying Wat Pho, which is a terrible shame.

Wat Pho is the oldest, and largest, temple in Bangkok. It houses the largest reclining Buddha image and the largest single collection of Buddha figures in the kingdom. It was the site of the first school in Thailand and still boasts the best centre for teaching traditional Thai massage. Its history goes back to at least the 16thC, though most of the architecture you see now dates from a renovation in 1781.

The grounds of Wat Pho are divided east to west by Jetuphon Road, and the northern compound holds most of what tourists will find interesting. More than a hundred separate structures dot the compound, including 91 small chedis, which house the ashes of more than two centuries of revered monks. The ashes of the first four kings of the Chakri dynasty are here, as is a large Buddhist library, a hall housing the 46-m-long Reclining Buddha and a gallery with 394 gilded Buddha images.

The **Reclining Buddha** of Wat Pho depicts the Buddha on his death bed, in the instant before he attained Nirvana, the state of being wherein there is no desire, and thus no suffering. He is made of plaster applied to a brick core, and finished with gold leaf; his eyes and feet are inlaid with mother-of-pearl, and on the soles of his feet are pictograms outlining the 108 *laksanas* or auspicious physical attributes by which a Buddha may be recognized.

The Buddha prohibited making graven images of himself. Therefore, at least theoretically, all Buddha images actually depict the potential Buddha-hood that exists within us all. This is why a Chinese Buddha figure will look Chinese, a Japanese statue will look Japanese, and so on.

Some of the *laksanas* that you may look for when viewing a Buddha figure are: his toes will be of equal length and so will his fingers; he will have tightly curled hair; long ear lobes; a big nose, and a large mole or growth between his eyebrows.

• *Wat Arun – pages* 144-5.

The galleries which extend between the four main chapels of this part of Wat Pho are, I believe, the most interesting element of the temple. They feature the Buddha as realized by several hundred different artisans over several centuries, including many depictions of the Buddha when he was an ascetic, and thus before actually becoming the Buddha. These can be recognized by the emaciated, starved condition of the figure.

WAT PHRA KAEW AND THE GRAND PALACE

On Charoen Khrung Road, by the Chao Phraya River. This amazing collection of temples and palace buildings is probably the most photographed site in Thailand, and with good reason. Construction began in 1782, the year Bangkok became the capital and the Chakri dynasty assumed the throne. Restorations and additions have continued (the latest in 1982) and the complex you see today is a beautiful example of everything that is unique and wonderful about Thai architecture and art.

Any tour of the grounds must include three separate sites, so plan to spend most of a day there. The palace itself is only used by the King on special occasions, since his residence is now Chitlada Palace in the northern part of the city. Visitors may not enter the palace, but merely walking around the outside of its several buildings is worth the effort. (There are four main ones: French-inspired Borobiman Hall; Amarindra Hall, used for coronations; tripled-winged Chakri Mahaprasat, designed by British architects and built in 1882 in an Italian Renaissance-Thai style; and Dusit Hall, latterly a royal funeral hall.) The best view of the palace is actually from a boat on the river, and that's the view that graces a million postcards.

The **Temple of the Emerald Buddha (Wat Phra Kaew)** is arguably the most holy site in Thailand, and the figure itself, which is made from a type of jade, rather than emerald, is considered a lucky charm for the whole kingdom. It was carved some time before the 15thC in the Lanna Thai kingdom of northern Thailand, from whence it was captured and moved by various armies until brought to Bankok by General Chakri, who went on to become King Rama I of the current Chakri Dynasty.

The murals which circle the walls of the temple date from the reign of King Rama III (1824-50) and depict scenes from the *Ramakien*, the Thai version of the Indian epic *Ramayana*. They have nothing to do with Buddhism, but tell the story of the eternal struggle between good and evil, as personified by Prince Rama and Totsagan, the evil giant with 20 heads who kidnapped Prince Rama's bride Nang Seeda. Divided into 178 sections, the cycle begins at the north gate and moves in a clockwise direction around the compound.

Also on these grounds is the **Royal Thai Decorations and Coins Pavilion**. Ancient Thai coins are especially prized by numismatists, but the cool and comfortable atmosphere inside the hall, and the attractive and well-displayed coins, make this a welcome respite for anybody from the heat and long walks of the palace grounds.

Admission to the temple and palace grounds is at time of writing B100 for foreigners and free for Thais. When visiting any Thai place of worship, tourists must observe a few simple rules on dress and etiquette - see page 18.

But while photography is allowed in temples all over Thailand, in the Temple of the Emerald Buddha it is forbidden. And the guards outside the gates will often find fault with a female tourist's dress, saying the skirt is too short or the blouse too revealing, and order her to go and buy a dress from one of the many street vendors who set up shop outside the palace.

WAT RAJANADDA

Across Mahachai Road from Wat Saket. Interesting to Buddhist historians for its inspired architecture, this temple also appeals to casual visitors because of its amulet market. The Thais place great faith in the powers of these icons, and some of them, guaranteed to bring love, success, health or protection from bullets, bombs or knives, will astonish the non-believer by their high prices.

As you wander down the rows of open-air stalls, notice the buyers of these mystical totems. Most will be either boxers, policemen, soldiers or politicians, hoping for protection in dangerous occupations.

WAT SAKET

At junction of Mahachai and Larn Luang Roads. This small temple has the distinction of being famous because of a failed construction project in its grounds. During the reign of King Rama III an enormous pagoda collapsed when the marshy swamp land underneath the building could not hold the weight. The ruins were left as they fell until King Rama IV built a small pagoda on the crest of the man-made hill.

King Rama V added a larger pagoda to house a Buddhist relic from India given to him by the British government, and during the Second World War concrete walls were added around the hill to stop erosion.

Now the hillock is visited for its views of the surrounding city.

WAT TRIMITR

Yaowarat Road at Charoen Krung Road. There are two reasons to visit this temple, the first being the 5-tonne solid gold presiding Buddha image, the second being the story behind that image.

In the late 1950s the statue, which was then covered in a layer of plaster or stucco, was being moved by crane into a new building. A rope slipped and the holy image came crashing to the ground, cracking the plaster and revealing the gold underneath.

Locals would have you believe that

OTHER INTERESTING SHRINES

Although Thailand is officially a Buddhist nation, it has long encouraged religious tolerance, and currently more than 70 religions and cults are practised. Prominent among them are Islam, Christianity, Hinduism, Sikhism, Taoism, Animism and Ancestor Worship. Each of these faiths has left some sort of mark on the Bangkok landscape, and the Thai love of heroes has resulted in a plethora of monuments to generals, historic dates, ideas and ideals. Below is a short list of some of the more interesting.

Wat Intarawihan, on Wisut Kasat Road north of the Banglamphu district, is an example of ancient Buddhist iconography rendered in a modern style. The 32-m high standing Buddha is thoroughly contemporary, and, I think, extremely ugly. There is an air-conditioned shrine in a hollowed-out pagoda boasting a very interesting representation of Luang Paw Toh, a venerated former abbot of the temple.

The Democracy Monument, in the traffic circle at Ratchadamnoen Road and Tripetch Road, is not very beautiful, but it is important to the Thais because it symbolizes the struggle for democracy that began in 1932 and continues to this day. In 1973, 1976 and 1992, ordinary Thai citizens paid for the struggle with their lives.

Sao Ching-Cha, just south of the Democracy Monument, is known by the name 'The Giant Swing', which more or less sums it up. Originally the site of a festival in honour of the Hindu god Shiva, the swing ceased to be used in rituals during the reign of King Rama VII. Today it is in almost constant use by tourists as a photo opportunity.

San Phra Pom, in front of the Hyatt Erawan Hotel, is a shrine to the four-faced elephant-headed patron saint of artisans and craftsmen. Every day hundreds of worshippers leave offerings of fruit, flowers and incense. Or, to give thanks for truly big favours, such as winning the lottery or placing a daughter in a

• *San Phra Phrom shrine, by Grand Hyatt.*

respectable marriage, troupes of traditional dancers and acrobats may be hired to perform for the god, and passers-by.

Every hotel, just like every Thai home, will have a **spirit house**, reflecting the original animist beliefs of pre-historic South-East Asia. The house is usually in front of a building, but in a spot where the shadow of the building will not fall on the spirit house, or vice-versa.

Offerings are left at the shrines in order to placate the spirits that live in a property's trees, rocks and earth. If not appeased, the spirits will act like a European poltergeist, causing problems for the human residents. Perhaps the most interesting spirit house in a hotel is at the Hilton International, off Wireless Road. Here dozes of carved stone and wooden lingam (phalluses) receive offerings from a steady stream of young women hoping for fertility.

In **Thonburi** are dozens of smaller Buddhist temples which have the advantage of seeing fewer tourists than the better-known ones on the Bangkok side of the rover. One of my favourites is **Wat Kamlayanimit** with an enormous Buddha image and the biggest bronze bell in Thailand. And for the bird watcher with a day to kill in Bangkok, from December to June thousands of open-billed storks nest in the grounds of **Wat Phailom** on the banks of the Chao Phraya in Pathumthani Province.

nobody knew the true material of the Buddha, though workmen must have known something was amiss when they began to move it, since it would have been five times heavier than a normal brick and plaster image.

The image is in the Sukhothai style, dating from some time before the 13thC. Historians theorize that it was hidden under its layer of stucco to protect it from one of the waves of Burmese invaders that plagued the old capital at Ayutthaya. Whatever the truth about its genesis, the image is the largest solid gold artifact in Thailand, and of immeasurable value.

WEEKEND MARKET

At Chattuchak Park in Saphan Khwai district across from the Northern Bus Terminal. This market operates every Saturday and Sunday of the year, and to see it all you need two days. Spread over an enormous area are thousands of vendors' stalls, ranging in size from a single card table displaying ten fake Rolex watches to huge tents filled with children's clothing. The emphasis is on

THAI BOXING

There are two major boxing stadiums in Bangkok: Lumpini on Rama IV Road near South Sathon Road and Ratchadamnoen on Ratchadamnoen Nok Road, next to the Thai Tourism Authority offices.

If you've never attended a Thai boxing match, here is what you've missed: first, you sit down in a crowded arena that's hot enough to grow orchids in and smells of old socks. You are jammed in with about a thousand of the worst characters in the province, all of whom who have had their personalities modified for the evening by whisky and blood lust. There is a dress code for the evening: every spectator must wear clothes that he has slept in for at least three nights.

Your ticket will bear the number of a seat in some stadium damaged by Allied bombers in 1944, so you claim a spot on a hard wooden bench at random, and sit on your programme in order to keep out the smaller splinters. Even before the boxers appear, the crown will be shouting and screaming and arm-waving. The yelling is in reference to the projected odds of the first fight; the arm-waving is aimed at the mosquitoes that are drawn to the oceans of blood spilled at these events.

Soon the first pair of gladiators are led out into the ring by their *phi liang*, which translates as 'nanny' or 'nursemaid'. At this point, the band kicks in. The orchestra at a Thai boxing match consists of three ancient and venerable men playing even older instruments: drum, cymbals and flute. Their job is to provide a noise like a train wreck, only louder and more prolonged.

The boxers begin a series of semi-graceful movements designed to pay homage to their dance teachers. They circle the ring, dipping and bowing, posturing and posing. Then they are given a rest period during which the crowd begins betting. This is illegal, so everyone does it surreptitiously, by waving handfuls of money in the air and screaming out their bets at maximum lung power. A few bet on the outcome of the fight, but most bet on which fighter will be the first to jump the ropes and start beating up the orchestra.

Eventually, the two combatants are brought to the centre of the ring and the referee explains The Rule. There is only one rule in Thai boxing: you cannot poke your opponent in the eye. Since people who make their living in this way cannot be too bright, they are made to wear thickly padded gloves in case they break The Rule. The fighters return to their corners, do some more stylized praying and bowing, and get a few last-minute tattoos appplied by their coaches. The band wheezes up to a squeaky crescendo, the gong sounds, and the fight is on.

A Thai boxer's uniform consists of a pair of polyester trunks that go from his ribs to his knees, in any of a large assortment of unattractive colours. The trunks are large because they need to accommodate numerous advertisements. Many of the products are in the health-care field, such as tobacco or alcohol, as befits an athletic event. The size of the trunks and the weight of the appliquéd corporate logos will dictate a fighter's household goods: pots, pans, basins, kithen utensils, bedding and clothes, but the market also stocks everything and anything that is on sale anywhere else.

Most designer-labelled products, such as blue jeans, electronics, computer software, compact discs, cassette tapes and watches are obviously faked, though in many cases they are just as good as (and usually indistinguishable from) the originals. Problems only arise when something is defective and you try to return it: you'll be met either with derisive laughter or open hostility. This is definitely a case of 'let the buyer beware'; but for the discerning and dedicated shopper with time to bargain, it is a fantasy come true.

Remember that this is still an Asian market: which means that any animals you see for sale are intended as groceries, not pets. This applies to cats and dogs, as well as to monkeys, snakes and turtles. In fact, virtually anything that is an ingredient in somebody's favourite recipe will show up for sale in Chattuchak Market.

style. Some fight with one hand, holding up the trunks with the other; while some prefer to throw a flurry of blows with both hands, then back off and pull up their trunks.

In Thai boxing you are allowed to hit your opponent with anything except pieces of furniture, so there is much kicking, elbowing, kneeing and butting with the head. Betting continues until the last round, or until one of the fighters, or someone in the audience, attacks the band.

A win is achieved by knock-out or by points given by a panel of referees, based on an arcane system of judgement taking into account form and technique. When a victor is announced, both fighters raise their hands in triumph, and strut around the ring bowing to the people who bet on them, then fall into each other's arms like brothers. They stumble out of the ring into an ambulance and everyone throws peanut shells at the band until the next fighters appear.

An evening of Thai boxing goes on as long as there are contestants willing to fight. They are carefully paired by weight and height. While you or I may or may not enjoy the fights, it's probably not fair to begrudge fans their infatuation with the sport. Is it any stranger than American football, a game that boxing fans say is for wimps because of the amount of protective gear worn by the players? You have to agree with Thai boxing fans that it takes guts to climb into the ring wearing nothing but a pair of gaudy bloomers and face the music.

SIGHTS OUTSIDE BANGKOK

ANCIENT CITY, THE

Reached by public bus no. 25 to Samut Prakan and then a local taxi to the park; or any tour agent can arrange a visit. Open 8 am to 6 pm, admission B300 at time of writing.

This is where the the tourist should go if he or she has only one day in which to see Thailand, or if very interested in architecture. If you have more than one day, and a pedestrian interest in architecture, give the Ancient City a miss.

Covering some 80 hectares in Samut Prakan, 33 km from Bangkok on the Sukhumvit Highway, the Ancient City houses reproductions of some of the kingdom's most famous sites, particularly temples and palaces, set in a kind of Disneyland environment. There are quite knowledgeable guides and brochures which do an excellent job of explaining the exhibits and of putting them into some sort of historical and social context. There are clean restaurants and WCs, and the inevitable souvenir stands and money changers.

AYUTTHAYA

About 86 km N of Bangkok. Buses from Bangkok's Northern Bus Teminal every 20 minutes between 5 am and 7 pm, journey time about two hours. If arriving by bus from somewhere other than Bangkok or a nearby city, then you may be dropped at the long-distance bus station, some 5 km E of the Pridi Damrong Bridge at Highway 32.

Ayutthaya was the capital of Siam from 1350 until it was sacked by invading Burmese in 1767. It was the seat of 33 kings from several dynasties, and according to contemporary European travellers, one of the most splendid cities in the world.

The Ayutthaya you will see today is a busy, modern market town and bears little resemblance to the city of the ancient legends. However, for the tourist interested in Thai history, the ruins of the old city are fascinating. The Ayutthaya period marks the high point of old Thai civilization, and the mixture of Khmer and Siamese influences in what is left of the temples and palaces makes for a style not seen elsewhere. The fact that Ayutthaya hosts far fewer travellers than Bangkok ensures much more leisurely and hassle-free sightseeing.

Ayutthaya is located at the confluence of three rivers: the Chao Phraya, the Lopburi and the Pa Sak. There is a canal which circles the city, crossed by five bridges, which happily makes it almost impossible to get lost. Most of the interesting sights are in the northern and north-eastern parts of town, though they are not really within walking distance of each other.

Two museums, both usually full of well-behaved groups of Thai schoolchildren, each give a useful overview of the city's history: The **Chao Sam Phraya National Museum**, near the intersection of Rotchana Road and Si Sanphet Road opposite the town hall, is open from 9 am to 12 noon Monday to Friday, also 1 pm to 4 pm Wednesday to Sunday. The entry fee of B10 at time of writing is well worth paying.

The **Chan Kasem Palace** built by the seventeenth king of Ayutthaya, Maha Thammurat, is itself a museum-piece, but it is also a repository of splendid exhibits including gold treasures from Wat Phra Mahathat and Wat Ratburana. You will find it in the north-eastern corner of the city near the Pa Sak river. Hours and entry price are the same as for the Chap Sam Phraya National Museum, and interesting maps of the historic city are available here for B25. (Maps of Ayutthaya are sold everywhere, but these are especially complete.)

Visitors with little time, or with flagging energy, may enjoy the convenience of touring Ayutthaya through the exhibits in these two museums, rather than slogging on foot through the ruins themselves. And in some cases, the displays in Chan Kasem Palace are actually more informative than the displays, or even the multi-lingual guides, at the sites.

Most of the ruins that remain in Ayutthaya are temples, preserved because of their religious significance. Though they see little worship today, visitors are still advised to follow the guidlines for respectful behaviour (see page 18). Some of the more interesting ruins are: **Wat Phra Si Sanphet**: in the 14thC this was the largest temple in Ayutthaya and the main place of royal worship through several dynasties. It is notable for its collection of chedis, often cited as definitive examples of the Ayutthaya style.

Wat Phra Mongkok Bopit was built in 1956 and is thus the youngest of Ayuttaya's tourist attractions. Its giant Buddha image is one of Thailand's largest.

Wat Phra Chao Phanan Choeng: there is controversy over who actually built this temple on the banks of the Chao Phraya River south-east of the main city. Since it predates Ayutthaya's becoming a Thai capital, it was probably built by the Khmer, but this theory is not popular in nationalistic modern Thailand. Whoever built it, seeing the 19-m seated Buddha, for which the temple is named, is well worth the short drive necessary to reach the temple.

Wat Phra Meru, reached by bridge from the Old Palace at Wat Phra Si Sanphet, was the only structure not razed by the Burmese in 1767. It is in remarkable shape, and gives a more complete picture than any of the sites of what life was like in the city 200 years ago; a must.

KHAO YAI NATIONAL PARK

About 200 km from Bangkok. Take a bus from the Northern Bus Terminal (they leave every 15 minutes from 5 am to 10 pm) to Pak Chong, journey time less than three hours. From there take a songthaew to the park gates. Tours can be arranged through any agent in Bangkok.

This is a beautiful 2,168-sq.-km forest preserve, one of the four sites in Thailand listed on the United Nations World Heritage List. Attractions include interesting birdlife (hornbills and other species), gibbons, elephants and night safaris. Weekends and public holidays bring in crowds.

The **Khao Yai Hotel, B** offers accommodation ranging from crowded dormitories through standard hotel rooms to bungalows and cottages. You can even pay B15 (at time of writing) for a plot on which to pitch a tent. There is an adequate coffee shop in the hotel, and noodle stalls and restaurants in Pak Chong. There are no restaurants in the park itself, although there is a golf course.

Walking and trekking are the main attractions, and a guide can be hired all day for B150 and upwards, no matter how large or small the group.

Sadly, the fact that this is a National Park and a World Heritage Site does not reduce the economic exploitation of the place. Tourism cannot come close to supporting the local population, so there is still logging, mining and commercial hunting in the Park.

KHLONG DAMNOEN SADUAK

See Floating Markets, pages 141-2.

RECOMMENDED HOTELS

AYUTTHAYA
There are plans to build large, Western-style hotels in Ayutthaya, and given the pace of construction in Thailand they may well be open by the time this guide is on sale. But most of the small, informal hotels and guesthouses offer cleanliness and security typical of Thai hospitality at its best. They include:

The Thai Thai, B; 13/1 *Naresuan Road; tel.* 035 251505.
   Pleasant air-conditioned rooms.

The Cathay Hotel, B; U *Thong Road; tel.* 035 251562.
   Very quaint, with extremely friendly management. Rooms with ceiling fan are low-priced by any standard.

The U Thong Hotel, B; U *Thong Road; tel.* 035 251136.
   The best-known hotel in town, it has seen better days. Still, the staff are used to foreigners and speak some English. Air-conditioned and fan rooms, at fair prices.

The U Thong Inn, BB; *Rotchana Road; tel.* 035 242618.
   My personal choice: peaceful, clean, quaint, with honest food and great service. Choice of fan or air-conditioned rooms.

Budget accommodation - guesthouses
As anywhere in Thailand, the quality of a guesthouse in Ayutthaya depends on the quality and ambition of the owners. Since these places tend to change hands often, especially in a tourist centre, it is hard to single out particular establishments. However, my current selections are:

Pai Thong Guest House, B; U *Thong Road; tel.* 035 241830 and **BJ Guest House, B;** *Naresuan Road; tel.* 035 251512. The latter is low-priced.

BANGKOK
Note on prices: the top end of our price band scale (see page 12) is low

for Bangkok. Expect to pay B2,000-3,000 for a room in the BBBB hotels listed below, even in low season. Check the price when booking.

Tourism is the single largest earner of foreign exchange in Thailand, and so Bangkok has probably more, and greater variety of accommodation than any city of its size. These selections concentrate on quality, in the upper two price bands; for cheaper accommodation, see below under Khao San Road guesthouses.

The Oriental, BBBB; 48 *Oriental Avenue; tel.* 02 236 0420; *cards* AE, DC, MC, V.

More than a century old, the Oriental is often said to be the best hotel in the world, and I for one have no reason to argue with that. Not only does it boast royal-class cuisine and luxurious rooms, but a sense of history as well, especially in the Author's Lounge where pictures of Joseph Conrad, Graham Greene and Somerset Maugham drinking at the bar are displayed over that same bar. It is also the most expensive hotel in Bangkok.

The Dusit Thani, BBBB; 956 *Rama* IV *Road, at intersection of Silom and Rama* IV *Road; tel.* 02 238 4790; *cards* AE, DC, MC, V.

It makes up for truly bad architecture with top-flight service and accommodation. The location on Silom Road makes this the most convenient hotel for shoppers and its proximity to Lumpini Park gives residents a convenient release from big-city stress.

The Grand Hyatt Erawan, BBBB; 494 *Ratchadamri Road; tel.* 02 254 1234; *cards* AE, DC, MC, V.

An elegant building with services and amenities to match, this place is probably best known as the location of the shrine to Phra-Phom, the elephant-headed saint of artisans and craftsmen, that stands in front. Worshippers flock to the shrine every day, and because of the god's affiliation with artists, devotees will often commission bands of traditional musicians or singers to perform for the statue, and delighted passers-by.

Grand Inn, BBB-BBBB; 2/7-8 *Sukhumvit 3; tel.* 02 253 3308; *cards* AE, DC, MC, V.

A central location and clean, safe, comfortable rooms makes this excellent value.

Ambassador Hotel, BBB-BBBB; *Soi* 11, *Sukhumvit Road; tel.* 02 254 0444; *cards* AE, DC, MC, V.

Another Sukhumvit hotel, this boasts 1,050 clean, modern rooms and staff who at least display some proficiency in English. It is competitively priced with other mid-range hotels in the area, though with any Sukhumvit address, expect to pay more for taxis, both coming and going.

The Airport Hotel, BBB-BBBB; *opposite Don Muang Airport; tel* 02 566 1020; *cards* AE, DC, MC, V.

The best thing about this hotel is that you don't have to enter Bangkok to get a bed. For knowledgeable travellers, who consider Bangkok merely a gateway to Chiang Mai or Phuket, this is a distinct advantage.

Khao San Road guesthouses, B

In the Banglamphu area centring on Khao San Road is an almost endless list of guesthouses. They range from the frankly dangerous and lice-infested dumps that charge around B50 for a cot in a dormitory full of round-the-world backpackers to about B500 for a pleasant corner room with bath and ceiling fan in a crumbling turn-of-the-century Chinese mansion. This is my current best selection:

VIP Guest House; *tel.* 02 282 5090.
Bonny Guest House; *tel.* 02 281 9877.
Top Guest House; *tel.* 02 281 9954.
Palace Hotel; *tel.* 02 282 0578.
Charoen Sukh Hotel; *tel.* 02 281 9872.
Lek Guest House; *tel.* 02 281 2775.
Hello Guest House; *tel.* 02 281 8579.
Central Guest House; *tel.* 02 282 0667.
Sweet Guest House; *tel.* 02 281 6756.
Prasuri Guest House; *tel.* 02 280 1428.
Bovorn Youth Hostel; *tel.* 02 281 6387.
Noi Guest House; *tel.* 02 282 2898.
James' Guest House; *tel.* 02 280 0362.
River Guest House; *tel.* 02 280 0876.
Trang Hotel; *tel.* 02 282 2141.

RECOMMENDED RESTAURANTS

Note on prices: all the restaurants recommended below are well into the BBB range, because, as with hotels, prices are higher in Bangkok than elsewhere in Thailand. A plate of *kwaytiaw*, the standard labourer's meal of noodles with fish balls, costs about B20 in the city today. Add B7 for a soft drink, and you are only B3 below our B price band. By the time you get to any sort of restaurant where you can actually sit down, the same plate of noodles is B50. We've not recommended any places in this category because there's so little to set any of them apart from the ten thousand others like them in the city.

Eat little and often: people who live in hot climates tend to eat smaller and more frequent meals than people who live in cool climates. The Thais seem to be dedicated to proving this axiom, and wherever you are in Bangkok, at whatever time of day or night, you will not be more than a dozen metres from someone selling food or drink.

If you follow the local example, and nibble on snacks all day long instead of eating three large meals, you'll find that you are less debilitated by the heat. You'll also discover a wide range of local food, and you may also save money.

The food scene in Bangkok: dining choices in Bangkok range from the exclusive and expensive La Normande French Restaurant in the Oriental Hotel to an old woman selling peanuts wrapped in banana leaves, picked that morning from her kitchen garden, on the corner of Silom and Patpong Roads.

A vogue for drinking fine wines is currently sweeping Asia, making the meal to be had at La Normande finally equal to one you'd eat in Paris. And the Thai compulsion for cleanliness makes eating off street stalls a safer bet than in South America or Africa. Which way you go depends on your budget, your taste, and why you came to Thailand.

How the Thais eat: rice is the staple of Thai diet, so much so that the phrase *Kin khao ru yang* or 'Have you eaten your rice yet?' means 'How are you?'.

Every diner is served with a personal plate of this wonderful grain, then adds spoonfuls of *kap khao* or 'with rice' dishes to his plate from communal bowls in the centre of the table. Listed are some of the better Thai food places:

Bussaracum, BBB; 35 *Soi Pipat, 2 Silom Road; tel.* 02 246 2147; *cards* AE, DC, MC, V.

One of Bangkok's best-known classical Thai restaurants. Attentive service, fine food and a happy atmosphere.

Sala Rim Nan, BBB; Oriental Hotel (*see page 154 for address*); *tel.* 02 437 6211; *cards* AE, DC, MC, V.

As with anything connected to the Oriental, there is a price to pay, but it's worth it. The view over the Chao Phraya River is stunning, the service and the food is magnificent, though prepared for the foreign palate. Classical Thai dance shows nightly.

Silom Village, BBB; 286 *Silom Road; tel.* 02 234 4448; *cards* AE, DC, MC, V.

Because of its proximity to the shopping district, this is a favourite with upper-class housewives. Excellent Thai food with traditional *gamelan* music.

Tanying, BBB; 10 *Pramuan Road, Silom; tel.*02 236 4361; *cards* AE, DC, MC, V.

Quality Thai cuisine set in a beautifully restored Thai house.

Whole Earth Restaurant, BBB; 93/3 *Soi Langsuan, Phloenchit Road; tel.* 02 252 5574; *cards* AE, DC, MC, V.

Specializes in vegetarian food served Thai style. Even if you're not vegetarian, you may find light cooking helpful while travelling. Honest service and guitar music in the evenings.

Monkorn Luang, BBB; Bangna Trat Road, *km* 1.5; *tel.* 02 398 0037; *cards* AE, DC, MC, V.

Allegedly the world's biggest restaurant, with more than 500 tables and waiters zooming around on roller skates. Seating is in various galleries, on platforms floating on an artificial lake, or on balconies circling a tower overlooking the city. There are Thai dance and music shows, and the food is adequate.

Northern Thailand

Chiang Rai and Region

250 km; map Nelles 1:1,500,000; Guide Map of Chiang Rai by V. Hongsombud
(a detailed map of the region, towns, and routes; various scales)

Chiang Rai, at the northernmost tip of Thailand, is the gateway to the Golden Triangle, covered in detail by Thailand Overall: 2. Although Chiang Mai, 185 km to the south-west, has long been the tourist Mecca of the north and the unrivalled heart of the trekking industry, Chiang Rai is starting to make its own mark on the scene as travellers seek somewhere quieter, smaller and less commercialized than Chiang Mai. If you're exploring the Golden Triangle on your own, you're likely to pass through or to end up in Chiang Rai at least for a night. On this itinerary, it's the getting there which is the exciting bit.

There are actually three routes to Chiang Rai. The quickest (around four hours by bus) via Wiang Papao on the new Highway 1019 (previously 118) is the one the tour buses favour. The longest (about seven hours), on Highway 11 via Lampang to the south-east, then north along Highway 1, is a less likely choice, unless you're starting from Lampang or want to include it in the trip. The third, the travellers' traditional favourite, and the route I suggest here, heads directly north along Highway 107. It is the only one with the thrill of a river trip at the end, in a long-tail boat from Tha Ton along the Kok River to Chiang Rai.

If you're pressed you can do this trip in a day from Chiang Mai, leaving by 7 am at the latest. But most people stay overnight in Fang or Tha Ton before catching the boat. And an enlightened few are discovering that the Tha Ton area itself is worth more than a passing glance. Close to the Burmese border, it's still surprisingly unspoilt and offers the opportunity of some independent trekking, based at guesthouses run by hill-tribe people themselves – a refreshing alternative to the Chiang Mai packaged trekking scene.

TRANSPORT

Direct buses to Tha Ton take around four hours from Chiang Mai's Chang Puak bus station, leaving five times a day (currently 6 am, 7.20 am, 9 am, 11.30 am and 3.30 pm; check the schedule with the TAT office or bus station). Or you can catch one of the more regular buses to Fang which leave every 30 minutes and take three hours. There are regular songthaews making the 40-minute hop from Fang to Tha Ton.

The public long-tail boat leaves Tha Ton daily at 12.30 pm for the four- to five-hour trip. Alternatively, there are buses from Tha Ton to Chiang Rai (taking about two hours via Mae Chan) as well as air-conditioned minibuses a few times daily. You can also reach Mae Salong and Mae Sai by bus from Tha Ton.

1:1,500,000

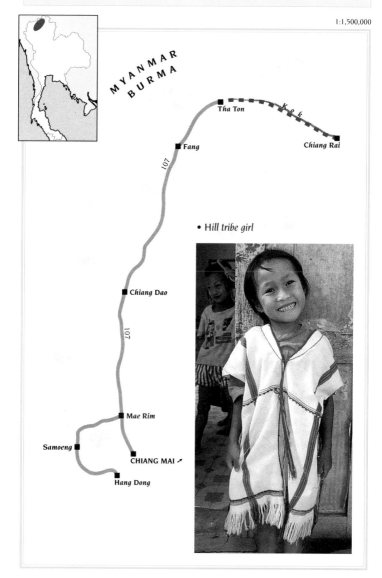

• *Hill tribe girl*

SIGHTS & PLACES OF INTEREST

CHIANG DAO

The Chiang Dao caves, *78 km north of Chiang Mai, just off Highway 107*, is a complex of caverns digging deep into the limestone hill of Doi Chiang Dao. Several of the caves, which are open to the public, have become religious shrines containing Buddha images – hence their popularity among Thai devotees and monks. A couple of these are illuminated; to explore the three others – some with fantastic rock formations – you'll need to hire a guide with a lantern. You can easily visit the caves *en route* to Fang and Tha Ton: just get off the bus at Chiang Dao and pick up a songthaew for the last 5 km.

CHIANG MAI

See Thailand Overall: 1, pages 36-9.

CHIANG RAI ⌫ ✕

About 185 km NE of Chiang Mai. Surprisingly low-key for the Golden Triangle's closest big city, Chiang Rai – the capital of Thailand's most northerly province – is a pleasant place for an overnight stop or to recharge your batteries after a trek. Although it was founded in 1263 by King Mengrai, historical sites are thin on the ground: apart from a couple of interesting temples, the town has little to match Chiang Mai's cultural glamour. Perhaps that's why it's so relaxing: you can walk along the broad streets, many bordered by plane trees girdled with orchids, without feeling any sight-seeing pressure.

The city spreads out south of the River Kok with the main bus station in the far south and the pier for boats from Tha Ton in the north-west of town, close to the guesthouses (although occasionally boats will inconveniently dock on the north bank and you'll need to get a samlor into town). The best way to get around is by samlor, tuk-tuk or bicycle which can be rented from your guesthouse.

Chiang Rai's major claim to cultural fame is its **Wat Phra Kaew** on Trairat Road. It's here, so the story goes, that the renowned Emerald Buddha (now in Bangkok) was discovered when lightning struck the temple's chedi in 1434, splitting it open to reveal the precious image inside. An almost exact jade copy (it's deliberately a millimetre smaller in height), was installed here in 1991 and can be seen in the wat's elegant main *viharn*.

Worthwhile for its hill-top views rather than for any architectural merit is **Wat Phra That Doi Thong**, on the wooded hilltop in the north-western edge of town. As you climb up here, you'll also pass **Wat Ngam Meuang** – pop into the workshop beside the main hall and you'll find wood carvers crafting intricate friezes and panels. Wat Doi Thong is important as the site of the city's *lak meuang* – the pillar representing the seat of a town's guardian spirits. A new stone *lak meuang* was erected here in 1988 at the centre of a striking design symbolizing the universe: circular stone platforms with replica lingams on every level, all surrounded by a narrow channel of water.

Down to more prosaic matters, some of Chiang Rai's most enjoyable **shopping** is done at night time when the new, blatantly tourist-oriented **night bazaar** next to the bus station (just off Phahonyothin Road) bursts into life with performances of song and dance and a range of stalls selling tribal handicrafts and souvenirs. For some reason it's not as bad as it sounds, perhaps because it still has none of Chiang Mai's night bazaar frenzy (or perhaps because the beer is so cheap).

But for quality tribal handicrafts in more sober surroundings, you're better off visiting the **Hilltribe Museum & Education Centre** at 620/25 Thanalai Road (open Monday to Saturday from 8 am to 5 pm, tel. 053 713410). It's operated by the Population & Community Development Association, which is well known for its family planning and AIDS-prevention campaigns, and for its 'Cabbages & Condoms' chain of restaurants (there's one of them here – see Recommended Restaurants, page 163). Upstairs, you'll find a small shop and museum – a great place to come before going on your trek: the display of hill-tribe clothes and domestic implements, models of typical houses and explanatory notes on various beliefs is supplemented by an excellent 25-minute slide show about the six main tribes, their history and traditions. Profits from the restaurant, shop and museum go towards AIDS education and community projects for the hill-tribes.

• *Right: Long-tail.*

The PDA also organizes two- to five-day 'jungle treks', elephant safaris and regional sightseeing trips.

FANG

A thriving market town with a long history (it was founded by King Mengrai in the 13thC), Fang gets overlooked these days by travellers who zoom past on their way to Tha Ton, 23 km further up Highway 107, where boats leave for the trip down the Kok River to Chiang Rai. Unless you're a drug baron (Fang is reputed to be one of the main entrepôts for the shipment of heroin from Myanmar into Thailand) there isn't actually any compelling reason to stop here, but if you've left Chiang Mai too late to go any further, you'll find adequate accommodation. Songthaews make the 40-minute trip to Tha Ton regularly throughout the day.

MAE RIM

This small town, *15 km north of Chiang Mai on Highway* 107, marks the start of

• *Below: elephant camp.*

NORTHERN THAILAND BY MOTORBIKE

Getting around Thailand by motorbike is increasingly popular with visitors – and nowhere more so than in the north where the mountain scenery and hill-tribe villages, comprehensive road network and plentiful accommodation and tourist facilities make touring by motorbike a highly attractive option. Although there are some sensitive no-go areas along the border with Burma (and biking anywhere at night is never recommended) motorbike travel here is generally safe. The main things to be wary about are Thai driving 'rules' (such as the biggest vehicle has right of way); and unscrupulous dealers trying to fob you off with an unreliable bike.

You can find bikes to hire in almost all the major towns: most common are the 100cc Honda Dream scooters (about 100B to 150B a day) but more suitable for long trips are the 125cc to 250cc Hondas or Yamahas (200B to 500B a day).

For advice on rental, roads and recommended routes, breakdowns, repairs, and accidents, pick up a copy of *General Touring Information, Northern Thailand* by David Unkovich, an Australian motorbike expert living in Chiang Mai who has also published two other useful publications, *Motorcycle Touring in North Thailand,* and *The Mae Hong Son Loop, A Touring Guide.*

The Chiang Mai Motorcyle Touring Club at 21/1 Ratchamankha Road Soi 2 (tel. 053 210518) can also help with information as well as renting out bikes and equipment.

a popular excursion through the **Mae Sa valley** to the west, following Route 1096 for 35 km to **Samoeng** and looping back along Route 1269 to Hang Dong, just south of Chiang Mai. On the way are Chiang Mai's most popular daytrip attractions – orchid farms and butterfly parks, elephant camps and rose gardens. The landscape is pretty enough, but with all the resorts and tourist developments it's hardly Northern Thailand at its best. As long as you know what to expect, however, some of the attractions – especially the elephant camps and the butterfly park – can provide an enjoyable day out, especially if you've got kids in tow.

Most travel agents in Chiang Mai offer Mae Sa day trips, or you can catch a bus or songthaew from the Chang Pheuak bus station. Best of all, rent a motorbike. David Unkovich, the region's motorbike expert (see box, this page) says this is 'the best 100-km ride in North Thailand – which everyone should do'.

SAMOENG
See Mai Rim, above.

THA TON ⇌ ✕
This small village straddling the Kok River, *179 km and four hours by bus north of Chiang Mai,* is becomingly increasingly popular not only as the starting point for raft and long-tail boat trips down the river to Chiang Rai but also as a base for independent or organized treks in the region. At the moment it's still a surprisingly quiet place with little development: there's not much more to the village itself than a couple of restaurants and shops on either side of the river, and a temple above the road on the southern side. Even the few guesthouses and resorts, and a strip of tourist souvenir shops by the river where the boats leave have had little impact on the generally low-key atmosphere – which becomes positively *sotto* after the flurry of tourists have left on the 12.30 pm boat.

The village has had a long history of being tossed between Burma and Thailand. The border is now a few kilometres upstream, but during the late 19thC, when Tha Ton was a thriving trading point for goods going to Chiang Rai or Chiang Mai, the border was the river on the village doorstep: the north bank of Tha Ton was considered to be in Burma, the south bank in Thailand. Shan Burmese moved in to inhabit the northern side while the Thais inhabited the southern areas. The distinction has remained to this day, with the north bank population still predominantly Shan.

Scattered in the nearby hills and fertile valleys are other hill-tribes who were originally attracted to the region's prosperity – Yao, Lisu, Lahu, Hmong, Karen and Akha, as well as pockets of Kuomintang Chinese Nationalists who fled here from the Chinese communist revolution of 1949 (see Thailand Overall: 2, page 55).

The influence of the Chinese is nowhere more obvious than at **Wat Tha Ton,** whose four giant Buddhist images built on the hillside include two that are typically Chinese in style. The wat is a ten-minute climb from the road by the bridge and is a fine place to visit at sunset in order to enjoy the hazy views over the river and rice paddies. It's also a useful source of information about tours and treks: the wat organizes its own three-hour tour to the Lahu village of Gaeng Dtoom near the Burmese border, with profits going directly towards a three-year reforestation, education and medical project that started in 1994.

Another enterprising project that has come from the wat is a useful little booklet called *The Road from Thaton to Mae Salong,* which provides plenty of ideas for independent exploration of the area and its villages. It was produced by Randy Gaudet, an American who first came to Thailand with the U.S. Air Force in 1969 and who later returned to teach at Chiang Mai University. His latest job, teaching English and computer literacy to the monks at Wat Tha Ton, has led to the instigation of projects to help the hill-tribe villagers directly by encouraging them in their efforts to set up home-based guesthouses in their own villages and teaching them how to become environmentally responsible trekking guides.

Previously, Randy Gaudet told me, "People like Asa of Asa's Lisu Guest Home (near Tha Ton) were getting only 10 per cent of what the tour company received from tourists visiting their village. The tour operators were getting richer and the hill-tribe people were getting the shaft. Asa now has a profitable guest home of his own and every village he visits with the traveller enjoys their company. No hands out for money, candy, or pictures. He donates a portion of his earnings to buy things such as school books, pencils, shoes, clothes and so on."

Such direct involvement in the tourism industry doesn't make the local middlemen tour operators happy, says Randy, but it certainly benefits both the villagers and the tourists.

The **long-tail boat trip** to Chiang Rai is still Tha Ton's biggest draw, at its best after the rainy season, from November to January, when the river is high. And it's undoubtedly the most exciting way to reach Chiang Rai (there are air-conditioned buses from Tha Ton taking half the time, but they're not even half as much fun). Mind you, this way of travel isn't for everyone: the regular boat (which leaves daily at 12.30 pm) can take up to five hours and is often packed (there are no individual seats). There's no shade on board, either, so you'll need to bring sunscreen or a sunhat that won't blow off. And be prepared to get drenched, or at the very least sprayed: there are plenty of hair-raising rapids and swerving manoeuvres round shallows and sandbanks and sometimes the boatman doesn't get it quite right (though I've yet to hear of a boat overturning). At least armed bandit attacks seem to be a thing of the past, though you'll still have to sign in at a police checkpost at Mae Salak (where Akha women flock to harrass you into buying strings of beads and bangles).

A couple of hours after leaving Tha Ton, the scenery becomes quite dramatic, with the hills closing in on both sides. Fishermen stand up to their waists in the river, tossing nets by hand, while villagers paddle by in dugout canoes. Closer to Chiang Rai, however, you'll encounter more day trippers in their chartered long-tail boats or rafts. The Karen village of **Ban Ruammid** is one of the most popular stop-off points, with elephants waiting for tour group rides. But from here you can trek by yourself to nearby villages which, while used to *farangs*, are not overly exploited. There is usually someone in the village happy to put you up for the night for a small charge.

Taking a **bamboo raft trip** to Chiang Rai is a much more appealing option if you like to take things slowly: the rafts (with pilot and cook) can accommodate up to eight people and take three days and two nights to reach Chiang Rai, with one night usually spent in a nearby hill-tribe village. There are several guesthouses and tour operators in Tha Ton which can arrange these trips for you.

RECOMMENDED HOTELS

CHIANG RAI

Mae Hong Son Guest House, B; 126 Singkhlai Road.

Better run than the original guesthouse in Mae Hong Son – thanks to motherly and efficient Khun Pannee (the half-Burmese, half-Thai aunt of the MHS operator). Travellers flock here for the cosy garden café, laid-back atmosphere and simple cheap rooms (have your ear-plugs ready: the walls are thin). Tits (that's his name) is at hand to arrange treks in the region, including three-day motorbike treks.

Ben Guest House, B; 620/25 Thanalai Road; tel. 053 716775.

A fairly recent operation, with rooms in a new Lanna-style teakwood house. It's in the south-west of town, but the English-speaking owners often meet the boat from Tha Ton.

Mae Kok Villa, B; 445 Singkhlai Road; tel. 053 711786.

Once you've managed to get past the horde of dachsunds, and found your way behind a dour puce-coloured house through an unkempt garden, the airy spacious rooms in the villa behind are a delight. There's plenty of room here for kids to run around.

The Golden Triangle Inn, BB; 590 Phahonyothin Road; tel. 053 711339; fax 053 713963; credit cards MC, V.

Justifiably popular (you'll need to book ahead), this town-centre hotel is an oasis of greenery and good taste, with rooms arranged around a lush Japanese-style garden and featuring northern Thai decoration and ambience. Under Thai-U.S. management, its staff are unfailingly polite.

Wiang Inn, BBB; 893 Phahonyothin Road; tel. 053 711543.

Several notches higher in facilities than the Golden Triangle – including a swimming pool and disco – but with less original atmosphere.

Dusit Island Resort, BBBB; 1129 Kraisorasit Road; tel. 053 715777; fax 053 715801; credit cards MC, V.

The deluxe choice, isolated from the low life by its island situation in the Kok River across from the town centre. Try bargaining for a discount if the isolation and luxury take your fancy.

THA TON

Thip's Travellers House, B; by the S side of the bridge, on the main road; tel./fax 053 459312.

Run by the enterprising Mrs Thip, this long-established traveller's favourite has simple fan rooms in a tiny garden. A new branch has opened 4 km up the road with new bungalows overlooking garlic fields and fruit orchards. Mrs Thip also organizes one- to seven-day treks in the region, as well as bamboo raft trips and elephant rides.

Garden Home, B; 236 M. 3 Ban Tha Ton; tel. 053 459287.

On the north side of the river, overlooking the wat, this delightful place has just five comfortable bungalows well spaced out in a neat orchard of lychee and mango trees. The shy gardener-owner, Pomchart Tit, knows only a little English but you can always go to Thip's (above) for travel information.

Asa's Guest Home, B; Louta village, 14 km NE of Tha Ton (30 minutes by songthaew, then a motorbike taxi for the last 2 km - well-signposted).

One of the first independent hill-tribe guesthouses in the area, this has had rave reviews: English-speaking Asa offers accommodation and meals in his Lisu village (listen to Paw playing his Lisu banjo) as well as 'jungle adventure' treks (sleep in a made-to-order bamboo and banana-leaf house, eat wild herbs and jungle vegetables).

Karen Farm House, B; Ban Meuang Ngam, 16 km NE of Tha Ton (30 minutes by songthaew, then motorbike taxi for last 4 km - well-signposted).

If you want to find out about life in a typical Karen village (or simply want some undisturbed days), this is the place to come: there are two Karen villages here – the first is Catholic, the second Buddhist. Once you've passed the church of the Christian village, and the surrounding chilli and soybean fields, you'll come to the Buddhist village and the Karen Farm House. It was opened in early 1995 by a southern Thai, Sommart, who previously worked with the International Red Cross and the U.N. When he married his local Karen wife, Amornrat, he fell in love with the area, too, and devoted his energies to establishing this guesthouse.

There are four bungalows with a wonderful view over the misty valley and forested hills. Sommart (who speaks excellent English) can take you on day treks or suggest places you can go on your own: there are Yao, Lahu and Lisu villages all nearby.

Maekok River Lodge, BBB; N *riverside, Tha Ton; tel.* 053 459328; *fax* 053 459329; *credit cards,* MC, V.

The best up-market choice if you want a place with character: designed and run by tattooed and T-shirted Irishman, Shane K. Beary (ex-Zimbabwe SAS), it's an attractive woody lodge with palm trees forming part of the interior decoration. An animal sanctuary in the grounds (now sheltering mostly macaques and gibbons) is for animals rescued from illegal traders or from people who can't afford to keep them. For the guests, there's a pool and landscaped gardens.

Shane's unique range of 'Track of the Tiger Company' soft adventure tour programmes are ideal for those who like their adventures to be comfortable (African safari style) – with a base camp that can ensure white linen on the table at the end of a day, plus ice and lemon in the G & T.

RECOMMENDED RESTAURANTS

CHIANG RAI
Phetburi Restaurant, B; 421 B*anphaprakan* Road.

There are several open-to-the-street restaurants along this road, but Phetburi has the most tempting array of dishes on display. Every time I've gone here I've struck lucky with my point-and-guess method of choosing: the last time I hit the jackpot with a fish mousse wrapped in a banana leaf that was so delicious I had to have two more, much to the amusement of the girls serving.

Cabbages & Condoms, B-BB;
620/25 T*hanalai* Road; *tel.* 053 719167.

One of three in this chain (the others are in Bangkok and Wiang Papao) with a family planning theme, operated with cheeky humour by the Population & Community Development Association. Fortunately its witty tags – 'Our food is guaranteed not to cause pregnancy' and 'You are now entering the rubber triangle' are two of the more memorable – don't extend to the names of dishes on the menu: it's traditional, fine-quality Thai food here at reasonable prices.

As you leave, you won't find the usual tray of free mints on offer, but – yes, you're right – free condoms, thoughtfully provided in Thai or 'international' sizes.

Mae Ui Khiaw, B-BB; 106/9 N*gam Meuang* Road.

Justifiably popular for its simple northern Thai dishes. Only open for lunch.

THA TON
As well as the restaurants serving standard travellers' fare in the guesthouses, there are several cheap restaurants serving Thai and Chinese dishes near the bridge, pier, and bus stop (north side of the bridge). For deluxe dining, your best bets are the **Maekok River Lodge** (see this page) which has an excellent menu and riverside view; or the **Thaton River View Hotel** further along the same riverside road.

Northern Thailand

The Northern Highlands of Nan

325 km; Nelles 1:1,500,000

Mountainous, forested Nan Province in Northern Thailand is one of the most remote and least-visited in the country. Until 14 years ago, you would have been advised to stay well clear: this area near the Laos border was a hotbed of Thai communist activity, where the People's Liberation Army of Thailand (PLAT) based their armed insurgency.

Since the disintegration of PLAT and the Communist Party in the 1980s, and the building of roads to link Nan with its neighbours, the province has shed its decades of isolation to emerge as an up-and-coming area for tourism. You won't find fancy facilities here, but if you're prepared for simple, rough travel, you will find some stunning mountainous scenery and unique hill tribes. Trekking and rafting tours are both possible. And culturally, the temples and textiles are among Thailand's finest.

The itinerary starts from Chiang Mai, 325 km west of Nan, suggesting stops in Lampang and/or Phrae (it's a seven-hour bus ride without stops). Take a look at Thailand Overall: 1 for details of the Lampang-Chiang Mai section. And Phrae? Hardly anyone bothers to stop here, but I think it's one of the friendliest places in Northern Thailand (perhaps because they see so few visitors), with its own unique cultural attractions. Just 23 km from the Den Chai train station (which is on the main north-south railway line), Phrae is also a convenient first stop if you're coming up from the south.

Including at least a couple of days once you reach Nan, this makes a fascinating three- to five-day trip. And if you can't stomach mountain roads all the way back, you can always fly: Chiang Mai is just 45 minutes away.

TRANSPORT

You can fly to Nan from Chiang Mai, Phitsanulok, Phrae or Bangkok, but travelling overland is much more exciting: buses from Chiang Mai take around seven hours, or two to three hours from Phrae.

Phrae is only 23 km north of Den Chai, a stop on the main north-south railway line.

1:3,000,000

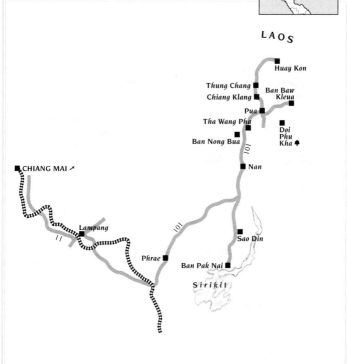

• *Above and left: Nan – page 167.*

Nan, thanks to its famous temple and its fine hand-woven cloth. *Located about 35 km N of Nan, off Route 1080*, just before Tha Wang Pha (also a major weaving centre), it's fairly easy to reach by songthaew from Nan: get off just before Tha Wang Pha, cross a bridge over the Nan River and continue 3 km further to Ban Nong Bua.

One of the villagers here has opened up his house as a show room where you can buy locally-woven items; or you can follow the sound of the clacking looms and see women weaving the cloth in their homes nearby.

The reason why this Thai Lu village is so attuned to visitors is the popularity of its temple, **Wat Nong Bua**. In traditional Thai Lu style, with a two-tiered roof and naga lintels, it has *Jataka* murals – now sadly faded – painted by the same artists who decorated Nan's Wat Phumin. (*Jataka* are tales of the lives of Buddha.)

SIGHTS & PLACES OF INTEREST

BAN BAW KLEUA
The area north-east of Nan is speckled with salt wells, and in this village close to the Laos border the Htin inhabitants (see box, bottom of page 168) make a living from extracting the salt.

It's not easy to get here, even with your own transport – the village is at the end of the rough and winding Route 1256 – but day trips from Nan which are organized by local tour agencies sometimes include Ban Baw Kleua on their itineraries.

BAN NONG BUA
This Thai Lu village is one of the most popular destinations for day trips from

DOI PHU KHA NATIONAL PARK
Only recently established, this national park lies *about 75 km NE of Nan, off Route 1080* (infrequent songthaews go to the park headquarters from the nearby village of Pua).

On the forested slopes below the

park's 1,980-m-high **Doi Phu Kha** summit are several hill-tribe villages, but there are few established trails to these or to the park's waterfalls. You can enquire at park headquarters about hiring guides. It's not recommended to go wandering off on your own into the wilds: there are said to be unexploded mines around from the communist insurgency days. But just getting here is fun, with spectacular views on the way up to the summit.

If you don't mind rough roads, you can return to Nan via Ban Baw Kleua (see page 166) and Route 1081.

HUAY KON
See Treks and Day Trips from Nan, page 169.

NAN 🛏 ✕
When you first arrive in this small provincial capital by the Nan River, just *50 km from Laos,* you may be disappointed: instead of some lawless frontier post with a wild and notorious past, you'll find a typically dull modern town centre. Give it a few days: you'll find the place grows on you.

Far from being rough and ready, its temples reflect a 14th to 15thC heyday of independence and civilization: once called Waranakhon (Excellent City), it was a powerful independent city state which became part of the Lan Na Thai (Million Thai Fields) Kingdom of Chiang Mai. In the 16thC, the Burmese seized control of the area, and Nan fell into decline until the 18thC. Even then, it remained aloof from the rest of Thailand, and was ruled by its own 'governors' right up until 1931.

The rich history of Nan is best understood with a visit to the excellent **Nan National Museum** (open Wednesday to Sunday from 9 am to noon, 1 pm to 4 pm) on Pha Khong Road in the southern part of town. Housed in the former palace of the local rulers, its two floors of exhibits are intelligently displayed and cover everything from the region's unusual ethnic groups to the distinctive Nan style of Buddhist art. Don't miss the weird black elephant tusk on the second floor, which is said to have been a talismanic present to a Nan ruler more than 300 years ago.

Just south of the museum is Nan's finest temple, **Wat Phumin**, whose 16thC cruciform bot seems to be car-

ried by two great glass-glittering nagas (mythical serpents). Inside, murals done in the 19thC when the bot was being restored take your breath away with their bold, brazen scenes. There's everything here, from stories of Buddha's previous lives to contemporary 19thC snapshots of hunting, fishing and weaving; lovers and musicians, bawdy monkeys and gruesome torture methods. My favourites are the noblewoman (on the east wall) laden with bangles and rings, and the men with extravagant tattoos on the west wall. The doors themselves are worth a close look, too, for their incredible carvings of animals, birds and flowers. In the midst of it all stands an elaborate altar with four Buddha images facing in each direction.

Across the road from the museum is another impressive temple, **Wat Phra That Chang Kham**, whose *viharn* was built in 1458. The murals here are slow-

• *Harvest, Tha Wang Pha.*

FESTIVALS IN NAN

Nan's most popular festival takes place at the end of the Buddhist Lent (mid-October to mid-November) when dragon boat races are part of the festivities celebrating **kathin**, when robes are ceremonially offered to the monks. Although similar boat races take place elsewhere in the country, Nan's event ranks as one of the best: dozens of brightly-painted, 30-m-long boats take part in the races, cheered by onlookers crowding the banks of the Nan River. For exact dates, contact the Chiang Mai or Chiang Rai TAT office.

The healthiest festival of the year is the Golden Orange Festival (December to January) which celebrates the local harvest of oranges with the inevitable parade of orange-adorned floats and, of course, an Orange Queen.

The ethnic minorities have their own calendar of festivals, too. One of the most important for the local Thai Lu of Nong Bua is their dramatic festival to pay homage to their ancestral spirits. Held only once every three years (the next will be in December 1996), the two-day event features processions, spirit offerings, feasts and buffalo sacrifices.

ly being uncovered from a previous whitewash ordered by a puritan abbot. But it's the chedi behind the *viharn* which grabs the attention: probably dating from the 14thC, it has chunky elephant buttresses similar to chedis in Si Satchanalai and Sukhothai.

Visiting **Wat Phra That Chae Haeng**, a couple of kilometres southeast of town, makes a worthwhile afternoon excursion. This highly revered wat, dating from 1354, overlooks the surrounding valley from its hill-top position and is approached by an appropiately dramatic avenue of rippling nagas. Within the wat's walled enclosure is an extravagant bot whose fabulous multi-tiered roof is edged with white dragon reliefs. The doors are topped by swirling stucco dragon designs. Nearby is an equally eye-catching gilded chedi, gleaming in the sunlight and surrounded by gilded umbrellas.

For a down-to-earth contrast, you can visit the park next door, which has dismal caged animals and wandering deer looking for food hand-outs from visitors. Best to ignore them all and peer through the trees at the sweeping views of the valley below.

Within Nan itself there are some excellent **handicraft shops**: local textiles are among the best in Thailand, especially the Thai Lu (see box, below) hand-woven cloth with its distinctive red-and-black

NAN'S ETHNIC GROUPS

There are several ethnic minorities living in the Nan area whom you are unlikely to come across anywhere else in the kingdom. The one which has had the most cultural influence on Nan is the **Thai Lu**. The group migrated from southern China's Xishuangbanna province some 200 years ago and mostly settled in the area north of Nan. Some of the most important temples in and around Nan have distinct Thai Lu architectural characteristics, and much of the high-quality weaving and silver jewellery you'll find in the handicraft shops will have been done by Thai Lu villagers.

Less well-known, the **Khamu**, who also migrated from Xishuangbanna, live mostly north of Nan, near the Laos border. Skilled metal workers, they keep to their own traditions.

You'll probably hear about the **Htin** because of their skill in making intricate bamboo baskets and grass mats (on sale in Nan's handicraft shops). A Mon-Khmer people, they live in remote valleys north of Nan.

Most unusual of all are the **Mrabri** (Forest People), whom the Thais exotically call **Phii Thong Luang** (Spirits of the Yellow Leaves) because they move on from their huts of branches and leaves as soon as the leaves turn yellow. The last truly nomadic hunter-gatherer tribe in Thailand, they inhabit the remote mountain area between Nan and Phrae and probably number less than a hundred. Few of the tribes people, in fact, now follow the traditional lifestyle, working instead for Hmong or Mien hill-tribe groups in exchange for food.

designs, very similar to that woven in the Thai Lu homeland of Xishuangbanna in southern China.

Also worth buying are embroidery by the Mien hill tribe and Hmong appliqué pieces. Try shops along Nan's main shopping street, Sumondhevaraj Road, such as the gift shop in **Nan Fah Hotel** at number 438; **Jantragul**, at number 304, which has a wide selection of textiles, made up into purses, bags, clothes and table runners; and **Nan** at 21/2 Sumondhevaraj Road, which is several notches classier, its display housed in a beautiful old building furnished with Lanna Thai antiques. For Mien silverware – stunning chunky bracelets, belts and buckles – visit **Nan Silverware** at 416 Sumondhevaraj Road.

If you want to support the local weavers and hill tribes more directly you might prefer to purchase textile goods from the non profit-making **Thai Payap Assocation** at 290 Sumondhevaraj Road or 24 Jetraboot Road: originally established in a refugee camp, the association now works directly with 31 local villages helping them to produce high-quality items mainly for export, with all profits going back to the villages.

PHRAE 🛏 ✕

More like a village in atmosphere than a town, this historic provincial capital 122 *km SW of Nan (and 23 km N of the train station at Den Chai)* is refreshingly free of tourist trappings. It's famous among Thais for carvings in teak and for its quality **seua maw hawm**, the popular indigo farmer's shirt. But just wandering around the old walled part of the city, by the Yom River, you'll also come across traditional old teak shophouses, unusual temples and a little-known horde of folk artifacts, all of which make a short visit here very pleasant.

Wat Luang is the place to start. Set in quiet, shady grounds, this fine old wat dates back to the town's founding in the 12thC: you'll enter through a chunky remnant of the original city wall (note the shrine against the wall with a statue of an early ruler, Chao Pu, decked in coloured garlands).

Behind the main *viharn* is a Lanna-style chedi with elephants on all corners. But most eye-catching of all is a lovely little teak house across the grounds, with beautifully carved lintels and stairway. Part of the wat's extensive museum, it

TREKS AND DAY TRIPS FROM NAN

To appreciate fully the remoteness of Nan and its surroundings you should consider taking a trek into the hills. Most of the guesthouses organize these, or you can check out the itineraries offered by Fhu Travel Service, 453/4 Sumondhevaraj Road (tel. 054 710636). One-day options include a northern tour towards the Laos border, visiting Thai Lu villages; a six-hour trek to local hill tribes; a jeep tour of Doi Phu Kha National Park; or a boat ride down the Nan River. Challenging two- to four-day treks are also possible.

If you have your own transport (motorbikes can be rented from Oversea, 88 Sumondhevaraj Road), or are prepared for some time-consuming songthaew travel, you can get to these and many other places yourself. Heading south for 110 km, **Ban Pak Nai** fishing village, on the northern shores of a lake formed by the Sirikit Reservoir, makes a great goal (there's even a small guesthouse here). On the way you can detour a few kilometres to see the weird earth pillars of **Sao Din**, just south of Route 1083.

Going north, you can visit the mainly Thai Lu villages of Tha Wang Pha, Pua (famous for its silver crafts) and Thung Chang. Further up the road is the border pass at Huay Kon: there are rumours that foreigners may soon be able to cross into Laos here (ask for details at Fhu Travel).

Back towards Nan, you can visit Silaphet Falls just south-east of Pua, or Doi Phu Kha National Park (see pages 166-7).

houses all kinds of wooden artifacts, from cow bells to spinning wheels.

Next door, in a modern building, is the main **museum**, a fascinating hotchpotch of curiosities and antiquities. On the ground floor, don't miss the old photos of the Mrabri tribe and the former royal family of Phrae, and a gruesome 19thC shot of an execution by decapitation. Upstairs is a horde of religious items including finely-carved meditation

Phae Meuang Phii or Ghost Land is what the locals call this area of bizarre rock formations 18 km NE of Phrae. Caused by erosion, the giant pillars of rock rear up from the dry land like stunted primeval peaks. Now a popular spot for day trippers, there are even picnic tables and food vendors.

The area lies about 9 km up Highway 101 towards Nan, and then 9 km off the highway: if you're using public transport, you can catch a bus towards Nan for the first 9 km; a songthaew can then get you to within a couple of kilometres of the park entrance.

screens, embroidered hangings edged with sequinned elephants, and a lovely 16thC seated Buddha.

In the adjacent building is yet more loot – old record players and chests of cloth, cabinets of lacquerware and a standing Buddha image in a gilded throne – all overshadowed by the interior's massive teak pillars and glowing teak floor.

If you spotted a pretty colonial-style mansion in the faded black-and-white photos in the main museum, you'll probably be as startled as I was when you pass the real thing in a back street near Wat Luang: **Vongburi House**, once the residence of Phrae's ruling family, looks as dainty as a French provincial villa, all pink and white with dozens of narrow windows and wooden shutters and a fringe of white wood carving so delicate

DETOUR – WAT PHRA THAT CHAW HAE
This hill-top wat, 8 km SE of Phrae, is highly revered for its 33-m-high gilded chedi, said to contain a hair of the Buddha: **chaw hae** refers to the cloth that devotees wrap around the chedi each year.

The wat is believed to date from the 12th or 13thC and also features an ornate bot with a lavish gilded ceiling. Because of its popularity as a pilgrimage site, the wat is easy to reach by songthaew from Phrae (but they run less frequently in the afternoon).

it looks like broderie Anglais. Now a private residence belonging to Khun Wannee Vongburi, it's not officially open to visitors (you can gaze at it from the gateway), though there are said to be plans to establish a small museum here.

Nearby **Wat Phra Non** is famous for its reclining Buddha image (phra non), housed in a dull viharn (you can ask the friendly monks to open it up if it's closed). But although the gilded, patterned stone pillows on which the Buddha lies look as elegant as the real versions in Wat Luang's museum, it's the façade of the adjacent 200-year-old bot which is far more spectacular: gilded and carved with Ramayana scenes, it rivals the triple-tiered roof and two-tiered portico in splendour. Behind the viharn is a yellow chedi dating from the 18thC. It has quaint, brightly-painted warrior figures at each corner.

But when it comes to carvings – and for teak carvings on a truly ostentatious scale – you should really see **Pratubjai House** on the western edge of town. Assembled from nine old teak houses and opened in 1985, it's little more than a glorified souvenir shop of locally-carved wooden decorations. If you've always wanted a life-size wooden Alsatian dog, a guardian elephant or decorative teak gnome, here's your chance. More interesting is the part of the private upper floor which is open to visitors, revealing the family clutter (and yet more lavish teak furniture) belonging to the wealthy owners of Pratubjai, the Chaivannacoopt family.

A total contrast in aesthetics is offered by the Shan Burmese-style **Wat Jom Sawan** near the bus station on the north-eastern edge of the new town. Built early in the 20thC, the spacious wooden viharn-cum-bot, with its central multi-tiered wooden tower, has an almost homely appearance, with pots and wooden cowbells hanging from the verandah's eaves. Among its horde of treasures (cabinets of coins, alms bowls and amulets, old guns and irons, even armadillo skins) is a precious set of Buddhist scriptures engraved on ivory (you'll have to ask to see it).

SAO DIN, THA WANG PHA AND THUNG CHANG

See Treks and Day Trips from Nan, page 169.

RECOMMENDED HOTELS

NAN

Doi Phukha Guest House, B; 94/5 Sumondhevaraj Road, Soi 1; tel. 054 771422.

The most attractive guesthouse in town, run by Yai ('Big'), a genial young woman (and yes, a little plump). There are six rooms in this pleasant wooden house and a cosy clutter of family knick-knacks. Bikes are available, too, and plenty of travel information. Expect to be woken by the sound of a cock crowing and monks chanting from the wat next door.

Nan Fah Hotel, BB; 438 Sumondhevaraj Road; tel. 054 771697.

Nan's first hotel, built some 40 years ago, is a spacious old wooden building with gleaming floors and ceilings and large air-conditioned rooms. A pity that its city-centre location and downstairs bar (plus live band) makes it so noisy.

Dhevaraj Hotel, BB-BBB; 466 Sumondhevaraj Road; tel. 054 710094; fax 054 771365.

Nan's best (don't get excited) with a choice of fan or air-conditioned rooms: decent enough, but not really worth the extra baht.

PHRAE

Dao Phin Guesthouse, B; 105/29 Chaw Hae Road.

Phrae's only guesthouse with a handful of cheap rooms. Enquire here, too, about the three-day off-road motorbike tours organized by Enduro Club (or radio tel. 01 9500683).

Thung Si Phaibun, B; 84 Yantarakitkoson Road; tel. 054 511011.

Typical Chinese-style hotel, with rows of rooms overlooking an inner courtyard. Pretty basic, but OK at a pinch.

Nakorn Phrae Hotel, BB; 118 Ratsadamnoen Road; tel. 054 511122; fax 054 521937; credit cards, MC, DC, V.

Large but friendly hotel near the old city, with an old wing for fan rooms and a new wing opposite for air-conditioned and deluxe (TV) rooms.

• *Food festival, Nan Province.*

RECOMMENDED RESTAURANTS

NAN

Suan Isaan, B-BB; off Sumondhevaraj Road, near Nan Fah Hotel.

Northern fare in a clean and well-run eaterie.

Da Dario Restaurant, BB; 37/4 Rajamnuay Road, Ban Pra Kerd; tel. 054 750258; closed Sundays.

Swiss-Italian, Paolo Ferrini, used to run Nan's farang-favourite Tiptop Restaurant but gave it up to return to Switzerland with his Thai wife and son, Dario. Now he's back (for good, he says) and has opened this typically Italian restaurant on the north-western edge of town (get a card from Fhu Travel to find it). Luxuries (for Nan) include steak au poivre and pizzas, ravioli and lasagne.

PHRAE

Malakaw Restaurant, BB; 28 Ratsadamnoen Road; tel. 054 511391.

Popular with young Thais, this pleasant open-air garden restaurant with a jungle of wooden decoration and plants is run by Bangkok-educated Tick Nopporn. Try his delicious chicken laap or mushroom salad.

Night market, B; just inside the old city walls, Rawp Meuang Road.

Plenty of room here for a hassle-free night of snacking under the stars.

North-Eastern Thailand

Isaan's Khmer Temple Ruins

343 km; map Nelles 1:1,500,000

The main reason for coming to Isaan, the north-eastern hinterland of Thailand, is to see some of the magnificent Khmer temple ruins which are scattered in the southern part of the area. This section has been designed to help you choose which temple complexes to visit, from the most famous and most easily accessible to the wildest, least-restored, and most atmospheric. Be sure to use this section in combination with Thailand Overall: 3, which provides an overview of the whole Isaan region.

The two temples at the top of everyone's list are Phimai (near Khorat) and Phanom Rung (near Buriram but also accessible from Khorat and Surin). Allow at least a full day each for those, but if you base yourself in Surin or Si Saket you could well be tempted to spend several more days exploring further afield, to lesser-known ruins in the area, either by yourself or with a tour from your hotel. Such trips take you deep into unspoilt Isaan countryside and indeed to the still-sensitive Cambodian border region, an area not to be explored without prior advice or guidance.

The nearly 200 ruins in this southern part of Isaan date from the 10th to the 13thC when the powerful Khmers of Cambodia expanded their empire from their base in Angkor to Vietnam, Laos, southern China and north-eastern and central Thailand. The rulers, who merged their Hindu (and later Mahayana Buddhist) faith with the cult of a god-king, commissioned the building of hundreds of prasats, huge castle-temples, to emphasize both the power of their rule as well as the power of the Hindu god Shiva (or later, Buddha). The sandstone carvings that adorn these temples are among the most spectacular that you'll see anywhere in Thailand. If you can't get to Cambodia's Angkor Wat (which was actually built later than many of these temples) this itinerary is ample compensation.

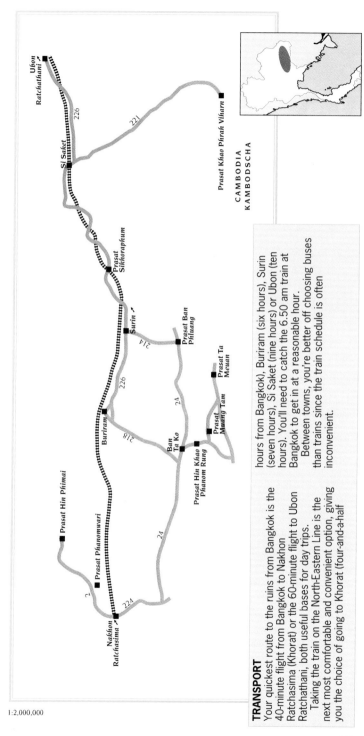

Ubon Ratchathani

226

221

Si Saket

Prasat Khao Phrah Viharn

CAMBODIA
KAMBODSCHA

Prasat Sikhoraphum

Surin

214

Prasat Ban Phluang

226

Prasat Ta Meuan

Buriram

2A

218

Ban Ta Ko

Prasat Muang Tam

Prasat Hin Phimai

Prasat Phanomwari

Prasat Hin Khao Phanom Rung

2

24

224

Nakhon Ratchasima

TRANSPORT

Your quickest route to the ruins from Bangkok is the 40-minute flight from Bangkok to Nakhon Ratchasima (Khorat) or the 60-minute flight to Ubon Ratchathani, both useful bases for day trips.

Taking the train on the North-Eastern Line is the next most comfortable and convenient option, giving you the choice of going to Khorat (four-and-a-half hours from Bangkok), Buriram (six hours), Surin (seven hours), Si Saket (nine hours) or Ubon (ten hours). You'll need to catch the 6.50 am train at Bangkok to get in at a reasonable hour.

Between towns, you're better off choosing buses than trains since the train schedule is often inconvenient.

1:2,000,000

173

• *Prasat Hin Phimai.*

SIGHTS & PLACES OF INTEREST

BURIRAM 🛏 ✕

Although Buriram province contains more than a hundred Khmer ruins – including the grandest and most extensively restored of them all, Prasat Phanom Rung – visitors tend to base themselves in Khorat or Surin rather than the provincial capital. There's nothing much wrong with the place, except that it's rather dull. Still, there's a fair range of accommodation and Phanom Rung is just 64 km south, accessible by songthaews that leave from the market every morning, or by bus to Ban Ta-Ko followed by motorbike taxi.

NAKHON RATCHASIMA (KHORAT)
See Thailand Overall: 3, pages 65-6.

PHIMAI 🛏 ✕
This small town, *about 60 km (and one hour by bus)* NE *of Khorat* is the focus of nearly all tours to Isaan, thanks to its beautifully-restored Prasat Hin Phimai, one of the finest examples of classical Khmer architecture in Thailand. Surrounded by the River Mun and its tributaries, the well-protected and well-irrigated area was inhabited long before the Khmers came on to the scene (Neolithic pottery and jewellery dating back to the 6thC have been found), but the Khmers are the ones who have left the greatest mark. There's nothing of interest about the modern town, though a couple of kilometres north-east down Route 206 you'll come across another popular tourist site, the **Sai Ngam** (Beautiful Banyan), Thailand's largest banyan tree. It's quite enormous, and has spread its trellis of branches over a vast area, surrounded by a small reservoir. If you stay the night in Phimai (a pleasant guesthouse makes this a tempting option, see page 181), you'll find a late-afternoon walk to the banyan pleasant light relief after temple-touring. But on a day trip from Khorat you'll find more than enough to keep you occupied at the prasat itself.

Like many Khmer temples, **Prasat Hin Phimai** (open daily from 7.30 am to 6 pm) was built and adapted over a long period of time, probably from the late 10thC reign of King Jayavarman V to the late 12thC under King Suriyavarman VII, by which time it had changed from a Hindu to a Mahayana Buddhist sanctuary.

At the height of the Khmer era, a road ran 240 km south-east from Phi-

• *Central prang carvings,*
Prasat Hin Phimai.

mai direct to the capital at Angkor, linking other important prasats, including
Muang Tham and Phanom Rung. In fact,
Phimai's prasat predates Angkor Wat
and probably influenced some of
Angkor Wat's design (particularly the
design of its gateways). It's significant,
too, that Phimai faces south-east (most
other Khmer monuments face east) –
which is the direction where Angkor lay.
Compared to Prasat Phanom Rung,
Prasat Hin Phimai is not a large site, but
it is extraordinarily impressive, the 28-
m-high white sandstone main prang surrounded by smaller coral-pink prangs
and all enclosed within a walled complex. If you want to experience the full
effect, you should enter through the
main south-eastern Victory Gate (built
to be large enough for an elephant to
pass through) which lies just south of
the bus terminal. This leads to one of
the four gopuras in the sanctuary's
outer walls.

Between here and the inner walls is a
raised pathway which would have originally crossed four ponds of water.

Through another gopura, set in a
gallery of pink sandstone, and you
enter the main sanctuary. There are
three prangs here, the main 11thC
white sandstone prang, and two smaller late 12thC prangs: the laterite prang
Phromathat, on the right, originally
housed a statue of King Jayavarman VII
(it's now in Phimai's National Museum
just north of the complex), while the
pink sandstone prang **Hin Daeng** is on
the left. Just behind this there was once
a Hindu shrine.

But it's the main, **central prang**
which steals the show, with its fantastic carvings and monumental porticos,
restored to its full glory after 20 years
of laborious jigsaw work. Topped by a
lotus bud decoration, the prang has a
cruciform design and four symmetrical
openings, the south-eastern one being
the main entrance. Take a good look
at the **lintel sculpture** over these doorways – they're some of the finest exam-

ples of Khmer art in existence. Particularly striking are the lintels over the most important **south-eastern gateway** which shows a dancing Shiva and, inside, a meditating Buddha lifted by a protective naga over flood waters – a fascinating combination of Hindu and Buddhist art, revealing the Khmer empire's shifting, merging faiths.

The minute detail of some of these carvings provides a striking contrast to the megalithic blocks of burnished red laterite which make up the walls and entrance paths, reflecting a balance of power and artistic skill.

If you're curious to see some carvings close-up, the **National Museum** (open Wednesday to Sunday, 9 am to 4 pm) is worth a visit. It contains carvings from some of Isaan's best Khmer temples, as well as the **statue of King Jayavarman VII** found at Phimai.

PRASAT BAN PHLUANG

See *Prasat Ta Meuan, page 180*.

PRASAT MUANG TAM

One of the dreamiest ruins in Isaan while it was still unrestored, this small 10thC temple lies 5 *km* SE *of Prasat Phanom Rung*, and can easily be combined with the visit to Phanom Rung (motorbike taxis are your only option if you're relying on public transport).

Prasat Muang Tam, or 'Lower City Temple', was probably completed during the reign of the Khmer King Jayavarman V, in the late 10thC, which would make it older than Prasat Phanom Rung. It features a surrounding laterite wall, four massive gopuras at each compass point and four L-shaped

> ### KALA
> Wherever you see carvings in Khmer sanctuaries (and particularly at Prasat Phanom Rung) you'll find the forbidding Kala head – the God of Time and Death – looking down at you. Also called Kiratimukha, the Kala head depicts both the lunar and solar eclipse: he was believed from ancient times to be the most powerful god because he could swallow anything, even the sun. He is always represented as a face to show that he is also able to swallow his own body.

ponds, guarded by nagas. Before the Fine Arts Department started restoration work here, everything was crumbling – prangs and lintels, gopuras and galleries. Carved sandstone blocks lay scattered in the grass, nagas tilting precariously towards their pools. Few tourists ever came here. The contrast with glamorous Phanom Rung was particularly striking.

I can't help feeling sad that the poignant atmosphere of the past will surely be lost when the restorers finish tidying up the place. But at least you won't have to cross your fingers when you step beneath the precariously leaning gopuras or continually stub your toes as you stumble over another carved masterpiece in the grass.

PRASAT HIN KHAO PHANOM RUNG

Situated 64 km South *of Buriram*, Prasat Phanom Rung is the largest and finest Khmer temple complex in Thailand. It dominates the surrounding plains from its position on top of an extinct volcano, and overlooks the Thai-Cambodian border to the south, marked by the Dongkrek mountain range. Its Khmer name, meaning 'big hill', has been reinforced by the Thai addition of *khao*, also meaning hill, while *hin* refers to the stone of which the temple is built.

You can visit the prasat on a day trip from Khorat, Buriram or Surin: catch a bus that goes via Ban Ta-Ko on Highway 24 and then either wait for a songthaew or take a motorbike-taxi (about B150 round trip) for the 12-km ride to the temple. (If you have the time, it's worth paying the taxi extra to include Prasat Muang Tam (see this page, opposite), which lies about 5 km south of Phanom Rung).

The first thing that strikes you about Phanom Rung is its grandeur. This was a temple built to impress and to please the gods, specifically the Hindu deity, Shiva. Constructed between the early 10th and 13thC, everything about it is on a majestic scale, enhanced by its hill-top position. Close up, the sense of mass and power, so typical of Khmer architecture, gives way to refined artistry, with exquisite carvings covering every lintel, pediment, prang and antechamber.

It is not clear who actually started the construction of Phanom Rung, though one of many inscriptions in the sanctuary refers to a great religious leader turned hermit called Hiranya who carved statues, stone inscriptions and images of the gods and was renowned as a meditator. It's thought that Phanom Rung could either have been initiated by him, or completed under his spiritual direction.

But whoever was responsible for the design certainly knew how to create a sense of majesty. Most dramatic of all is the **approach**, beginning with a stone avenue of sandstone lotus-bud pillars leading 160 m towards the temple, the symbolic mountain home of the gods. Three **naga bridges** link the world of man and gods, the first (the finest in Thailand) in a cruciform featuring 16 five-headed nagas. Climbing a series of **monumental stairways** past four small ponds (probably used for ritual ablutions before entering the temple) you reach the second bridge in front of the main, **east-facing gopura** which is beautifully sculpted. Three other gopuras, one on each side, are set in the sandstone rectangular wall which surrounds the inner sanctuary.

Inside the wall, sandstone galleries (laterite on the north side), with false windows and curvilinear roofs, also shield the sanctuary on all four sides.

The **main prang**, a few steps away from the east gopura via a last naga bridge, is where the main lingam was once enshrined. It is notable for its magnificent stone carvings. One of the most famous is the **Phra Narai Lintel**, a relief of a reclining Vishnu above the eastern entrance: this was stolen in the early 1960s and discovered years later on display in the Art Institute of Chicago. Not until restoration work at Phanom Rung was nearing completion in May 1988 did the escalating public outcry force the Institute to return the lintel (in exchange for a substantial fee, of course).

Other outstanding carvings to look out for are the one of a **dancing Shiva** (above the Phra Narai Lintel, at the eastern entrance); **Shiva and Uma riding their bull** (at the southern entrance); and the **abduction of Sita by Ravana** (on the northern pediment). The carved lintels over the porticoes represent some of the finest examples of Khmer art in existence, certainly as impressive as anything at Angkor Wat. You'll also notice some rougher, older

PRANGS, PRASATS, KUS AND NAGAS

When visiting the Khmer ruins you'll come across some specific architectural terms. The most common is prasat: this refers to a temple sanctuary or complex, often translated loosely as a castle or palace (though no king would ever have lived there). Prang is a Khmer temple tower. Often there's only one in the complex, but sometimes several. The central or main prang contains the temple's most sacred image, originally a lingam (the phallic symbol of the Hindu god, Shiva), and later a Buddhist image. Prangs are often elaborately carved and feature rounded tops in the style of a corn-cob.

Many Thai and Lao-speaking people tend to confuse the issue by calling a prasat a ku or prang ku, though these terms can also refer to smaller Khmer-style prangs.

But there's no confusion over nagas: these are the mythical dragon-headed snakes which in Buddhist mythology protected the Buddha from the rain. According to Cambodian legend, the kings of Cambodia were believed always to marry a daughter of the Naga King, who then protected the son-in-law's throne. In Khmer architecture, the nagas are represented as wonderful coiling lengths of stone, often in the form of naga stairways or bridges which symbolically bridge the worlds of gods and mortals. At the top of the stairway you'll be greeted by a gopura, an ornamental covered gateway or porch which can be as big as a small chamber. There are usually gopuras surrounding the main prang on four sides.

The material used for building many of the Khmer temples is laterite, a reddish pock-marked stone which hardens when exposed to the air: one of the reasons the ruins have lasted relatively well for so long.

FESTIVAL FOR THE GODS

Hill-top temples and festivals go well together in both Hindu and Buddhist belief: Mount Meru is considered to be the home of the gods, and festivals commemorating the gods are an essential part of the religious calendar. Prasat Phanom Rung combines both at April full moon, the time of the **Songkran New Year Festival**. It is thought that this was the day which marked the auspicious start of building work at Phanom Rung, for it's only then that you can stand at the westernmost porch of the gallery and see the sun rising through all 15 doors. Nowadays the celebrations include day-time processions to lay offerings at the Buddha's footprint in the prang noi, and, at night, dance-dramas and a *son-et-lumière* show, enough to keep all the gods happy.

structures inside the sanctuary: two laterite *viharas* (libraries) in the north-east and south-east corners, dating from the late 12thC; and two square brick prangs to the north-east of the main prang. These date from the early 10thC and are thought to be the oldest structures in the prasat. There's also a small, early-11thC prang (**prang noi**) in the south-western corner which was either never completed or partially torn down to make way for the building of the main prang.

Often overlooked is a sandstone and laterite hall just to the north of the far eastern end of the avenue. Although known as the **White Elephant Stable** by locals it was probably used as a common hall for daily ceremonies, where offerings and presentations were prepared. These days, it's the prang noi which receives most of the pilgrims' offerings since it now contains a stone Buddha footprint. During the Thai New Year festival in April (see box, above) this is the focus of the celebrations.

PRASAT PHANOMWAN

Just 15 *km* NE *of Khorat*, this small temple site, still mostly in ruins, is rarely visited. If you find Phimai and Phanom Rung too tidy and tourist-oriented, Prasat Phanomwan might make a suitably untamed alternative, especially if you walk the 6 km from the Highway 2 turn-off (ask the bus to stop at Ban Saen Meuang). There's supposed to be a songthaew service from this turn-off – locals confidently told me there would be one coming 'very soon' when I was there, but our ideas of time were obviously days apart because I never saw one. Perhaps it was just as well because the walk turned out to be delightful, passing several sprawling villages of bamboo and wood houses, surrounded by rice paddies. Every time I asked the way, I was given friendly (mostly incomprehensible) instructions by the villagers and several times offered a snack to keep me going.

After all this effort, Prasat Phanomwan could have been a big disappointment. But its crumbling ruins, now set in the grounds of an active wat, and surrounded, almost hidden by trees, made an instant impression, so dramatic was the contrast of this millenia-old monument with its rural surroundings.

Although smaller and far less ornate than Prasat Hin Phimai, Prasat Phanomwan has a similar style and rectangular layout. In fact, it is probably older: remains of brick towers in the courtyard date to the 9thC reign of Yasovarman (a stele bearing his name was found among the rubble). Most of the prasat, however, was probably built during the 10thC reign of Suryavarman I, with later 11thC additions (especially the carved lintels).

Most of the lintels were removed long ago to museums in Phimai and Bangkok, but the one over the north entrance to the main sanctuary is still in place. There's also evidence of the moat that once surrounded the sanctuary and even in the dry season you can usually see water in the reservoir pool to the east, both of which were built to symbolize aspects of the Hindu universe.

Now the atmosphere is distinctly Buddhist, with several Buddha images inside the sanctuary, venerated by the monks from the nearby wat and the local villagers. Restoration work which is now under way may well drag Phanomwan from the shadows of Phimai and create a well-documented tourist attraction, but in the meantime there is plenty of scope here for the imagination to roam.

PRASAT TA MEUAN

If you fancy some off-the-beaten-track adventures in the search for Khmer ruins, this is the one for you. Prasat Ta Meuan, and several other nearby ruins, are all along the Cambodian border, *about 60 km south of Surin*.

You shouldn't come here lightly: beyond the cleared pathways around the monuments the jungle is still full of landmines and undetonated hand grenades left by the Khmer Rouge (the skull-and-crossbone signs mean what they imply). And just a few kilometres across the border there are frequent skirmishes (or worse) between the Cambodian Army and the Khmer Rouge or the Cambodian and Thai Armies.

When the Cambodians try to cross the border to attack the Khmer Rouge from the Thai side, all three armies get involved. In a border fracas in March 1995, two Thai paratroopers were killed by the Cambodian Army and at least a dozen Cambodians by the Thais. This happened near Prasat Khao Prah Viharn (see page 180), not far to the east along the disputed border. So if you do want to visit this area, ask in Surin beforehand about the current situation – or better still, take a guided tour from Pirom's Guesthouse. If Pirom's tours aren't going, neither should you. If you get the all-clear, don't

● *Sai Ngam – page* 174.

be surprised to come across several army checkpoints along Route 2121 or even have an armed escort assigned to you. Distant sounds of shelling are considered quite normal.

The small laterite Prasat Ta Meuan was built in the 12th to 13thC reign of Jayavarman VII as a resting place for pilgrims on their journey between Phimai and Angkor. The nearby **Prasat Ta Meuan Tot** is a larger and more impressive monument, now tangled amongst the roots of trees. Also dating from Jayavarman VII's reign, it's believed to have been attached to a hospital, one of many built on the king's orders.

Right on the border and built on a small hill is **Prasat Ta Meuan Thom**, obviously once a major temple on the road to Angkor. Badly damaged by recent warfare and occupation by the Khmer Rouge (as at Angkor, they find the temples useful as shelters as well as for target practice), the sandstone sanctuary has a stairway leading south towards Angkor: Cambodian territory is just a few steps away.

The southern gate is also the most ornate, though you have to look around elsewhere for some pieces of its design, haphazardly re-arranged in a short burst of restoration enthusiasm. Crumbling and sinking, and surrounded by jungle, with the occasional shell-burst to break the silence, this temple has an unbeatable aura of danger and decay.

Moving into safer ground to the north, a couple of kilometres south of Prasat village off Route 214, you'll come across the tiny **Prasat Ban Phluang** (open daily 7.30 am to 6 pm). Dating from the 11th to 12thC, it has been extensively restored, revealing some fine carvings, especially on the eastern pediment and porch.

PRASAT SIKHORAPHUM
This sizeable Khmer sanctuary, 30 km NE of Surin on Route 226 (and accessible from Surin by bus or train) is notable for its five **brick prangs surrounded by moats**, and the beautiful **carvings** from Hindu mythology on the tallest, central prang. In Angkor Wat style, they date from the late 11thC. As with most Khmer temples, this one now houses Buddhist images in the main prang.

PRASAT KHAO PHRA VIHARN
One of the grandest monuments in South-East Asia, Khao Phra Viharn (known as Preah Vihear in Cambodian) has the misfortune to be situated in the thick of current Khmer Rouge battles with the Cambodian Army, just across the Thai-Cambodian border. At the time of writing, the 10thC temple had recently been taken over by a small force of Khmer Rouge rebels, with élite Thai troops keeping close watch just 2 km away across the border. See warnings about travel to the area, under Prasat Ta Meuan, page 179.

Practically inaccessible from the Cambodian side, and for many years the subject of a border tug-of-war between Thailand and Cambodia, it was finally declared to be on Cambodian territory by the International Court of Justice in the 1960s and opened to the public in 1991 – only to close promptly again when the Cambodian Army started its annual dry-season offensive against the Khmer Rouge. If the situation has calmed down and the border has re-opened (check with TAT), it's easiest to reach the site on a day trip from Si Saket or Ubon Ratchathani, 106 km or 150 km to the north. If you're coming from Bangkok, it might

be worth enquiring about weekend train-and-accommodation tour packages from Hualamphong Station, previously organized by the State Railways, although the weekend crowds are certainly not conducive to calm appreciation of the place.

The most dramatic aspect of Phra Viharn is its position, on top of a 600-m-high hill, with a view of the Thai plains to the west and a sheer drop to the Cambodian jungle to the south. The hill itself was considered sacred centuries before the Khmers began building the present temple in the 10thC (nearly a hundred years before Angkor Wat).

The complex extends north to south for 850 m with a naga avenue rising 120 m from the bottom of the hill to the sanctuary at the top. Five gopuras line the route, leading to a ruined prang within a courtyard, surrounded by galleries, although those on the north and south sides have crumbled. There obviously hasn't been much chance yet for extensive restoration work – much of the naga balustrade and two gopuras lie in a heap of laterite and sandstone blocks – but the carvings everywhere indicate the former splendour of the sanctuary. Note especially the **lintel** on the second gopura's southern doorway, showing Shiva and Uma sitting on Shiva's bull; and on the second gopura, a finely-executed **lintel of Vishnu** in the Hindu creation myth.

If Khao Prah Viharn is fully restored, it will undoubtedly be one of the most prized sites in the region, an outstanding legacy of Khmer craftmanship.

SI SAKET ✕
Situated 61 km West of Ubon Ratchathani, and easily accessible by train from Bangkok, this provincial capital is waiting for nearby Prasat Khao Prah Viharn to open to tourists in order to reap its rewards as a suitable base for visitors. Meanwhile, no one bothers to stop here. But if you want to stay somewhere quieter and simpler than Ubon while you explore little-known Khmer ruins or Isaan countryside in the area, Si Saket will suit you well.

SURIN
See Thailand Overall: 3, page 69.

UBON RATCHATHANI
See Thailand Overall: 3, pages 70-2.

RECOMMENDED HOTELS

BURIRAM
Tepnakorn Hotel, BB; 139 Jira Road; *tel. and fax 044 613400.*

On the south-eastern edge of town, so not brilliantly convenient for bus connections, but if you need a few modern comforts after tramping round the ruins, this has the goods. Rooms are all air-conditioned.

Buriram Hotel, BB; 148 Niwat Road; *tel. 044611740; fax 044 612147.*

Another edge-of-town hotel (this time to the north-west), Buriram is a newer, posher reincarnation of the old Krung Rome Hotel.

The air-conditioned rooms here are decent enough, if a little dull.

Thai Hotel, B-BB; 38/1 Romburi Road, *tel. 044 612462; fax 044 612461.*

The best of the bunch in the town centre, with a wide range of fan or air-conditioned rooms.

PHIMAI
Old Phimai Guest House, B; Mu 1 *Chomsudasapet Road – off the main road to the ruins; tel. 044 471725.*

For budget accommodation, this beats anything in Khorat: attractive rooms in an old wooden house, with a friendly owner and great atmosphere. Rooms (and dormitory accommodation) are fan-only.

Phimai Hotel, B-BB; 305/1-2 *Haruthairom Road – near the bus station; tel. 044 471689.*

If you need air-conditioning, or rooms with attached bath, this is your only choice in town. There are more modest fan-rooms, too, but you'd be better off staying at the Old Phimai Guest House for those.

SI SAKET
Phrom Phiman, B-BB; 849/1d Lak *Meuang Road; tel. 045-611141.*

Your best budget bet: a choice of fan or air-conditioned rooms in a simple, friendly hotel.

Kessiri Hotel, BBB; 1102-5 Khukhan *Road; tel. 045 614007; fax 045 612144.*

Incongruously up-market, boasting city frills such as a roof-top swimming pool and satellite TV.

RECOMMENDED RESTAURANTS

BURIRAM
Phawn Phen, B-BB; Romburi Road, *near the Thai Hotel.*

For cheap and delicious Thai or Chinese dishes, this town-centre restaurant is a reliable, popular choice.

Beer House, B-BB; Romburi Road.

Just down the road from Phawn Phen, this is a relaxing open-air place specializing in barbecued seafood.

Night market, B; *junction of Samatakan and Thani Roads.*

Great for people-watching and soaking up the local atmosphere, as well as snacking on Isaan or Chinese fare.

PHIMAI
Baiteiy, B-BB; Chomsudasapet Road.

The most popular place in town, especially among travellers (you can pick up useful travel information here, as well as rent bikes). The mostly Thai dishes are excellent and there are also a few vegetarian choices.

Night market, B; *at the south-eastern edge of the ruins.*

Try this for cheap Thai and Isaan dishes, and for whiling away the evening hours.

Sai Ngam, BB; *beside the huge banyan tree, a couple of kilometres north-east of town.*

A favourite day-tripper's place for lunch, so prices aren't cheap, but the location beside the banyan and lake is very pleasant.

North-Western Thailand

The Mae Hong Son Loop - Part One

460 km; map Nelles 1: 1,500,000

Mae Hong Son is Thailand's most north-westerly province, hugging the Burmese border behind a shield of mountains. Its remoteness and its landscape of cool forested hills are the main reason for coming here: the provincial capital, Mae Hong Son, is an increasingly popular centre for hill-tribe treks, though it's still just a small town, delightfully quiet and low-key, with none of Chiang Mai's razzmatazz. With daily flights from Chiang Mai, it's easily accessible, too, though you should really travel overland at least one way to make the most of the mountains.

There are two choices of route. This itinerary follows the southern one from Chiang Mai along Highway 108: it gives you the chance to detour to Doi Inthanon National Park, which boasts the country's highest peak and some of its most spectacular waterfalls. Mae Sariang, near the border, gives you your first taste of Burmese influences which gradually increase as you head north to Mae Hong Son, populated by many Burmese and Shan immigrants.

If you have the time and the stomach for long, winding mountain roads, the northern route back to Chiang Mai on Highway 1095 completes one of the most spectacular loops in Thailand, with more possibilities for trekking (and caving and river rafting) on the way. Local Explorations: 5 gives the details.

For the itinerary described here, you should allow at least four days (including overnight stops in Doi Inthanon and Mae Sariang). And if you're a really keen trekker, you might even want to commit yourself to another seven days and walk all the way back to Chiang Mai.

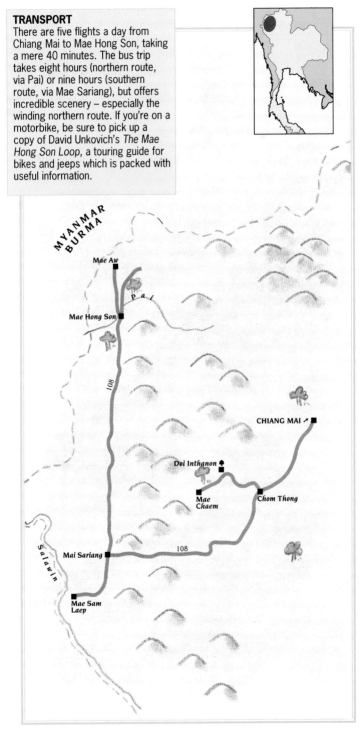

TRANSPORT
There are five flights a day from Chiang Mai to Mae Hong Son, taking a mere 40 minutes. The bus trip takes eight hours (northern route, via Pai) or nine hours (southern route, via Mae Sariang), but offers incredible scenery – especially the winding northern route. If you're on a motorbike, be sure to pick up a copy of David Unkovich's *The Mae Hong Son Loop*, a touring guide for bikes and jeeps which is packed with useful information.

1:2,000,000

SIGHTS & PLACES OF INTEREST

CHIANG MAI
See Thailand Overall: 1, pages 36-9.

DOI INTHANON NATIONAL PARK 🏨
This vast 1,000-sq.-km park SW *of Chiang Mai* covers an area of mist-shrouded hills and forested mountain ranges, including the country's highest peak, the 2,565-m **Doi Inthanon**. Popular among visitors for its waterfalls and hiking trails, it also attracts many serious naturalists and ornithologists: there are nearly 400 bird species to be found in its moist evergreen forests, including the ashy-throated leaf warbler and lesser white-throat pigeon, found nowhere else in Thailand, and the yellow-bellied flowerpecker, the largest of its kind in the country.

Wild fauna hasn't survived so well (what the hunters haven't got, the destruction of the habitat has finished off) but the rare Assamese macaque and Phayre's langur are believed to hide out here still, as well as two tiny Himalayan species – Père David's vole and the Szechuan burrowing shrew, found only at the summit. Flowers flourish, especially at the higher elevations, where you'll find orchids, moss and other epiphytic plants. An unique sphagnum moss bog, which is just below the summit, is particularly rich in both bird life and flora.

The park's mountain slopes are also home to several thousand Hmong and Karen hill-tribe villagers whose terraced rice and vegetable fields can be seen along the road to the summit, a winding 47-km route from Highway 108 that starts at **Chom Thong**, 58 km southwest of Chiang Mai. You can pick up regular buses from Chiang Mai to Chom Thong where songthaews go up to Doi Inthanon. Some turn off 10 km before the summit for Mae Chaem, 20 km to the south-west. Others stop at the first major falls, **Mae Klang**, where you have to pick up another songthaew. Overall, you're better off with your own wheels (or on a tour from Chiang Mai).

Mae Klang Falls are just 8 km from the highway, which means that they are crowded and commercialized. (The **visitors' centre** with maps and bird lists is just a kilometre beyond.) But keep going another 11 km and you'll find the

dramatic **Vachiratan Falls**, crashing down a granite escarpment. The **Siriphum Falls**, in another 11 km, near the park headquarters, are twin falls (named after King Bhumiphol and Queen Sirikit) forming a dramatic backdrop to the park bungalows. You can also detour off the road to the summit just a couple of kilometres after the turn-off from the highway, to reach the spectacular **Mae Ya Falls**, 14 km to the south-west along a rough track. Reputed to be the highest in Thailand, they plunge over 250 m to the river below. There are five more waterfalls along the road to Mae Chaem, including the pretty and rarely crowded **Mae Pan Falls**.

If you're more interested in the hill tribes, you'll find several rough trails off the road to the summit leading to their villages. One of the most interesting and easiest to follow starts at Km 23 and passes several Karen villages *en route*, including the large village of **Ban Pha Mon**, before rejoining the summit road at Km 31.

Trails near or towards the summit are among the most beautiful for trekking (but watch out for leeches in the wet season). These currently require guides: ask at the headquarters for details.

As for the summit itself, don't raise your hopes: an ugly Air Force radar station and car park crowns the peak, though Thais still like to come here to visit the shrine and stupa containing the ashes of Chiang Mai's last sovereign, King Inthawichayanon (after whom the peak is named). Another chedi, **Phra Mahathat Naphamethanidon**, 5 km before the summit, is an even more incongruous eyesore, a lavish modern monument built by the Air Force to commemorate King Bhumiphol's 60th birthday.

Be sure to bring a sweater or jacket if you visit Doi Inthanon in the cool season (the best time): it can get surprisingly cold in these high, misty hills.

MAE AW
See Treks and Day Trips from Mae Hong Son, page 185.

MAE HONG SON 🏨 ✕
This isolated mountain town, *270 km (and around eight hours by bus) NW of Chiang Mai*, took a long time to come on to

TREKS AND DAY TRIPS FROM MAE HONG SON

Nearly every guesthouse and hotel in Mae Hong Son, as well as the tour agencies in town, offer treks and day trips. The most common day trip attraction is to the **'long-neck' Padaung tribe** on the Burmese border. The women of this small hill tribe – refugees from Burma – have traditionally worn brass rings around their necks (adding more as they get older) making their necks look abnormally long. In fact, it's their collarbones and ribs which are pushed down with the weight. These days, only a few women still continue the custom and most of these are under the control of Karen and Thai operators who charge tourists an exorbitant fee for the dubious privilege of photographing and staring at the women.

Less controversial is the trip to **Mae Aw**, 22 km to the north, off Highway 1095. This Chinese Kuomintang village, high on the Burmese border, is home to former Nationalist soldiers and their families who fled China after the communist takeover. Now it's main attraction is its fantastic views over Burma. You can easily get to Mae Aw yourself – songthaews leave Mae Hong Son in the morning for the two-hour journey – but check beforehand that the coast is clear: there are occasional skirmishes in this area with drug warlord Khun Sa's Muang Tai Army. *En route*, and often included in organized tours, are several hill-tribe villages; the wild and roaring **Pha Sua Falls**, 15 km before Mae Aw; and **Tham Plaa (Fish Cave)**, just off the highway. The cave's underground lake has giant blue carp, who live a fat and happy life, constantly fed by devotees seeking merit.

The best mountain views south of Mae Hong Son are from the Hmong village of **Ban Maekovafe** (yes, it does sound like microwave – it's named after the radio mast on the peak), about 36 km south-east of Mae Hong Son. Its dramatic panorama of the Burmese hills make it a popular destination for day trips. Included on the way back are the **hot springs**

• *Padaung woman.*

near the Shan village of Ban Phabong.

River rafting trips on the Pai River are increasingly popular. The favourite day-long outings start either from the pier at **Ban Huay Deua**, 8 km south-west of Mae Hong; or a shorter down-river excursion from **Sop Soi**, 10 km north-west, to Soppong (not the village of the same name on Highway 1095). Some agencies can organize outings on the less-visited Samat River to the south-east of town.

Many of the organized **treks** from Mae Hong Son also include some rafting (and/or elephant rides), although it's the local hill tribes who are usually the main attraction. The most popular three-to-four day treks are to the north-west border area, passing Karen, Hmong and Shan (Thai Yai) villages. The areas towards Soppong and Pai are becoming over-crowded with visitors.

If it's the trekking not the tribes you want, you can always consider the six-to ten-day marathon to Chiang Mai – it really will test your leg muscles.

Tour agencies in Mae Hong Son have had a tendency to come and go, but two of the longest-established are **Namrin Tour**, 5/2 Khunlun Praphat Road (tel. 053 611857), run by the enterprising former Bangkok native, 'Dam' Banlang Pantarak; and **Don Enterprises**, 77/1 Khunlun Praphat Road (tel. 053 612236 and fax 053 611682), whose formidable white-bearded Burmese boss, Aswin Bunyodayana, oversees a staff made up entirely of Karen Burmese.

the travellers' scene. A small settlement was first established here in 1831 by the Prince of Chiang Mai who had sent expeditions into the area to search for the highly-revered white elephants. But it was only in 1968 that a paved road connected Mae Hong Son to Chiang Mai and only in 1989 that the first traffic lights were installed. In the 1990s Mae Hong Son started to get into the limelight as a refreshing, more peaceful alternative to Chiang Mai, with daily flights from Chiang Mai and a few deluxe resorts and hotels catering to tour groups on quick visits. Even Hollywood has discovered the place, filming several blockbusters in the area, including *Air America* starring Mel Gibson.

But you'd hardly call Mae Hong Son glamorous. Though the trekking business is growing, this is still a backwater, with little actually to do in town. It's the tranquil and cool mountain setting which is its greatest allure (bring a sweater for the chilly nights and misty mornings), and the Burmese influence which is the most intriguing part of its atmosphere. In addition to the many Shan inhabitants (a large ethnic group,

• *Wat Si Boonruang* – page 188.

also called Thai Yai, who make up Burma's north-east Shan State) there have been more recent influxes of Burmese refugees (both Karen villagers and students) fleeing from Burma's military rule. Chances are that you'll meet some of them during your stay as many are now unofficially involved in the tourism and trekking business, thanks to their excellent English and in-depth knowledge of the area.

The Burmese-style temples are the most obvious cultural influence. In the south-east of town, just off the main Khunlun Praphat Road, you'll find the atmospheric heart of Mae Hong Son: the **Jong Kham Lake** (almost small enough to be a pond) with two photogenic temples on the far side, their typically Burmese multi-tiered wooden spires framed against a mountainous backdrop. **Wat Jong Kham** (the one to the east) was built in 1827 by the former Shan ruler of Mae Hong Son and boasts a gilded, sparkling sermon throne set in a typically spacious *viharn*.

Next door, in the same compound, is **Wat Jong Klang,** which has some exquisite small glass paintings of the *Jataka* (stories of the Buddha's previous lives), reminiscent of Indian miniatures, in the far left corner. The room behind has an intriguing collection of wooden figures representing the *Jataka* and brought over from Burma in the late 1850s. They include some endearing characters, especially the tattooed men and the beautifully-dressed women. Don't miss the equally endearing sign at the entrance to the room: 'Please switch on electric lamp, get in sightseeing after that be off it offering meritorious deed for electricity. Thank you for your generosity.'

After the lake, my next favourite haunt in Mae Hong Son is the **market**, at the north end of town on Phanit Wattana Road. It's especially lively in the early morning when you can feast on hot soy milk and fresh doughnuts for just a few *baht* and rub shoulders with hill-tribe women as they shop, poring over mounds of melons and piles of pigs' trotters.

Back towards the main road, pop in to see **Wat Hua Wiang** whose renovated bot is as fancy as a Christmas tree decoration, its three-tiered wooden tower edged with lacey white woodwork. Inside, within a wood-panelled, iron-grilled cage sits a magnificent Buddha image in Mandalay style. Called the **Chao Phlakakhaeng**, it's swathed in saffron cloth, from the ends of his dangling earlobes to the tips of his elegant fingers.

The **main street** itself is now mostly devoted to restaurants and tour agencies, souvenir and handicraft shops. But there are still a few old cavernous Burmese-style shophouses, including the wonderful treasure trove of junk and antiques called **Chokeakradet** at number 65. Opened in 1978 by Sitichai Kalpanaprai (a native of Nakhon Sawan) it's chockablock with loot from Burma, including antique wall clocks and 100-year-old German pressure lamps, as well as specialities such as Japanese Samurai swords and Thai Yai lacquerware and image tables. Sitichai's weakness is obviously for rusty bits of metal: piles of the stuff lie inside and outside the shop. You could probably find just the thing you need to cobble together your

• *Soppong, selecting beans.*

ropey motorbike or truck. But the best items are at the very back of the warehouse, past the old china and typewriters, bells and alms bowls. Take a peek here at towering Burmese drums, dangling puppets and beautifully carved dancing figures. Prices are by no means cheap, but Sitichai accepts Visa card purchases if you get seriously tempted.

At dusk, the best place to be is at the **Wat Doi Kong Mu**, built 150 years ago at the top of the 1,500-m-high hill on the western edge of town. The two chedis here are locally revered, but the view is even more alluring, stretching over the hills and fields below and confirming Mae Hong Son's sense of rural peace and isolation.

MAE SAM LAEP

Before the Burmese Army finally captured the rebel Karen National Union's headquarters at Manerplaw in early 1995 (see page 89 in Thailand Overall: 5), it used to be a fun adventure to hop on a songthaew from Mae Sariang for the rugged 46-km journey to Mae Sam Laep on the Salawin River border, and then take a long-tail boat to the Manerplaw area. For a time, there was even a small guesthouse by a beautiful riverside beach for the crazy *farangs* who made it this far.

Now the Burmese Army are in control of the area, though at the time of writing skirmishes are continuing with the diehard KNU. Even a month after the takeover, however, the morning songthaew was still leaving for the busy smuggling village of Mae Sam Laep, but you'd be advised to check at your guesthouse in Mae Sariang on the current situation before making the trip. If all's quiet and safe, the Riverside Guesthouse even organizes its own trips to Mae Sam Laep during the dry season. There's not actually much to see once you get here – it's the arduous journey fording dozens of rivers which is usually more exciting than the village itself – but if blackmarket frontiers give you a *frisson*, this is as rewarding a place as any along the Burmese border. The best approach is simply to sit back in one of the restaurants and watch the shady goings-on.

MAE SARIANG ⋈ ✕

If you've come all the way from Chiang Mai in one day you'll be glad to reach Mae Sariang: it may be only 183 km and four hours away by bus, but the tortuous mountain roads make it seem much longer.

Mae Sariang itself is a one-traffic-light frontier town which has obviously prospered from trade (legal or otherwise) with nearby Burma. As you walk along the two main north-south roads alongside the Yuam River, you'll notice plenty of incongruous evidence of wealth: smart suburban-style villas among old-fashioned teak shophouses whose cool dark interiors are furnished with reclining wooden chairs, typically Burmese.

Other Burmese influences are particularly obvious in the town's two temples just south of the bus station: **Wat Sri Boonruang** has a typically Burmese multi-tiered **bot** while the adjacent **Wat Utthayarom's** teak floor positively glows from decades of bare-feet polishing.

Other than Mae Sam Laep (see above) nearby hill-tribe villages (mostly Karen) are Mae Sariang's only other day-trip attractions: some are within walking or songthaew distance, but for others you'll need your own wheels (preferably a motorbike). Check at the Riverside Guest House, too, for details of their own tours.

RECOMMENDED HOTELS

DOI INTHANON NATIONAL PARK

Adequate National Park bungalows (sleeping at least four) are set in a leafy area by the park headquarters. You'll have to book ahead (tel. 02 579 0529) if you want to stay during weekends or holidays. Tents and blankets are also available if you fancy camping.

MAE HONG SON

Holiday House, B; *Pradit Jongkham Road; tel. 053 611146.*

Run by a Burmese student refugee couple – Chocho and 'Moscow' – who speak excellent English, this is a simple guesthouse just across the road from the lake and its Fitness Park. Moscow will be happy to whizz you around by motorbike if you want to see the sights.

Jongkam Guesthouse, B; *U-Dorn-chaointesh Road.*

A great budget location for families: the row of rooms and individual bungalows here are in a spacious grassy area on the north side of the lake, a step away from the Fitness Park. Facilities and information are better at the sister-establishment next door (Prince's) though the standard of cleanliness is about as low.

Prince's Guesthouse, B; *37 U-Dorn-chaointesh Road; tel. 053 611137.*

Pleasantly Bohemian, with an upstairs patio with great views of the lake and plenty of cushions for lounging on. The friendly lads who run the place tend to be more interested in chatting up the girls and strumming their guitars than doing any housework.

Friend House, B; *20 Pradit Jongkham Road; tel. 053 611647.*

Six clean and spacious rooms in a renovated teak house on the north-western corner of the lake, run by the friendly Kookai. The upstairs rooms have balcony lake views.

Piya Guesthouse, B-BB; *1/1 Khunlun Praphat Road; tel. 053 611260; fax 053 612308.*

Smart and orderly bungalows with

air-conditioning and attached bathrooms, or cheaper fan rooms at the back overlooking a scruffy garden are both available.

Baiyoke Chalet Hotel, BB-BBB; 90 Khunlun Praphat Road; tel. 053 611486.
Comfortable rooms with all the usual facilities in a businesslike establishment.

Holiday Inn Mae Hong Son, BBBB; 114/5-7 Khunlun Praphat Road; tel. 053 611390, Bangkok reservations, 02 254 2614.
Best hotel in town, with all the frills tour groups expect, including a swimming pool and tennis courts.

Rim Nam Klang Doi Resort, BB-BBB; 108 Ban Huey Daer; tel. 053 612142; fax 053 612086.
One of several resorts several kilometres south-west of town favoured by Thais, this is a delightful retreat if you have your own transport. A range of rooms and thatched bungalows are set in a beautiful riverside location, with loads of space for kids to run around in. Avoid weekends and holidays when the place gets packed with Thai tour groups.

MAE SARIANG
Riverside Guesthouse, B; 85 Laeng Phanit Road; tel. 053 681188.
Set beside the Yuam River, this old travellers' favourite has so-so rooms but an unbeatable riverside view and terrace. When I last visited, at the time of the major Burmese Army offensive against the Karens, refugee rebels were crowded into the thatched bungalows across the river and the place was buzzing with journalists. Come here for up-to-date news on the latest developments, and travel information (or tours) to sensitive border areas.

See View Guest House, B; 70 Wiangmai Road; tel. 053 681556.
Chances are that See View's owner, Aekkasan Wiruchsilpa, will be waiting with his pick-up van when you stagger off the bus from Chiang Mai or Mae Hong Son, hoping to scoop you up for a stay at his guesthouse just across the river.
The new set of spacious clean rooms (with bathrooms) are fair value, though they're in an unattractive concrete block in a rather arid riverside setting. The thatched dining area gets higher marks for aesthetics.

RECOMMENDED RESTAURANTS

MAE HONG SON
Padeem Restaurant, B; 84 Khunlun Praphat Road; tel. 053 620205.
Always packed with both locals and farangs, this is a cheap and cheerful eaterie, with standard Thai and Chinese fare.

Khai Muk, B-BB; 23 U-Dornchaointesh Road; tel. 053 612092; credit cards MC, V.
Attractive pavilion-style restaurant with efficient service. The house speciality, duck with crispy basil leaves, is so good it's hard to recommend anything else, but the fried spare ribs with honey and the eggplant salad come pretty close.

Fern Restaurant, BB; 87 Khunlun Praphat Road; tel. 053 611374; credit cards, AE, MC.
Smart and slick, with pleasant open-air dining area at the back and an extensive, often imaginative menu: try the river fish curry or fried spicy pumpkin patties.

MAE SARIANG
Inthira Restaurant, B-BB; 170/1 Wiang Mai Road; tel. 053 681529; credit cards MC, V.
Almost as popular as the Renu Restaurant opposite, with a tempting choice of dishes and pleasantly casual atmosphere.

Nong Boor Farm (also called Hnong Bua Garden Restaurant), BB; Ban Tung Leng, across the bridge, 1 km W of town; tel. 053 681237.
The sort of 'rural' restaurant Thais love, with individual thatched pavilions set among lychee trees and coconut palms and rather grubby lotus ponds. The English menu lists some intriguing items: how about a 'marine pizza Thai style' or 'water mimosa salad in lime juice'?

189

North-Western Thailand

The Mae Hong Son Loop: Part Two

Map Nelles 1: 1,500,000

The northern route between Chiang Mai and Mae Hong Son along High-way 1095 is one of the most dramatic in north-west Thailand, twist-ing through the mountains up to several high passes with panoramic views of the Burmese hills to the west and the cultivated valleys below. Combine it with the southern route between Chiang Mai and Mae Hong Son described in Local Explorations: 4, and you have a superb circuit of the north-west border country.

Much of Highway 1095 was originally built by the Japanese during the Second World War for moving troops and supplies to Burma. Now that it's paved all the way it's an increasingly popular route for adventur-ous travellers who are discovering it's more than just a thrilling way to reach Mae Hong Son, the mountain town and trekking centre at the end of the highway.

Around Pai and Soppong is an area that's fast becoming the adventure travel heartland of Northern Thailand: as well as trekking to hill-tribe vil-lages you can also go rafting on the Khong and Pai Rivers, rock climbing on the limestone cliffs, or spelunking in some of the most spectacular caverns and cave systems in Asia.

You can of course follow the Mae Hong Son loop in either direction, or just do one part if time is short. For this section you should allow at least three days, stopping in Pai and/or Soppong for treks and cave explorations. Serious speleoligists will want much more: there are more than 200 caves and more than 50 km of subterranean passageways in the limestone hills, and most of them have yet to be thoroughly explored.

TRANSPORT

Buses run six times daily on this northern route between Mae Hong Son and Chiang Mai via Pai and Soppong. They take about eight hours (four between Chiang Mai and Pai, three-and-a-half to four between Pai and Mae Hong Son). In addition there's one daily minibus doing the route from Pai, but unless you're desperate to get there in a hurry, I wouldn't recommend risking your life with their crazy drivers on this hair-raising mountain road. Bicycles and motorbikes are available for rent both in Pai and Mae Hong Son.

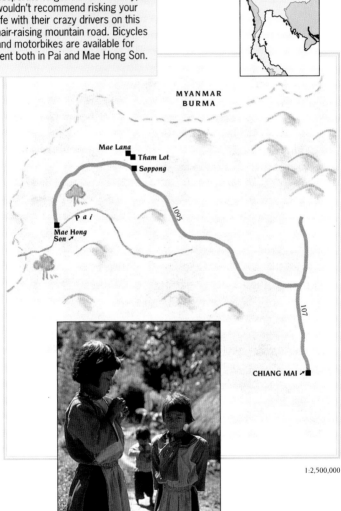

1:2,500,000

SIGHTS & PLACES OF INTEREST

BAN NAM KHONG ⌘

Just a couple of kilometres N of Highway 1095, down a dirt track just E of Mae Suya (40 km NE of Mae Hong Son), Ban Nam Khong is worth heading for if you want a base for exploring two of the most daunting caves in the Nam Khong valley: Tham Pha Daeng and Tham Nam Lang. The simple Wilderness Lodge here (see Recommended Hotels, below) can provide reliable information on the caves (as well as suggestions on walks to hill-tribe villages in the area).

Tham Pha Daeng is the easier of the two caves to explore, a 1.4 km through-cave which requires some low crawling and wading in neck-high water – which is why you should only tackle it during the dry season. The reward for your two-hour effort is the fabulous limestone formations and **coffin caves** – caverns where ancient wooden coffins have been found. Similar hollowed-out coffins have been discovered in many of the region's caves, and though their exact origins are unknown they have been found to date back at least 1,700 years – the oldest yet found was 2,200 years old. Local lore claims they were built by *pi man* cave spirits, but some coffins at least have been found to contain pottery, jewellery and bronze implements indicating a more human involvement.

Tham Nam Lang is a giant. At 9 km, it's one of the longest caves in South-East Asia, with vast chambers, magnificent crystal flowstones and a stunning entrance chamber. It should only be tackled by experienced cavers with proper equipment, in the dry season. For more details, contact Wilderness Lodge or Cave Lodge (see Recommended Hotels, page 193).

RECOMMENDED HOTELS

BAN NAM KHONG
Wilderness Lodge, B.
The best place to base yourself if you want to explore caves in the Nam Khong Valley. Huts and beds are basic, but the remote setting is wonderful. This is a sister-establishment to Cave Lodge (see page 193).

MAE LANA
Mae Lana Guest House, B.
On the edge of the village, this simple little guesthouse has plain rooms and dormitory accommodation and can serve up surprisingly ambitious fare.

PAI
Pai River Lodge, B; *riverside lane, south-east of the bus stop.*
A dozen huts in a spacious, grassy riverside location makes this a great budget choice for travellers with kids. The drawbacks are a dozy staff and occasional outbreaks of noise, due to a school sports' hall next door and the town's PA system which blasts you awake at 6 am (but still, it means you can watch the sun rising over the hills).

Pin's Huts, B; *a short walk towards the river from the bus stop - follow the signs.*
Pin and his new German wife, Katie, have made this cluster of huts in a beautiful spot by the river a very friendly, relaxing hideaway. Some guests end up staying stay here for months.

Charlie's House, B; *9/3 Rungsiyanon Road; tel. 053 699039.*
Particularly popular with German visitors, this is a spic-and-span complex of rooms and bungalows in a tiled, paved setting in the town centre. There's even a twee bungalow for honeymooners, called Romantic House. Pity about the surly young staff.

Rim Pai Cottage, BB; *17 Moo 3 Viang Tai; tel. 053 699133; fax 053 699234.*
The most enchanting place in Pai, with comfortable A-frame bungalows and rooms in a longhouse set in a lush garden near the river. The 'Thai Yai' two-room wood-panelled complex, with shared bathroom, is perfect for families. My favourite is the riverside tree house, wrapped in red and white bougainvillea. Prices include breakfast.

Pai Mountain Lodge, BB; *7 km north-west of town near the Maw Paeng Falls.*
A favourite with Thais, this is a delightful retreat: comfortable bungalows are geared for a minimum of four which make them a bargain for families.

CHIANG MAI
See Thailand Overall: 1, pages 36-9.

MAE HONG SON
See Local Explorations: 4, pages 184-7.

MAE LANA 🛏

This Shan (Thai Yai) village lies 61 *km* NE *of Mae Hong Son, 6 km up a steep track off* Highway 1095. If you want a simple base for some remote hill-tribe treks, Mae Lana is ideal: there's a couple of small guesthouses in the village, one of which (see Recommended Hotels, page 192) can provide maps and valuable information on where to go.

Within a day's walk there are Red and Black Lahu villages including one, **Ban Huay Hea**, very close to the Burmese border, which also has simple accommodation. (The Red and Black Lahu are two of the five main groups of the Lahu hill-tribe, so-called after the predominant colour of their dress and/or shoulder bags.) If you fancy some more strenuous exploration, you can even walk all the way to Soppong via Tham Lot, a 20-km route to the south-east.

The scenery is stunning around here and the whole area still largely unspoilt, although it's already popular with trekking tours from Mae Hong Son. Even Hollywood has discovered its appeal: an entire Vietnamese-style hill village was built near Mae Lana for the filming of *Operation Dumbo Drop*, and was subsequently used in the more recent filming of *The Quest*. Unless another director takes a fancy to it, it's supposed to be turned into a boy scout camp.

Be sure to check at the guesthouse on the current border situation if you're heading north into remote areas (and always tell someone where you're going): drug warlord Khun Sa and his Muang Tai Army aren't far away across the border (see page 55 in Thailand

SOPPONG
Kemarin Garden Lodge, B; *just off the main road.*
A simple, friendly guesthouse run by the articulate Udon.

Jungle Guest House, B; 1 *km* W *of town.*
A well-established favourite, with dormitories and huts. This is a useful place for information on treks in the area, too.

Cave Lodge, B; *Ban Tham, near Tham Lot; radio tel.* 536 11711, *ext.* 822.
Run by Australian John Spies and his Thai wife, this was one of the first guesthouses in the area, offering simple dormitory beds, bungalows and meals. It's the best place for information on caves and treks in the Pangmapa area: John has been exploring here since 1984 and together with Australian caver John Dunkley has discovered and mapped hundreds of caves and subterranean passageways.

==================================
RECOMMENDED RESTAURANTS
==================================

Most of the guesthouses above (especially the more remote ones) provide meals, sometimes communal style. For more exotic fare, Pai is your best bet:

PAI
Nong Bia, B-BB; *Chaisongkhram Road.*
A long-established favourite with the locals, serving up tasty Thai and Chinese dishes at reasonable prices.

Thai Yai Restaurant, B-BB; 12 *Rungsiyanon Road; tel.* 053 699093.
The first *farang*-style restaurant in Pai (opened in 1990), it's still one of the best. Local-born, half-Shan Tao and his Scottish wife Andrea provide all the travellers' classics (mueseli, pancakes, fresh brown bread, locally-grown coffee) as well as other *farang* favourites such as home-made carrot cake and delicious sandwiches (also some great Thai dishes). Open to the street and with a small library of books, it's a perfect place for long lazy breakfasts and lunches.

Chez Swan, BB; *Rungsiyanon Road, tel./fax* 053 699111.
If you've been dreaming of steak *au poivre*, a bottle of wine and a taste of real French camembert during your trek in the hills, you'll find the real thing right here. Frenchman Guy Gorias and his Thai-French wife have added a touch of class to Pai with this restaurant.

• *Nort-west border landscape.*

Overall: 2). Apart from the risk of getting caught in crossfire between the MTA and the Thai or Burmese Army, there's always the possibility you may be mistaken by the MTA for an agent of the U.S. Drug Enforcement Agency – or by the Thai Army as a drug-runner.

PAI 🛏 ✕
After a rollicking four-hour bus ride from Chiang Mai along a winding mountain road, Pai comes as a welcome rest stop, conveniently situated about half way from Chiang Mai to Mae Hong Son (which is 111 km and another three to four hours further along Highway 1095).

This laid-back, originally Shan town situated by the Pai River has increasingly geared itself to the growing traffic of young travellers by opening a bunch of cheap guesthouses, restaurants and trekking agencies. There's no better place to take advantage of the trekking, rock climbing or river rafting activities in the area. Or for simply hanging out for a few days: the back lanes are fragrant with jasmine, bright with bougainvillea, and the riverside often busy with local Lahu or Lisu hill-tribe villagers tending their garlic fields.

There are several easy walks you can do around town, including one heading east across the river to the modern hill-top temple of **Wat Phra**

That Mae Yen which isn't particularly interesting but a great spot for gazing over the Pai Valley. If you're here between December and February you may also be able to join organized visits to Lisu or Lahu villages celebrating their New Year festivals. Other ways to relax include a **traditional massage** by graduates of Chiang Mai's Old Medicine Hospital at their house in the riverside lane; and **Thai cookery classes** at Sidewalk Kitchen Restaurant (next to Home Style Kitchen Restaurant, off Chaisongkhram Road).

For more strenuous activities, check out the **treks or river rafting trips** organized by the guesthouses and tour agencies found along the main Rungsiyanon or Chaisongkharm Roads. The two- to four-day treks visit local Lisu, Karen or Lahu villages, sometimes including river rafting and elephant rides on the way, (try **Northern Green Tours** at 87 Chaisongkharm Road, or **Karen Trekking** in Rungsiyanon Road). Tougher trekking (including a five-day trek to Mae Hong Son, with some rafting) is also available at the appropriately-named **No Mercy Trek**, run by the energetic Karen local, Pin of Pin's Huts (see Recommended Hotels, page 192) and his brother Sith. This is also the place to book an elephant ride at the nearby hot springs, 6 km from Pai.

The rainy season (July to December) is the best time for rafting down the Pai River. Frenchman Guy Gorias (of Chez Swan Restaurant) runs the most professional operation in town, **Thai Adventure** (tel./fax 053 699111), using high-tech rubber rafts for a two-day trip to Mae Hong Son (minimum four people). Real white-water fans may be a little disappointed by the lack of wild rapids, but the surrounding landscape is stunning, with several highlights *en route* such as the **Pai Kit** gorges and the 20-cascade **Susa Waterfall**.

SOPPONG 🛏

Some 70 km E of Mae Hong Son, this small busy village on Highway 1095 is increasingly a travellers' haunt, especially for those attracted to the network of caves in the surrounding area known as Pangmapa.

The most famous cave – and now a popular destination for day trippers from Mae Hong Son and Chiang Mai – is **Tham Lot**, about 8 km north of the highway (motorbike taxis in Soppong can speed you there for around B40). Now part of a national park (open 8 am to 5 pm daily), Tham Lot is a spectacular 1.6-km tunnel cave formed by the Lang River pushing its way through a limestone hill. It's relatively easy to explore: guides with lanterns are available for about B100 to take you on the standard two- to three-hour tour, which includes crossing the subterranean river half a dozen times – sometimes by using bamboo bridges, other times by hiring a raft.

The cave's most dramatic attractions are its three higher-level caverns reached by rustic ladders: **Big Column Cavern**, on the right soon after you enter the stunning entrance chamber, features an immense stalactite that's joined a stalagmite to create a 20-m-high, millenia-old column. **Doll Cave**, the second cavern, has hundreds of doll-shaped stalgmites. Nearby is a rare example of prehistoric cave painting: a picture of a deer and a bow and arrow. The final cavern, **Tham Pi Man**, is named after the hollowed-out wooden coffins (see Ban Nam Khong, page 192) which locals believe were made by *pi man* spirits. There are ten here,

• *Lisu girl.*

some propped up by poles.

Tham Lot's exit is even more dramatic than its entrance – especially if you're here at dusk when hundreds of thousands of swifts swoop into the cave's vast exit chamber to swoop resting places with the thousands of bats who simultaneously leave for their night's feeding activity. It's an incredible show after the stillness of the cave.

But if it's the coffins which have grabbed your interest, you might want to visit another easily-accessible cave, **Tham Pi Man** (just north of the highway near Pangmapa village) which has several chambers containing the eery handiwork of the *pi man*.

Other caves that don't demand much spelunking experience are **Tham Long Yaow**, near the Karen village of Ban Muang Paem; the impressive 1-km-long **Tham Pang Kham** through-cave (accessible in dry season only) near the Shan village of Ban Pang Kham; and the dry series of caverns in the cave of **Tham Nam Rin**, near Ban Nam Rin. Local guides are always available from the villages, but if you want more information, contact Cave or Wilderness Lodges (see pages 193 and 192).

THAM LOT

See Soppong, this page.

<u>Western Thailand</u>

The River Kwai Bridge and Three Pagodas Pass

343 km; map, Nelles 1:1,500,000

Most people who head west from Bangkok make Kanchanaburi their only goal. This riverside town is just 128 km west of Bangkok (two to three hours by bus) and a popular weekend destination for both Thais and foreign tourists. They come not only to see the Bridge over the River Kwai (in Thai, Khwae) – built by Allied prisoners of war during the Second World War and made internationally famous in the David Lean film of the same name – but also to visit some of Thailand's most popular national parks, including Erawan and Sai Yok, which boast some of the country's most spectacular waterfalls.

This section, however, takes in a great deal more besides Kanchanaburi, revealing a dramatic corner of the country which still receives surprisingly few visitors. On the itinerary is a recently-cleared part of the jungle-clad Death Railway built by the POWs; a remote 13thC Khmer outpost; a stunning 227-km journey to the mostly Karen and Mon town of Sangkhlaburi, and – at the end of the road in Thailand – a visit to the black market frontier village at the Three Pagodas Pass where you can visit Burma (Myanmar) for the day.

With its unusual (and cheap) raft accommodation on the Khwae Yai River, and its variety of day trips, Kanchanaburi itself could detain you for at least a couple of days, and if you want to make the most of the waterfalls, you'll need another day for each of the national parks. The intriguing border town of Sangkhlaburi, much quieter and less developed than Kanchanaburi, is an ideal place to hang out for a few more days, to enjoy the town's lakeside position and Burmese influences.

If you're heading north afterwards, you can avoid Bangkok by hopping across to Lopburi from Kanchanaburi via Suphanburi. You can then pick up Thailand Overall: 1 to Chiang Mai.

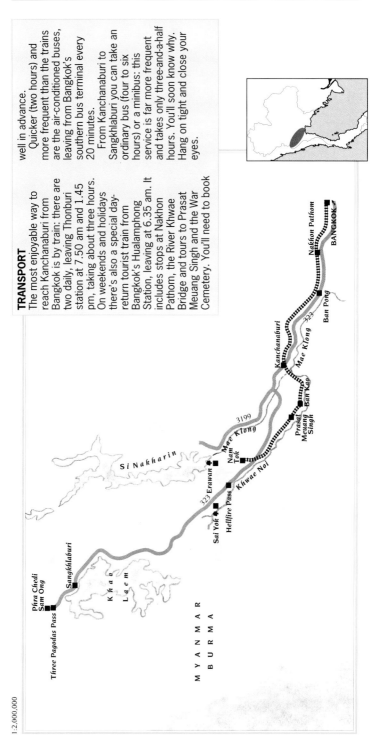

TRANSPORT

The most enjoyable way to reach Kanchanaburi from Bangkok is by train: there are two daily, leaving Thonburi station at 7.50 am and 1.45 pm, taking about three hours. On weekends and holidays there's also a special day-return tourist train from Bangkok's Hualamphong Station, leaving at 6.35 am. It includes stops at Nakhon Pathom, the River Khwae Bridge and tours to Prasat Meuang Singh and the War Cemetery. You'll need to book well in advance.

Quicker (two hours) and more frequent than the trains are the air-conditioned buses, leaving from Bangkok's southern bus terminal every 20 minutes.

From Kanchanaburi to Sangkhlaburi you can take an ordinary bus (four to six hours) or a minibus: this service is far more frequent and takes only three-and-a-half hours. You'll soon know why. Hang on tight and close your eyes.

1:2,000,000

197

SIGHTS & PLACES OF INTEREST

BAN KAO MUSEUM

This small museum (open 8 am to 4.30 pm, from Wednesday to Sunday) is 35 km W of Kanchanaburi and houses neolithic artifacts found in the region, some dating back 10,000 years. It was a Dutch prisoner-of-war, archaeologist Van Heekeren, who, while labouring on the Death Railway during the Second World War, first stumbled on evidence that prehistoric man once made this fertile river valley his home. He returned in the early 1960s with a Thai-Danish team and established that prehistoric 'Mesolithic' man (belonging to a period 10,000 to 4,000 years ago) had lived in rock shelters near the Kwae Noi River and made a mound near Ban Kao both his residence and burial ground.

Among the objects on display here are beautiful coral-coloured stone beads some 3,000 years old; polished stone axes and ornaments of shell, animal bone, bronze and glass (some from a later site) as well as a Mesolithic skeleton and curious tripod-shaped burial jars. One of the most curious displays is the collection of wooden boat-shaped coffins in an annexe outside. Similar ones have also been found in Mae Hong Son in Northern Thailand as well as in China and the Philippines. Though they are thought to be coffins, their boat shape is still something of a mystery.

• Death Railway.

Ban Kao is just 7 km south-east of Prasat Meuang Singh (see pages 203-4) and is best visited at the same time (an hour each is about enough). Although Meuang Singh is near the Tha Kilen railway station, Ban Kao is trickier to reach: you can either hope for a songthaew or motorbike taxi from the station, or hitch, or walk. Best of all, rent a motorbike from Kan'buri or join an organized tour.

ERAWAN NATIONAL PARK ⊨

Situated in the Tenasserim hills 65 km NW of Kanchanaburi, and bordered on the eastern side by the Khwae Yai River, this is one of the most popular national parks in Thailand, thanks to its stunning seven-level waterfall – at its best during or just after the rainy season. The name of the park comes from the rock formation above the falls, said to resemble the three-headed elephant (erawan) of Buddhist-Hindu mythology. The one and only trail in the 550 sq.km park winds up around the falls from the visitor's centre. It's a 2-km walk and scramble (bring sturdy shoes) to the final level. The top is the most secluded spot, with one of the most alluring pools for swimming, though you'll find similarly enticing jungle-clad places for a dip at every level. At weekends, levels one and two in particular are packed with Thai picnickers; come on a weekday if you want a peaceful ambience.

Another popular picnic spot is a couple of kilometres to the north, on the edge of the **Si Nakharin Reservoir**, created when the Khwae Yai River was dammed. A lesser-known attraction in the park is **Phrathat Cave**, 12 km north-west of the visitor's centre (catch a songthaew from the market place near the centre), whose domed chambers positively bulge with stalagmites and stalactites.

Because of the park's popularity, buses and minibuses go there frequently throughout the day from Kanchanaburi, a one- to two-hour journey (most guesthouses have daily tours). Don't leave too late, though: you'll need a full day for enjoying the emerald-green pools, and the last bus back leaves at 4 pm.

HELLFIRE PASS

During the construction of the Thailand to Burma Death Railway (see box, page 202) from 1942 to 1943, the prisoners-of-war encountered some appallingly difficult terrain: dense, malarial jungle and mountains of solid rock through which they had to cut with the most primitive tools.

One of the worst sections was at Konyu, about 80 km north-west of Kanchanaburi and 18 km from Nam Tok. Here, not only one but seven mountain cuttings had to be made within a 3.5-km stretch, as well as embankments and timber trestle bridges. The POWs were made to work round-the-clock; at night, looking down at the skeletal men working by the light of candles and fires in the deepest and most devilish cutting at Konyu, it was like looking into the jaws of Hell – hence the name the POWs gave to this 100-m-long Pass. It took the mostly-Australian POWs 12 weeks to dig and blast and drill through the 17 m of rock. Even today, with the most modern equipment, it's said the work couldn't be done any quicker. By the time it was finished, 69 men had been beaten to death by the disciplinarian guards and more than 600 men had died.

Today, Hellfire Pass is perhaps the most striking war memorial experience in Thailand. A memorial path, first established by the Australian-Thai Chamber of Commerce in 1987, has recently been improved and extended by Australian Rod Beattie, a former civil

• *Erawan National Park.*

engineer living in Kanchanaburi who has hacked through the jungle to find further remains of the track. Rod has ambitious plans to extend the present path on a rougher trail for another 7 km, following the old track all the way to Hintok, site of the infamous Pack of Cards trestle bridge – so-called because it kept collapsing. You can still see bits of original sleepers and remains of concrete supports and stone embankments along this jungle path, but it's the view of the valley below and the realization of how nightmarish the experience must have been that are the most memorable aspects of the site.

For now, you can follow a cement path on a 90-minute circular walk, along part of the track the POWs used to get to work from their camp at Konyu. Another camp was at Hintok, several kilometres away down in the Khwae Noi River valley: the day's 12-hour shift often began with hauling timber through the dense jungle. Hellfire Pass itself stands as an eery memorial surrounded by thick bamboo forest: part of the original rail track was replaced here in 1989 and there is now also a memorial plaque on the rockface in honour of Sir Edward 'Weary' Dunlop, 'the surgeon of the jungle', whose ashes were scattered in the area in April 1994. Rod recounts a hair-raising story about the time they put up the plaque: "We had to return to Kan'buri for some more tools and by the time we got back, it was dark. Suddenly we saw two bodies lying in Hellfire Pass. They turned out to be early arrivals for the ANZAC day ceremony due to start at dawn next morning; they were so exhausted by the time they arrived they had fallen asleep, but they certainly gave us a nasty shock."

Another plaque at the far end of the cutting lists the number of Allied POWs who died during the construction of the Death Railway. A further part of the trail then winds up around the cutting so you can see it from above.

To get to Hellfire Pass by public transport, take a Kanchanaburi to Sangkhlaburi bus along Highway 323 and ask to be let off at **Suanthahaan**, the Army farm behind which the trail begins. The farm is just beyond an old steam engine on the left-hand side of the road.

For one of the best organized tours to Hellfire Pass, contact ex-soldier Danny, an Englishman who runs the Punnee Bar & Café with his Thai wife Punnee (2/15 Ban Nua Road; tel. 034 513503). Either he or Rod Beattie usually leads the day-long tours, which not only include the memorial walk but also take in a visit to Sai Yok, and lunch at a restaurant overlooking the dramatic trestle bridge at the Wang Po viaduct.

KANCHANABURI ⌂ ✕

Just a couple of hours from Bangkok, 'Kan'buri' is a delightful contrast to the big city, surrounded by cave-pitted limestone hills and sugar cane plantations, and situated by the confluence of the Khwae Yai and Khwae Noi Rivers which become the Mae Klong at the southern end of town.

Although Kan'buri's fame rests largely on its role as a prisoner-of-war camp during the Second World War – the Bridge over the River Kwai and the Allied War Cemeteries are its major historical sites – it is also very popular as a base for day trips to nearby attractions such as Erawan and Sai Yok national parks, (see pages 198-9 and 204; try to avoid weekends, when everywhere is packed with Thai tourists).

Arriving by train, you'll find samlors waiting to take you to your guesthouse – those north of the town centre are close by, others are a couple of kilometres to the south of the station. The air-conditioned bus terminal is at the southern end of town, near the useful TAT office on Saengchuto Road (tel. 034 511200). For organized tours, ask at your guesthouse or at one of the private tour operators such as Part Group Travel on Mae Nam Khwae Road (tel. 034 512135). This is a new operation run by U.K.-trained 'Apple' who offers everything from three-hour river trips to day-long cave and waterfall adventures or three-day treks in the Sangkhlaburi region.

Sunrise is the best time to visit the famous **River Kwai Bridge**, which is 4 km north of the town centre (rent a bike or catch a samlor to get here). Later in the day the commercialization of the place (souvenir sellers, hawkers, tour buses disgorging hundreds of day trippers) can ruin your impressions. Not that the steel-arched bridge itself is very dramatic; but when the first train of the day from Kan'buri to Nam Tok (there are only three services daily) arrives at the bridge soon after 6 am and disappears along the misty-morning track you catch a sense of the drama of the place.

When the bridge was first built, in February 1943, it was made entirely of wood. Three months later, a steel bridge – made from materials brought from Java by the Japanese Army – was finished. Twenty months later, the middle section was destroyed by Allied bombing.

After the war, the steel bridge was repaired; part of the structure you see today is still the original. There are also some original Second World War steam locomotives parked just before the bridge: one was found in the early 1970s near the Thai-Burmese border by a team of Australians using a wartime Japanese map. They sold it to the State Railway of Thailand which later sold it to wartime driver Kazumi Sasaki who drove the train from Thonburi to Kan'buri in October 1976.

The most important event of the year for both Kan'buri and its bridge is the ten-day **River Kwai Festival** starting every November 28 to commemorate the Allied bombing of the bridge. With son et lumière and firework shows nightly, and steam engines puffing across the bridge, it's a spectacular occasion which attracts crowds of people. You should book transport and accommodation well in advance if you fancy coming to Kan'buri to see the action.

The gaudy-looking **World War II Museum & Art Gallery** (open 9 am to 4.30 pm daily) just south of the bridge has simply cashed in on the bridge's popularity by throwing together an odd assortment of artifacts in one building (everything from Buddhas and ancient weapons to pots and paintings); and Second World War relics displayed in another building – the most gruesome exhibit being a collection of skeletons of some of the Death Railway's Asian labourers.

For a far more evocative war-time memorial, head back into town to visit the **JEATH War Museum** (open 8.30 am to 6 pm daily) in the grounds of Wat Chaichumpon, beside the Mae Klong River (just west of the TAT office). Established by the wat's abbot, the small display of photographs, paintings and wartime newspaper clips are housed in a reconstructed hut, similar to the ones which housed the Allied POWs. JEATH stands for the six countries involved in the Death Railway: Japan, England, Australia/America, Thailand and Holland.

Perhaps the most horrifying of the exhibits are the crudely-painted scenes (based on sketches done by the POWs) showing the maggot-infested latrines, the torture methods of the Japanese and the Death March of POWs carrying their colleagues who were dying of dysentery and cholera.

Of the 16,000 POWs who died in the outrageous saga of the Death Railway, nearly 9,000 are buried in Kan'buri's two war cemeteries. The larger and more impressive of the two is the **Kanchanaburi War Cemetery** at the north end of Saengchuto Road opposite

DETOUR – WAT THAM SEUA AND WAT THAM KHAO NOI

These ornate hill-top temples, right next to each other, lie *about 15 km SE of Kanchanaburi* and make a pleasant excursion into the countryside. From the temples' main terraces you get a wonderful view of the surrounding rice fields, river valley, and distant mountain ranges.

Wat Tham Khao Noi (Little Hill Cave Monastery) is traditionally Chinese in design and more richly decorated than its Thai-designed neighbour. Steps leading up to the seven-tiered Chinese pagoda on the top level pass several halls and shrines on different levels. The first houses a glass-encased laughing Buddha, surrounded by cabinets of gilded, gaudy figures; the next a glass-encased Kuan Yin (Goddess of Mercy), and the third – the most impressive – has gilded black doors revealing a gilded seated Buddha, with tiled panels covering the walls. The pagoda itself, tiled in blue, green and yellow, is cool and inviting, its window niches popular with lovers who gaze out in silence over the River Khwae valley below.

A few steps away, but deliberately kept apart by a concrete wall, is the Thai-style **Wat Tham Seua** (Tiger Cave Monastery). You have to go all the way down to the bottom again to climb up here – either tackling the steep naga stairway or the more gentle back steps which lead past the cave itself (which is really more of an alcove than a cave, and contains Buddha images).

If you can't face either option, there's a cable car to whisk you to the top. The main chedi here is still under construction, but it's the huge seated Buddha on the terrace outside which grabs the attention: all shimmering gilt, with sparkling Wheels of Life engraved on its palms and sheltered by a flamboyant naga hood. Passing before the Buddha is a mini conveyor belt carrying money and candle-lit offerings. Adjacent is an even more elaborate bot with a rather kitsch interior. Seen with the Chinese pagoda behind, the ornateness of the whole complex seems like an extraordinary piece of one-upmanship. At dusk, the simple silhouettes of pagoda and chedi across the nearby Meuang Dam reservoir are almost more impressive than either of the temples' glittering day-time splendour.

Many tour operators include visits to the temples on day tours of Kan'buri. By public transport it's easiest to hire a tuk-tuk or motorbike taxi from town.

the train station. Set in well-cut lawns among miniature flowering shrubs are the graves of 6,982 POWs, in neat rows according to their nationality. Many of the small tombstones carry the same simple memorial: 'His duty nobly done – ever remembered.' Some have full details of names and rank, and often have bunches of fresh flowers laid beside them – offerings from relatives, friends or colleagues. Other graves are unmarked, the remains unknown.

Chung Kai Allied War Cemetery is across the river, a couple of kilometres south-west of town (it's easy, and pleasant, to bicycle here, by first taking the public ferry across the river from the pier at the end of Lak Meuang Road). Once the site of a POW camp, it's now a peaceful final resting place for 1,750 POWs. If you have time, you can continue south along the river another km to visit the cave temple of **Wat Tham Khao Pun**, though it's not

worth making a special trip to see this rather garishly-decorated thin cave (more like a tunnel) adorned with various Buddha images, the largest and most elaborately lit at the very bottom. A more impressive cave temple south of town on the other side of the Mae Klong River is **Wat Tham Mongkon Thong** (easily accessible by songthaew across the new Chukkadon Road bridge). Actually, it's not the series of limestone caves up in the hillside which is the most famous attraction here, but a septuagenarian 'floating nun' who likes to meditate while floating in the temple pool. Popular with Thai devotees and Taiwanese day trippers, she makes rare appearances these days. The caves are a rather disappointing subsitute, though they're more substantial than those at Wat Tham Khao Pun, with a pleasant view of the valley below at the end. They require a degree of agility and a tolerance for

THE DEATH RAILWAY

The Bridge over the River Kwai – and its bombing by Allied warplanes – is one of the most infamous episodes of the Second World War. In fact, the bridge only represented a small part of the appalling labours the Allied prisoners-of-war had to face in building the 415-km line from Thailand (then called Siam) to Burma during 1942 and 1943.

The Japanese wanted the rail link to connect and supply their newly-conquered (and yet-to-be-conquered) territories in western Asia, rather than having to depend on the longer sea route from Japan to Burma's port at Rangoon. The route chosen – through the Khwae Noi River Valley from existing terminals at Nong Pladuk in Thailand to Thanbyuzayat in Burma – couldn't have been more demanding: dense, malarial jungle and mountainous terrain, hard rock and impenetrable forest. The Japanese estimated that it would take at least five years, given their limited labour resources.

But that was unacceptable to the high command. So they brought in some 60,000 Allied POWs (mostly British, Australians and Dutch) who had been captured in Singapore and

other territories, and put them to work. They later added more than 200,000 Asian labourers. Construction began from both ends of the line in June 1942. By the time the Death Railway was finished, just 16 months later, an estimated 16,000 POWs had died, and up to 100,000 Asians.

It was a combination of the harsh conditions and the disgraceful treatment by the Japanese and Korean guards that killed most of them: in particular, dysentery, cholera and malaria preyed on the weakened, malnourished men who were made to work 12 to 18 hours a day on meagre rations.

The lines finally met just south of the Thailand-Burma border in October 1943, and the railway was immediately put into use. But just 20 months later the Allies bombed the bridge, and in August 1945 the Japanese surrendered. Most of the line disappeared soon after, sold by the Thais as scrap or carried off by the Karen and Mon tribespeople to use elsewhere.

Many of the POW victims of these war crimes are buried in cemeteries in Kanchanaburi – see page 201 and above.

bats and guano smells: they're at the top of a long steep naga stairway, and become quite narrow in places – be prepared for some crawling on hands and knees.

NAM TOK

If you do nothing else while you're in Kan'buri, don't miss the two-hour train ride along the infamous Death Railway to the end of the line at Nam Tok, *77 km to the* NW. Not only is the scenery dramatic, with the line running beside the Khwae Noi River past jungle-dense hills, but it's also an eye-opening experience to see the difficulties the prisoners-of-war faced in building the track. The most spectacular section is just beyond Tha Kilen station where the train inches past the cliff-face and crawls over the **Wang Po viaduct**: peer out of the train window to your left and you'll see the intricate wooden trestle bridge below. The original structure cost the lives of many POWs. Now it's the focus for tourists staying at floating raft resorts on the river below.

Nam Tok town itself (called Tarsao during the war) has little of interest: it's mainly used as a jumping-off point for tours going on to their river resorts or to Sai Yok National Park (page 204). If you don't want to wait for the next train back, you can catch a bus to Kan'buri from Highway 323, about 500 m south of the train station.

There are three trains daily to Nam Tok from Kan'buri: 6.10 am (from Kan'buri only), 10.55 a.m. (starting at Thonburi at 7.50 a.m.) and 16.26 p.m (starting at Thonburi at 13.45 p.m.). The first is the most atmospheric, with the train slipping through the misty dawn landscape with only a few villagers aboard. The 10.55 is packed with tourists – especially in the B100-per-seat carriage. I went local price (B17) and found myself squeezed among dozens of jovial Thai students, larking about, roaring with laughter, sharing food and drink and having so much fun that they infected the whole trip, and I almost forgot about the Death Railway's associations.

For the best river and viaduct views, try to get a seat on the left-hand side. And don't be surprised if you see a *farang* train driver taking the controls: it's probably Englishman Michael Cox, steam engine fan and Thai Railways'

honorary driver, who often visits Kan'buri, especially during its River Khwae Festival. If you want to talk trains past or present, you can usually track him down at Punnee's Bar & Café in town (see Recommended Restaurants, page 207).

PRASAT MEUANG SINGH

Meuang Singh (City of Lions) was once an important trading outpost of the Khmer Empire. *Situated on the Khwae Noi River, some 43 km W of modern Kanchanaburi*, it was probably at the Empire's westernmost limits. The 12thC ruined temple complex that remains is best seen on a day trip from Kanchanaburi that takes in nearby Ban Kao Museum too (page 198); it's scarcely worth coming all the way to see either of these on their own. It's best to come by train: the Tha Kilen Station is just 1.5 km from the site, now an Historical Park and open from 8 am to 4 pm daily.

The site covers some 80 hectares of various shrines surrounded by remains of ramparts and moats, but you don't need to tramp round it all: the main central shrine, Prasat Meuang Singh, is the one that has been most extensively restored and is the most impressive. Approached directly from the entrance by a long laterite walkway past sweet-smelling frangipani trees, the central prang towers above the grassy compound. It faces east, towards Angkor, and is enclosed within chunky laterite walls and galleries.

Unlike other Khmer ruins near Nakhon Ratchasima, Prasat Meung Singh can boast few *in situ* carvings on its lintels or doorways, although there's a stucco carving of a figure assumed to be the Mahayana Buddhist figure of mercy, Avalokitesvara, on the inside of the northern gallery wall. A statue of the same figure stands in the centre, with only the stumps of his eight arms left. If you look closely you'll notice that his torso is covered with hundreds of tiny carvings of the Buddha. Like the much smaller Prajnaparamita figure of wisdom nearby, the statue is draped in yellow cloth, and there are offerings at his feet – evidence of the unbroken centuries of worship.

Another complex to the north-east has only the foundations remaining, but probably would have been similar, with *gopuras* on all four sides and a surrounding gallery. The nearby modern pavilion is worth a look: it houses a small collection of carvings and statues from the shrines, including fragments of huge carved claws and a wing – perhaps pieces from an enormous *khut* or mythological eagle.

SAI YOK NATIONAL PARK ⌁
Almost as popular as nearby Erawan National Park (pages 198-9) for its inevitable waterfalls, (especially the **Sai Yok Yai Falls** which cascade into the Khwae Noi River), this 500-sq.-km park lies *about* 100 *km* NW *of Kanchanaburi* and is most easily accessible by direct bus from Kan'buri (taking about one hour). Other buses *en route* for Sangkhlaburi will stop at the entrance to the park, 3 km from the visitors' centre by the river. Trails to the falls are well-marked and easy to follow, but as always with these popular waterfall sites, they can be unbearably crowded at weekends. Short boat excursions or overnight **raft trips** along the Khwae Noi are available from near the Sai Yok Yai Falls, and often include visits to **Daowadung Cave**, about 5 km further upstream. Keeping to firm ground you can also follow a 2-km trail inland to the **bat cave** (**Tham Khang Khao**), named after its tiny residents, the rare Kitti's hog-nosed bat. Weighing just two grams, it's the world's smallest mammal and was discovered by a Thai scientist, Professor Kitti, as recently as 1973. The bats are very hard to spot, though; you'll have more luck tracing the remains of the Death Railway which crosses the trail to the cave and, just before this, a pile of bricks which were apparently used by the Japanese as cooking stoves during the construction of the railway.

SANGKHLABURI ⌁ ✕
Relatively few tourists make the 227-*km trip from Kanchanaburi* NW *to Sangkhlaburi, at the end of Highway* 323. It's not just the long journey that puts people off (around five hours by bus or three-and-a-half by minibus). Nor the increasingly winding mountain road – especially wild and treacherous for the last 74 km, from the town of Thong Pha Phum. It's the sense that you're entering lawless land: Sangkhlaburi is just 23 km from the border outpost of Three

Pagodas Pass, long notorious for black market smuggling and skirmishes between Karen, Mon and Burmese armies keen to control this important border crossing.

All of this makes the journey sound very enticing indeed if you're the adventurous sort. In fact, though smuggling still goes on, the border point and village (now called Payathonzu) has been calm since the Myanmar Government

---

THE FALLEN MONK
On your way to Sangkhlaburi you'll pass the **Sunyataram Forest Monastery**, 32 *km* N *of Thong Pha Phum*. This large meditation retreat hit the headlines in 1994 when its founder, Yantra Amaro Bhikku – a famous monk with a following of thousands – was accused by one of his woman disciples of fathering her child. For months, the handsome monk denied the charges. But then more surfaced: allegations of sexual indiscretions during his frequent overseas trips, including claims by a Cambodian that she had had sex with the monk on the deck of a cruise ship in Scandinavia. A Danish harpist who met the monk in Denmark, and a German psychologist added their own equally spicy tales.

The scandal rocked Thailand, a staunchly religious country: speaking out against the Buddhist priesthood is considered highly improper. 'It has divided Buddhism and Thai society as never before,' commented a Thai newspaper. 'In this painful episode we can see the faults of Buddhism being paraded for public scrutiny, and it isn't a pretty sight.'

Finally, in early 1995, came more substantial proof: counterfoils from credit cards showing visits to brothels in Australia and New Zealand in 1991 and 1992. At the end of March 1995, the Sangha Supreme Council, Buddhism's highest authority in Thailand, ruled that Yantra should be defrocked for violating several Buddhist disciplines and doing 'worldly things'.

Not surprisingly, the Sunyataram Forest Monastery is rather cagey these days about receiving visitors.

fought off the Karen and Mon in 1989. The most dangerous thing you're likely to experience these days is the maniacal driving of the minibus men who routinely overload their vehicles and then roar along the mountain road between Kan'buri and Sangkhlaburi ('Sangkhla') with brakes screeching on every corner. I rank my own trip on this route recently as the most hair-raising I've ever had in Thailand, surpassing the experience years ago on an out-of-control charging elephant.

Still, if you manage to get to Sangkhla in one piece, it's a charming place. The main attraction is its location on the northern edge of the huge Khao Laem Reservoir. This was formed when the Khao Laem Dam was built near Thong Pha Phum in 1983, flooding several villages, including the original Sangkhlaburi town. In the dry season you can still spot the tips of a former temple peeping above the water. The black skeletons of tree tops are a constant rather ghostly presence.

The new town itself isn't very attractive, but as it's mostly inhabited by Mon, Karen or Burmese it has an intriguing atmosphere: try the central market in the morning – also worthwhile for its cheap Burmese cheroots, sarongs and sunscreen powder. Or, even better, stroll across the intricately-constructed **wooden bridge** (which is reputedly the longest of its kind in Thailand) to the **Mon settlement** the other side of the lake, which feels more like Burma than Thailand. The residents fled from Burma and are restricted to staying and working in the Sangkhla area. *Farangs* still cause something of a stir here: stop to talk to schoolkids on their way home, and they'll giggle and blush before practising their few words of English. There's a ragged little market here too, and several small jewellery workshops along the dirt track from the bridge.

Dominating it all is the hill-top **Wat Wang Wiwekaram,** whose huge central stupa is in the style of the stupa at Bodhgaya in India and whose monks are mostly Mon. The surrounding pavilion, with an eye-catching red corrugated roof, houses a market of tacky trinkets and made-in-Burma souvenirs for the bus-loads of tourists and pilgrims who dash here on day trips. The best time to come is at dusk, when the tourists have gone, and the view over the lake and surrounding hills is at its golden-mellow best.

Further up the road from the village is a new **extension of the temple**, with five halls (the last still under construction), featuring glittering chrome and green-glass pillars and Burmese-style sequinned panels among their other many ornate decorations. A great deal of money has obviously gone into their construction, but in a place like Sankghla it's probably wise not to ask where the funds have come from.

Sangkhla's other attractions mostly revolve around the lake: you can rent canoes from most guesthouses, take an organized **boat trip** up the Pikri River followed by an elephant ride, or a visit by boat to the nearby **Mon refugee camps.**

SI NAKHARIN RESERVOIR

See *Erawan National Park, pages* 198-9.

THREE PAGODAS PASS

This exotically-named pass lies *about* 23 *km* NW *of Sangkhlaburi* and is now easily accessible from Sangkhla by regular songthaews which take 40 minutes to follow the broad, paved road into the mountains, past several Mon and Karen villages. The pagodas themselves (**Phra Chedi Sam Ong**) aren't worth more than a glance: small and insignificant, they're stuck in the middle of the road just before the border point. They are believed to have been built in the 18thC – either by the Burmese as a rallying point for their raids on Thailand's capital, Ayutthaya, or by the kings of Burma and Thailand as symbols of future peace together.

Peace certainly hasn't been a feature of the place recently: as the most important border crossing for hundreds of kilometres, the pass has been fought over for decades by Karen and Mon insurgent armies who both used it for collecting tax on goods crossing the border to fund their resistance activities against the Burmese government. Since the government army wrested control in 1989, and even more recently entered into negotiations with rebel Karen and Mon factions, they have tried to transform the border town, renamed **Payathonzu**, into a market outpost attractive to both Thai traders and tourists. The border is open from 6 am to 6 pm and foreigners are allowed to cross for a fee of B130 – but at the time of writing only as far as the next check post, 2 km down the road.

Most of Payathonzu's legitimate trade is in furniture construction: almost every workshop you pass along the road to the market is making Burmese-style reclining wooden chairs. The market itself is also worth a lingering look, especially in the early morning when Burmese women, their faces

RECOMMENDED HOTELS

ERAWAN AND SAI YOK NATIONAL PARKS

Spartan official bungalows are available at both parks, though they're geared to groups of Thai trippers, accommodating up to as many as 15 people, and ranging in price from B500 to B1000. Far more attractive for individual travellers are the rafts and bungalows at **Erawan Guest House Resort** (*tel. 034 513001*) just before the Erawan park entrance; or the Saiyok View Raft not far from the Sai Yok Yai Falls (there are several smarter river raft resorts, popular with tour groups and Bangkok expats, along the Khwae Yai: enquire at Kan'buri's TAT office). Food stalls and/or simple restaurants are available at both parks.

KANCHANABURI

Budget travellers are well catered for here, with dozens of cheap raft and bungalow operations on or beside the river (choose those north of town for the most peaceful nights, especially at weekends). Samlor drivers meet trains and buses and often try to lure you to their own choice: if it's not what you want, bargain politely and be firm.

Bamboo House, B-BB; 3-5 *Soi Vietnam, off Maenam Kwai Road; tel. 034 512532.*

The most serene spot along the river thanks to its location several kilometres north of town, just before the bridge (you can rent a bicycle from the shop next door). Run by Phun Pimchanok (call her 'Ow') and her mother, it has only ten rooms: six in simple raft huts, a couple (with attached bathrooms) on the riverside lawn (great for kids) and two deluxe air-conditioned rooms. At night it's so quiet you can hear the frogs plop into the water.

Rick's Lodge, B; 48/5 *Rong Hip Awy Road; tel./fax 034 514831.*

Closer to town but still away from the main drag, this is a popular, friendly place run by Kitt Thepsuwan and his Australian wife, Julie. The A-frame huts (all with bathroom) are more stylish than most in this area and there's an enticing riverside restaurant.

River View Guesthouse, B; 42 *Rong Hip Awy Road; tel. 034 512491.*

This place has a jolly backpackers' atmosphere, with 45 bungalows (many with attached bathroom) spread out along the riverbank and connected by boardwalks. Splash out some extra *baht* for the two-storey bungalow (there's only one) at the far end.

Kasem Island Resort, BB; 27 *Tambon Ban Tai; tel. 034 513359 or Chukkadon wharf office, tel. 034-511603.*

An up-market version of the budget raft operations, with air conditioned 'house boats' or bamboo cottages on an island in the Mae Klong River (private ferries go from Tha Chukkadon pier). There's a swimming pool, too, and floating restaurant.

Felix River Kwai Resort, BBBB; 9/1 *Mu 3 Tambon Thamakharm; tel. 034 515061; Bangkok reservations, tel. 02 255 3410.*

Kan'buri's first deluxe international resort, with all the frills: pool, fitness centre, jogging track, golf course, all set within 30 acres of beautifully landscaped gardens (including the world's largest rock garden). You can't beat the location, either: across the river just beyond the Bridge (private boats shuttle guests to and fro).

SANGKHLABURI

P. Guesthouse, B; 81/1 *Tumbon Nong Loo; tel.034 595061; fax 034 595139.*

Run by the formidable local-born Darunee (her father is Mon, her mother half Karen, half Thai), this is the most popular budget place in town: the setting is magnificent, with huts on a grassy slope above the lake. A new restaurant (built by Darunee's carpenter streaked with powder against the sun, sell chickens, fruit and vegetables, while nearby Burmese teahouses are crowded with cheroot-smoking men and women. You could spend another couple of hours poking around the

dusty back alleys or sitting in one of the café-restaurants eating Burmese curry. Don't wait until the border closes if you're dependent on songthaew transport: the last one back to Sangkhla leaves around 4.30 pm.

husband Paiboon) will have a prime lakeside view. Darunee can organize anything – including boat tours and elephant rides led by her ebullient sister Kumsai (Darunee is the only person in town to 'retain' a fleet of 20 elephants for guests and visiting tour groups).

Burmese Inn, B; 52/3 *Tumbon Nong Loo; tel.* 034 595146.

A smaller, more modest place than P's, with simple huts tucked into a gulley (some overlooking a stream). Thai Meo runs the place with her Austrian husband – there's a pleasant, relaxed family atmosphere. Tours and boat trips are available here, too.

Sri Daeng Hotel, B; *in the town centre, by the market; air-conditioned buses to Kan'buri leave from here.*

There's not much point coming to Sangkhlaburi if you don't stay by the lake; but if you're desperate for air-conditioned rooms, this will do.

it's a great place to pick up information (there's a small library of guidebooks and paperbacks), rent bikes or change money.

Rick's Lodge, B-BB; 48/5 *Rong Hip Awy Road; tel.* 034 514831.

Among the more attractive guesthouse restaurants, right by the river and pleasantly low-key. Owner Kitt does some great fish dishes. (And the shakes with whisky are a novel experience.)

Solo's, BB-BBB; *by River Kwai Bridge; tel.* 034 511311; *credit cards,* AE, MC, V.

One of many riverside restaurants catering largely to tour groups and Thai day trippers, this one at least has the view of the bridge. The menu is strong on prawn and fish dishes – try the steamed pomfret with plums.

Night market, B; *near the junction of Saengchuto and Lak Meuang Roads.*

Worth seeking out for cheap takeaways or sit-down snacks. You'll also find food vendors and shady places to sit along the river in Song Khwae Road.

RECOMMENDED RESTAURANTS

KANCHANABURI
Isaan, B; 269/1-2 *Saengchuto Road.*

A noisy roadside location, but the affable manager, Chatchai Chumsuwan, provides a warm welcome and the north-eastern dishes makes a delicious change from guesthouse *farang* fare. Try the stir-fried wild boar with fresh chilli and basil leaves; or the old favourite freshly-grilled chicken, sticky rice and spicy papaya salad.

Punnee Bar & Café, B-BB; 2/15 *Ban Nua Road; tel.* 034 513503.

The first *farang* bar in Kan'buri, run by British ex-paratrooper Danny (who also dabbles in real estate and sapphires) and his Thai wife Punnee. It's a favourite among resident expats, boasting the coldest beer in town ("if it was any colder you could eat it") and other home-sweet-home specialities such as 'mom's apple pie'. As well as the beer and food

SANGKHLABURI
P Guest House, B-BB; 81/1 *Tumbon Nong Loo; tel.* 034 595061.

My memories of this relaxing lakeside restaurant will for ever be associated with the groans of a young Israeli who had injured his arm while riding his motorbike: the local herbal doctor was rushed in – an elderly Burmese whose only words of English were "I love you." The Israeli was laid out on the restaurant floor while the doctor administered scalding bricks of cloth-wrapped herbs, and forced the arm back into shape. Screams were matched with shouts of "I love you" while we tried to eat our Burmese curry (it's delicious, by the way). At the end of two hours, the Israeli staggered up, grimly smiling, his arm once again able to raise a beer to his lips. The doctor slapped him on the back, shouted one last "I love you", and disappeared.

Hua Hin Area

293 _km; map_ Nelles 1:1,500,000

This area – the northernmost part of southern Thailand – makes one of the best short trips from Bangkok. There is a varied menu: some unpretentious beach resorts, excellent temple art and architecture, and a protected area of rainforest. None of the main towns are more than four hours away by bus or train from Bangkok. If time is tight you can just choose one for a day-and-night trip from Bangkok or combine a couple for a longer expedition. The full itinerary would take at least four days.

Travelling south from Bangkok, the first major stop is Phetchaburi, about three hours by bus or rapid train. One of Thailand's oldest historic towns, it's renowned for its many fine temples dating from the 16th to the 18thC. Another hour and 70 km down the rail line lies Hua Hin, the country's first seaside resort and a favourite with the royal family since the 1920s. Still relatively low-key, it's the kind of place that will appeal if you're looking for a simple seaside holiday where the seafood is cheap, the sunshine plentiful and the sand just right for building sandcastles.

By catching an early bus from Bangkok you can visit Phetchaburi _en route_ to spending the night at Hua Hin (avoid weekends when hordes of Bangkokians escape to frolic by the sea). But be prepared to give yourself time in Hua Hin: I've never managed to tear myself away in less than two days.

Discovering the two national parks in the area will take some time and perseverance (and leg muscle), unless you take advantage of the day tours organized by companies in Hua Hin. Trekkers and wildlife enthusiasts who want to tackle them independently, however, will find that this section provides useful basic information on getting the most out of the coastal Khao Sam Roi Yot National Park and the 3,000-sq.km Kaeng Krachan National Park, two of the country's best.

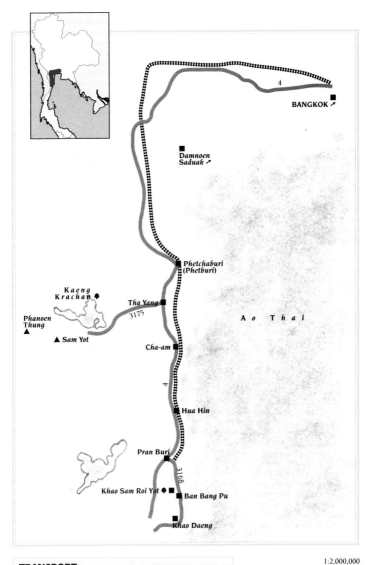

TRANSPORT
The main destinations on this route are easily reached by both train and bus: seven trains a day leave from Bangkok's main Hualamphong Station for the south, arriving in Phetchaburi about three hours later, and Hua Hin about four hours later. Air-conditioned buses for these towns leave from Bangkok's Southern Bus Terminal, on Pinklao-Nakhonchaisi Road, every 45 minutes (from 6 am to 8 pm) and take three to three-and-a-half hours. Non-air-conditioned buses leave every 25 minutes. The two national parks are best reached by rented car or motorbike.

1:2,000,000

SIGHTS & PLACES OF INTEREST

BANGKOK
See pages 134-55.

CHA-AM 🛏 ✕
This small beach resort, 178 km S of Bangkok, is an easy bus hop from Hua Hin or Phetchaburi (which are both on the main rail line from Bangkok). Unfortunately, that's too close to the big city for its own good: in the last few years, Cha-am has become increasingly popular with Bangkok residents, and shown signs of going down the same neon-lit road to ruin as Pattaya, with a rash of new hotels, 'condotels', condominiums and weekends of non-stop beach parties to the sound of roaring jetskis. On weekdays, however, the seafront is so quiet it's almost boring, although many people prefer this laid-back Thai atmosphere to the constant activity of nearby Hua Hin, whose bars and restaurants are much more geared to farang tastes. Not that Cha-am can ever rival Hua Hin in charm (see below). Cha-am has always been the royal resort's poor cousin, but what it lacks in atmosphere and historical associations, it makes up for in a range of excellent accommodation (especially for groups or families) and a silvery beach lined with casuarinas which provide welcome shade. (Hua Hin can be scorching by comparison.) Unfortunate-

• Top and above: Hotel Sofitel Central, Hua Hin.

ly, a busy beach road mars the tranquillity. On weekdays you can get bargain rates in the five-star hotels and miles of sand to yourself. At weekends the pace and the prices escalate.

There's not much of a town to explore, nor sights to see, except an abandoned royal residence, **Maruek-khathayawan Palace**, built by King Rama VI in 1924 a couple of kilometres south of town and usually open to visitors. For action-packed days your best bet is to base yourself in one of the deluxe resort hotels which offer a wide variety of sport facilities both on land and at sea. The tourist office is at 500/51 Phetkasem Road, tel. 032 471005.

HUA HIN 🛏 ✕
S of Cha-am. I've never been much of a beach lover, but there's something about Hua Hin which always manages to win me over. Long billed as the sim-

• *Hua Hin.*

plest, most charming seaside resort in Thailand, it's now shedding its dozy, old-fashioned ambience for a much livelier lifestyle, with a recent proliferation of hotels, bars and restaurants, nearly all geared to the tastes of its many foreign (and predominantly middle-aged) visitors. But it's still surprisingly low-key: facing the sunrise side of the Gulf of Thailand, Hua Hin is also at the opposite end of the horizon from Pattaya: you'll find no hard-core sleaze here, no glitz, and little glamour, though hotel and condominium development is eating up the coastline, and golf courses continue to multiply (there are already six nearby).

Hua Hin is the mother of Thai resorts: it's been around longer than any other in the kingdom, and has an unrivalled claim on royal affections. Its charms were first uncovered in 1910 by King Rama VI's brother, who started a fashion for building elegant villas by the beach. In 1927, King Rama VII put the final royal stamp of approval on Hua Hin by building his Klai Kangwon Palace (its name means 'Far from Worries') just north of the town's fishing piers. Although worries proved to be far from banished (the King was staying here in 1932 when he heard of the *coup d'état* which dethroned him), the palace has continued to be a favourite summer residence for the royal family.

The earliest visitors to Hua Hin had to make the 230-km journey from Bangkok by bullock cart and canal boat. These days the train gets here in three to four hours, dropping you at a little station which features a dainty Royal Waiting Room on the platform and a 1920s American steam engine across the tracks.

One of the grandest sights in Hua Hin is the Railway Hotel (now tediously called the **Hotel Sofitel Central Hua Hin**) which was built in 1923 by the State Railway of Thailand a year after they opened the rail link to Bangkok. Overlooking the beach, the colonial-style hotel, complete with *fin de siècle* ceiling fans, fancy fretwork decoration

---

THE BLOODLESS REVOLUTION

When King Rama VII built his summer palace in Hua Hin in 1927, he named it Klai Kangwon – Far from Worries. But it was only five years later that worries reached the palace door: on June 24 1932, while the King was at Klai Kangwon, a junta of soldiers and civilians in Bangkok seized power and declared the end of absolute monarchy.

There was no resistance. The King immediately accepted the new terms, writing to the junta, 'For the sake of peace, and in order to save useless bloodshed; to avoid confusion and loss to the country, and, more, because I have already considered making this change myself, I am willing to co-operate in the establishment of a constitution under which I am willing to serve.' It proved harder than he thought: three years later, Rama VII abdicated in favour of his young nephew, the ten-year-old Prince Ananda Mahidol.

COCONUT CUSTARD FESTIVAL
One of the major cottage industries of the Phetchaburi province is collecting sweet palm juice to make traditional Thai sweets: Phetchaburi town is particularly famous for its *khanom maw kaeng* (egg custard) desserts. Perhaps to counteract the provincial capital's villainous reputation, the local authorities have come up with an unique festival celebrating the area's sugar-and-sweet activities. The highlight is a palm-tree climbing competition between man and monkey to collect the palm juice. Last year's score? Man: 1. Monkeys: 3.

and vast teak verandas, was completely restored in 1986 and is now one of the finest historic hotels in Asia. (It gained fame in its role as Hotel Le Phnom in the film, *The Killing Fields*.) Even if you can't afford a room here, be sure to take a stroll through the grounds to admire the finely-sculpted topiary – everything from pudgy rabbits to massive elephants, complete with tusks. And that's about it as far as famous sights go – which is why Hua Hin (billed as 'The Queen of Tranquillity') is so relaxing. If you've got energy to burn you can try out the **Royal Hua Hin Golf Course** – the first golf course in Thailand, designed by a Scot in 1926; take a pony ride along the beach, or a day-tour to one of the national parks (see below and page 213). Tourist information for the area is available at the Cha-am office (see page 210).

Or you can simply slide into Hua Hin mode and meander south for a few kilometres along the beach past discreetly hidden private villas until you reach **Khao Takiap** (Chopstick Hill) with its large standing Buddha looking out to sea and its new resort developments. (Women are advised not to go this far alone – there have been a couple of incidents in this surprisingly isolated stretch of beach.)

At dusk or dawn, head north for the **fishing pier** to watch the jaunty little fishing boats gather their nets or deposit their catch. In the morning, particularly, it's a marvellous, raucous

scene of hollering fisherfolk and bargaining tradesmen, the pier stacked with boxes of flapping fish. Fresh seafood in Hua Hin is superb value, with restaurants selling dishes of kingfish, perch, squid and crab for rock-bottom prices.

On weekend nights, the beach is the playground for Thai families who order steamed crab, mussels and shrimp from nearby vendors to eat with vast quantities of Mekong whisky and beer. Even drunkenness seems innocent here: one of my favourite memories of Hua Hin was when I was serenaded on the beach by a group of very tipsy Thai boys. Surrounding me with smiles, they beat a foot-tapping rhythm on drums and tambourines before disappearing, giggling, into the darkness, leaving behind their footprints outlined in silvery aquamarine.

KAENG KRACHAN NATIONAL PARK ⇔
Thailand's largest national park (3,000 sq. km) lies *about 60 km SW of Phetchaburi and 63 km NW of Hua Hin*, stretching towards the Burmese border.

Several tour agents (try Hua Hin's Western Tours at 11 Damnoenkasem Road, tel. 032512560; or Toodtoo Tours, 128 Kor Naretdamri Road, tel. 032 512209) organize day trips to the park's popular **Kaeng Krachan Dam**, but if you prefer to go under your own steam by public transport it's easiest from Phetchaburi: take a bus along Highway 4 to Tha Yang (18 km) where occasional songthaews turn off along Route 3175 to the dam. There's a **Visitor's Centre** about 8 km further on where you can ask about bungalow accommodation if you fancy staying the night, or hire guides (probably with minimum English) for treks into the rainforest (come prepared for chilly nights and

PHETCHABURI'S DARK SECRET
It may seem a laid-back little place, famous for its culture and custard cakes, but Phetchaburi is actually a hotbed of crime. A powerful network of Thai mafia exists here, with assassins who regularly carry out their own effective method of voting during elections. Fortunately, they have no interest in tourists.

rough trails). Reaching and exploring the park is far simpler, of course, if you have your own wheels: both motorbikes and jeeps can be rented in Hua Hin for about B250 or B1,200 a day respectively (the efficient Sai Bour has one of the largest fleets: you'll find her open-air 'office' at the end of Damnoenkasem Road, near the beach).

One of the best ways to get the most out of the Park on a short two-day visit is to climb the **Phanoen Thung** mountain: it is a six-hour trek to the summit from the trail head. You can camp for the night at the top (fantastic views, especially at dawn). Even if you're not lucky enough to see elephants, black bears or barking deer, you're bound to hear the eery call of gibbons and see spectacular hornbills, butterflies and bee-eaters. With more time, energetic hikers can continue for another 15 km through the rainforest to the dramatic 18-level Tothip Waterfall. Guides are advisable for both trips.

KHAO SAM ROI YOT NATIONAL PARK ⌘

Only 98 sq. km in size, this protected coastal area 45 *km S of Hua Hin* still manages to pack in more varied and accessible attractions than any other park in the country – lagoons and marshes (ideal for spotting waterbirds); beaches, caves and boat trips (keep an eye out for dolphins); and dramatic hilltop panoramas (the park's name means Mountain of Three Hundred Peaks). It's not as 'protected' as it should be, however: private prawn and fish ponds are gradually encroaching on the marshland, threatening the future of the water birds which breed here.There are organized day tours to the park from Hua Hin (see Kaeng Krachan, page 212, for contacts), but it's not too difficult to get here by public transport: from Hua Hin take a bus 25 km to Pranburi, where you can charter a motorcycle taxi or songthaew for the remaining 38 km to the park headquarters.

Make sure your driver takes you to the park, not to the village by the same name located just outside. More convenient is transport by rented motorbike or car. At weekends Khao Sam Roi Yot can get busy, especially around **Laem Sala Beach** (about 10 km northeast of the park headquarters), where you'll find the main visitors' centre,

restaurant and bungalow accommodation. If you're using public transport, this beach is most easily reached by hired boat from **Ban Bang Pu**, a village connected to Pran Buri by regular songthaew. But if you go on a weekday and stay the night you'll find you have much of the park to yourself. Even on a short visit you'll be able to see most of the park's best attractions: to reach the top of **Khao Daeng** mountain, for instance, only takes half an hour or so from the park headquarters (try it at sunrise or sunset for the best views and greatest chance of seeing the shy, goat-like serow) or you can do a half-hour walk or boat trip from near Ban Bang Pu to **Phraya Nakhon** cave which features a pavilion built in 1896 for King Rama V.

The **visitors' centre** has detailed background information on the local flora and fauna: the park is especially well-endowed with crab-eating macaques and dusky langurs as well as hundreds of migratory and marsh birds, including the rare spotted greenshank. Guides can be hired at the office for about B100 a day. Bring plenty of insect repellent: this area is notorious for its mosquitoes.

PHETCHABURI ⌘ ✕

Once known as Muang Phribphli, this historic provincial capital 160 *km S of Bangkok* is refreshingly free of tourists: tour groups only come here on rapid day trips from Bangkok (visiting the floating market of Damnoen Saduak *en route* – see page 142) and make little

---

KHAO SAM ROI YOT AND RAMA IV

King Mongkut, Rama IV, an eminent astronomer, excelled himself in Khao Sam Roi Yot – and also met his end. On August 18 1886, he led a group of European VIPs into the marshy lands of Khao Sam Roi Yot to witness the eclipse of the sun. Mongkut's prediction of its timing was just four minutes out – considered amazingly accurate for those times. But the King's forecasting skills unfortunately didn't extend to his own health: he caught malaria during the trip and died two months later.

• *Hua Hin.*

impact. Delve into the old-fashioned back streets and you'll find you're the only *farang* around.

The best place to get your bearings is the central **Chomrut Bridge**. Buses from Bangkok will either deposit you near here or (if they're going on to another destination) on the edge of town. The train station is a short samlor ride away to the north-west.

Phetchaburi (sometimes spelled Phetburi) is one of the oldest towns in Thailand, renowned for its salt trade as early as the 12thC.

Its golden era was during the Ayutthaya Period (1350-1767), and the dozens of well-preserved temples dating from this time are the major reason to visit the city today. If you're here in February, it's also worth checking with the tourist office in Bangkok or nearby Cha-am to see if you can time your visit to coincide with the fun **Coconut Custard Festival** (see box, page 212) or **Phra Nakhon Khiri Fair** which features *son et lumière* and classical dancing.

The temples, of course, are always around: you can do a walking tour of the five best in about two hours, though it's more relaxing if you hire a samlor. Start with **Wat Yai Suwannaram**, directly east of Chomrut Bridge, on Phongsuriya Road. This temple was built during the reign of King Rama V and is the loveliest in town, set in peaceful, shady grounds. The first building to catch your eye is an old teak hall with an elegant roof line and elaborately-carved doors: at this point, your samlor driver (if he's anything like mine) might enact an energetic mime to demonstrate why there's a sword-gash in one of the doors. My old man had some difficulty portraying the villains (invading Burmese) and the exact date (1760), but I got the gist. Next to this hall is the bot (main chapel) where rare Ayutthaya-period murals of celestial beings (most of them sadly faded) cover the walls: the best are on the back of the entrance doors. Prettiest of all in this temple complex is the dainty little wooden scripture library perched over an adjacent pool (originally to keep insects from eating its manuscripts).

Passing Wat Borom and Wat Trailok across the road (their wooden dormitories on stilts are worth a look), you'll reach **Wat Kampaeng Laeng**, the oldest wat in town. Its five large 12thC Khmer prangs (probably originally built as Hindu monuments) are a startling sight: great chunks of laterite dominating the bougainvillea-adorned grounds, they're still far more impressive than the modern white wat which the resident monks will proudly open up to show you. Two of the prangs now house Buddha images (the largest still has some stucco decoration); the others, in varying states of ruin, house a

squabbling family of pigeons, guinea-fowl and dogs.

By far the most popular wat among today's devotees, however, is **Wat Mahathat** in the centre of town. Its five brilliantly white prangs (Khmer in style but dating from the late Ayutthaya period) grab the most immediate attention, but it's the *viharn* and bot which are actually more interesting, their rooflines a fantastic display of lively stucco work, as fussy as a wedding cake.

Inside the *viharn* are elaborate, well-restored murals and three gleaming, golden Buddha images, highly respected, the tallest in Ayutthaya style. Devotees crowd in throughout the day. During my visit there was even a special ceremony involving a ragged troupe of silk-clad attendants bearing offerings and incense to the sound of drums and cymbals, just like a scene from an amateur Chinese opera.

A fine way to end the day is to visit **Phra Nakhon Khiri**, more often called **Khao Wang** (Palace on the Mountain), a palace and temple complex on a hill-top just west of town, about 30 minutes' walk from the centre (the feeble can resort to a cable-car which runs to the top from 8 am to 5.30 pm daily from Phetkasem Hotel on Highway 4).

Khao Wang was built by King Rama IV in 1858 as a holiday retreat, instantly giving Phetchaburi the status of a classy place to visit, like the royal-favoured seaside resort of Hua Hin further south. The recently restored palace is a quaint combination of Western (particularly Mediterranean) and Oriental styles, housing a mildly interesting

• *Cha-am.*

collection of royal paraphernalia, but one of the best reasons for coming up here is for the sunset view of Phetchaburi and the distant forested hills. In other parts of the complex you'll come across a haphazard sprinkling of wats and chedis and pavilions and even an observatory tower used by the royal astronomer, Rama IV.

> DETOUR – **CAVES OF KHAO LUANG AND KHAO BANDA-IT**
> About 5 km north of Phetchaburi, on Route 3173 (and most easily reached from town by samlor or motorbike taxi) is the cave shrine of **Khao Luang** which reached its height of popularity during the 19thC when it became a fashionable place for visits by Thai royalty and Western tourists. It still makes a pleasant outing, its main cavern – spotlighted by rays of light from holes in the cave roof – stashed with Buddha images which devotees regularly plaster with gold leaf (an act of merit-making). A couple of kilometres west of town is **Khao Banda-it**, another complex of cave shrines and an Ayutthaya-period temple which consists of a chedi, flanked by a bot and a *viharn*. Local lore reports that a wealthy merchant paid for the chedi, his first wife built the bot and his concubine the *viharn*. Local wags point out that the chedi undeniably leans towards the *viharn*.

RECOMMENDED HOTELS

CHA-AM
The Regent Cha-am Beach Resort, BBBB; 849/21 Phetkasem Road; tel. 032 471480; fax 032471492.

One of the best resorts in Cha-am, with acres of space, and dozens of facilities including squash and tennis courts and fitness centre. On weekdays you may get a 40 per cent discount.

Santisuk Bungalows & Beach Resort, B-BB;
Cha-Am Beach; tel. 032 571211.

Great location opposite the beach, with two- and three-room modern bungalows on stilts in spacious grounds (including a kids' playground). Ideal for families, though midweek it's so empty it's rather soulless.

HUA HIN
Hotel Sofitel Central Hua Hin, BBBB, plus B800 supplement in peak season; 1 Damnernkasem Road; tel. 032 512021; fax 032511014; all credit cards.

This impressive colonial-style hotel, dating from 1923, is still a cut above the rest in Hua Hin (and arguably of any of its peers in Asia). Australian General Manager Richard Kaldor maintains a genial high-profile: stay for a while and he'll be greeting you like an old friend. With all the hotel's nostalgic luxury, its facilities and activities (staff members provide day-courses on everything from fruit and vegetable carving to Thai cookery and language lessons) you hardly ever need to step beyond the 16 hectares of landscaped gardens. In addition to the original colonial wing (cheaper and more romantic than the new wing), there are also one- and two-bedroom beach bungalows across the road.

Chiva-Som Health Resort, BBBB;
73/4 Petchkasem Road, just south of Hua Hin; tel. 032 536536; fax 032 511615; credit cards, MC, DC, V.

Feeling fat or stressed-out? In need of a little pampering and special treatment – like flotation pools, bust-firming and facials, aqua aerobics and a gourmet health diet? Chiva-Som is Thailand's newest and most luxurious answer, billed as Asia's first dedicated health spa. Under General Manager Ana Maria Tavares, and an expatriate staff who have all trained at England's élite Champneys health resort, Chiva-Som offers individual pampering in a superb beach-front location. There's only one drawback: it costs U.S.$400 a day (including meals and consultations). Treatments are extra.

Ban Boosarin Hotel, BB; 8/8 Phoonsuk Road; tel. 032 512089.

One of several middle-range, modern hotels, this is particularly welcoming and intimate, with just ten spotless rooms, all with air-conditioning.

Parichart Guest House, BB; 162/6 Naresdamri Road, near the beach; tel. 032 513863.

There are dozens of cheap guesthouses along Naresdamri Road, so you can afford to shop around. Parichart is slightly smarter than most with some rooms boasting air-conditioning.

Phuen Guesthouse, B; 4a Soi Binthabart Phoonsuk Road; tel. 032 512344.

Call me sentimental, but even with all the smart, comfortable new hotels in town, I still prefer my favourite old wooden two-storey guesthouse, even if the single rooms are box-like and the street-facing rooms are now plagued by noise from the soi's strip of bars. But you can't beat the cosy, family atmosphere: Ta Sangawan and her family live downstairs, invariably watching TV (her husband is a samlor driver, so there's transport available at the door). Double rooms are fairly spacious, and all are clean.

KHAO KRACHAN AND KHAO SAM ROI YOT NATIONAL PARKS
If you want to stay a night or two in either of these parks, especially if it's during a weekend in peak season (November to April) it's best to phone the main national park reservations office in Bangkok in advance: tel. 02 5794842. Accommodation is usually in Spartan concrete bungalows (with

two to four rooms) for about B500 a night. You may also pitch tents on specified sites.

PHETCHABURI

Accommodation here is poor compared to what's available in nearby Hua Hin or Cha-am, but if you've arrived too late to go on, try:

Phetkasem Hotel, B-BB; 86/1 *Phetkasem Road, on the north-west edge of town, near the cable car to Khao Wang;* tel. 032 425581.

A dull-looking place, but the rooms are among the best the town can offer (with a choice of fan or air-conditioning) and the service is always friendly.

Chom Klao, B; 1-3 *Phongsuriya Road, next to Chomrut Bridge;* tel. 032 425398.

Don't expect anything wonderful here, but at least it's conveniently central, the rooms are cheap (some even boast private bathrooms), and the staff know how to smile.

RECOMMENDED RESTAURANTS

CHA-AM

Restaurant Khan Had, B-BB; 241/8 *Cha-am Beach Road, near Sripoom Minimart;* tel. 032 471312.

One of the few restaurants along Beach Road with an English sign, this casual restaurant, open to the street, prides itself on its squid. 'Mama' Som Phong can cook it whichever way you like – fried with chillies, dunked in soup, 'charcoaled', or stuffed with pork. (She can cook most other things, too, but squid is her passion.)

HUA HIN

Chatchai Market, B-BB; *Dechanuchit Road, west of Phetkasem Road.*

For real Thai food, morning or night, cheap or cheerful, this market is unbeatable. For only a few *baht* you can breakfast on freshly-fried batter sticks dunked into hot soy milk, or cups of sweet, gooey coffee.

At night there are dozens of open-air stalls selling excellent cheap dishes. My favourite stall (and that of many other visitors) is the one with a large jovial waitress called Porntip (she's used to jokes about her name). It's on the corner of Sasong and Dechanuchit Roads and is the only one with an English name: Moo Sea Food. Come back a few times and you'll find you're part of the family, receiving especially huge servings of Moo's delicious steamed pomfret with chilli.

If you prefer more salubrious surroundings for a seafood dinner, try:

Saeng Thai, BB-BBB; *Naresdramri Road, near the fishing pier;* tel. 032 512144; *credit cards*, AE, MC, V.

A long-established favourite for large groups and parties, with a pleasant open-air seafront setting, and a jolly transvestite wait(er)ress. As with all seafood restaurants in Hua Hin there's a table groaning with fresh seafood out front where you can make your choice. I recommend *plaa kapong* (perch), *plaa meuk* (squid), *plaa samlii* (kingfish) or *puu* (crab).

Le Chablis, BB-BBB; 88 *Naresdamri Road;* tel. 032 531499.

One of the new crop of *farang*-run eateries, this offers the best-value French food in Hua Hin, thanks to Frenchman (and Polish-speaker) Reginald Malek and his Thai wife. A romantic little candle-lit nook, it conjures up nostalgic memories of France with the first sip of Beaujolais.

PHETCHABURI

Lamiet Cake Shop, B; *Damnoen Kasem Road, almost opposite Wat Mahathat.*

The place to try the town's famous *khanom maw kaeng* (egg custards), sold in little cake tins at B30 each.

Rabieng Restaurant, B-BB; *Phongsuriya Road, near Chomrut Bridge.*

A typically casual eaterie with all your favourite Thai dishes at reasonable prices.

Southern Thailand

Phuket

Map Nelles 1: 1,500,000

Phuket is one of Asia's most unique pieces of real-estate: with a tiny and ever-shrinking fishing fleet, soil too infertile to grow anything except coconuts, rubber and pineapples, the economy of the island depends almost entirely on tourism. Its former source of wealth, tin ore, discovered in the island in the 17thC, has been of little service since the price of tin collapsed.

In the 19thC, when the Industrial Revolution increased the demand for tin, Phuket suddenly became important to Thailand's central government, which had been moved to Bangkok after the Burmese sacked Ayutthaya in 1767. Chinese labourers were brought to Phuket by the thousands to dig the tin out of the ground, and since only males were allowed to immigrate, they quickly intermarried with the locals. During the first half of the 20thC, Phuket was the world's fifth largest producer of tin ore, with a growing population.

The advent of plastic technology, shortly after the Second World War, undermined the demand for tin and caused a depression on Phuket. The island languished in unemployment and poverty until the mid-1970s, when legions of European back-packers discovered her and she began to develop a tourism industry.

Today Phuket is so organized for tourism that it offers a range of accommodation and activities attractive to almost any holidaymaker. While the back-packers can still find cheap bungalows and noodle stands, vacationing rock stars and European royalty hide out from the *paparazzi* in five-star resorts and eat meals prepared by *Gault et Millau* star-rated chefs. And because the tourism industry on Phuket has grown up so recently, developers have to some extent learned a lesson from the mistakes made elsewhere: the beaches and roads are relatively unpolluted, and, as yet, the place is not over-developed.

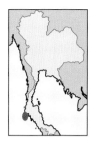

TRANSPORT

Because of Phuket's size, and the rudimentary nature of its public transport, you should rent a car or motor bicycle if you want to see more of the island than the beach you're staying on. *But*: Phuket's roads have the highest fatality rate of any province in Thailand: be *extremely* cautious, especially since many vehicles for hire are in poor condition.

A ring road circles the island, offering breathtaking vistas of bays and sunsets over the Andaman Sea on the western coast and of picturesque fishing villages and luxurious yacht basins on the eastern coast. Because of the distances involved, and the narrow, crowded roads, bicycling is not recommended, though within the small communities that line each western bay, travel by foot or by bike is often the most enjoyable option.

If you rent a motorbike, the safest option is to deal with one of the major car rental agencies, such as Hertz or Avis.

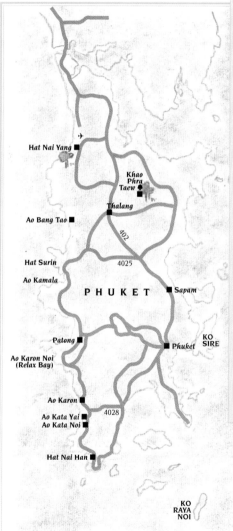

1:500,000

SIGHTS & PLACES OF INTEREST

EASTERN COAST
Because of the topography of the island, Phuket's eastern bays are marked by either deep-water commercial ports or mud flats. The shallow beaches make for poor swimming, and the ports are most popular with yachtsmen. Thus the eastern side of Phuket offers little in the way of accommodation for the average traveller. However, it is from this side that most dive trips and fishing charters leave the island, so if you've booked a tour, expect to ride in a van for half an hour before you board the boat.

Phuket Town ⇔ ✕
It was once a lovely provincial capital full of Chinese shophouses and Sino-Portuguese mansions straight from a Somerset Maugham novel, but the current economic boom has seen many of these deserted or demolished to make way for new, ugly, glass-and-brick banks, shopping centres and hotels. The town is plagued with traffic on its narrow streets, unbelievably hot in the afternoon, and not very interesting to walk around. To be honest, the only things worth recommending in Phuket Town are the island's one **English-language movie theatre** and **bowling alley**, both next door to the Pearl Hotel in Montri Road.

GIBBON REHABILITATION PROJECT
Do you know the difference between monkeys and apes? You should. Monkeys have tails; apes, like humans, don't. Most monkey species are not endangered, all ape species are. Thailand is the last remaining wild habitat of the white gibbon, but unfortunately, due to the apes' popularity with tourists, their numbers are declining very rapidly.

The Thai government's Phuket Gibbon Rehabilitaion Project at **Khao Phra Taew National Park** rescues gibbons from sad existences in bars and restaurants and returns them to the wild. The Project is supported entirely by voluntary donation and sales of T-shirts and the like.

It's well worth visiting the Project at the Park, if only as a gesture of solidarity with your animal cousins. If you don't

DIVING
Though the reefs close to Phuket were destroyed by tin mining in the early 20thC, the outlying islands offer some of the most beautiful diving in the world. For dedicated divers with time to invest, the Similan Islands, one day's sail north of Phuket, are a marine sanctuary only opened to sport divers in the last few years.

Each of the nine islands has a completely different eco-system and offers a unique diving experience. For further details, including access from the mainland, see Thailand Overall: 7, page 113; and page 224 in this section.

Siam Divers on Kata Beach (tel. 330 936) and Fantasea Divers (340 088) offer 'live aboard' trips to the Similans.

go, help the apes by refusing ever to have your photograph taken with an ape (or indeed any other wild animal) in Thailand, and never patronize a business that keeps wild animals in chains or in cages.

KHAO RANG HILL AND OTHER VIEWPOINTS
The word *bhukit* means mountain in Malay, and the hilly geography of Phuket lends credence to many an academic's theory that this is how the island got its name. **Khao Rang Hill** in Phuket town offers stunning views of the city and eastern coast, and there are two recommendable restaurants up there together with a lovely park.

Phrom Thep Cape over Nai Harn Bay is the favoured spot from which to view sunsets over the Andaman Sea and boasts a very good restaurant.

The lobby of the **Raya Pacific Resort** over Kata Bay is the only public spot on the island where you can view both coasts at once.

VEGETARIAN FESTIVAL
Usually late September or early October; list of events available from the TAT office in Phuket Town.

Each year downtown Phuket becomes a scene of unbridled weirdness which reminds visitors that the island had a history before the resorts were built. During the first nine days of the ninth lunar month, devotees, most of Chinese descent, abstain from sex, drugs and meat at the start of the 'Taoist Lent' to purify their bodies sufficiently to host spirits. When these spirits take possession, during five large parades on the last five days of the festival, the spirit mediums will prove their supernatural powers by feats of strength and endurance. Lips, tongues, cheeks and pectorals are pierced by an astonishing array of objects and bare-footed, white-clad believers walk over hot coals and climb ladders made of swords. Not for the squeamish, but the festival is still worth attending if only for the wonderful vegetarian restaurants that open their doors just at this one time each year.

WESTERN COAST
Each of the bays that dot Phuket's western coast has a unique ambience, making it fairly easy for first-time visitors, with a little time for exploration, to find a place that suits their particular tastes

Hat Nai Yang
At the northern tip of the island, this is an enormously long beach with only one hotel and a few small bungalow complexes.

Ao Bang Tao
Just as long as Hat Nai Yang, but home to the Laguna Complex, with five luxury resorts, 1,300 guest rooms, 200 condominiums, 50 restaurants and bars, ten swimming pools and 18 holes of golf. This development is built on the site of an old tin mine, which had rendered the area unfit for any kind of development, according to a 1972 United Nations survey. The eco-friendly design of the Laguna Complex, and its miraculous reclamation of the moonscape left by the miners, has won several awards from environmental groups since its opening.

Ao Kamala and Hat Surin
These bays are relatively undeveloped, and each still harbours a traditional, mostly Muslim, community of locals. They are quaint, lovely, cheap and a bit boring for the average traveller.

Patong 🛏
Its reputation (deservedly) is as Phuket's Sodom and Gomorrah. It is the most developed beach on the island, and has dozens of hotels, hundreds of restaurants serving every type of cuisine, hundreds of shops selling everything from Burmese teakwood carvings to satellite dishes, a transvestite review in a state-of-the-art theatre and more

---

PHUKET'S EARLY HISTORY
The original inhabitants of Phuket were probably negrito fisherfolk who were extirpated or absorbed by the Tai/Mon tribes that migrated south from China some 1,700 years ago. The original name for the island was Thalang, and that is still the name for the northernmost of the three *amphur*, or administrative districts, that make up the island.

The earliest known map of the area, drawn by Ptolemy the Greek historian in the 2ndC AD, shows a peninsula called Junk Ceylon where Phuket is today. The name was probably a bastardization of *Ujong Salang*, the Malay for Salang Headland, but whether Alexander the Great's favourite cartographer misdrew an island as a cape, or whether the cape was separated from the mainland by a later earthquake

(Phuket sits next to a major fault line) is unknown.

From the 7th to 13thC, Indian and Arabic traders colonized the area, bringing Buddhism and Islam with them. For most of Phuket's early history, it was administerd by Malaysian sultans who paid tribute to the Thai kings in Ayutthaya. With the discovery of tin deposits in about 1640 AD, the island was made a province of Siam and put under the direct control of the Thai kings.

Through the 1700s Phuket was subjected to numerous invasions and counter-invasions by the Burmese and Siamese armies, and today there is a monument on the main inland road, which is seen by every tourist who visits the island as they travel south from the airport, to two women who saved the island during one such invasion.

• *Opposite: 'James Bond Island'.*

than two hundred massage parlours, discos, Karaoke bars, beer bars and go-go bars.

The traditionally lenient attitude of Thai governments towards the world's oldest profession has made possible what, in this writer's experience, is a unique red light district in Patong. The usual formula is a small, open-air bar, serving beer and local whisky, staffed by between five and twenty bored women, from very young to very old, and all available for periods from 15 minutes to six months. The 'special services industry', as the government and local press calls it, is fairly well regulated and relatively cheap, by western standards, but see the warning on page 26.

It does promote a negative, and false, reputation for Thai women, which is suffered by the waitresses, room maids, desk clerks and even female executives who work in the legitimate businesses on the island. Though most popular with the infamous 'sex tourists', Patong Beach

สนาม กอล์ฟ
GOLF COURSE
1 กม. KM.

is also a favourite place for normal people who want to go and watch a type of lifestyle they'll never see at home.

The beach is lined with umbrellas and vendors, the beach road with shops selling dive trips or yacht charters. Aged crones give massage on blankets on the sand, and young men urge tourists to rent a jet-ski or try para-sailing. The vendors of Patong are the most insistent on Phuket, though nowhere near as strident as their counterparts in Bali or Jamaica.

Patong can also be a shopper's paradise, with every imaginable kind of merchandise being sold out of chic boutiques or off push-carts. *Laissez-faire* capitalism is enjoyed by Thailand's legions of small business people, and it is easy to find a bargain, or to be cheated, on any block in Patong. The huge volume of tourist trade on the beach has drawn large hotel chains such as Holiday Inn and Amari, and in low season some of the best deals on accommodation can be found there.

Ao Karon, Ao Kata Yai and Noi 🏖 ✕

These are smaller, quieter versions of Patong, with the same beach scene but fewer hotels, restaurants and shops. The Kata Beach Tourism Association petitioned the provincial government in 1994 to stop issuing licences to businesses that promote the sex industry, and became the first community in the kingdom to do so. The government is currently considering the request.

Ao Karon Noi (Relax Bay) and Hat Nai Harn 🏖

Unique on Phuket, perhaps unique in Thailand, each of these beautiful bays has only one hotel on it (The Phuket Yacht Club on Nai Harn and Le Meridien Phuket on Relax Bay), with access to the beach limited by that hotel, effectively circumventing the Thai law against private beaches. These are both five-star resorts, very exclusive and very luxurious, with nothing around them to lure the tourists, and their money, away from the hotel.

GOLF ON PHUKET

Over the past decade, Asians have become enamoured of the sport of golf. Phuket has three excellent courses at the moment, with many more on the drawing board. The best is **The Blue Canyon Country Club,** site of the 1994 Johnny Walker Classic, but unfortunately this course is only open to members or guests of members. **The Phuket Country Club** is the oldest course on the island, pitched to provide an interesting game for pros and duffers alike.

The Banyan Tree is most notable for what it provides for the family while Daddy is on the links: a modern health spa with every conceivable treatment including several kinds of massage therapy, saunas, jacuzzis and health food restaurants.

DAY TRIPS

Perhaps one of Phuket's greatest advantages is in its convenience as a jumping-off place to see the outlying, and less developed, areas of southern Thailand. Because of the destruction caused by off-shore tin mining in the first half of the 20thC, there is not an intact reef anywhere around Phuket. So all diving trips start with a boat ride, and fishing charters must motor miles off the coast to find fish.

The nine islands knows as the **Similans** (the word *similan* means 'nine' in Malay) are a National Marine Wildlife Sanctuary, and as such provide some of the most spectacular diving anywhere in the world. Unfortunately, it's a full day's boat ride to get there, and one back, so you've got to be a pretty dedicated diver to invest the time. *See also* Diving, *page* 220, *and for further details, see box,* Thailand Overall: *7, page* 113.

Ko Phi Phi (pronounced Pee-Pee) is actually two islands, with reefs so beautiful that they almost take your attention away from the outrageous environmental destruction that has taken place on the islands themselves since tourists began coming in numbers about five years ago. *For full details, see* Local Explorations: 9, *pages* 230-2.

Ko Raya Yai and **Ko Raya Noi** are relatively undeveloped, fairly large islands where a few Muslim families have given up the family coconut plantations in favour of selling pineapple slices and cold drinks to the boatloads of divers coming from Phuket. They are favourite spots for divers in the May to October monsoon season, when strong winds and heavy seas preclude the usual trips out into the Andaman Sea.

Krabi, on the mainland opposite Phuket, is what Phuket was like ten years ago: still small and quiet, with few hotels and restaurants, lovely scenery and pristine, empty beaches, but with a smell of imminent development hanging in the air. Accommodation is clean, safe and cheap, and around Krabi are caves which house ancient Buddhist shrines and even more ancient Neolithic cave paintings. Krabi is tailor-made for honeymooners or any travellers wishing to find a quiet retreat, but how much longer it remains so is yet to be seen. For full details, see *Local Explorations:* 10, *pages 237-8.*

Phang Nga, the gulf in which Phuket nestles, is famous for two things: its name, unpronounceable by most westerners; and the dramatic limestone 'karsts' which were immortalized in the James Bond movie *Man With the Golden Gun.* The Phang Nga Bay Resort plays this movie, over and over, 24 hours every day, on its in-house video channel, and has done so ever since 1975.

In fact, you may recognize the karsts from Chinese scroll paintings. They rise vertically from the sea bed and are carved into eerie shapes by the wind. The ones in Phang Nga Bay are the tail end of a chain that stretches up through Cambodia, Laos, Vietnam and China, and it is the dust of their erosion that makes the bay as shallow and calm as it is.

One of the most exciting tours on Phuket is hosted by **Phuket Sea Canoes** (tel. 212 172 / 212 152; they'll pick you up from your hotel). It takes small groups of visitors in inflatable kayaks through caves into the hollow interiors of the karsts. Each *hong* (which is the Thai word for 'room') hosts its own distinct eco-system, and the *hongs* can only be reached by narrow fissures during certain windows of opportunity in the tide table.

Sea Canoes is an environmentally friendly company that strictly polices its guests to ensure minimal impact on the *hongs*, (they also provide the best food this writer has ever eaten on a boat); but beware of copy-cat companies that charge more and actually encourage guests to pull stalactites off the cave walls or play loud music inside the *hongs*.

RECOMMENDED HOTELS

AO KATA
The Boathouse, BBB; *Kata Beach;*
tel. 66 76 330 015 or E-mail to
the.boathouse@phuket.com.

Definitely Phuket's most unique
hotel, this intimate 36-room boutique
resort boasts one of the best kitchens
on the island, and surely the best wine
cellar. Set on the quiet southern end
of Kata Beach, The Boathouse is
Phuket's culturual centre, and hosts
regular wine tastings, gallery openings, book signings and Thai culinary
courses.

PATONG
The Holiday Inn Phuket, BBB;
Patong Beach; tel. 66 76 340 608.

This hotel offers the peace of mind
you get from staying in a chain hotel.
It's safe, clean, competitively priced,
and the staff speaks excellent English.
It is in the middle of Patong Beach, a
useful base from which to explore the
island's most diverse night life.

HAT NAI HARN
The Phuket Yacht Club, BBBB;
Nai Harn Beach; tel. 66 76 381 156.

This five-star resort is the host of
the annual King's Cup Regatta, and in
December when Nai Harn Bay fills up
with hundreds of the most beautiful
boats in Asia, the view from the Club's
Quarterdeck restaurant is spectacular. It's not cheap, but it shares its
beach with no other hotel and the food
and service are impeccable.

Guesthouses and bungalows
There are hundreds of these on the
island, and the best way to select one
that's right for you is by visiting several and asking for room tours. You
can expect to pay between B300 and
B1,200 per night, depending on style,
whether air conditioned or cooled by a
ceiling fan, and proximity to the
beach.

If you don't want to spend time
doing this, the following are all worth
trying:

**The Kata Tropicana Bungalows, B,
Kata Delight Hotel, BB** and **Sea**

Beas Bungalows, B; all three at Kata
Beach; **The On-On Hotel, B** in
Phuket Town; **The Expat Hotel, BB**
and **Viset Hotel, BB,** both at Patong
Beach.

RECOMMENDED RESTAURANTS

AO KATA
**The Boathouse Wine and Grill,
BBB;** *Kata Beach; tel. 66 76 330 015.*

This restaurant has been written
about in publications worldwide, and
with reason. It specializes in Thai
food, though the European *cuisine* is
just as good. The wine cellar is actually the private reserve of a member
of the Thai nobility, who also owns the
place, and there are labels there you
can't find in Singapore or Bangkok.

AO KARON NOI
Le Meridien Phuket, BBB; *Relax
Bay; tel. 66 76 340 480.*

This classy hotel boasts several
fine restaurants, including **Ariake**
(Japanese), **Le Phuket's** (French) and
Wang Warin (Thai). European management, a huge staff, and sky-high
prices guarantee a memorable culinary experience.

PHUKET TOWN
Kajoke See, BB; *2/2, Takua Pa Road.*

This tiny, funky place is a gay bar at
weekends, and the best place for
quality Thai food in Phuket Town the
rest of the time. There are only six
tables, so if you want to be sure of
one, call in person – there's no phone.

The Pearl Hotel, BBB; *42, Montri
Road; tel. 66 76 211 044.*

The eleventh floor of the second
oldest hotel on the island is the best
Chinese restaurant in the southern
provinces. Expect to wait a while for
your food; they are used to serving
huge family gatherings or business
meetings and the chef can't be
rushed.

Southern Thailand

Ko Phi Phi, Ko Lanta and other Andaman Islands

50 km; map Nelles 1:1,500,000 and Guide Map of Krabi 1:300,000

The two Phi Phi islands – Ko Phi Phi Don and the smaller Ko Phi Phi Leh – lie almost equal distances from Phuket (48 km to the north-west) and Krabi (40 km to the north-east), close enough to be drawn into the area's burgeoning tourism scene. In fact, their breathtakingly clear waters and stunning scenery have become so popular lately (especially among scuba-divers) that many visitors now prefer to come here than to Phuket.

Both islands are part of the Hat Noppharat Thara-Ko Phi Phi National Marine Park, though you wouldn't know it to look at the rampant development that is now transforming (some would say ruining) the formerly pristine Ko Phi Phi Don into a major tourist and scuba-diving destination. The uninhabited Ko Phi Phi Leh is luckier: its sheer cliffs are home to thousands of sea swallows whose nests are so highly prized by Chinese gourmets for birds' nest soup (see page 232) that the island and its lucrative nest-collecting business receive special protection. Day-trips to see the island's caves and snorkel in the surrounding waters are on most visitors' agendas, but no-one is allowed to stay overnight.

If you find Ko Phi Phi too crowded and trendy, up-and-coming Ko Lanta would be a far better choice, though its scenery is less dramatic and its accommodation less glamorous. For those who really want to get away from it all, there's Ko Jam or tiny Ko Bubu or Ko Hong, with nothing but the sound of the cicadas and surf and little to do but enjoy it.

Note that in monsoon season (May to October) the seas can be rough, boat services reduced and the diving often disappointing. On the other hand, accommodation is cheaper and the islands quieter. For many old-Andaman hands, this is the best time.

TRANSPORT

The most popular route to Ko Phi Phi is from Krabi: boats usually leave three times daily (less often in monsoon season), taking two to two-and-a-half hours. From Patong, on Phuket, boats leave at least twice-daily, taking from 40 minutes to three hours, depending on the boat used. And from Ko Lanta there's a daily service taking two hours. During the monsoon season, the Krabi service is the most frequent, but don't go if the weather looks rough.

To Ko Lanta your easiest choice is from Krabi: in high season (November to May), two boats daily take one to one-and-a-half hours to reach Ban Sala Dan on the island's northern tip. A shorter (one-hour) crossing (used year-round) is from the port of Ban Baw Meuang (about 80 km south-east of Krabi) to Ban Lanta village on the island's east coast.

In high season, at least one boat daily leaves for Ko Lanta from Ko Phi Phi.

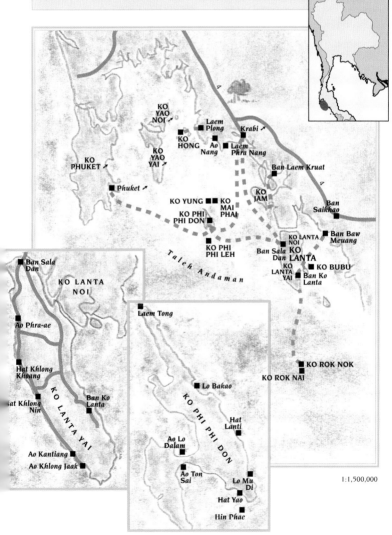

1:1,500,000

SIGHTS & PLACES OF INTEREST

KO BUBU
Blink and you'd miss it: this speck of an island lies *about 6 km E of Ko Lanta* and is so small that it hosts only one set of bungalows (dormitory accommodation is also available). You can get here either from Ko Lanta itself (long-tail boats leave for the 20-minute ride from the east coast pier at Ko Lanta village), or from the mainland coastal village of Ban Baw Meuang, about 80 km south-east of Krabi. For more information about other transport possibilities contact Thammachat Guest House in Krabi (tel. 075 612536).

KO HONG
Also known as Ko Bele (*hong* refers to the giant cliff-lined lagoon on its north side), this is a tiny island *7 km off the Krabi coastline* that not many people have even heard of, let alone visited. It's perfect for a day-trip of snorkelling and swimming: there are three fantastic beaches, on the north, east and south sides of the island (the southern one is the most spectacular), with coral reefs off all of them.

There's nowhere to stay on Ko Hong but you can camp on the beach (the eastern one has a cave for shelter). Long-tail boats can be chartered from Ao Nang or near Laem Plong, about 26 km west of Krabi.

KO JAM
Just 13 km off the Krabi coastline, and about 22 km S of Krabi town, Ko Jam (sometimes called Ko Pu) frequently gets overlooked by tourists intent on reaching the more famous Ko Phi Phi or Ko Lanta islands lying to the west and south.

Ko Jam's low profile is due partly to its lack of suitable beaches: the northern end of the island is a knot of wooded hills and the eastern *coast* (where there's a small fishing village) is a tangle of mangrove swamps.

But the west coast is sandy enough for those with simple seaside tastes, and the lack of any other attractions is a major draw for those who have had enough of the bright lights. There's only one place to stay, Joy Bungalows (radio tel. 01 7230502), on the island's southern tip: no electricity, of course, and no fancy food. Just a few bamboo huts and the sound of silence. Joy, indeed (well, for some, anyway).

In high season you may find a direct boat service to Ko Jam leaving from Krabi; if not, take a songthaew to the pier of Ban Laem Kruat, about 30 km south-east of Krabi, from where a boat leaves daily (usually at 1 pm). Alternatively, in peak season, you can take the Krabi-Ko Lanta boat and ask to be dropped off *en route* (Joy Bungalows usually operates its own long-tail boat service to collect visitors from the Ko Lanta ferry).

KO LANTA YAI ⌫ ✕
Ko Lanta actually refers to a group of 52 islands off the Krabi coastline, although only one – **Ko Lanta Yai** (*yai* means big) – is the focus of tourist attention. Few of the others are even inhabited. No-one bothers with the *yai* when they talk of Ko Lanta, but this is the island they mean when they say they've found the perfect alternative to crowded Ko Phi Phi: a place where tourism is still in its infancy, where the sand and the snorkelling are just as magnificent as Phi Phi's and the lifestyle still charmingly simple.

How long it will last is anyone's guess, but already land prices are soaring as property developers move in. Concrete roads and grid electricity will probably exist by the time this book is published and certainly there will be more tourists and more bungalow resorts. The fact that the southern part of Ko Lanta (in addition to several southern islands) was made part of a Ko Lanta National Marine Park a few years ago is no guarantee of protection, of course. All one can hope for is that the island's residents (mostly descendants of Muslim Thais and *chao naam* (sea gypsies) will see the effect that over-development has had on nearby Ko Phi Phi and try to protect their own island from a similar fate.

For now, however, Ko Lanta is a hot destination among budget travellers. Almost as large as Ko Samui (it's 25 km long and about 5 km wide), its west coast is one long beach with over 20 bungalow resorts ranging from primitive to surprisingly posh. The east coast is mostly clogged with mangroves, so rarely sees tourists, though if you wanted to hop across to tiny Ko Bubu (page 228) you would have to come here in order to take a boat from Ban Ko Lanta.

The easiest way to get to Ko Lanta is on the twice-daily boat service from Krabi (which takes about two hours). The ferries dock at **Ban Sala Dan**, on Ko Lanta's northern tip, a small Muslim fishing village and the most important on the island, with the district offices, a money exchange service and several restaurants overlooking the bay towards Ko Lanta Noi.

Bungalow touts invariably meet the boats to lure you to their resorts with the offer of free transport, but if you've arrived at the end of the season and the touts are thin on the ground, you'll probably have to walk or hitch a ride to the resort of your choice. (It's worth noting that many of the resorts close during the low season, May to October, though you'll always find a few open year-round in Hat Khlong Dao.)

One of the best beaches lies on the west coast just a couple of kilometres south from Ban Sala Dan: **Hat Khlong Dao** is a beautiful 3-km stretch of sand where you'll find most of the island's accommodation and its liveliest night life (mostly in the form of barbecues and cocktail bars).

Keep walking south, past a headland with a triple-trunked coconut tree well-loved by the locals, and you'll reach **Ao Phra-ae** (or Palm Beach) with several more resorts facing a dazzling stretch of white sand. **Hat Khlong Khoang**, a few kilometres further, is the next fine stretch, with shelving sands and superb sunset views. In another 5 km (with no resorts yet built *en route*) you'll reach *Hat Khlong Nin* (or Paradise Beach) whose southern end becomes rather rocky. **Ao Kantiang** has poor accommodation but a superb little beach which is one of the quietest and most secluded on the island (not surprisingly, since it's about 20 km from Ban Sala Dan). The final place to stay, the Waterfall Bay Resort at **Ao Khlong Jaak**, just 1 km south of Ao Kantiang, is better than its rather poor beach, but the advantage of staying here is that you're close to the **national park**, at the southern tip of the island.

The most exhilarating way to reach the park is to follow the coastal cliff path that winds 3 km from Waterfall

SEA GYPSIES

On many islands and coastal areas of southern Thailand and the Malay peninsula there are often communities of semi-nomadic fisherfolk or sea gypsies known as *chao naam* or *chao ley*. Ethnically distinct from southern Thais, with their own language and customs, they have traditionally moved from place to place. Those who have long ago settled on some of the most beautiful islands in the Andaman Sea now find their land in demand from eager resort developers. Sometimes they sell out for high prices; sometimes they're simply ignored or kicked out. The *chao naam* are skilled divers and climbers, descending to great depths to collect shells and pearls, and climbing sheer rock faces to harvest the precious sea swallows' nests.

Animists by belief, they hold an unique festival at the end of the fishing season in which they fill a small boat with symbolic items of ill luck and launch it out to sea, thereby ensuring a fresh start to the new year.

Bay Resort past deserted bays and beaches (in a couple of places the trail is quite steep). There's also a pleasant walk which takes you inland a couple of kilometres to a waterfall.

Walking along the laterite coastal road is one way to expend energy on Lanta (motorbikes are easy to rent, too, though beware of the potholes). But it's the off-shore attractions which lure most visitors. Atlantis Diving (radio tel. 01 72330868; fax 01 70220106) in Ban Sala Dan is one of the more reputable scuba diving operations, offering one- to five-day PADI courses. Or you can join one of the day-long snorkelling trips (organized by most bungalow resorts) to nearby islands.

The Rok islands, **Ko Rok Nok** and **Ko Rok Nai**, some 30 km to the south, are part of the National Marine Park and are especially beautiful for their coral and white-sand beaches. Other trips go to Ko Phi Phi or islands east of Lanta. Incidentally, one way of helping to preserve these islands' coral reefs is to

ensure that the long-tail boat taking you on these day trips anchors at a buoy, not in the fragile coral: already, some of the Rok islands' best coral has been destroyed by anchor damage.

KO PHI PHI DON, KO PHI PHI LEH ⊭ ×

When you see pictures of **Ko Phi Phi Don**, *a couple of km* N *of Ko Phi Phi Leh*, with its stunning twin-crescent bays almost meeting across a lush tropical isthmus, it seems too gorgeous to be true. Ten years ago, the fantasy no doubt matched the reality. Now, sadly, the worst effects of the tourism industry – pollution, litter, coral destruction, ugly concrete developments, and noisy nightime entertainment – have started to ruin the island's charm. What those pictures don't show are the strips of bungalow resorts all along the isthmus and the southern beach, the construction debris and piles of plastic water-bottles at the back of the resorts, and the dirty wells from which villagers collect polluted water.

Nevertheless, it's also true that when your boat enters the main bay of Ao

• *Ko Phi Phi Don.*

Ton Sai, the clarity of the turquoise waters and the sight of those palm-fringed beaches takes your breath away. The scuba-diving in this area is among the best in Asia: nearby wrecks, reefs, islands and rich marine plant life have established Ko Phi Phi as an internationally acclaimed diving centre. There are at least a dozen diving shops now operating here, and many visitors come just to dive.

Others come to climb the sheer limestone cliffs that tower over **Ao Ton Sai**. Big game fishing, yachting trips to Malaysia, sea kayaking, snorkelling or simply lazing on the beach and eating fabulous seafood dinners in classy restaurants or at open-air barbecues – it's all here. No wonder the place is so popular. As long as you don't expect pristine beauty, isolation and innocence (or cheap accommodation in peak season) you could have a great time.

Ao Ton Sai is on the south side of the narrow handle connecting the two hilly ends of the island. It's the busiest and most crowded bay, where boats from

Krabi and Phuket dock and where long-tails leave for the other beaches (alternatively, you can walk: there's no road transport on the island, but there is a coastal path south-east around the bay which you can follow for about 30 minutes to reach the resorts at Hat Yao).

Dominated by the up-market PP Islands Cabana Resort to the west of the pier, the beach of Ao Ton Sai is no longer suitable for swimming. But just a few minutes' walk across the handle you reach **Ao Lo Dalam**, Ao Ton Sai's twin crescent bay, popular for its shallow water (without any long-tail traffic) and great sweep of sand. Many of the larger, more expensive resorts line this beach, with live bands playing on the sands nightly. At the far eastern end, above Viewpoint Bungalows, a steep hillside path leads, after half-an-hour's clamber, to the island's most dramatic **viewpoint**, overlooking both bays. This is where photographers get those dreamy, deceptive photos. Dawn or dusk are the best times to be here. There's a little park with flowering shrubs set around the hilltop's rocky viewpoint, and a small drinks stall open until just after dusk.

Coming down, choose the sealed path which leads south to the village instead of west to Ao Lo Dalam, and you'll enter the hippy heartland of Ko Phi Phi where villagers' shacks and cheap accommodation huts are crammed beside stalls selling beads, belts and bangles, and open-air shops where *batik* artists, masseurs and hair-braiders operate. This is where the lifestyles of locals and travellers meet in a good-natured jamboree. At night, lights flash in the trees to the sound of frogs, cicadas and generators and the occasional blast of a live band or video programme.

The village's main lane, which leads to the pier, is more orthodox, with dozens of cafés and restaurants, dive operators and tour agents. Following it to the south-east will lead you out of the melée, past a tree wrapped in cloth by the locals out of respect for the tree spirit which they believe lives there, to various bungalow resorts and eventually to a secluded stretch of beach, **Hat Yao** (Long Beach: also accessible by regular long-tail boats from the pier). There are resorts here, too, but they are few and relatively far between.

Hat Yao's main attraction, apart from its greater sense of isolation, is its deluxe coral reefs (especially around a nearby rock known as **Hin Phae**), swarming with a kaleidoscope of butterfly, parrot and angel fish, less than 50 m offshore.

The east coast bays of **Lo Mu Di** (accessible from Hat Yao) and **Hat Lanti** (take a rocky path down from the viewpoint) are also worth exploring, though there's no accommodation here yet. Surprisingly large chunks of the island are undeveloped or off-limits to most tourists: the western 'dumbbell' is so hilly that it's practically uninhabited, while the northern tip of Laem Tong is where the remaining *chao naam* (sea gipsies) live. The north-east bays of **Hat Laem Tong** and **Lo Bakao** are the preserve of very exclusive resorts.

However you decide to spend your time on Ko Phi Phi, there's one trip you shouldn't miss: the day-long snorkelling trip offered by nearly all bungalow resorts that includes a visit south to the stunningly beautiful **Ko Phi Phi Leh**, and north to **Ko Mai Phai** (Bamboo Island) and **Ko Yung** (Mosquito Island).

Ko Phi Phi Leh

Lying just a couple of km south of Ko Phi Phi Don (20 minutes by boat), this rugged little island is famous for its coral reefs, caves and sea swallow nests. It has become the focus of nearly all snorkelling trips from its northern neighbour and of many trips from Phuket, too.

Unfortunately, that has led to much anchor damage and litter, especially in its most dramatic east coast bay, **Ao Phi Leh**, which is practically an inland lagoon, as it's almost entirely enclosed by cliffs.

Just north of here is the **Viking Cave**, so-called because of its paintings of Viking-like ships (they're actually Chinese junks) which are either prehistoric or only a century old, depending on who you ask. Just as bizarre is the activity that goes on inside the cave: it's here that the local *chao naam* (sea gipsies) risk their lives to collect the nests of sea swallows for the Chinese restaurant business in Hong Kong, Taiwan and Singapore. In order to reach the nests – which the swallows like to build as high up into the cave as possible – the *chao naam* have to climb a precarious network of bamboo and vine scaffolding.

Most day-trips to Ko Phi Phi Leh combine visits to the cave and lagoon with snorkelling in the western bay of **Ao Maya**, by far the best spot for spectacular coral formations.

KO ROK NOK AND KO ROK NAI
See Ko Lanta Yai, pages 229-30.

KO RAYA NOI AND KO RAYA YAI
See Phuket, Local Explorations: 8, page 224.

KO YUNG AND KO MAI PHAI
See Ko Phi Phi Don, page 231.

BIRD'S NEST SOUP
Eating a soup of bird's saliva may not sound very appealing, but to wealthy Chinese gourmets in Hong Kong, Taiwan and Singapore there's no better delicacy for boosting your libido. The saliva is secreted by female sea swallows (*Collocalia esculenta*) to bind their nests together. Cooked in chicken broth, the nests soften to look like fine noodles. Bird's nest soup is believed to have a range of medicinal properties, which help to cure loss of energy, skin and lung problems as well as a faltering love life.

Since the swallows sensibly build their nests as high up as possible, either inside caves or in crevices of sheer rock faces, gathering them is a precarious business. Collectors – usually native *chao naam* (sea gypsies) – have to be both brave and agile, clambering up flimsy bamboo scaffolding to scrape the nests off the walls.

There's money at stake: a hundred top-quality nests (weighing a total of about a kilo) will eventually be sold for up to U.S. $2,000.

Since the business is so lucrative, it has to be strictly controlled: harvesting is only allowed twice a year (usually between February and May, and again in September) and only those who have a government licence are permitted to do it.

RECOMMENDED HOTELS

KO LANTA
Lanta Villa, B-BB; Hat Klong Dao; tel. 075 620629; credit cards, MC, V.

One of the smartest and most popular bungalow resorts on the island, with a range of bungalows at different prices. All have attached bathrooms, fan and overnight electricity. The spacious Thai-style cottages are ideal for families.

Sea House, B-BB; Hat Klong Dao.

The emphasis here is on cleanliness and comfort: even the garden is neat and tidy.

Relax Bay Tropicana, B-BB; Hat Phra Ae; radio tel. 01 7220089; fax 075 620618.

A very stylish place: large wooden bungalows in a shady, landscaped setting, with artistically Bohemian 'open-air' bathrooms so you can star-gaze in your shower.

Blue Lanta, B; Hat Klong Khoang.

Modern, charming bungalows under the shade of coconut palms.

KO PHI PHI
During the high season (November to February) budget accommodation (especially on the beaches) is often hard to find. You may have to spend a night in one of the grotty village rooms (or under the stars) before a room becomes available in the best-located budget resorts of Hat Yao. Avoid the PP Andaman Resort where there have been reports of theft by members of staff (its regimented rows of green huts are hideous, anyway).

Maphrao (Coconut) Bungalows, B-BB; W end of Hat Yao (Long Beach).

With only 25 bamboo bungalows (some with prow-shaped terraces) tucked up among the trees on the hillside, this is the cosiest and most secluded budget resort on the island. It was established by a young Belgian couple, Guy and Marie-Pia, eight years ago (their 16-year-old son is a fanatic diver and can tell you all the best places to go) and is famous for its well-stocked sea-view cocktail bar (get there for happy hour, 5 pm to 7 pm).

Paradise Pearl Resort, B-BB; *Hat Yao (Long Beach)p; radio tel.* 01 7230484; *credit cards (minimum B2,000)* MC, V.

More than 80 bungalows (the newest cottages are very smart), a large restaurant, diving and tour facilities, long-tail service to and from the pier, and a fabulous beach on your doorstep: no wonder this place is popular. Frederik Jurricause is the efficient Englishman (despite his name) who keeps the operation buzzing.

Charlie's Beach Bungalows, B-BB; *Ao Lo Dalam; radio tel.* 01 7230495; *tel./fax* 075 620615; *credit cards*, MC, V.

Pleasant thatched bungalows in a shady, floral setting, just a step away from the quiet Lo Dalam beach (the cheapest are much further back and uncomfortably close to the generator). Entertainment ranges from satellite TV in the restaurant to beach-side barbecues and live music every night.

PP Islands Cabana, BBBB; *Ao Ton Sai; tel./fax* 075 612132; *credit cards*, AE, MC, V.

The swankiest place on the island: elegant bungalows as well as a new 200-room hotel overlooking Ton Sai bay. The adjacent **Ton Sai Village** is the sister-resort, with pretty bungalows surrounded by coconut palms in the lee of the cliff.

=====
RECOMMENDED RESTAURANTS
=====

KO LANTA
If you're staying at one of the more remote beaches, you'll probably be restricted to eating at your own bungalow resort. But if you're in Hat Klong Dao you have much more choice (and the food is often better, too). The seafood barbecues (offered at nearly all the resorts) are superb value.

Danny's Restaurant, B-BB; *S end of Hat Klong Dao.*

Danny has made this a landmark in Lanta: his menu has 300-plus items, both Thai and international. And his

Sunday night eat-all-you-can for B70 buffets are legendary: get there by 7 pm to beat the crowds.

Team Bungalows, B-BB; *S end of Hat Khlong Nin.*

Healthy home cooking (using home-grown vegetables and herbs) in a beautifully landscaped garden.

KO PHI PHI
Mama's, BB-BBB; *Ao Ton Sai; tel.* 075 620078; *credit cards*, AE, MC, V.

When 35-year-old Angelo Rasamimanana (former barman, baker, guide and painter) and his Thai wife Ying opened this first seafood restaurant in Phi Phi nine years ago, it was a one-table, one-bench affair with no set prices ("We just asked customers what they thought was reasonable"). Now it's one of the largest and best, offering a wide choice of fresh seafood, temptingly displayed outside every evening, as well as Australian steaks and other international fare (and wines). The waiters (especially the fellow who looks like a Rastafarian) are a jolly lot. Go early to grab a street-side table (great for people watching).

Garlic 1992, BB; *Ao Ton Sai.*

A pleasant choice for Thai fare (especially north-eastern), also for seafood. The prawn kebab with pineapple fried rice is a favourite.

Pee Pee Bakery, B-BB; *Ao Ton Sai; credit cards*, MC, V.

Very popular for breakfasts (it's packed by 8 am), this is the place to gorge on *baguettes* and chocolate brownies, banana cakes and *capuccino*. You can even buy birthday cakes here.

Krabi and Region

56 km; maps Nelles, 1:1,500,000; also Guide Map of Krabi by V. Hongsombud

Not so many years ago, tourists had hardly heard of this area. Nearby Phuket kept them enthralled. But with a similarly stunning coastal scenery of limestone crags and mountains, and with dozens of islands offshore in the Andaman Sea, it was only a matter of time before the province began to lure travellers to its shores.

Krabi town is now the centre of a whole new area of discovery, a jumping-off point not only for the highly popular Ko Phi Phi and up-and-coming Ko Lanta islands (see Local Explorations: 9) but also for the spectacular beaches of the nearby Laem Phra Nang headland, with its dramatic karst formations, caves and dazzling, clear seas. Most visitors base themselves here, though if you're interested in exploring the little-known interior of tropical forests and mountains, you'd be better off staying in town for a few days.

Birdwatchers, naturalists and rock climbers will get a special buzz from this area: the rare Gurney's pitta (once thought to be extinct) has been spotted in several places including one of the last remaining areas of lowland rainforest in Thailand, 56 km south of town, while jungle safaris in the Khao Phanom Bencha National Park, 25 km north, will give you the chance to discover virgin rainforest and dramatic waterfalls. Laem Phra Nang, meanwhile, has become something of a cult destination for rock climbers who tackle (sometimes by spotlight) the sheer limestone stacks that tower above the beach.

Be prepared for this intoxicating cocktail of attractions to seduce you: whether you just loll in the sun or go jungle trekking, birdwatching, island-hopping, scuba diving, canoeing, or rock climbing, you'll need at least a week before the spell starts to fade. If you're exploring the area in depth (for instance by motorbike) it's worth picking up the detailed *Guide Map of Krabi* by V. Hongsombud, available in Krabi town. Note that the south-west monsoon can make the seas choppy and access to some beaches and islands tricky (or impossible) from May to October.

TRANSPORT

The quickest way to Krabi is to fly from Bangkok to Phuket (nearly a dozen flights daily, taking 75 minutes) and then take a bus or minibus (two hours). The cheaper option is to take the overnight train (giving you a nine-hour sleep) to Surat Thani, arriving soon after dawn for a three-and-a-half-hour bus ride to Krabi. Air-conditioned buses all the way from Bangkok take about 14 hours.

From Ko Phi Phi there are usually three sailings a day to Krabi and two daily from Ko Lanta.

1:1,500.000

SIGHTS & PLACES OF INTEREST

AO NANG ⚓ ✕

Easily accessible by road from Krabi town (songthaews make the 45-minute, 17-km run through the day), this bay has become one of the most developed in the area, with middle- and upper-range resorts and hotels that cater largely to the post-backpacker generation. But it's still a mostly low-rise, low-key development, and Ao Nang's main attractions – its long sandy beach and panorama of offshore craggy islands – remain as appealing as ever.

In addition to easy access, another advantage of staying here, rather than the more remote Laem Phra Nang, is that the long seafront road has everything you'll need for a stress-free holiday by the sea: restaurants, shops and cafés, tailors, minimarts and exchange facilities, as well as tour operators and various outfits encouraging you to take to the seas.

Among the more unusual of these are two **sea canoeing** operations (Sea Canoe Thailand, based at Phra Nang Inn, and Krabi Canoe Tour, at Gift's Bungalows) which offer outings to nearby rock outcrops and mangrove canals. Sea Canoe's 'back to nature adventures' can last up to ten days. There are also half-a-dozen **scuba diving** shops which cater for both novices and experienced divers. You may find diving prices higher here than in Phuket or Ko Phi Phi, but the attractions are said to be well worth the extra cost: within a 20 to 60-minute boat ride you can reach some excellent sites, especially around **Ko Poda** and **Ko Hua Khwan** (known as Chicken Island), which lie just south of Ao Nang. Many hotels and guesthouses here and in town also organize day snorkelling trips to these and other nearby islands.

From Ao Nang, too, there's a daily sightseeing and snorkelling trip to Ko Phi Phi on the *Ao Nang Princess* ferry, though you don't actually get much time to see the island. Easier day trips which you can do yourself are around the headland to **Ao Rai Leh** and **Laem Phra Nang**: long-tail boats nip to and fro regularly throughout the day on a spectacular 15-minute ride past the coastline's limestone crags. These boat trips usually only run from November to April: during the monsoon season you'll find Ao Nang deserted, many of its hotels closed and its seas too rough for trips.

A couple of kilometres north-west of Ao Nang (jump on a Krabi-bound songthaew to get here) is **Hat Noppharat Thara** beach, part of the Hat Noppharat Thara-Ko Phi Phi National Marine Park. While Ao Nang beach caters very much for foreign tourists, this one attracts a predominantly local clientèle who come here to paddle in the shallow seas, stroll along the pine-shaded beach, and snack on the seafood and spicy north-eastern food sold at various stalls at the far end of the beach. It's a relaxing spot, and with few tourists, especially around the Khlong Son River (past the food vendors and the useless park Visitor's Centre) where long-tails and fishing boats are drawn up to the shore. It's across this estuary, too, that you'll find some of Krabi's most secluded beach accommodation: to get there, hail a long-tail ferry to take you across.

The much-touted **Shell Cemetery (Su-Saan Hawy)**, 19 km west of Krabi, isn't worth a special trip: it sounds exciting – a shoreline of shell fossils 75 million years old – but the reality is disappointing and dull, with the compressed fossils looking like a heap of paving stones. It's far more thrilling to catch a glimpse of it from your long-tail boat as it races dramatically across the sea from Krabi to Laem Phra Nang.

KHAO NOR CHUCHI

This area of lowland rainforest – the last significant patch in southern Thailand – lies *some 56 km SE of Krabi* and incorporates the **Thung Tieo Nature Trail**, a 2.7-km easy and well-signposted walking route through the forest from the village of Ban Bang Tieo. Established in 1990 by the Khao Nor Chuchi Lowland Forest Project (a joint project between Bangkok's Mahidol University and the International Council for Bird Preservation) the trail gives you the chance to see one of the world's rarest birds: Gurney's pitta, a brightly coloured ground-living bird, which exists in small pockets of Thailand's southern rainforests. It is only a chance, though: the bird is so shy and reclusive it was thought for many years to be extinct.

But there are more than 308 other bird species in these forests, as well as barking deer, wild pig, civets, monkeys, squirrels, flying lizards and thousands of butterflies, so any visit here is a delight for nature-lovers, even if the pitta fails to put in an appearance. An added attraction if you want to be here at dawn (the best time for bird-spotting) is that you can stay overnight – all services for visitors such as meals and accommodation (in thatched huts) are arranged by Project workers, with profits going to the Project's work of reforestation, wildlife research and rural development.

Getting here is easier by rented motorbike than by public transport: you first have to get to the town of Khlong Thom (40 km south of Krabi on Highway 4), then turn off (or take a motorbike taxi) to Ban Bang Tieo, 16 km east. Or you can ask Chan Phen Tour in Krabi to arrange a taxi songthaew all the way.

KHAO PHANOM BENCHA NATIONAL PARK

This pocket of mountainous rainforest 25 *km* N *of* K*rabi* may be small – the park is just 50 sq. km in size – but it's packed with precious wildlife: more than 150 species of birds (including Gurney's pitta, see Khao Nor Chuchi, page 236 and above) and 32 recorded species of mammals including the Malayan sun bear and tapir, clouded leopard and wild boar, Asiatic black bears, macaques and civets.

To most Thai tourists, however, the park is best known for its 11-tiered Huay To Falls and Huay Sadeh Falls, both close to the park headquarters and popular picnic sites at weekends. If you're energetic enough for further exploration, you can follow a couple of trails (also near the park HQ) for an hour's steep climb up into the interior.

Sadly, the park's lush primary rainforest, which supports hundreds of plant and tree species, is increasingly at risk from illegal loggers and lowland farmers: the surrounding lowlands have already been decimated, stripped of their indigenous trees and converted into money-making plantations of rubber trees and oil palms. If the destruction continues, soon there will be nothing left.

Visits from tourists can only help keep the park in the public eye. The easiest way to get there is with one of the hotels, guesthouses or tour operators in Krabi (for example, Dawn of Happiness Resort or Chan Phen Tour on Utarakit Road) which run day-trip 'jungle safaris' to the park, giving you time for a swim in the waterfall pools. Under your own steam, it's only really feasible by rented songthaew or motorbike: from the Talaat Kao crossroads on Highway 4 north of Krabi, turn right for 1 km and then left for 20 km to Ban Huay To and the nearby park entrance. Motorbike thefts at the waterfall parking site have been a problem recently: be sure to chain up your bike or ask a park official to keep an eye on it.

KRABI 🖂 ✕

Getting to Krabi is a good deal more exciting than the place itself: the surrounding landscape is an army of Tolkienesque peaks, with fingers and fists of forested rock towering over plantations of rubber and coconut palms. It's a hard act to follow and Krabi initially comes as something of a disappointment. Considering the number of travellers now passing through on their way to Ko Phi Phi and Ko Lanta, this small provincial capital, *directly across the Andaman Sea from Phuket* (180 *km by road*) is still surprisingly low-key. It was originally situated 5 km further north, at Talaat Kao, but King Chulalongkorn apparently suggested that the town should be moved to its present location, near the mouth of the Krabi River.

It's a relaxing spot, though, and grows on you if you give it a few days. Most tourists don't, of course, since the nearby islands and beaches (Ao Nang and Laem Phra Nang are just 45 minutes away) have far greater appeal. But although the town itself has nothing much to offer in the way of cultural interest, there is a wide choice of accommodation and restaurants and efficient tour operators who can arrange day trips to nearby forests and national parks.

One of the easiest and most popular trips (especially with birdwatchers) is to the **mangrove swamps** along the Krabi River estuary. Any of the long-tail boatmen just north of the main pier can give you a one-hour tour (expect to pay around B100-200). However, the best man to get is Khun Dai (ask at Chan Phen Travel): he knows just where to go to find the most birds. He'll probably want to start early, around 7am. It's not just the birds that make this trip enthralling. The mangrove swamps are a fascinating world of fiddler crabs and mudskippers (a kind of fish that loves nothing better than squirming about in the mud), otters and crab-eating macaques.

For a contrast, take a songthaew from town to **Wat Tham Seua** (Tiger Cave Temple), about 8 km to the north-east (motorbike taxis waiting at the highway turn-off will take you the last few kilometres for B10). Built among limestone cliffs and woods, this forest wat and its young abbot, Ajaan Jamnien, are well known throughout Thailand and at weekends the place is packed with devotees and sightseers.

The main bot, on your left as you arrive, is built into a low, deep cave, decorated not only with portraits of the smiling, rotund abbot but also with macabre photos of corpses with smashed skulls, and a glass cabinet containing a skeleton. Like some ghoulish Victorian fairground attraction, they draw a crowd of fascinated visitors, but their real purpose is as visual aids to meditating on the frailty of life. Even more gruesome photos of dissected corpses await you in the heart of the complex – though this isn't what you'll remember about this extraordinary spiritual enclave.

You reach it by climbing a short hill by the gaudy statue of Kuan Yin (the Chinese Goddess of Mercy), beyond the bot. On the other side of the ridge you enter a dense forest enclosed on all sides by cave-pitted cliffs. This is where the monks live, in individual little huts (called *kutis*) set alongside various recesses and caves, some of which serve as chapels, complete with Buddha images. As you follow the path through the jungle woods with their towering trees draping thick liana roots, you feel

GETTING TO LAEM PHRA NANG
One of the reasons this headland west of Krabi is so dramatic is that it's only accessible by long-tail boat, either from Krabi (45 minutes) or from Ao Nang (15 minutes). The sea gets very choppy in the afternoon (be prepared to get drenched), and so rough during the monsoon season (May to October) that long-tails rarely brave the Ao Nang crossing and will usually only go from Krabi to Hat Rai Leh beach. The journey costs B40 per person from Krabi, or B20 per person from Ao Nang.

DETOUR – **THAN BOKKHARANI**
This national park *off Highway 4, 50 km NW of Krabi and just a kilometre S of Ao Leuk*, is a delightful detour on the way to or from Ao Phang Nga and Phuket. Set in a forest of tall trees, a series of small waterfalls cascades down from a cliff, interspersed by pools where you can bathe. At weekends, locals love coming to 'Than Bok' (also sometimes spelled Thanboke Khoranee), but on weekdays it's enchantingly quiet.

Day-tours from Krabi usually concentrate on the caves within the park boundaries, notably **Tham Hua Kalok**, in a hill above a canal, which features 2,000-year-old cave paintings. If you want to get here yourself, rent a motorbike since there's no public transport: the cave is only accessible by chartered boat from Tha Baw Thaw, 6 km southwest of Than Bok.

utterly cut off from the world outside. In reality, the monks are well catered for – electricity lines lead down to their *kutis* and there are even a couple of washing machines around – but the sense of isolation and tranquillity is overwhelming. Deeper into the forest, deeper sinks the silence: at the heart of the wood in the most sacred, sun-spangled spot of all, you'll come across two giant trees, their vast buttressed roots wrapped in offerings of coloured cloth.

As I was leaving the wat, I stopped to buy a drink at a stall. A beautiful young nun served me. Her name was Tay, she told me, and she had come to the wat from Surat Thani several months ago because she was suffering from a "broken heart". She didn't live in the woods – that was only for the monks – but she walked there every day. "And would she stay for long?" I asked. She smiled, and her face radiated serenity. "For ever," she said. "This place has given me back my happiness." After walking in the woods, I knew what she meant.

LAEM PHRA NANG 🛏 ✕
This headland is one of the most spectacular corners of the Krabi coastline. Its three beaches – Hat Tham Phra Nang, Hat Rai Leh and Ao Rai Leh – are now

densely packed with bungalow resorts (and one very up-market hotel), with long-tail boats zipping to and fro throughout the day. But the drama of the setting remains extraordinary.

The most photographed beach is **Hat Tham Phra Nang**, sometimes also called the Bay of Phra Nang or **Ao Phra Nang** (not to be confused with Ao Nang, page 236). It's a tiny pocket of sand dominated by huge limestone stacks towering a hundred metres high. Just off shore is another craggy outcrop, surrounded by reefs in a crystal-clear sea. In the cliff at the eastern end of the beach is the **Tham Phra Nang** itself – the **Princess Cave** which is believed by local fisherfolk to be the palace of a mythical sea princess. At the entrance you'll see wooden phallic offerings made to ensure successful catches.

You can clamber inside the cave (from an entrance along the wooden walkway to Hat Rai Leh beach) to the **Princess Lagoon (Sa Phra Nang)**, though be prepared for a tough 45-minute descent, using ropes for help. A left fork along the way will take you to a viewpoint in the cliff overlooking the two Rai Leh beaches.

Of these, **Ao Rai Leh (or Sunset Beach)** is the best: a long sweep of fine sand, with a dramatic backdrop of coconut palms and craggy cliffs. The best budget accommodation is here, too, in a series of bungalow resorts set back from the beach. Walking through the Railey Bay Bungalows complex for five minutes will bring you to **Hat Rai Leh (Sunrise Beach)** the other side of the headland, where long-tails often dock (especially during the monsoon season). You can forget the beach: mangroves and mud, litter and construction debris make it a dismal contrast to the other two beaches. But you will find many of the long-term residents who organize rock climbing or diving courses based in the bungalows here: Phra-Nang Adventures, for instance, operates from Railey Bay Bungalows 2, offering rock climbing, trekking and abseiling courses, while the Phra Nang Diving School is based in the Viewpoint Resort, and Baby Shark Divers in Sunrise Bay Bungalows.

Hat Rai Leh can also boast the **Inner Princess Cave (Tham Phra Nang Nai)**, a trio of caverns with dazzling stalactites in a cliff at the northern end of the beach. It's not always possible to

---

BIRDS OF THE KRABI AREA

The sea may be startling, the landscape magnificent, but for dedicated twitchers, it's the birdlife which is the most exciting thing about this area. The Birdwatchers' Comments Book kept at May & Mark Restaurant in Krabi gives full details of what's flying where. For instance:

Tara Park, Krabi: *black-shouldered kite, bar-tailed godwit, black-capped kingfisher, black-naped oriole.*

Mangrove swamps, Krabi: *common and greater crested tern, curlew sandpiper, Nordmann's greenshank, Pacific reef egret, white-bellied sea eagle, mangrove pitta, dollarbirds, nightjars and mangrove blue fly catcher.*

Ao Nang: *Malaysian plovers, woodcock, blue rock thrush, red-throated fly catcher, blue-throated bee eater.*

Khao Nor Chuchi: *Gurney's pitta, bushy crested hornbill, emerald dove, Diard's trogan, ruddy kingfisher.*

Khao Phanom Bencha National Park: *vernal hanging parrot, chestnut-breasted malkoha, white-crowned hornbill, argus pheasant, bronzed drongo, striped wren-babbler, bulbuls, Asian paradise flycatcher.*

Ko Phi Phi Don: *bridled tern, lesser frigate, pied imperial pigeon, sea eagle, greater racket-tailed drongo, greater-breasted Booby.*

Ko Lanta: *silver-rumped swift, oriental dwarf kingfisher, Wallace's hawk eagle, brown shrike, oriental scops owl.*

---

gain access: ask at your guesthouse for the latest information or a guide.

The narrow boardwalk which connects the southern end of Hat Rai Leh with Hat Tham Phra Nang by hugging the Princess Cave's cliff passes Laem Phra Nang's most salubrious accommodation, the Dusit Rayavadee, whose two-storey pavilions have been discreetly built among the coconut groves. You'll know when you've strayed on to their land because a guard will tell you so; but apart from an ugly W.C. block (the Dusit's 'gift' to Laem Phra Nang's tourists), this large luxury complex has managed to remain relatively unobtrusive.

WAT THAM SEUA

See Krabi, page 238.

RECOMMENDED HOTELS

AO NANG
Ao Nang Thara Lodge, BB; Mu 2, Tambon Ao Nang; tel. 01 7230517; credit cards, AE, MC, V.

In a peaceful hillside setting five minutes' walk from the seafront melée, with grand views of Hat Noppharat Thara and the surrounding cliffs. The thatched-roof bungalows are in somewhat regimented rows but softened by trellises of bougainvillea: very pretty. You'd need to book well ahead in season – this is a popular place with Europeans, especially Germans.

Phra Nang Inn, BBBB; Ao Nang; tel. 075 612173; fax 075 612174; credit cards, AE, MC, V.

Bagging the best place at the southern end of the bay, this luxury resort has a bizarrely rustic appearance, with thatched roofs and a coconut bark exterior. The gnarled wood furnishings and rooms with shell-encrusted walls border on *kitsch*, but it's saved by a profusion of interior greenery and spectacular views of the bay's limestone cliffs.

KRABI
K.R. Mansion Hotel, B; 52/1 Chao Fa Road, Krabi; tel. 075 612761.

Despite its name, this is actually a modest little guesthouse five minutes' walk south-west of the town centre. Efficiently run by young Klang (he's the one with the cross-shaped earring dangling from his left earlobe) it provides everything a traveller needs: decent rooms and food (the curries are legendary), ticketing, travel information and local tours (ask for Mr Dum, the guide).

Grand Tower Guest House, B; Utarakit Road, Krabi; tel. 075 612948.

A popular travellers' haunt close to the post office and town centre, with six floors of rooms at various prices (the most expensive have private bathrooms).

Viengthong Hotel, BB; 155 Utarakit Road, Krabi; tel. 075 611188.

A typical hotel, huge (150 rooms) and rather impersonal, but with the best riverside location in town and rooms that can boast carpeting, air-conditioning, phone and refrigerator.

Dawn of Happiness Beach Resort, BB; Ao Nam Mao, Krabi; tel. 075 612730; fax 075 612251.

Situated off the road to the Shell Cemetery (Route 4204), 17 km west of Krabi, this family-run resort is notable for its environmentally-conscious approach: no sewage into the sea, no litter on the grounds and educational tours arranged to rubber plantations and national parks. Naturally, the thatched bungalows are environmentally-friendly, too, made of local materials and with no superfluous synthetic luxuries (in other words, they're very simple).

LAEM PHRA NANG
If you're looking for rock-bottom budget accommodation on the cape, be careful to check where the generators and video-bars are: your humble little seashore haven may be ruined by the night-time noise. There's one place, however, where such intrusions are the last thing you need worry about:

Dusit Rayavadee Resort, BBBB; Hat Tham Phra Nang; tel. 075 620740; fax 075 620630; credit cards, AE, MC, V.

If you don't mind feeling as if you're in a different world from the backpackers on the adjacent beaches (which you are, of course), this deluxe resort, complete with tennis and squash courts, swimming pool, exercise and water sports centre, offers you the best accommodation on the Krabi coastline: the resort's unusual circular bungalows are set in 26 acres of landscaped gardens just a few steps from Hat Tham Phra Nang beach. High season rates *start* at B9,000.

Viewpoint Bungalows, BB; East Rai Leh beach.

At the far northern end of the beach, this modern white building looks oddly out of place among the scruffier bungalow resorts. Geared to Thai visitors, it boasts fan-cooled rooms with modern bathrooms. There's an excellent restaurant here, too.

Railey Bay Bungalows, B-BB; West
and East Rai Leh beaches; tel. 075 611944,
ext. 41; fax 01 7220112.

One of the largest bungalow complexes on the headland, stretching
across to both Ao and Hat Rai Leh
beaches, and featuring a variety of cottages and bungalows in different price
ranges, as well as a minimart, gift shop
and efficient tour counter.

Railey Village Bungalows, B-BB;
West Rai Leh beach; tel. 075 611944, ext.
27.

Very similar to Railey Bay, with a
choice of cheap thatched huts (away
from the beach) or modern concrete
cottages with attached bathrooms.
Check out Buck and Sonya's *batik*
painting lessons, given outside their
hut, number 410 (the cheap, hippy end
of the complex).

Ya Ya Bungalows, B-BB; East Rai Leh
beach.

The most unusual bungalows on the
headland: three- to four-storey wood
and bamboo constructions like tree
houses, surrounded by papaya trees
and coconut palms and facing a
secluded little area. If possible, choose
a room away from the generators.

RECOMMENDED RESTAURANTS

AO NANG
At the northern end of the beach (just
past Route 4203 as it heads to the
Krabi Resort and Ao Nang Thara
Lodge) is a little seaside lane known as
Soi Sunset which has a lively bunch
of open-air bars and restaurants. This
is the place to head for in the evenings
(go early to get a beach-side table).
Sala Thai Restaurant is my personal
favourite, but they all serve delicious
(though rather expensive) seafood,
kebabs and Thai curries.

Gift's, B-BB; Ao Nang Beach; tel. 01
7231128.

The aroma of freshly-baked bread
from Gift's Kitchen & Bakery is enough
to lure bread-deprived travellers off the
streets in droves. There's plenty more
on the menu, too, of course, and fresh
seafood every evening. This is the sort

of place where they serve drinks decorated with orchid flowers but aren't
too stuffy to serve hippies too. The
Vietnamese waiter is particularly welcoming to one and all.

KRABI
Ruen Mai Thai, BB; 319 Uttarakit Rd;
tel. 075 611365.

Traditional Thai food in a delightful
setting: either inside a house built from
teak and furnished with antiques, or
outside in the garden. Long favoured
by locals for its excellent seafood. The
owner is planning to move to a new
location just outside town: ask around
if you can't find it here any more.

May & Mark, B-BB; 6 Ruen Rudee
Road; tel. 075 612562.

Run by the always-jolly Khun Kittiya
(the restaurant is named after her children) this is a favourite haunt for both
travellers and ex patriot residents, with
a mouth-watering menu: home-made
brown bread and yogurt, *enchiladas*
and *tacos*, even caviar on toast. You
can get tour information here, too
(birdwatchers should ask for the
detailed Birdwatchers' Comments
Book) – and make 'over seacalls'.

Roti & Curry Muslim Café, B; Preusa
Uthit Road; closes by 6 pm.

The best place in town for
Malaysian-style curries (the chicken
and potato curry is especially tasty)
and freshly-made *roti* (flat bread). Try
it for breakfast or lunch.

Night market, B; Khongkha Rd, near
the Chao Fah pier.

Cheap and delicious seafood, deep-
fried snacks, mussel omelettes, fresh
fruit, colourful desserts – and a breezy
riverside setting.

LAEM PHRA NANG
Coco's, B-BB; East Rai Leh beach.

You may not want to stay at Coco's
(the bungalows are pretty basic) but
you should definitely eat here: not only
is the food excellent, but the setting is
delicious, combining tropical, open-air
ingredients with just the right flavour
of background music. Go early to be
sure of getting a table.

The East Coast to Ko Chang

400 *km*; *map* Nelles 1: 1,500,000

Ko Chang is Thailand's second largest island after Phuket: 492 sq. km of mostly virgin forest, hills and beaches, waterfalls and coconut plantations. But relatively few visitors make it this far round the east coast (almost to the Cambodian border), and the island remains remarkably unspoilt, an ideal low-key getaway with enough decent accommodation to make life comfortable. It's not hard to get to, just time-consuming: about six hours by bus from Bangkok, followed by a two to three-hour boat ride. You can actually do it in a day from Bangkok if you leave early enough.

But there are plenty of places *en route* which could tempt you to spin the trip into several days. Thailand Overall: 6, following the first part of the east coast, combines well with this itinerary if you're keen to dawdle by the sea. And on this Local Exploration, a major place of interest is the gem-trading town of Chanthaburi, fascinating not only for its shops of sapphires and rubies but also for its Catholic Vietnamese influences.

With the Cambodian border so close it's also worth taking a day-trip from Trat through some dramatic landscape to the end of Highway 318 where the border town of Khlong Yai offers a peep at the huge amount of trading (and smuggling) that goes on between Thailand and Cambodia. For fine scenery and rainforest hikes, there are a couple of national parks with very pretty waterfalls less than an hour from Chanthaburi.

Note that both inland and on Ko Chang especially, malaria is rife: be sure to bring plenty of mosquito repellent and a net.

TRANSPORT

Air-conditioned buses from Bangkok's eastern terminal run to Chanthaburi every half hour and to Trat every one or two hours, taking around five and six hours respectively. You can also reach Chanthaburi direct from the north-east town of Khorat, a five-hour bus journey.

Boats leave regularly from Laem Ngop (25 minutes' songthaew from Trat) for the various beaches of Ko Chang, at least three times daily during high season to the popular west coast beaches. During the monsoon season (May to October) the seas are sometimes too rough for boats to venture round to the west coast, but overland transport should be available from the east coast Hat Sai Tong pier. You can get to Ko Chang from Bangkok within a day if you leave by 8 am.

During the non-monsoon season (November to May), boats leave once daily from Laem Ngop for Ko Mak, Ko Khlam and Ko Wai. For the other islands you may have to take a coconut boat from the canal pier at Trat or charter a boat. Enquire at your bungalow resort in Ko Chang or guesthouse in Trat.

1:1,500,000

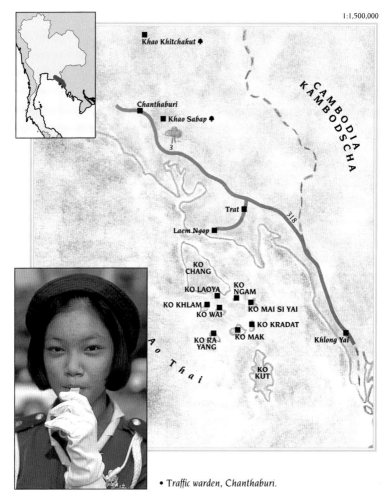

• *Traffic warden, Chanthaburi.*

SIGHTS & PLACES OF INTEREST

CHANTHABURI ⌂ ×

Known as the City of the Moon, Chanthaburi is the undisputed gem capital of Thailand. Tucked into a bend of the Chanthaburi River, *some 300 km E of Bangkok*, this provincial capital has attracted gem miners and traders for centuries: major deposits of rubies and sapphires have been found in the hills behind. In many places the land is now pockmarked with mines and stripped bare of its trees, leaving gashes of raw red earth.

The first big gem rush in the 19thC attracted an influx of Cambodians, Burmese and Vietnamese, but it was actually anti-Catholic persecution in southern Vietnam which brought many more Vietnamese to Chanthaburi at this time. Later waves of Vietnamese fled from French and then Communist rule. The gem market and Vietnamese part of town are still the main reasons for visiting Chanthaburi, though if you like fruit you'll also be able to sample some of the country's best durian, mangosteen and rambutan from dozens of stalls in the market.

Arriving by bus (from Bangkok, air-conditioned buses leave every half-hour for the five-hour journey) you'll be dropped at the terminal on Saritidet Road, a short samlor hop north-west of the town centre. The **gem market** spreads along Tok Kachang and Thetsaban 4 Roads, not far from the river. Here you'll see traders haggling

with Bangkok dealers over piles of red and blue gems; craftsmen cutting and polishing and shopkeepers evaluating individual gems through microscopes. Fakes abound: don't try to buy anything here unless you can tell the difference. Many of the stones don't even come from the area any more, but from Cambodia, Burma, or Australia.

A short walk north-east from the market, across a footbridge over the river, brings you to Chanthaburi's **Catholic cathedral**, the largest in Thailand. It was reconstructed by the French from a smaller chapel in the late 19thC. It's not very attractive but it's certainly the most significant piece of architecture to emerge from the era of the Vietnamese Catholics' arrival. Other, more picturesque architectural evidence – old wooden-shuttered shophouses and residences – can be found if you walk along the town side of the river and north of the cathedral.

KHAO KHITCHAKUT NATIONAL PARK

One of Thailand's smallest parks, just 58 mountainous square kilometres of semi-evergreen rainforest, Khao Khitchakut harbours a surprisingly large number of birds and mammals – largely because of its proximity to the much larger Khao Soi Dao Wildlife Sanctuary to the north. Unfortunately, you're unlikely to see much of this wildlife since there are no trails for exploring the park's interior, although the dirt road to the top of **Phrabat Mountain** (an arduous three-hour climb) takes you deep into one part of the forest. Thousands of pilgrims follow this route every February to pay homage at the footprint of the Buddha engraved on a rocky outcrop at the top; according to legend, a hunter discovered the footprint more than 200 years ago when he stopped for a drink and was miraculously healed of a skin disease. The belief in the waters' medicinal qualities (as well as its easy access) makes the nine-level **Krathing Waterfall** the park's most popular sight, especially at weekends. A trail 300 m from the park entrance leads half a kilometre to the highest level.

To get to the park, which is *about 30 km NW of Chanthaburi*, hop on a songthaew at the market in town. This will take you to within 1.5 km of the park

---

DETOUR – SAPPHIRE-RING MOUNTAIN

Just 4 km N of Chanthaburi, off Route 3249, is Khao Phloi Waen, a small hill topped by a Ceylonese-style chedi which was built in the 19thC during the reign of King Rama IV. The hill gets its name, of course, from the sapphires which were once found here by the basketload. Now the mines have been abandoned and the search for gems moved elsewhere, notably across the border in Cambodia. Watch your step if you wander off the path: there are still plenty of treasure-hunters' holes around.

RECOMMENDED HOTELS

CHANTHABURI

Kasemsan I Hotel, B; 98/1 *Benchamarachutit Road; tel.* 039 312340.

The air-conditioned rooms here are better value than the street-facing fan rooms. Don't confuse this place with Kasemsan II, which has a noisy market location.

Mark's Travelodge, B-BB; 14 *Raksakchamun Road; tel.* 039 311531.

On the edge of town, but the large, comfortable rooms are value for money.

KO CHANG

During peak season (December to January) many of the cheaper bungalow resorts here are full, especially on the popular Hat Sai Khao.

Be prepared to walk or take a motorbike taxi until you find an available hut, or spend a night on the sand with the sand-fleas until there's a vacancy.

White Sand Beach Resort, B-BB; *Hat Sai Khao.*

Separated from the rest of the pack on the beach by a little rocky headland, this has a choice of ordinary or up-market huts (plus bathroom).

Ban Rung Rong, B; *Hat Sai Khao; tel.* 039 597184.

Well-run, with useful facilities such as currency exchange. Huts come in the usual range of spartan to simple.

Coconut Beach Bungalows, B-BB; *Ao Khlong Phrao.*

A pretty little beach without many other bungalows around, attractive huts and a conveniently close pier make this a popular hideaway.

Ko Chang Resort, BBBB; *Ao Khlong Phrao; tel.* 01 3290434; *or Bangkok reservation, tel.* 02 2761233/2541574; *fax* 02 2770975/2541573.

Incongruously smart, with 70 air-conditioned bungalows and all the frills. Naturally, the resort has its own boat and road transport so you don't have to mingle with the masses.

Kaibae Hut, B; *Hat Kaibae; tel.* 01 3290452.

My personal favourite, run by the jolly Khun Lek and kids. It's worth splashing out for the better huts with bath.

Sea View Resort, B-BBB; *Hat Kaibae; tel.* 013 210055; *Bangkok reservations, tel.* 02 4113605, *fax* 02 4114662.

Another enclave of luxury, at the southern end of Hat Kaibae, with a surprisingly wide range of huts. The large bungalows up above the beach are the best.

TRAT

Max & Tick Guest House, B; 1-3 *Soi Luang Aet, Lak Meuang Road - behind the market; tel.* 039 520799.

A backpackers' favourite, run by the friendly and informative Max & Tick.

RECOMMENDED RESTAURANTS

CHANTHABURI

Chanthaburi is famous for its rice noodles: you'll find many stalls selling them along the riverside road (keep an eye out for Vietnamese spring rolls, too).

KO CHANG

Most people eat at their bungalow resorts, but for something special it's worth taking a beach stroll to:

Bubby Bong's, B-BB; S *of Hat Sai Khao.*

The first and still most famous *farang*-run eaterie on the island, with a fabulous hillside and seaview position, and a laid-back Californian atmosphere.

Kaibae Hut, B-BB; *Hat Kaibae.*

OK, I'm biased because I stayed here, but even non-residents give Lek top marks for her homely restaurant and great food.

• *Khlong Yai.*

entrance, at Km 24 on Route 3249.

KHAO SABAP NATIONAL PARK
The **Phliu Waterfall** is the major attraction in this park, especially during the June durian and rambutan season when tens of thousands of Thai fruit lovers also flock here for picnics. It's easy to get to: just *15 km SE of Chanthaburi, 2 km off Highway 3*. The falls are 400 m from the park entrance.

The Phliu falls have a romantic association with royalty. The future King Chulalongkorn first came here with his bride when he was a prince; they were so enthralled that they returned some years later. After the Queen drowned in a boating accident in 1876, the King had a chedi and stone triangle monument built at the foot of the falls in her memory.

KHLONG YAI
It's worth missing your boat to Ko Chang to make this day trip *from Trat to the Cambodian border, 74 km and just over an hour's songthaew ride* away through some dramatic sea and mountain landscapes. Khlong Yai is a bustling fishing port and major market town for cross-border trade (not all of it legal).

It's safe enough to come here, but it's not advisable to wander north along the border: illegal gems, timber and arms trading for the ruthless Khmer Rouge goes on in this region.

KO CHANG 🛏 ×
At 30 km long and 8 km wide, Ko Chang is Thailand's second largest island after Phuket. The similarity with Phuket ends there although if you had visited Phuket 20 years ago you can imagine the kind of charm Ko Chang possesses.

To get to this Robinson Crusoe of an island, *8 km off the coast of Trat*, you have to suffer a little first: at least five hours by bus from Bangkok to Trat, followed by a short hop to the pier at Laem Ngop and two to three hours by boat to the island's west coast.

This kind of inaccessibility is one reason why Ko Chang has remained largely undeveloped and unknown, though during the high season backpackers flock here. If you're looking for somewhere on the eastern seaboard that's simple, cheap and lovely, with a wide choice of beach accommodation (including a couple of sophisticated resorts) but no raving nightlife, this is the place to head for.

Unfortunately, it's unlikely to stay this way for long. At the time of my visit, there were no paved roads and no electricity except for small generators. But the dirt track that almost circles the island is already being converted into a 30-km paved ring road, to be followed by power lines (and then, no doubt, by the big resort developers).

Ko Chang is in fact only one island (though the largest) in a 52-island archipelago which forms **Mu Ko Chang**

National Park. Some 70 per cent of the island is virgin forest, with a mountainous interior that reaches 744 m at Khao Jom Prasat. Only a few thousand people live on the island, mostly fishermen or farmers in scattered villages.

The best place to head for is the string of fine beaches on the west coast. The east coast has few attractions or bungalow resorts, though it's easy to get to if you want to explore: just follow the dirt road round the northern tip of the island, by motorbike or jeep taxi (on foot it takes hours). Boats from Laem Ngop leave at different times for the various beaches and resorts: the most frequent departures (at least three times a day in high season) are to the west coast's **Hat Sai Khao** (White Sand Beach), **Ao Khlong Phrao** and **Hat Kaibae**.

(Don't make my mistake and fail to go to the loo before leaving: many of these converted fishing boats have no W.C. facilities.)

Hat Sai Khao, the northernmost west coast beach, 5 km south of the island's main village of **Khlong Son**, is the longest and prettiest, and most crowded with bungalows, but there are plenty of alternatives if you keep heading south. **Hat Khlong Phrao** beach, divided by an estuary, hosts the island's most expensive Ko Chang Resort, but my own favourite hideaway is at **Hat Kaibae**, 15 km south of Khlong Son. The beach here is slim and rather pebbly, but the atmosphere is wonderfully relaxed. The most secluded beaches are **Ao Bang Bao** and **Ao Salek Phet** on the south coast, and **Hat Yao** on the south-east headland, although only Hat Yao can rival the west coast beaches. It's most easily reached by boat from Ao Salek Phet.

To get around the island you'll either have to walk along the dusty track (be warned: the beaches are often many kilometres apart), hire a motorbike taxi (which can be pricey), or rent your own mountain bike or motorbike (available at many resorts).

If you're a walker you'll find that some of Ko Chang's most enjoyable excursions are on foot to its inland waterfalls. The **Khlong Phu Falls** are just 45 minutes inland from Ao Khlong Phrao and there's a pleasant little pool beneath the falls where you can take a dip and cool off.

• *Catholic-Thai wedding, Chanthaburi.*

From the east coast village of Ban Dan Mai or Tha Than Mayom (site of the park's headquarters) you can also reach the **Than Mayom Falls**, a series of three waterfalls, the first about 45 minutes' climb from the coast, and the last about 3 km further on.

There are now several diving and watersports operations on the island, and many places offering day snorkelling trips to other islands in the park south of Ko Chang, such as **Ko Mak, Ko Ngam, Ko Wai, Ko Laoya** and even the more distant **Ko Kut**. You can reach some of these islands yourself direct from Laem Ngop, although accommodation is limited and often expensive.

TRAT 🚄

Most people just whizz through Trat on their way to *Laem Ngop, the small port 20 km away* where boats leave for Ko Chang (songthaews depart regularly for Laem Ngop from Trat's Sukhumvit Road, near the market). But if you arrive too late to go on, this provincial capital is a pleasant place for an overnight stop, and the guesthouses have useful information on nearby places to visit, including gem markets.

If you fancy a stroll, head for the canal area south of the market, which has some funky old shophouses.

Ko Samui, Ko Pha-Ngan and Ko Tao

Map Nelles 1:1,500,000

Many tropical islands are reputed to be paradise destinations, sometimes with good reason, sometimes not. Ko Samui is, despite everything that has happened to it over the past decade, one such island: beautiful white sandy beaches. crystal-clear turquoise waters, stunning sunsets, dozens of water-falls and a glut of coconut palms.

However: in high season, finding accommodation can be a real problem, and prices soar. More bunga-low resorts and hotels open every year; with them come the inevitable hangers-on: money changers, supermarkets, discos and even go-go bars.

So is it still worth going? I'd say yes, because although Samui is not as laid back and easy going as it was ten years ago, there are still beau-tiful, secluded beaches hidden away, great jungle and nature walks to be found on the hilly slopes in the centre of the island and, of course, the famed seafood dishes, prepared with coconut milk and local spices.

Nowadays Samui offers all kinds of water sports, too, and after dark there is entertainment to suit all tastes, ranging from pulsating reggae and house music to video bars and, at the other extreme, peaceful little cafés. For the early risers there are day and overnight trips to other islands, wonderful lagoons and the best diving in the Gulf of Thailand.

When you really want to get away from it all, the neighbouring island of Ko Pha-Ngan is the place to be: one hour by ferry from Samui, it is com-parable to Ko Samui ten years ago.

Then there's Ko Tao, some three hours by boat from Pha-Ngan, and smallest of the group. When Samui becomes excessively expensive, and when Pha-Ngan gets too crowded, then Ko Tao will probably start getting spoilt too. Mean-while, it is rapidly gaining in popularity.

All three islands in this section are best visit-ed from January until the monsoon season starts in September. From October until late Decem-ber you can expect rain and thunder storms.

1:3,000,000

1:400,000

TRANSPORT

Boats leave four piers in the neighbourhood of Surat Thani (but only three are in use at any given time). Two ferry companies and one jet boat company offer services. Songserm Travel runs express boats usually from Tha Thong Pier, 6 km north-east of central Surat Thani, also night boats (slow) from Ban Dom Pier in the town. Samui Ferry Co operates from Don Sak or Khanom when the sea is rough. Which service to use? Rely on the touts at the bus terminal – they'll lead you to the one with the next sailing.

There is an express boat service from Tha Thong, from November to May.

By air: Bangkok Airways flies daily (one hour ten minutes) from Bangkok. Book well ahead in high season – sometimes the service is full six weeks ahead. There is a rumour that Bangkok Airways will start regular flights between Hua Hin and Samui. To Ko Pha-Ngan from Ko Samui: boats twice daily from Na Thon; or from Surat Thani, stopping at Na Thon.

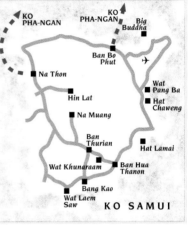

To Ko Tao: boats leave from mainland Chumphon and Surat Thani; also from Ko Pha-Ngan.

Exploring Samui is best done by rented motorbike or car – several outlets in Na Thon (B150 a day for a 100 cc bike. Samui's roads are well maintained and driving around is fairly straightforward. A word of caution: more and more people get involved in traffic accidents every year. Stay sober and wear trousers, shoes and a shirt to prevent minor scrapes in case of an unexpected accident.

If you want your own transport on Ko Pha-Ngan, hire an off-road motor bike in Thong Sala (about B300 a day).

On Ko Tao, use the pick-ups (B20 per trip by day), or long-tail boat, to any beach.

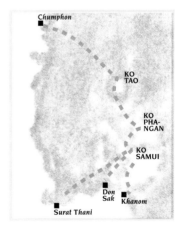

1:400,000

SIGHTS AND PLACES OF INTEREST

KO SAMUI

Island some 560 km S of Bangkok and two-and-half hours by fast boat from Surat Thani. Coconuts and palm trees, palm trees and coconuts... Ko Samui has a thriving coconut industry which forms, together with tourism, the main occupation for Samui's 35,000 residents. Nearly every part of the coconut is used: the milk for cooking, flesh for food and the fibres for thatching and bed stuffing. All over the island, but especially in the south-east, you will find people working with coconuts, and see trained monkeys climbing the trees to pick them. Millions of coconuts are shipped to Bangkok from Ko Samui every year.

Samui is Thailand's third largest island, 70 km in circumference and part of an archipelago of about 80 islands. Six, including Ko Samui, Ko Pha-Ngan and Ko Tao, are inhabited.

There is, of course, too much building and concrete on and around Samui's beaches. But because the beaches are long, the damage is not as bad as it might be – at any rate, there's nothing here yet to compare with, say, the Costa del Sol – if that's any consolation.

Lamai and **Chaweng** (see this page) are the two main beaches, and with good reason because, although the northern beaches such as **Ban Bo Phut** and **Big Budda Beach** are not as crowded, they are also not that great: they are smaller, the sand is not so white and they tend to be more rocky. If you really need to get away from people, the answer is to rent a motor bike and explore: perhaps the south-eastern part of the island where there are still beautiful little bays, especially near **Ban Hua Thanon**... but you do have to find them yourself.

Na Thon

Samui's main town is for many people no more than an arrival and exit point. The main post office, banks and money changers are here, and there are plenty of shops offering photo processing. There's an excellent market too. (Most of these facilities are also found on Lamai and Chaweng beaches.)

There are some pleasant restaurants in the town with gardens or terraces where you can relax while waiting for the ferry.

If you want to make an overseas phone call, do it at the main post office here – it's the only place that charges the normal rate.

Hat Chaweng

Some people prefer Chaweng Beach, others, Lamai. I prefer Chaweng: it's somewhat cleaner and the beach itself slopes gradually – it's enjoyable at low tide. The sand is whiter than Lamai's. Chaweng is 3 km long, with Chaweng Noi adding another kilometre to the south. At night, many restaurants, cafés, reggae pubs and discos come alive, and because of the competition, prices for food and drinks are fairly reasonable.

Hat Lamai

Lamai Beach is just as popular and as busy as Chaweng, but less up-market, with fewer three and five-star hotels. The people you find here tend to be the younger age-group, travelling independently.

As you go north from Lamai, the people thin out, but the beaches are less attractive.

Hin Lat and Na Muang Falls

Both these inland waterfalls are worthwhile expeditions, except in the dry season, when they may be disappointing. Hin Lat Falls are only 3 km south of Na Thon. Pick up the signposted trail from the main road about 100 m south of town, by the hospital.

Na Muang Falls are less visited, about 10 km from Na Thon: get a songthaew from Na Thon, Chaweng or Lamai.

Big Buddah Statue and Temple

A couple of kilometres north of the airport, on a tiny rocky island connected by a causeway. The 12-m-high statue is quite impressive; go at sunset for atmospheric views out to sea.

Shooting Range

North of Chaweng Beach, offering target practice with rifles.

Monkey Theatre

Also north of Chaweng Beach, you can witness the dubious spectacle of monkeys doing circus tricks and climbing

• *Ko Samui.*

coconut trees to collect the nuts.

Massage
Dozens of female masseurs ply the main beaches. It's difficult to say who is an expert, and who is not. Expect to pay B100-200 for an hour, and bargain the price.

Muay Thai
This Thai boxing ring is found at the northern outskirts of Na Thon. Some of the fights can be impressive, but they are essentially tourist entertainments: the big matches are staged in Bangkok and other centres.

Diving
Small dive outfits are found round the island. The cheap option is to dive from the beach – about B450 a day for equipment hire. A four-day introductory course may cost B5,000 or more. Some operators offer three-night diving trips to Ko Tao. The diving close to Ko Samui is generally not as good as Ko Pha-Ngan's or Ko Tao's.

Temples
Enthusiasts should make for **Bang Kao** village, at the southern end of the island, to view **Wat Laem Saw**; or for the northern end of Chaweng Beach to see **Wat Pang Ba**.

From the car park at Hin Lat Falls (see page 250) you can pick up a trail to **Suan Dharmapala**, a meditiation temple.

There is the ghoulish spectacle of a **mummified monk** at **Wat Khu-naraam**, between Ban Thurian and Ban Hua Thanom, off Route 4169.

Ang Thong National Marine Park
About 32 km west of Ko Samui, this park offers beautiful uninhabited islands, pretty lagoons and probably the best snokelling in the Gulf. On Ang Thong Island you can climb to the top of its 244-m high hill for a spectacular view of the whole group of islands, 40 in total.

You can make a day or overnight trip from Samui. Tours depart daily from Na Thon at 8.30 am and get you back to Ko Samui before sunset. For more information contact Samui Travel Service in Na Thon or at one of the other travel agencies on Ko Samui.

Other beaches
People tend to ignore the south-eastern beaches, such as Hua Thanon, near Laem Inn Bungalows, which is gently shelving and secluded. Explore this part of the island and you may well get a cove almost to yourself.

KO PHA-NGAN
By boat, about 50 minutes N of Ko Samui. Songserm Express boats depart Na Thon pier twice a day (typically 10.30 am and 4.30 pm, but check first). Return boats go from Pha-Ngan's Thong Sala pier around 12.30 pm and 6.15 pm. You can also go from Surat Thani, with a stop-over at Na Thon - see Ko Samui for further details.

In theory, Pha-Ngan is the simple,

mellow, peaceful, affordable alternative to Samui, with beautiful, deserted bays just for the asking, especially in the north-eastern part. In practice, anything written about the island is likely to become out of date before it is published, because as prices rise on Samui, pressure increases on its smaller neighbour.

The south-west of the island, in particular **Hat Rin,** is already a second Ko Samui, with video cafés, discos and the notorious Full Moon Parties, when once a month as many as 3,000 ravers party all night long on the beach to the latest music.

By contrast, the north-east is, at time of writing, accessible only by an unmade-up road. The 45-minute, bumpy ride by four- wheel drive taxi is good fun, and when you're there you can reasonably expect to find enough deserted, palm-fringed beaches to keep you happy.

The **diving** is excellent, with live coral formations.

The North-East

My favourite beach is **Ao Thong Nai Pan Yai**: white sand and aquamarine water. There are only three bungalow resorts so far and two small resorts, with delicious, bargain-priced food.

A hilly 15-minute walk on from Nai Pan Yai is **Ao Thong Nai Pan Noi**, almost as pretty, and a little larger and busier. A boat goes to both beaches once a day from Hat Rin beach.

Other unspoilt beaches in the north-east, accessible only by boat or on foot, are **Hat Khuat** (Bottle Beach) and **Chalok Lam.**

Hat Rin

This is actually two beaches, Hat Rin Nai and Hat Rin Nok, either side of a narrow isthmus. Bungalow resorts seem to be permanently under construction, but the beaches are undeniably beautiful, palm-fringed with white sand. Between here and Ao Thong Nai Pan Yai (see above) there are plenty of secluded beaches not served by roads

RECOMMENDED HOTELS

SAMUI

Arriving by boat, you'll be besieged in the usual Asian fashion by touts selling their bungalow resorts. Since most accommodation on Samui has 24-hour electricity and private bathroom and W.C., you could do worse than go with the most likely-looking tout for the first night. Next day, investigate what else is on offer.

Ikk Bungalows, B-BB; North Chaweng Beach.

This cosy little place situated in a secluded beach is great value. Only 12 bungalows, close to the beach, and only accessible via a small dusty road (or try swimming).

Laem Set Inn, BB-BBB; 110 Mu 2, Hua Thanon; tel. 077 424393.

Another secluded place to get away from it all, but more up-market than Ikk Bungalows. The restaurant is one of the best on the island and serves excellent local dishes. Value for money, especially the set menu at lunchtime, but don't forget to give the restaurant a day's notice in advance.

KO PHA-NGAN

There is a reasonable choice of hotels and bungalow operations at Hat Rin.

Honey Bungalows, B; Ao Ta Pa, Noi Bay.

The location is perfect, only 50 m away from the gently shelving beach. Cheap, plain bungalows, with electricity (most of the time), plus your own bathroom with W.C.

Panviman Resort, BBB; Ao Ta Pan Noi.

The best (air-conditioned) rooms in the north-eastern part of the island and a wonderful view of the bay; delicious barbecued seafood at very fair prices.

KO TAO

There are dozens of bungalow operations on Ko Tao, but they fill up quickly during the high season, especially those in the most accessible western and southern areas such as Mae Hat (the main village), Hat Sai Ri and Ao Chalok. The best solution is probably to take a tout's suggestion on arrival and then look around on your own the next day (if it's *really* full, you may have to sleep on the beach for a night or two). With new resorts opening all the time, it's also or other transport: it's well worth exploring on foot.

Thong Sala

It used to be a small fishing village; now it's the arrival point for Ko Pha-Ngan with moneychangers, a small post office, a couple of modest restaurants, some coffee shops and supermarkets. It's the only place on the island to organize onward tickets, hire motor bikes and buy souvenirs.

Exploring inland

Take the spectacular road to the northeastern part of the island for rugged country and untamed jungle. There are exotic birds, spiders, snakes and some huge lizards more than 1.5 m in length. The **Than Sadet** and **Phaeng Falls**, in the island's interior, are worth a visit.

Wat Khao Tham, near the village of Ban Tai, is a superbly sited cave temple on top of a hill. It was the eyrie of an American monk for ten years (his ashes are buried nearby); enquire about meditation retreats by writing, or by looking at notices on the information board at the temple.

KO TAO

Only 4 km wide and 8 km long, Ko Tao or Turtle Island (named after its turtle-like shape) has a resident population of around 750, still mostly dependent on fishing and coconuts for their income, although tourism is fast becoming an alternative source of employment.

It's a rugged little place with a long strip of west coast beach and one main village, **Ban Mae Hat**, where the ferries dock from Chumphon (see Thailand Overall: 7, pages 109-11, for details) and Ko Pha-Ngan – a daily boat, taking three hours, leaves Ko Pha-Ngan's Thong Sala pier around noon.

But it's not so much Ko Tao's simple island life which is drawing the crowds: it's the off-shore diving, in the clearest and most spectacular waters to be found in the Gulf.

worth checking with recent visitors on the latest situation. Some places have a nasty habit of throwing out guests who don't spend enough in their restaurants (you'll soon get to hear who they are). Others change hands and alter almost overnight. The following seem to have maintained their standards and reputations:

O-Chai, B; N *end of* Hat Sai Ri.
Cosy atmosphere and a range of bungalows from basic to simple, on Ko Tao's longest beach.

Crystal, B-BB; *just* N *of* Ban Mae Hat.
Some of the swankiest bungalows on the island, made from concrete and wood and even boasting attached bathrooms.

Sunshine, B-BB; Ao Chalok Ban Kao, a *couple of km south of* Ban Mae Hat.
Welcoming place, with an excellent restaurant, though the beach itself has become somewhat crowded with other bungalow operations.

RECOMMENDED RESTAURANTS

KO SAMUI
Bayview Restaurant, BB; Coral Cove Beach.
Situated on one of the highest coastal points on the island, this restaurant can claim the best views. The food is delicious, affordable and served outdoors on the terrace. Italian as well as Thai dishes. Try the Caesar's salad or the seafood dishes.

El Pirata Restaurant, B; Na Ampoe Road, Na Thon Town.
One of the oldest restaurants here, with a small garden and some great Spanish dishes as well as Thai food. Run by a Spaniard and his Thai wife.

KO PHA-NGAN AND KO TAO
Few places really stand out on these islands at time of going to press. You can rely on delicious fresh seafood almost anywhere. Three places at Hat Rin on Pha-Ngan are perhaps worth mentioning: **Sand**, **Crab** and **The Haadrin Bakery**. The first two have above-average food; the last offers a range of useful snack foods.

INDEX